Introducing Philosophy

GU00750745

Written for any readers interested in better harnessing philosophy's real value, this book covers a broad range of fundamental philosophical problems and certain intellectual techniques for addressing those problems. In *Introducing Philosophy: God, Mind, World, and Logic*, Neil Tennant helps any student in pursuit of a 'big picture' to think independently, question received dogma, and analyze problems incisively. It also connects philosophy to other areas of study at the university, enabling all students to employ the concepts and techniques of this millennia-old discipline throughout their college careers – and beyond.

Key features and benefits:

- Investigates the philosophy of various subjects (psychology, language, biology, math), helping students contextualize philosophy and view it as an interdisciplinary pursuit.
- Introduces students to various important philosophical distinctions (e.g. fact vs. value, descriptive vs. prescriptive, norms vs. laws of nature, analytic vs. synthetic, inductive vs. deductive, *a priori* vs. *a posteriori*) providing skills that are important for undergraduates to develop in order to inform their study at higher levels.
- Is much more *methodologically comprehensive* than competing introductions, giving the student the ability to address a wide range of philosophical problems – and not just the ones reviewed in the book.
- Offers a companion website with links to apt primary sources, organized chapter-by-chapter, making unnecessary a separate reader/anthology of primary sources – thus providing students with all reading material necessary for the course.
- Provides five to ten discussion questions for each chapter.

Neil Tennant is Humanities Distinguished Professor in Philosophy and Distinguished University Scholar at The Ohio State University. He has published widely in the philosophy of logic and language, metaphysics, philosophy of mathematics, philosophy of mind, and the history of analytical philosophy. He teaches classes regularly at Ohio State, from 100-level Introduction to Philosophy courses to Advanced Graduate-level Seminars.

Introducing Philosophy
God, Mind, World, and Logic

Neil Tennant

Routledge
Taylor & Francis Group

NEW YORK AND LONDON

First published 2015
by Routledge
711 Third Avenue, New York, NY 10017

and by Routledge
2 Park Square, Milton Park, Abingdon, Oxon, OX14 4RN

Routledge is an imprint of the Taylor & Francis Group, an informa business

Library of Congress Cataloging in Publication data
Tennant, Neil, 1950–
  Introducing philosophy : God, mind, world, and logic / Neil Tennant.
    pages   cm
  Includes bibliographical references and index.
  ISBN 978-0-415-53711-7 (hardback) – ISBN 978-0-415-53714-8 (pbk) –
  ISBN 978-1-315-73440-8 (ebk)
  1. Philosophy–Introductions.   I. Title.
  BD21.T39   2014
  100–dc23
  2014027493

ISBN: 978-0-415-53711-7 (hbk)
ISBN: 978-0-415-53714-8 (pbk)
ISBN: 978-1-315-73440-8 (ebk)

Typeset in Goudy
by Out of House Publishing

Printed and bound by CPI Group (UK) Ltd, Croydon, CR0 4YY

Contents

PART III
The Existence of God   211

Preface

This Preface is important for the reader who wishes to have, at the very outset, well-informed expectations.

Philosophy values highly the ability to analyze theories or points of view carefully, to assess arguments critically, to make useful and enlightening connections, and to bring some systematic order to our reflections on deep and important issues. Those who teach Philosophy wish, above all, to impart *these* abilities to their students.

This book is written in the hope that it may help to make such a wish come true. It aims to introduce the beginner, in a reasonably balanced and comprehensive way, to a certain broad range of *problems* with which Philosophy deals, along with certain *intellectual techniques*, or *methods*, for addressing those problems. The beginner will acquire a considerable battery of philosophical *concepts*, and an understanding of crucial *distinctions* that can be expressed by means of them. These help to define the main ingredients of important philosophical *positions*, or *theories*, or *world-views*, here labeled '*-isms*'.

As its subtitle indicates, the book introduces the beginner to some of the most important philosophical problems, and explains a variety of philosophical views and methods in response to them. The author hopes that it will attract students to the discipline, and then provide a continuing way *into* it, even after their first introductory course. The book is intended to be a resource for re-initiation and replenishment, as it were, in addition to being some kind of 'hook'. Instructors are therefore invited to pick and choose from the topics covered here, in a way that best suits their instructional needs.

For the beginner, a word is in order about how to cope with certain bits of material in this text. Different readers may have to pore over the material at different rates in different places. This is one of the ineliminable problems in teaching both Logic and Philosophy: it is impossible to make all material uniformly accessible without great variations in texture. Students will find large sections of this book easy to follow, even as the ideas they encounter are new and engaging. But they should also be prepared to read and re-read other sections very carefully in order to master the material. A good book on Philosophy is not at all like a novel. Philosophy texts are not page-turners. If anything, they are page-turner-backers! One needs to learn to savor the detailed moves, the distinctions, and the directions of argument more slowly than one does when simply following a story.

There are some important differences between this work and others that have aimed, in their various ways, to fill similar needs. The experienced Introduction to Philosophy instructor will know of various introductory texts that are all excellent in their own special ways. Especially noteworthy are the Michael Bratman, John Perry, and John Fischer anthology *Introduction to Philosophy: Classical and Contemporary Readings*; Thomas Nagel's *What Does It All Mean?: A Very Short Introduction to Philosophy*; and Kwame Anthony Appiah's *Thinking It Through: An Introduction to Contemporary Philosophy*.

This book is *not* an anthology of source papers, in which the author's or editor's contribution, apart from judicious selection, is to furnish introductory remarks that provide some context for the readings on different topics. It is, rather, what publishers call a 'singly authored textbook' – a description which, because of the morpheme 'text', implies a humbled sense of what it owes to all those singly authored, *original*, and *pioneering* works by the truly great philosophers who have gone before. This book cannot, therefore, confine itself to setting out the author's own 'reflective equilibrium' (*see* §1.1) on all the issues addressed. Rather, it must convey a sense of the great variety of opposing views, and their various merits and demerits, on matters of great importance. Like any singly authored work, however – and, in this regard, like the works just mentioned, by Nagel and by Appiah – it will take the liberty of presenting certain matters from its author's point of view. That, after all, is what makes any textbook interestingly different from any other.

The way the present work differs from the two just mentioned is that it provides a more methodical survey of the *basic tools for thinking* that the beginning philosopher must acquire. It tries to be methodologically *comprehensive*, but expositorily *clear*. It aims to provide the beginning student with the wherewithal to address even those philosophical problems that the text does not itself discuss (of which there are perforce many). A further distinguishing mark (see below) is its insistence on getting clear about the overall logical structure of the arguments involved.

With any work that furnishes an authorial point of view, one must immediately point out some obvious accompanying drawbacks. No philosophical author nowadays can claim expertise in every one of the sub-disciplines into which Philosophy has become divided. This is a mirror of the problem, to be mentioned again in §2.1, that no thinker nowadays can possibly master all the different disciplines in science; *there are no 'Renaissance' men or women any longer*. So, the author begs the reader's indulgence for what will inevitably be a slightly biased or personal selection of topics and methods. The book is largely silent also on the areas of Ethics (or Moral Philosophy), and Aesthetics. It could not have cast its net that wide without coarsening the mesh. Moreover, Ethics and Aesthetics tend, in American colleges and universities, to have their own introductory courses devoted to them, using appropriately specialized textbooks. So, while mention and broad description of those two areas of Philosophy are indeed included here in the interests of comprehensive coverage, the reader should be aware, at the outset, that the philosophizing undertaken here is more concerned with the topics of a 'core' introductory course in Analytical Philosophy: Metaphysics, Epistemology, Philosophy of Mind and Language, and Logic.

'Bias', of course, usually carries a pejorative connotation. But there is one feature of 'bias' in this work for which the author is unapologetic, and which was foreshadowed above. This is the pride of place given, and detailed attention paid, to Logic as the centerpiece of philosophical method. The author aims to show just how crucial Logic is to a proper grasp of the ongoing debates about major philosophical problems. And this is so in two regards.

First, there is the matter of judging the internal logical correctness of passages of philosophical argumentation, when their validity is at issue (ordinary logic being brought to bear within the philosopher's 'object language', as it were). We do not shrink from the hard but enlightening work of actually regimenting certain arguments, revealing in minute detail every step taken, so that each step is either obviously correct even to the skeptic's eye, or revealed as formally wanting, and even fallacious.

Secondly – and extremely important also, in the author's estimation – we seek to impart a working knowledge of how certain major results in *metalogic* and in foundations can be brought to bear on central philosophical problems. (*Metalogical* results are rigorously proven results *about* logical systems and formal languages.)

In this latter regard – the explanation and applications of metalogical results – the author has sought to impart a personal stamp to the material, by seeking to explain these results in the most accessible possible way, but without doing so at excessive length. The aim is to equip the motivated reader, who is willing to put in some extra intellectual effort, with the most succinct and lucid exposition possible of the major results that are so often merely mentioned and not fully explained. The author hopes that this text will be judged at least in part by the extent to which this aim has been achieved.

Various logical themes recur within the text. The extent of their reprise, with variations, is an intentional part of this composition. For the book has been written in the realization that many students might be called upon to use it only in part, because their instructor teaches from several different texts. For that reason, the author has taken the liberty of repeating the basic lessons of Logic that are relevant to major themes. The dedicated reader who starts at the beginning and works all the way through the text to the end will notice the recurring *Leitmotif* of the contrast between proof in mathematics, and hypothetico-deductivism in science. The contrast is so vital that it cannot suffer from repetition.

Another recurring *Leitmotif* is the *method of diagonal argument*. This is a beautiful and pervasive technique that finds application in many areas of logical, mathematical, and metamathematical reasoning that are of significance for the philosopher and foundationalist.

The method of diagonal argument is one formal refinement of that peculiar cast of mind whose native deployment is so often a sign of philosophical talent on the part of a beginning student: that tendency to question a position by first checking to see whether it *applies to itself*. It is often known as the 'reflexive trick', and it is a hallmark of philosophical thinking. Confronted, say, with a proposed Principle of Verifiability, one can ask: *Is that Principle verifiable by its own lights?* Or, of a proposed criterion of cognitive significance, one can ask: *Is that criterion cognitively significant by its own lights?* It is no accident that the method of diagonal argument in logic and mathematics should have been forged by thinkers who were profoundly *philosophical* in their approaches to their subject matters: Georg Cantor (1845–1918) in set theory and analysis; Bertrand Russell (1872–1970) in the foundations of mathematics; Alan Turing (1912–54) in the foundations of computer science; Alfred Tarski (1901–83) in the foundations of formal semantics; Kurt Gödel (1906–78) in metamathematics. Throughout this text we shall have occasion to draw the reader's attention to the beautiful power, elegance, and simplicity of diagonal argumentation.

The author approaches Philosophy with a past grounding in Mathematics, which inspired his first interest in philosophical, logical, and foundational matters. He was trained in the analytical method, with an emphasis on problems as currently conceived and handled. This differs from the hermeneutical tradition of trying to interpret past texts in order to make sense of how thinkers in *other* historical periods conceived of the problems they were bequeathing us. This is not to imply, however, any measure of disregard for the importance and value of our continuing study of the History of Philosophy. It is only to say that that is not how this particular author cut his teeth in the subject.

Of course, historical figures and certain central features of their thought are important in setting out the philosophical problems treated here. That having been said, however, it should be noted that historical coverage here is limited, in the main, to providing a suitable *context* for our appreciation of the depth of a central problem. This is not a work in, nor even an introduction to, the History of Philosophy as such. It is, rather, a more personal tribute to the tradition. It takes the form of an explanation – which, it is to be hoped, is accessible – of certain main philosophical problems. They are the ones that the author finds both engaging and tractable by the intellectual methods that he has available, as someone coming from a background of logic and foundations within Analytical Philosophy. They are also ones which, the author has found, resonate with many beginning students. Space permits a reasonably thorough introductory examination only of the main topics mentioned in the subtitle: the existence of God; knowledge of the external world (including the problem of induction); the mind–body problem (including the problem of free will); and logic (as both tool and topic throughout).

There is one aspect of this work that bears emphasis, and which perhaps sets it apart from other introductory texts. This is that the author makes uninhibited use of logical analysis, schematization, and regimentation in order to *clarify* important views or methods as they are laid out. (This is the first of the two regards mentioned earlier, in which Logic is relevant to Philosophy.) It is the author's sincere conviction that professional philosophers often err by being too reluctant to actually deploy the logical methods to which they pay a great deal of pedagogical lip-service. It is one thing for philosophers in colleges and universities to teach 'baby logic' to their first-year students, and then to move on to the fundamentals of first-order logic for the more advanced student. It is quite another to employ these logical methods, as a matter of first instinct and intellectual habit, when addressing thorny philosophical issues involving intricate reasoning. A philosopher who shies away from formal analysis is like a surgeon who ignores the need for basic hygiene.

This work aims to enliven Logic a little, by applying it closer to home. Invoking logical analysis helps one to understand important techniques in Philosophy, such as the provision of analyses (and criticisms thereof) of *individually necessary and jointly sufficient conditions* for the application of a given concept. The same holds true for more general intellectual methods or techniques whose *logical* structure needs to be properly appreciated before they can be deployed successfully. This is particularly the case with the *hypothetico-deductive method* in science, and the method of *inference to the best explanation*.

The beginning student will not, of course, be able to understand right away what all the italicized phrases in the previous paragraph mean, let alone appreciate the importance of the methods they denote. In this regard, they might be relieved to learn, they keep company with virtually all thinkers before the latter part of the nineteenth century. For we owe mainly to the philosophers of science Charles Sanders Peirce (1839–1914), Rudolf Carnap (1891–1970), Karl Popper (1902–94) and Carl Hempel (1905–97) our contemporary understanding of what may be called the 'logic of scientific explanation'.

This book is both the author's attempt at overview and a disclosure of the author's own views at times. It is an invitation to the beginner to get more deeply involved in the discipline. The author believes that many of his own intellectual biases and preferences are shared by many other contemporary philosophers, even if not every one of them is shared by a majority – let alone that a majority shares all of them. This book will have succeeded even if the reader goes on to take issue with many, even all, of the author's more idiosyncratic views whenever they are disclosed within the text. This is a familiar fate for, and a fate familiar to, all philosophers of a certain age. For Philosophy is that field in the humanities that prizes, above all, independent, creative, and original thought; and does the most to encourage any intellectual rebel *with* a cause.

Acknowledgements

This book owes its existence to the initiative, encouragement, and patient guidance of Routledge's Philosophy Editor, Andrew Beck. I am grateful to the several anonymous readers involved at various stages, from original proposal, through draft chapters to penultimate draft, for their carefully considered and very helpful comments. Any remaining defects are entirely my responsibility.

I want to thank my many past students. Among them there have always been an inspiring few, year after year, who have been committed to entering the life of the mind. My interactions with them began back in my Edinburgh days, when I conducted tutorials (or what in the USA are called recitations) for first-year students taking the introductory Philosophy course taught by the distinguished Kant scholar W. H. Walsh. Further cohorts of skeptical and commonsensical young Scots helped to refine my philosophical sensibilities whenever I taught the large introductory course at Stirling on Theories of Human Nature. Thereafter, at the Australian National University, I had the benefit of yet more down-to-earth feedback from students in a first-year course that I inherited, with the engaging Platonic title *Dialectic*. Some of them may recognize here traces of my notes that were circulated for that course. My largest accumulated debt to student reaction has accrued during my time at The Ohio State University, the USA's largest campus. Here I have had the rewarding privilege of teaching Introduction to Philosophy on many an occasion, and amassing incontrovertible evidence, through Student Evaluations of Intructors, that while one can satisfy some of the people some of the time, one cannot possibly satisfy all of the people all of the time.

Much of the current text was written on the psychic energy released by the Ethiopian and Costa Rican brews provided by Boston Stoker at Neil and 11th, just south of the Oval on the main campus of The Ohio State University. My thanks go to baristas Erik Fenstermacher, Kasey Kimble and Alicia Nunez.

I also thank my long-deceased maternal grandmother. (If some of her metaphysical views were correct, she will be in a position to appreciate this.) Her contribution to my interest in the Philosophy of Mathematics was as follows. Around the age of four, I was sitting in her kitchen, next to her huge iron log- and coal-burning stove, looking at a tin (or, for my American readers, a can) of baking soda whose trademark picture on its side was of – *itself*. This meant that the picture of it that it had on its side contained a part that pictured its side, which of course contained a picture of it that ... . The visibly shrinking, but pairwise discernible pictures of 'the' tin immediately prompted the conception of an ω-series. It was a series with a double interest. First, it afforded the intuition of unboundedly many distinct things. Secondly, it did so by exploiting the ancillary intuition that space is infinitely divisible. That gorgeous tin gave the little boy his first grasp of both infinity and infinite divisibility. When he excitedly asked his grandmother if she could see that the tins-within-tins would just go on and on, *forever*, she impatiently exclaimed 'Why, don't be silly, little boy, you can see it just ends with that blob there!', as she pointed to the fourth (or was it the fifth?) place in the series, at which ordinary vision gave out and a certain intellectual microscope would have to be turned on. Rebuffed, I went back morosely to my toast with dripping. If she had prevailed, I would have become, not an intuitionist – which is deviant enough, by today's insufficiently criticized, orthodox standards – but a wretched *finitist*.

I dedicate this book with a deep sense of gratitude to my own teachers at Cambridge, for whom the world of ideas was their oyster, and whose lectures or tutorials shaped my way of thinking: Jimmy Altham, Elizabeth Anscombe, Thomas Baldwin, Renford Bambrough, John Conway, Edward Craig, Ian Hacking, Casimir Lewy, Adrian Mathias, Hugh Mellor, Timothy Smiley, and Bernard Williams. Even those who have passed on remain part of the Great Conversation.

The Plan of this Book

Parts I and II provide groundwork, orientation, and wherewithal: concepts; distinctions; characterization of important '-isms'; and philosophical methodologies such as analysis, explication and thought-experiment.

Parts III–V provide applications of these methods to famous philosophical problems, concentrating in the main on the existence of God; the mind–body problem; and the limits of thought and language. Both Part III and Part IV provide standard coverage, aiming to be both comprehensive and balanced. Part V is where the author offers some of his own original ideas, and presents some standard material in his own preferred way.

The book can therefore be used as a 'dual-aspect' resource, either for the basic explanation of the terrain in Parts I and II, or for the discussion of particular philosophical problems in Parts III, IV and V (or for both). It can therefore supplement other texts of the instructor's choice; or serve as a sole text for an introductory course.

The chapters number thirty in all. They also vary in length. Some care has been exercised, however, to constrain variation in this regard, and the remaining variation reflects, in the author's estimation, the 'difficulty density' of the topics involved. Shorter chapters, by and large, will take more time per page to digest. Each chapter, therefore, can be commended as background reading for a single meeting of an introductory course. The book should thereby be able to cater both for a ten-week, term-long course with three meetings each week, and for a fourteen-week, semester-long course with two meetings each week.

Judicious selection of chapters (or more demanding imposition of longer readings) will be required for a ten-week course meeting twice a week. And for a fourteen-week course meeting three times a week, the text can be supplemented with primary sources.

Each chapter (except for the final two) is furnished with a set of problems. The problems can serve different purposes. Readers can use them to test their comprehension and recall once they have read the material in that chapter. The problems can be used as the basis for group discussion of the material in class; they can be used for take-home assignments, or for examination questions; and they can also serve to provoke further interest in the topic, perhaps leading to some independent and original research. A few of the problems are not for the faint-hearted. They have been included in order to help instructors identify those students who 'have what it takes'.

The final two chapters are free of problem-sets because the author would not want the student who has read either of these chapters to do anything but meditate on the enormity of the *a priori* lesson that they have just learned ... and then re-read it.

Part I

The Nature of Philosophy

1 The Main Features of Philosophy

1.1 Philosophy as a conceptual and reflective discipline

Philosophy is a *conceptual* discipline. Its method is introspective and reflective. It is based on our intuitions and on our grasp of the meanings of our words. Yet it aspires now, after two and a half millennia of refinement, refutation and re-thinking, not to be provincial to any particular language. Nor is it confined to any particular historical period, cultural milieu, socio-political system or religious affiliation. Philosophy strives to be of *universal* appeal, to any rational intellect, human or otherwise. In that regard, it is a lot like Mathematics. Philosophy tries not to depend on empirical considerations, even though one of its main contemporary aims is to come to mutually enlightening terms with natural science. There has been increased interest of late in so-called 'experimental philosophy'. This purports to be a form of Philosophy while being a branch of empirical inquiry. 'X-phi' strikes this author, however, as a straightforward branch of social psychology or sociology or anthropology. For it involves the use of surveys and questionnaires to find out what ordinary people think about certain philosophical issues. (And when the survey-respondents are chosen from within the philosophical community, X-phi is a poor substitute for simply reading the journals.)

The archetypical philosopher (and henceforth we drop the adjective) does not perform real-world experiments, or make observations in the field, or conduct opinion polls. The philosopher's tool-kit contains no measuring rules, no scales, no clocks. The most one will find, in the literal sense of 'tool-kit', is paper and pencil – or, nowadays, a laptop computer. In the more figurative sense, what one would hope to find in the philosopher's tool-kit is a mind wide open, ready to turn on the searchlights within. The philosopher must be prepared to mull over words, stretch concepts to their limits, imagine far-fetched, bizarre situations, and consider principles of the highest level of abstraction and the widest domain of application.

Philosophical method in its purest form is, in one simple phrase, *a priori*, not *a posteriori*. The cliché for this is 'the armchair method'. Another hackneyed expression is 'putting one's thinking-cap on'. Methods of investigation, and the knowledge they enable us to obtain, are called *a priori* when they do not depend in any way on our sensory experience. Also, truths are called *a priori* when they can be known in that way. By contrast, *a posteriori* truths are those that can be known only by appeal to sensory experience.

A closely related distinction is that between analytic and synthetic truths. A sentence is said to be *analytically* true just in case it is true solely in virtue of its meaning, quite independently of any appeal to 'facts about the world'. Mere *a priori* reflection on one's grasp of the meaning of such a sentence should be enough to enable one to recognize that it is indeed true. Thus analytic truth is *a priori*. Put another way, it is truth that is accessible 'merely by reflecting on the meanings of the words involved'. Simple examples are 'All red things are colored' and 'Every bachelor is unmarried'. *Once one has grasped the concepts and/or the meanings of the words involved*, one can tell that these sentences are true without any further recourse to sensory experience. And *that* last observation is true regardless of the fact that one needed sensory experience *in order to acquire* mastery of the concepts involved (or knowledge of the meanings of the words involved).

Truths that are not analytic are called *synthetic*. Given the foregoing characterization of analytic truths, it is clear that a synthetically true sentence must owe its truth not only to its meaning, but also to 'facts about the world'. Thus synthetic truths *tell us something informative about the world*. A firm grasp of both these distinctions is vital for a proper appreciation of philosophical debates that took place in the twentieth century – including debates over the question whether the two distinctions are of any value at all. For more detailed discussion of this issue, see §5.2.

We have stressed that Philosophy is done *a priori*. Philosophy is also fundamentally *argumentative*. It seeks to establish conclusions firmly, with the help of logic, from clearly stated premises. A critic can disagree with such argumentation in two important ways. (This holds good for *any* intellectual discipline, not just for Philosophy.) One can reject a premise – or, at least, refuse to accept it. Alternatively, one can demur at a particular step within the argument, complaining – very often with justification – that it is fallacious. A fallacious step of reasoning is one that cannot be guaranteed always to transmit truth from its immediate premises to its conclusion.

The intellectual aim of philosophizing is to achieve *reflective equilibrium*. This the philosopher does by synthesizing, integrating, and reconciling all our immediate intuitions, important insights, arduously deduced results, and inspired hypotheses. The philosopher seeks to resolve paradoxes and eliminate inconsistencies, and to provide proper foundations where appropriate. The aim is to attain some overarching understanding both of the human condition within the natural cosmos, and of the connections among thought, language, and the world; emotion and reason; fact and value; being and truth.

1.2 The main areas of Philosophy

The five main areas of Philosophy have traditionally been Metaphysics, Epistemology, Logic, Ethics (also known as Moral Philosophy) and Aesthetics.

(A recent, and disappointing, departure from this tradition has been the comparative neglect, of late, of Aesthetics among the ranks of professional philosophers. This may be because theorizing in Aesthetics has migrated to other university departments catering to students with appropriate interests, such as Literature, Music, and Art History. If so, this is a pity, for it incurs the risk of aesthetic theorizing becoming less general and systematic. One hopes that the trend might be reversed.)

Here are some general comments about, and sample questions from, each of these respective areas.

1.2.1 Metaphysics

The area of Philosophy known as Metaphysics is concerned with the necessities and possibilities governing existence. The name of this area derives from the Greek word 'meta', meaning 'after': the relevant book by Aristotle (384–322 BC), which attended to these deeper concerns about existence, tended to be anthologized immediately after his book on physics.

Today, however, we understand the prefix 'meta' as indicating a sort of conceptual or theoretical ascent, 'going one step higher', in our contemplation of the world through particular 'lower-level' scientific *or philosophical* disciplines. In Metaethics, for example, one inquires into *what sort of facts* moral facts might be – indeed, whether there could be any such facts at all. There is even a branch of contemporary Philosophy called Metaphilosophy, concerned with the nature, purpose and direction of Philosophy itself.

Metaphysical questions typically arise 'at the edge' or 'at the limits' of scientific or mathematical inquiry. They concern 'ultimate' matters, to which some default answer is usually presupposed by the intellectual disciplines in question. So, for example, Physics can investigate what kinds of fundamental particles there are, and what laws govern their interactions. Most philosophers believe, however, that it lies beyond the reach of Physics, and of science in general, to explain why there should be something rather than nothing; or why there should be any regularities in nature at all.

Some sample metaphysical questions follow. Note that some of them are not entirely independent of scientific theorizing. For example, the question whether every event has a cause receives a negative answer from quantum physics. This is because of the random and completely unpredictable nature of the radioactive decay of individual fundamental particles. These uncaused events were discovered, however – by Marie Curie (1867–1934) – only about a century ago; so it has been only since then that the question whether every event has a cause has begun to strike some *cognoscenti* as a little dated.

By contrast, however, consider the question concerning how consciousness relates to the workings of mere matter. This question was stoutly maintained, by prominent European scientists and philosophers in the mid-to-late nineteenth century, and has been maintained by many Anglo-American analytical philosophers since then, to be, in principle, beyond the reach of any scientific determination. The phrase 'in principle' here, which is often used in such discussions, stresses that it is impossible for science to give an answer, *regardless of how our scientific theories could or might progress in the future*. (For more on this, and especially on the provenance of the epistemic pessimism involved, see Tennant (2007).)

The reader should be asking, of each of the other metaphysical questions below, whether its answer, too, might lie, in principle, beyond the reach of any possible future scientific theory. (Note that these are *meta*questions.) Any such scientific theory would, of course, have to be beholden to sensory experience – that is, empirical evidence – in the sense that it *could* be refuted by recalcitrant experience. We shall have more to say, in due course, about exactly what counts as a scientific theory, and what qualifies as properly scientific method. Such issues lie under the heading 'Epistemology', rather than 'Metaphysics'.

Here, then are the promised sample questions in Metaphysics:

1 Do individuals have *essences* – that is, clusters of properties that they must possess in order to exist 'as themselves' at all?
2 Is there more to a law of nature than its universal truth?
3 Does the world itself possess a causal structure, or is that structure something that the mind imposes in order to make sense of the world?
4 Does every event have a cause?
5 Does the universe exist for a purpose?
6 Must space have three dimensions?
7 Must time be linear?
8 Could there be time travel?
9 What is the relationship between mind and body?
10 How does consciousness relate to the workings of 'mere' matter? Are the facts of consciousness beyond the reach of science?
11 Are persons to be identified with their physical bodies, or with their streams of consciousness?
12 Is the Self a *thing*, or *individual substance*? If so, what kind of thing?
13 Is there an objective fact of the matter as to what it is like to be a bat, or any other kind of sentient creature, even if it is in principle inaccessible to us?
14 Could there be re-incarnation, or at least some kind of survival – of soul, or individual consciousness – after bodily death?
15 Is the future determined by the past?
16 Whether or not all events are pre-determined, can we exercise free will?
17 Does God exist? If so, does He/She/It exist necessarily?
18 Could there be thought without talk?
19 Are there abstract objects such as numbers? Or are all existents concrete – that is, physical – things?

One tradition in Metaphysics, due to Immanuel Kant (1724–1804), is that of so-called *transcendental philosophy*, which inquires after the *necessary pre-conditions*

for the very possibility of thought about, and knowledge of, an external world.
According to this tradition, mind has to be regarded as *constituted by* various
rules, norms, conceptual capacities, etc. These could be thought of as 'innate'.
Our possession of these capacities is what enables us to acquire certain kinds
of knowledge *a priori*. But – very importantly, for Kant – our knowledge of
both *mathematics* and *metaphysics* is *synthetic a priori*. Here, of course, one has
metaphysics blending into epistemology, the next area on our list.

1.2.2 *Epistemology*

Questions about different kinds of knowledge, its scope and limits, its proper
objects, its sources and its justification, are pursued in that branch of philosophy
known as *Epistemology* or the *theory of knowledge*.

The epistemologist is concerned, first, to establish the *possibility* of knowledge
of the external world (that is, to refute skepticism) and is then concerned to
elucidate the different kinds of knowledge to be had; how we acquire such
knowledge; and how we justify it.

The results of such inquiries are likely to depend on what kinds of objects or
states of affairs the knowledge in question is about. These include mathematical
entities; observable matters of fact; theoretical entities such as protons and
electrons; individual organisms; species; one's own states of mind; other people's
states of mind; and meanings of expressions of a language.

We might come to *acquire* such knowledge in different ways. Among these
might be introspection; direct observation; deductive inference; indirect or
inductive inference; and testimony of others. But what of ingrained habit? innate
endowment? subliminal exposure? flash of integrating insight? telepathy? Or even
divine revelation? religious prophecy? reading the Bible?

The knowledge in question might be *justified as* knowledge in different ways.
Among these are mathematical proof; the withstanding of severe experimental
tests; and causal links to the phenomena at the source. But might we include also
(say) appeals to papal authority?

The main questions faced by epistemologists in a long and venerable tradition
have been these:

1 Could there be truths we could not know?
2 Could we be systematically deceived, or hallucinating, in all our 'experiences'?
3 Are there any beliefs that are immune to revision in the light of experience?
4 Are any statements true solely by virtue of what they mean?
5 What is special about knowledge?
6 What distinguishes knowledge from true belief?
7 What sorts of propositions are our knowledge-claims ultimately based upon?
8 Which of our knowledge-claims, if any, are – or could be – *absolutely certain*,
   or *incorrigible*?
9 Can contingent ones be among these?

10   Are there limits to what we can know?
11   How is knowledge of abstract objects possible?
12   Is our knowledge of the external world based wholly on sensory perception?
13   Are there limits to self-knowledge?
14   Is it possible to organize our knowledge in a logical way, with the propositions that are most certain making up a firm foundation, and with the rest of our knowledge built on top of that foundation, by following strictly logical, or other inferential, methods?
15   Are the facts of subjectivity and consciousness inaccessible to the methods of objective science?
16   Can reason be naturalized?
17   Is there a single correct scientific method?

1.2.3 Logic

Logic is the study of *valid reasoning*, that is, transitions in thought (typically heralded by words like 'therefore') that aim to preserve truth from their premises, or starting points, to their conclusion, or end point. The premises, and the conclusion, are *truth-bearers* – declarative sentences, or statements, or propositions. (And much ink has been spilled debating which of these choices is optimal.)

Aristotle pioneered the discipline of formal logic, in his famous work *Prior Analytics*. In that book he crafted his theory of *syllogisms*. (For a detailed description of Aristotle's syllogistic, and a modernized version of it, see Tennant (2014a).) These are valid arguments of very specific forms, involving two premises and a conclusion. Perhaps the most famous of these can be represented as follows:

$$\frac{\text{Every M is P}}{\text{Every S is M.}}$$
$$\text{Every S is P}$$

Here, the horizontal line marks the deductive transition, from the sentences above it (the premises) to the sentence below it (the conclusion).

A quick aside about ways to display arguments. Because the sentences are quite long, we have just used the *vertical-stack* display option for the premises. This option also makes it easier to read the sentences separately from each other. An alternative would have been the *horizontal-stack* display:

$$\frac{\text{Every M is P} \qquad \text{Every S is M}}{\text{Every S is P}}\quad.$$

This, however, presents problems of 'sideways stretch' very quickly when we have more than two sentences above the line, adequately spaced so as to be easily read. Displaying premises horizontally is the better choice only when they are abbreviated symbolically, as with:

$$\frac{P_1 \quad P_2 \quad \ldots \quad P_n}{Q} \; .$$

In a case like this, the vertical-stack option would just be too space-consuming:

$$
\begin{array}{c}
P_1 \\
P_2 \\
\vdots \\
P_n \\
\hline
Q
\end{array}
$$

The reader is forewarned, though, that the horizontal-stack display option is the one that we prefer for stating *rules of inference* symbolically. Two self-explanatory examples would be:

$$\frac{A \quad\quad B}{A \text{ and } B} \qquad\qquad \frac{A \quad\quad \text{if } A \text{ then } B}{B} \; .$$

End of aside

Another well-known syllogistic form is:

$$
\begin{array}{l}
\text{No M is P} \\
\underline{\text{Every S is M}} \\
\text{No S is P}
\end{array} \; .
$$

These two syllogisms, to repeat, are *valid*. Put another way: their premises *logically imply* their conclusions. This relation of logical implication between a set of premises, on the one hand, and a conclusion, on the other, is the main relation studied in logic. Logical systems for a given language seek to furnish proofs, or deductions, for valid arguments in that language. Logical systems, which specify *norms* for deductive reasoning, are themselves beholden to two standards:

- **Soundness:** No invalid argument has a proof.
- **Completeness:** Every valid argument has a proof.

In order to understand these two standards, one needs to understand what sort of object a proof is.

　A *proof* is a finite arrangement of individually obvious and compelling *steps of inference* that take one from the premises of the proof to its conclusion. A proof has to be finite in order to be surveyable and checkable. A proof makes clear and indisputable that its conclusion really does follow logically from its premises. And one can 'read off' those premises (say $P_1,\ldots,P_n$) and that conclusion (say Q) from the proof itself (otherwise, one would not know what the proof was a proof of). *When there exists a proof of conclusion Q from premises* $P_1,\ldots,P_n$ we say that Q is *deducible* from $P_1,\ldots,P_n$; and we write

$$P_1,\ldots,P_n \vdash Q$$

to register this. The symbol '$\vdash$' is called the *single turnstile*, and it is perhaps the most important symbol in (Meta)logic.

The requirements of Soundness and Completeness, then, are to the effect that for any set of premises, all conclusions deducible from it should be logically implied by it, and vice versa. The requirements can be re-stated as follows, using our new symbol $\vdash$:

> **Soundness:**
> If $P_1,\ldots,P_n \vdash Q$, then the argument $P_1,\ldots,P_n/Q$ is valid.
> **Completeness:**
> If the argument $P_1,\ldots,P_n/Q$ is valid, then $P_1,\ldots,P_n \vdash Q$.

We owe to Aristotle the central and original ideas that:

(i)   Logic treats forms of deductive reasoning that arise in all disciplines, and in all areas of thought. So logic is *universally* applicable.
(ii) Arguments in natural language can be *symbolized* by using letters for longer expressions, and studying the patterns of their occurrences. These abbreviating symbols are of two distinct kinds: so-called *logical expressions*, which are always interpreted the same way; and so-called *extralogical expressions*, whose interpretations can vary.
(iii) The central idea in Logic is that of *valid inference*, as revealed by *perfected proofs*.

For Aristotle, the logical expressions were

> 'All …are __';
> 'Some …is __';
> 'No …is __'; and
> 'Some …is not __'.

His extralogical expressions were *predicates*, like '…is a man' and '…is mortal'.

Aristotle's guiding ideas informed all subsequent work in Logic. Interesting developments were accomplished by various medieval figures, but still, by the middle of the 1800s, the intellectual communities of the civilized world *had no canon of deductive reasoning adequate to the intricacies of inference already in evidence in ancient Greek mathematics.*

All that was changed in 1879, by a revolutionary breakthrough: the short monograph by Gottlob Frege (1848–1925), a philosopher, logician and mathematician in Jena, titled *Begriffsschrift* (trans: *Conceptual Notation*). The subtitle is worth mentioning too: *Eine der arithmetischen nachgebildete Formelsprache des reinen Denkens* (trans: *A formula language for pure thought, modeled after that for arithmetic*). We owe to Frege our modern ability to frame mathematical statements as sentences in formalized languages, and to manipulate them logically in all the ways justified by their internal structure.

Frege's technical achievement did not, however, dispose of all the philosophical questions and issues that surround the use of Logic, and its applications in mathematics and other areas of inquiry. Philosophers still ponder questions like the following.

1 What makes an argument from premises to a conclusion valid?
2 Can every valid argument be (compellingly) proved?
3 Is there a single correct system of logic?
4 How do scientific hypotheses relate to observational evidence?
5 Can we both say everything we want to say about certain infinite mathematical structures and also deduce every statement that follows logically from what we say?
6 Can all mathematical truths be proved from suitably chosen first principles?
7 Is it possible to prove, mathematically, that mathematics is consistent, i.e., free from internal contradiction?
8 Is *all* of natural language suitable for logical formalization, as far as its declarative sentences are concerned? Or does the recent success of modern Logic have to stop short at, and be limited to, the analysis of *mathematical* statements and their logical relations?
9 Are there formal 'logics' to be had of philosophically important concepts such as necessity and possibility? belief and knowledge? part and whole? causal relations and counterfactual dependencies? obligation and permission? time and tense?

1.2.4 Ethics

Virtually all the questions we have considered above from Metaphysics and Epistemology could be raised by two kinds of very non-human characters: *Star Trek*'s Vulcan Mr. Spock, who is devoid of all emotions and moods; and your favorite kind of alien, heartless brute (think: those glistening tentacled beings in *Independence Day*), who is devoid of any moral scruples in annihilating humankind. But we human beings, having evolved as social creatures in our little corner of the Milky Way, are very concerned about *values* – both moral and aesthetic. In addition to wanting to know *what the world is ultimately like*, we want to know *how we should conduct ourselves within it, and towards one another*. We raise questions about both the Good and the Beautiful. Ethics is concerned with the Good. Here are some of the questions that it raises:

1 Are there moral facts in the world? Or is morality just an expression of subjective opinions?
2 Is the goodness or badness of an action something that is based on, or determined by, only what turn out to be the *consequences* of the action, regardless of whether the agent intended them? Or does the action's moral status depend on the agent's *intentions* (even if the action fails to accomplish them)?
3 Do we 'create our values' through our actions? Or are our values things that we can *excogitate*, and that will (or *ought*, then, to) guide and constrain our actions?
4 Are there any basic principles about good and bad, from which one could work out which actions would be good and which would be bad?
5 Can science throw any light on questions about what is good and what is bad? Or will the application of scientific theory to questions of morals always be guilty of the 'is–ought' fallacy? (The fallacy in question is that of trying to derive *prescriptive* statements about what one *ought to do* from *merely descriptive* statements about *how things are*.)
6 Are our moral codes based on emotions, or on reason, or perhaps on a combination of both?
7 How do moral judgments motivate one to act? *Can* they?
8 Are morals absolute? Or might they be culturally relative? Might they be attuned to, or appropriate for, only a particular era, or place, or *Zeitgeist*, or phase of one's life, or stage of technological development?
9 Is there such a thing as moral progress? If so, how is it possible?
10 Is it necessary to base one's morality on some set of religious beliefs? Or can morality be utterly segregated from religious views, so that non-religious agents can be moral saints and paragons?
11 What creatures merit our moral concern? Only human beings? Only those human beings who are into their second trimester? Only those human beings who have been born? Only those among the latter who already talk, and can still talk? Or should the circle of concern be widened, to include not only human beings, but also all primates? or all mammals? or all vertebrates? or all creatures with rudimentary nervous systems?

With this last question, we see how Metaphysics, Epistemology and Moral Philosophy can intersect. *Is there something it is like to be* a creature of type X? Can it *suffer*? If so, oughtn't we to *care* about its well-being, for *its own* sake, and not just for ours?

1.2.5 Aesthetics

The other main area of so-called 'value theory' is Aesthetics, the study of artistic beauty and our judgments about it. The subject matter of Aesthetics is *prima facie* more variegated and chaotic than the subject matters of the other main areas of Philosophy already discussed above. Think for a moment about the baffling variety of artistic endeavor: literature (novels, short stories, poems, plays, …); music (covering both works embodied in scores, and performances that can be highly extemporized); theater (from tragedy to comedy … even unto stand-up comedy); painting and other graphic art-forms, such as engraving, etching, and printing; sculpture; textiles; architecture; dance; photography; film; … . Within each of these areas, art works vary from the more directly representational to the highly abstract; from celebration to harsh criticism; from the soothing or amusing to the terrifying; from the satiating or satisfying to the disgusting or revolting. *Why* and *how* is it, then, that the creative activities in these areas, and the various enduring products or fleeting performances that they result in, are almost universally recognizable, and *valued*, as *art*?

Art seems to be an extreme form of successful classification without any immediately recognizable 'necessary and sufficient conditions'. Art works are analogous in this regard to *games*, which were the favorite example used by Ludwig Wittgenstein (1889–1951) when he put forward his theory of 'family resemblances' as providing the threads that unite disparate items into a category that can then be conveniently labeled.

Art has played an essential role in a fulfilled and enriched life, not only in the civilized world, but also in the prehistoric world of our cave-dwelling ancestors. At this juncture of human development, however, we almost take for granted its pervasive presence in the environments that we create for ourselves, or in which we choose to live. But Philosophy is in part a project of questioning things that we take for granted, so as to attain a deeper understanding and appreciation of what they involve: their ultimate make-up or constitution; their relations to us; our perceptions of them; the concepts by means of which we organize our experience of them; and the value we derive from our interactions with them. Here are some of the questions that a philosopher might raise about art, art objects, the art world, and aesthetic value:

1 What is an 'art form'? Do all art forms have something specific in common?
2 What is good taste? Must we defer to 'experts' in matters of taste?
3 Does aesthetic judgment involve any kind of logic, any notion of evidence, or any conception of 'best' or 'simplest' explanation of the 'artistic phenomena'? Is the aesthete in intellectual pursuit of important *generalities* or *regularities* in the 'art world', when accumulating experiences within it, and arriving at aesthetic judgments about it? Or is the whole point about works of art that each of them is *utterly singular*, despite belonging to a *genre*?
4 Is one of the main aims of artists working at the frontiers of creative foment to continually *undermine* or *subvert* any systematic conceptions or

categorizations that critics or theorists have thus far arrived at, and to render false or irrelevant any generalizations based thereon, concerning what may count as art?

5   Are there unsuspected biases at work in our judgments of what counts as art? – in particular, gender biases, biases of historical remove, or biases of Western culture? (This question is explored by some of the essays in Korsmeyer (1998).)

6   What makes something a work of art? Are works of art at least partially constituted by their creators' intentions? or by social conventions?

7   Are there objective standards of beauty?

8   Can two observers be in extreme disagreement as to whether a creation is beautiful or ugly, yet unanimous in their judgment that it is *art* – even, indeed, *great* art?

9   What is the nature of 'artistic experience', both on the part of the artist and on the part of the beholder?

10   Are certain art forms 'higher' than others?

11   How can we be moved by works of art? Do art objects communicate emotion(s)?

12   Do works of art make moral statements? If so, does their aesthetic value depend on 'getting it right' (as to what is right)?

13   Is there any difference between erotic art and pornography?

14   How do judgments about what is beautiful relate to judgments about what is morally right, and to judgments about what is factually correct?

15   What is the aesthetic difference between an authentic work of art and a perfect fake?

16   What is the *value* of art (its creation and its consumption) in a world plagued by poverty, famine, disease, apocalyptic disasters, and wars?

17   Do aesthetic sensibilities and preferences have a role to play in the way we understand reality? Why do we prefer 'elegant' equations in Physics? Why is it that the world admits of such elegant descriptions? Why do scientific hypotheses, when mathematically encapsulated in an elegant fashion, enable us not only to know about the world at a deep level, but also to *marvel* at the *beauty* of its inner workings?

18   Can a work of art possess an intrinsic value or beauty that might forever elude, or go undetected and unappreciated by, anyone who experiences the work?

1.3 Philosophical questions as concerned with fundamentals

All the questions given above as examples from the five main areas of Philosophy involve very *fundamental concepts or distinctions*. Among these are *mind; body; causation; free will, knowledge; consciousness; concrete v. abstract; fact v. value; objective v. subjective; moral goodness; validity of argument; and beauty.* They seem to be the sorts of questions that one would like to have answered *before* undertaking any particular scientific investigations.

At this point we can raise an important *Metaphilosophical Question*:

> *Can* one – *should* one – try to answer these questions without the benefit of any light that scientific theories might be able to shed on them?

Philosophy, as a reflective discipline, contrasts with disciplines that rely more on the empirical method. Philosophy engages with very *fundamental* concepts and questions. The following question, for example, concerns all possible areas of human inquiry, or of thought about things-in-the-world:

> Are there properties in the world, over and above the things or individuals that 'have' them? Does the truth-condition for a statement like 'Socrates is wise' involve just the *individual* Socrates, or does it involve also the *property*, or *universal*, of wisdom?

This is known as the *Problem of Universals*. The question at issue is whether universals exist at all. If they do not, then the world contains (as the nominalist asserts) *only individuals*, like Socrates, whom we group or classify using different labels, such as the predicate '...is wise'. But if, in addition to individuals such as Socrates, universals (such as *wisdom*) exist (as the Platonist claims they do), then the world consists – to put it crudely – not just of things that we can grasp with our hands, but also things for whose grasp we have to use our minds. There is then an added depth to reality, to which only minds are granted access of any kind. If the Platonist prevails, then – who knows? – perhaps those erstwhile individuals such as Socrates may come to be 'seen' or 'understood' not as the flesh-and-blood individuals we unreflectively take them to be, but also rather as *clusters of the universals that they instantiate*. With the emphasis and focus on universals, perhaps one would wish to say, not that Socrates is wise, but rather that *wisdom Socratizes*. Might Jorge Luis Borges have been right in having his speakers of Tlön say, not *The moon rose above the river* but (whatever in their language was best translated as) *Upward behind the onstreaming it mooned*?

Problems

1 What are the five main areas of Philosophy? Can you think of any problems that can be solved only by combining certain concepts and methods from more than one of these areas?
2 What dependencies or logical relationships can you detect among possible answers to any of the questions listed under the five main areas? What questions *not* listed above would you wish to add, and to which list(s)?
3 Which of the questions listed under the five main areas strike you as the most intriguing? the most unusual? the most perplexing? the most important for your quality of life? the most pressing or urgent for the human condition? the most inconsequential? Give reasons for your offerings.

4 Do you think that any of the questions listed under the five main areas will ever receive a definitive answer? If so, will the answer(s) come from Philosophy, or from the sciences?

5 Are any of the questions listed under the five main areas absolutely unanswerable by human thinkers? If so, might they be answerable by *other* rational beings?

6 Should any of the questions listed under the five main areas be relegated to Religion or Theology, as matters for resolution by faith alone, without regard for observational evidence of any kind, and without relying on scientific method?

2 Philosophy's History and Legacy

This is an introductory text on the *problems* of Philosophy, not on the *history* of Philosophy. These problems, however, do have a history, and we should be mindful of that. Philosophy is the oldest and most venerable branch of human inquiry. Even though its problems, and the answers it tries to provide, have evolved over more than two millennia, they nevertheless remain profound mysteries that will always be there to fascinate us and our descendants.

2.1 The historical sweep of Philosophy

Many illustrious and influential thinkers of the past have been, first and foremost, philosophers. They have also been among the pre-eminent mathematicians and scientists of their day. The beginner in Philosophy will benefit from having some initial sense of the ancient roots of the discipline, so as better to be able to understand its relationship to other disciplines, especially Mathematics and the various empirical sciences. Moreover, the names of certain famous philosophers crop up so often in contemporary philosophical discussion that it is helpful to have some sense of the timeline of major developments, and the historical succession of famous philosophers and the philosophical systems named after them. To that end, the reader will find in Appendix A a chronological table of some of the greatest philosophers in the Western tradition, along with mention of some of their most important works, for each of the main periods customarily identified by contemporary historians of Philosophy.

The ancient cosmological systems, such as those of the Pre-Socratics (beginning in the sixth century BC), of Plato, and of Aristotle, sought to characterize completely the cosmos and the human condition. These ancient philosophers succeeded in formulating many of the main philosophical problems and conceptual distinctions that have occupied philosophers' attention ever since. To the ancient Greeks we owe the axiomatic method in Mathematics, as so magnificently founded for geometry by Euclid's *Elements*. To them we owe also the distinctions between appearance and reality; necessity and contingency; the senses and the intellect; substance and attribute; free will and determinism; knowledge and true belief; and between mechanical and teleological explanation – to mention but a handful. The ancient Greeks also initiated Philosophy's preoccupation both with the nature of the self and with the possibility of immortality. As Alfred North Whitehead once wrote, 'The safest general characterization of the European philosophical tradition is that it consists of a series of footnotes to Plato' (Whitehead (1929), p. 39).

Medieval philosophy (beginning in the late fifth century, and lasting until the fourteenth century) was, in the main, a project of reconciling the doctrines of the three great monotheistic religions, especially Christianity, with ancient Greek metaphysics – to which, as just noted, we owe the doctrine of the immortality of the soul. This is not to imply monolithic agreement among the ancients on this score. As with the contemporary philosophical community, there were representatives among the ancients of diametrically opposed views on the matters just mentioned. The Roman philosopher Lucretius (99–55 BC), for example, did not believe in the immortality of the soul, and argued that death was therefore nothing to be feared. Medieval philosophers such as Anselm (1033–1109) and Aquinas (1225–74) also bequeathed to the philosophical tradition some of the most famous arguments for the existence of God $((-\infty, \infty)$, should He/She/It exist). And quite apart from addressing theological and metaphysical questions, medieval philosophers also grappled with problems concerning the structure of language and logical reasoning.

Early Modern Philosophy (mid-sixteenth to mid-seventeenth century) began the movement that celebrated the individual's exercise of reason and judgment, even (and especially) when the results were in conflict with established superstition or authoritarian dogma or unquestioned tradition. It laid the foundation of political liberalism, and offered contractarian explanations of society and morals. Early Modern Philosophy also laid the foundation of modern scientific method. Modern science bases theories on observational evidence, and rejects theories that conflict with it. In doing so, it stands indebted to the 'early moderns'. This period saw the birth of experimental science, with a new emphasis on the priority of observation and experiment. It bequeathed to us the first major works on scientific method, as one based on the testimony of our senses, and using rational methods to explore the consequences of suggested explanations. The Copernican revolution in astronomy (*De Revolutionibus Orbium Coelestium*, published in 1543, as Copernicus lay on his deathbed), which ushered in our current understanding of the arrangement of the Sun and the various planets in our solar system, de-emphasized our position in the universe.

The era of so-called Modern, or Enlightenment, Philosophy (approximately 1650–1800) developed its impetus in the immediate wake of the Newtonian revolution in physical science, occasioned by the great *Philosophiae Naturalis Principia Mathematica* (1687) of Isaac Newton (1642–1727). This was shortly after the major founding figure of Early Modern Philosophy, namely René Descartes, had helped earlier to shape the intellectual climate in which Newton's work became possible. This era was dominated by the opposition of *Rationalism*, whose main representatives were Descartes, Baruch Spinoza (1632–77) and Gottfried Wilhelm von Leibniz (1646–1716), and (mainly British) *Empiricism*, whose earliest representatives were Francis Bacon (1561–1626) and Thomas

Hobbes (1588–1679), but whose most famous, mature representatives were John Locke (1632–1704), George Berkeley (1685–1753), and David Hume (1711–76). Rationalists took logical, mathematical, and theological knowledge as the standard to which all other forms of knowledge should be held; whereas empiricists claimed to the contrary that all our knowledge is based, ultimately, on the deliverance of our senses. The opposition between rationalism and empiricism that came thus to the fore was, however, but a reprise of these conflicting themes in the works of many of the ancients. It is, after all, to Sextus Empiricus (160–210) that we owe the label 'empiricism'.

This polar opposition between Rationalism and Empiricism in the Early Modern and Modern periods was resolved in the 'Kantian synthesis', also known as the 'Copernican turn' in philosophy. It ushered in the period now known as 'Post-Enlightenment' Philosophy. Philosophy was re-conceived as concerned with the *a priori and necessary pre-conditions* – concerning substance, cause, space, and time – for the very possibility of scientific knowledge.

One part of the mind, Kant held, contributed the 'forms of intuition' of space and of time, whose role is to impose spatiotemporal order upon the flux (or *Wirrwarr*) of our sensory impressions. This Kant called 'the field of apperception', consisting of our sensory *intuitions*. (Quine was later to call this a 'booming, buzzing confusion'. Note that it is very easy to mispronounce this.)

The flux of impressions would also be shaped by another faculty of mind, the understanding, so that it yielded *experience* as of enduring objects engaged in causal interactions with one another. This was courtesy of the *concepts of the understanding*, most prominent among them the concept of individual substance (or 'thing'), and the concept of causation. Kant's famous slogan was *Concepts without intuitions are empty; intuitions without concepts are blind.* This combination of '-isms' was new: Kant combined 'transcendental idealism', which emphasized the *a priori* structuring of experience provided by the mind, with 'empirical realism', which emphasized the mind's need to be supplied with sensory impressions of things in the external world. He then sought to investigate the limits of rational understanding, and the enigmas of self, freedom, morality and God.

Thinkers in the late nineteenth century grappled with the profound implications of the revolution in our understanding of the extremely long history of life on our planet that was provided by Charles Darwin (1809–82) in his masterwork *The Origin of Species* (1859). On Darwin's view, all living organisms, ourselves included, have descended over aeons, and by natural selection, from more primitive ancestors. Darwinian thought led to a de-emphasizing of humankind's position in the animal kingdom. It challenged teleological modes of thought, by offering a convincing prospect of explaining all aspects of nature by appeal only to efficient causes, and not by appeal to the intentions of an almighty creator or 'designer'. Through the participation of many different scientific disciplines in the ensuing 'neo-Darwinian synthesis' we now have the beginnings of what Richard Dawkins (b. 1941), has called an 'intellectually satisfying atheism'. (Dawkins, who gained fame with his first popular book, *The Selfish Gene*, is now retired from the Charles Simonyi Professorship in the Public Understanding of Science at the University of Oxford. He has been a vigorous proponent of atheism, and acerbic critic of what he regards as both the intellectual and the moral shortcomings of organized religions.)

Thinkers in the twentieth century likewise grappled with the implications and the presuppositions of the major scientific revolutions that followed Darwin: *quantum mechanics* and *relativity theory*. The former theory seems to paint an indeterministic picture of the world; and the latter theory seems to dissolve important distinctions such as those between space and time and between matter and energy. The late 1900s and the first two decades of the twentieth century also saw the birth of modern logic, with the seminal work of Frege mentioned above, and the first rigorous study of the foundations of mathematics. The movement known as Logical Positivism, centered on the famous Vienna Circle in the 1920s, reacted against Kantian metaphysics in light of these recent advances in metamathematics and science. Logical Positivism sought the 'elimination of metaphysics' – arguing, in particular, against Kant, that *there are no synthetic*, a priori *truths*.

Philosophy subsequently took the 'linguistic turn': language was seen as the source both of philosophical problems and of their solutions. This ushered in the era of linguistic or conceptual analysis. The task of philosophers was taken to be the study of analytic truths, or the conceptual connections that they expressed. There was further progress also in the biological and the 'soft' sciences. Molecular biologists discovered the genetic code. Advances in cognitive psychology and neuroscience began to undermine mind/body dualism. Intellectual conditions became ripe for the development of a materialist or naturalist metaphysics (and epistemology).

Ancient and medieval philosophers, and to a certain extent philosophers of the Renaissance, were able to be conversant with the full range of sciences of their day, because the knowledge gained thus far was quite limited. They sought to integrate what was known to them into one intellectually satisfying system. Today, however, it is impossible for any one mind to master fully all the discovered facts and explanatory theories that are available across the whole range of extant scientific disciplines. There is simply too much in the way of data, and there are too many different mathematical, statistical and computational techniques. There are too many specialized sub-disciplines for it to be possible any longer for a scholar, however naturally gifted and dedicated to the life of the mind, to earn the title 'Renaissance man (or woman)'.

This predicament, if not handled carefully, can make the intellectual position of the philosopher rather precarious. Modern scientists are quick to point out that Science itself has co-opted domains of knowledge and theorizing that once upon a time were regarded as special provinces of Philosophy.

For example, the study of mind itself has morphed into the scientific disciplines of cognitive and social psychology, and neuroscience. Philosophical accounts of the 'social contract' as the basis of morality, the law, and of institutions of governance have likewise morphed into modern political science, drawing on arcane methods from game theory and the theory of the evolution of equilibria in dynamical systems of interacting agents. In yet another scientific encroachment upon a sub-domain of Philosophy, evolutionary psychologists are beginning to probe, with *empirical* methods, the sources of our inner convictions that we are free to act as we choose. They claim to be in a position, now, to reveal that these common-sense convictions are, in all likelihood, false. Evolutionary epistemologists, likewise, have re-visited standard problems in the theory of knowledge, and have tried to 'naturalize' epistemology itself. Instead of pursuing epistemology as a branch of 'first philosophy', setting out the foundations for the possibility of any kind of scientific knowledge, evolutionary epistemology boldly applies current scientific theory to account for our ability to know things and truths about them. For the evolutionary epistemologist, the brain and our sensory transducers are cognitive organs. They have been shaped by natural selection because of the advantages that even more primitive versions of those organs would have conferred on the ancestral organisms that possessed them, in the competition for survival and reproduction.

The history of scientific encroachment, albeit with rapid budding off of ever more specialized sub-disciplines, has seen the old-fashioned philosophical agenda eroded in big chunks. Some of these chunks fall off the edges as they are overcome by the incessant pounding of scientific inquiry. Yet others, more centrally positioned, find their once-firm conceptual ground suddenly giving way to a new, gnawing sinkhole of science undermining the philosophers' claims to privileged intellectual status from within.

Some philosophers' reaction has been to *re-conceive the very role of Philosophy* in relation to Science. They have urged that the primary role of the philosopher is to clarify and to integrate the various findings of Science. This is a far cry from the conception of 'first philosophy', going back to Descartes, according to which one has to solve certain major philosophical problems in an *a priori* fashion before even being positioned to pursue any particular scientific inquiries. Pale imitation of that former role now comes with the contemporary philosopher being tasked with 'keeping Science honest' by critically assessing various aspects of scientific method as these change over time. This deferential reaction set in with the Logical Positivists, with Rudolf Carnap prominent among them. Deference to science was advocated also by Willard Van Orman Quine (1908–2000), who was heavily influenced both by Carnap and by the earlier American pragmatists, and whose (meta)philosophy has been extraordinarily influential in North America and beyond, in the latter half of the twentieth century.

2.2 The current legacy

The current legacy of all these developments is that Philosophy places a strong emphasis on intellectual *rigor*: it calls for exactitude and clarity in the way we express ourselves, and reason. It also has an overriding concern with *analysis of meaning*: getting clear about concepts by getting clear about the meanings of the words that express them.

Philosophers by intellectual inclination immerse themselves in the history of thought, for their tradition is a long and proud one. They are thereby in a position to offer enlightening perspectives on *conceptual evolution* and *theoretical revolutions*. It is fair to say that it is to philosophers such as Popper that we owe our contemporary awareness that even the most 'authoritative' science is at best tentative. There remains, of course, the tension between Philosophy's *aspiring to apriority* and its *systematic integration with the sciences*; and Philosophy needs new ways to cope with 'cannibalization by the special sciences'.

Philosophy in the twentieth century began to mount a rearguard action against this cannibalization by feeding off the cannibals one at a time, as it were. There was an interesting trend towards sub-specialization within Philosophy, as its practitioners acquired competence in particular disciplines X, and then developed the corresponding 'Philosophy of X'. The aim and effect was to show that each discipline X has its own particular philosophical problems, concerning its concepts, its foundations, and its methods. Also, each discipline X could provide interesting material for philosophical reflection on that part of the Big Picture that X sought to study. The relationship between X and the Philosophy of X could become symbiotic: each stood to gain illuminating material from the other. In this spirit, the twentieth century saw the development of the 'Philosophy of X' for X taking the values

> Logic; Mathematics; Science; Social Science; Physics; Chemistry; Biology; Archaeology; Art; Education; Sport; Medicine; Mind; Psychology; Perception; Action; Cognitive Science; Language; Linguistics; Information; Literature; Economics; Politics; Law; …

These 'Philosophies of …' are now well recognized as areas of specialization or competence on the part of well-trained graduate students in Philosophy who are entering the academic profession as teachers and researchers. Philosophy Departments in universities standardly list the so-called AOSs (Areas of Specialization) and AOCs (Areas of Competence) of their faculty members by drawing on entries from the foregoing list. The 'Philosophy of X's are routinely named alongside the five 'main areas' – Metaphysics, Epistemology, Logic, Ethics, and Aesthetics – as are the various Histories of (Western) Philosophy within the major periods identified in Appendix A (Ancient, Medieval, Early Modern, Modern, Twentieth Century).

As disciplinary boundaries expand and contract or are re-drawn, Philosophy within the universities continues to explore new opportunities to create synergies, and encourage cross-fertilization of ideas, from neighboring disciplines with which it engages. This means that the philosophers of the future – if they are to enjoy a continuing, and lasting, intellectual presence in our havens of higher learning – have to be not only intellectually honest and rigorous, but also versatile, interdisciplinary, open-minded, thirsty for new scientific knowledge, and intellectually catholic, with a small 'c'. This is a tall intellectual order, to stave off institutional short shrift.

One of the most valuable services that Philosophy can now render is to enable thinkers and leaders of the future to reflect on how science enlightens us as to the ultimate nature of things, and on the place of humankind in the scheme of things. We need continuing vigilance over the rationality of any proposed new scientific method, and we must continue to be able to identify the use of illicit philosophical assumptions when doing science. We need continuing vigilance also over the claims made by those who exploit the findings of modern science in order to create new technologies and therapies. It would appear that with ever-gathering pace, these technologies and therapies are generating ethical dilemmas because of their unforeseen and unintended consequences.

Thus ethicists have a unique opportunity to make the principled findings of their sub-discipline more vitally relevant to current concerns. *Ought we* to allow gene therapy to be performed on the unborn? *Ought we* to grow and eat genetically modified organisms? *Ought we* to allow our own blood and body tissues to be used in vast statistical studies whose results might end up being frightening chickens come home to roost? *Ought we* to continue to exploit and consume natural resources because of current demand and available technologies, without caring about the possibly devastating long-term effects on ourselves, on our water- and food-supply, on other species of life, and on our planet? Philosophy's renewed engagement with technology and medicine has given a great impetus to new subfields of Applied Ethics. This is also one particular area where the mainly *a priori* methods of the philosopher can fruitfully be combined with the *empirical* discoveries of the relevant sciences, to provide a context in which matters of ultimately *moral* import become more pressing. *What sort of life do we wish to lead?* – one in which we push for the short-term benefits (and corporations push for the short-term profits) that may result from the application of new technologies? Or one in which we are more circumspect – wiser, perhaps – in stressing our moral responsibilities and obligations to the as-yet-unborn, to preserve a planet that will be habitable by them? (The English word 'philosophy' comes, after all, from the Greek words 'philo', meaning *love*, and 'sophia', meaning *wisdom*. *Love of wisdom* … a precious commodity that is itself, like carbon-based fuels, in increasingly short supply.)

Also, metaphysicians and philosophers of science have a unique opportunity to make intellectual contributions to contemporary theoretical physics. Here, the concepts deployed are so arcane, and the new mathematics involved is so searingly abstract, that one begins to lose any intuitive grasp of what sorts of processes or interactions are being described. Philosophers of science can take a critical look at the sense in which the Big Bang might or might not be a 'creation event' with potential theological significance. They can involve themselves in advocacy or critique of 'hidden variables' theories in quantum mechanics, on whose existence or success the debate over the nature and extent of causation might turn. Philosophers of science can also contribute to debates about the possibility of emergent systems, and of 'top-down' causation, in the context of complex evolving systems whose behavior is highly non-linear, and subject to both phase transitions and 'catastrophic' qualitative change.

Philosophers of mathematics have joined forces with philosophers of mind, and of cognitive science, to explore the consequences of our conceiving of the mind in computational terms – as the 'software' of the brain that mediates between sensory input and motor output. The celebrated incompleteness theorems of the famous Austrian logician Kurt Gödel have been used by some 'transcendentalists' to argue that the human mind cannot possibly be conceived in these computationalist terms. They argue that a computational system *cannot* (as the human mind allegedly *can*) comprehend, and then transcend, the proven limits to the capacity of any formalized deductive system for mathematics. The human mind, they maintain, could always 'out-Gödelize' any formal computational system that might be put forward as a model of the mind's workings. Thus, they conclude, minds transcend machines; so Mechanism is false.

These are just a few examples of the challenges and opportunities that present themselves to the enterprising student of Philosophy who seeks to master its intellectual methods and then apply them to newly arising problems in a rapidly changing world.

Problems

1   Why do you think Philosophy has undergone the evolution briefly described in this chapter?
2   In the distant past, great philosophers were also among the great scientists of their times. Are any of today's great scientists still doing Philosophy?
3   What, in your view, is the proper role for Philosophy in relation to the contemporary physical, social, and human sciences?
4   Are any of the ethical precepts of established religions under threat from contemporary scientific findings?
5   *Must* Philosophy at least harmonize with the sciences, even if it is not itself pursued as an empirical discipline? How can contemporary scientific theories be made relevant to traditional philosophical problems?
6   Does the trend towards increasing specialization and fragmentation in every area of intellectual inquiry pose a special threat to Philosophy as an ongoing discipline? How would you argue for its continuing intellectual value against a skeptic who thinks there should not even be funding for it within a system of public education?

3 The Philosophical Temperament

3.1 Keeping an open mind

Philosophy, as we have seen, deals with fundamental concepts, and with important questions that can be posed by means of them. But both *mathematics* and the natural *sciences* have fundamental concepts, and pose important questions using them. How, then, does Philosophy differ from both mathematics and the sciences?

First, note that scientific or mathematical questions are ones that scientists and mathematicians think could, in principle, be definitively answered; or, at the very least, could be considered in the light of evidence and argumentation that would incline a rational thinker one way rather than the other.

A 'definitive answer' need not be one that we can confidently claim to know with complete certainty. Rather, it need only be one that we are strongly inclined to accept, on the balance of the evidence and on the strength of the arguments that marshal that evidence. This inclination, however, has to be *rational*; it cannot be a matter of arbitrary whim, or dogmatic insistence in the teeth of evidence to the contrary. This in turn raises the question *What is rationality?*, to which I hope some sort of answer will have emerged by the end of this book.

3.2 Philosophy contrasted with Mathematics and Science

Almost every beginner in Philosophy has had at least some exposure to Mathematics and various sub-disciplines in Science (physics, chemistry, biology, etc.). So the beginner in Philosophy can be helped by some initial foreshadowing of the ways in which philosophical questions, and the sorts of answer one can provide to them, differ from those with which they might already be familiar in Mathematics and Science respectively.

The main differences, in their most telegraphic form, are these:

1 *Mathematical* questions can be settled by proof from first principles.
2 *Scientific* questions can be settled by observational evidence and reasoning.
3 *Philosophical* questions are settled in a final *reflective equilibrium*; and there are potentially many of the latter.

Take a mathematical conjecture like 'Every even number greater than 2 is the sum of two prime numbers'. Is it true or is it false? This is a famous unsolved problem in number theory. It is named after Christian Goldbach (1690–1764), who first posed the question. Goldbach's Conjecture has the following significant features:

1   We would recognize a counterexample to the conjecture, if there is one.
2   We would recognize a proof of the conjecture, if there is one, within a system of currently accepted mathematical axioms.
3   We could also recognize a proof of *the impossibility of being able to settle the question within a given axiomatic system.*

This last would be an example of what metamathematicians call a 'natural independence result'. In the last two centuries such results have established the independence of the Parallels Postulate from the other axioms of Euclidean geometry, and the independence of Cantor's Continuum Hypothesis from the standard axioms of modern set theory, including the Axiom of Choice.

A counterexample to Goldbach's Conjecture would be a number n – and, if such a number exists, there would be a *least* such – that is not the sum of any two primes preceding n.

3.3 Scientific questions

There are many scientific questions that have one or the other of the following two basic forms:

1   **Existential.** 'Are there any Xs?' – we can imagine experimental and observational circumstances favoring an *affirmative* answer. We would need only to be presented with an X.
2   **Universal.** 'Are all Xs Ys?' – we can imagine experimental and observational circumstances favoring a *negative* answer. We would need only to be presented with an X that is *not* also a Y.

Someone presented with the basic principles of, say, Einsteinian relativity theory and cosmology could contemplate an Existential question such as 'Are there any black holes?' or 'Does the gravitational field of the sun cause light rays from some distant star to curve on their way to the earth?', and can imagine experimental and observational circumstances in which they would give a definite affirmative answer to the question. Or, in the case of scientific generalizations such as 'All planets move in elliptical orbits around the Sun', they can imagine what would be required, of observations of the orbit of a given planet, to *falsify* the generalization.

The philosophical generalization suggested by these examples from scientific practice is this: a scientific question is posed in such a way, and with such conceptual resources, as to permit the possibility of *definitely answering* the question one way or the other (Existentials affirmatively and Universals negatively).

3.4 Mathematical questions

The same holds true for Mathematics. Consider once again the simple, as yet undecided mathematical conjecture of Goldbach: *Every even number greater than 2 is the sum of two prime numbers.* No proof has yet been given; nor has any counterexample been found. But, while the conjecture is undecided, mathematicians would hesitate to say that it is, in principle, undecid*able*. For, they can imagine *what it would be to have a proof* of this conjecture; and someone, some day, might very well produce such a proof. On the other hand, they also know *what it would be to falsify the conjecture*: simply produce an even number greater than 2, which is not the sum of any two preceding primes. The status of such an even number, as a counterexample to the conjecture, could be settled in a finite time, by means of a finite (mechanical) computation.

So, in summary: scientific and mathematical questions are *essentially soluble*, in the sense that practitioners of those disciplines tend to have a good idea of what, in principle, would be required, by way of evidence and argument, in order to convince themselves of the truth, or the falsity, of any given statement using the conceptual resources available to them. When a correct solution is offered, the scientific or mathematical community eventually reaches consensus – no matter how deep or difficult the question being answered.

Answers to mathematical questions, when we attain them, are wholly objective and dispositive. Answers to scientific questions, when we first find them, are reasonably objective. Whether they are dispositive, however, will depend on their logical form. A properly evidenced affirmative answer to an Existential question ('Are there any Xs?') will be dispositive; and so too will be a properly evidenced negative answer to a Universal question ('Are all Xs Ys?'). But no finite amount of evidence can in principle provide a dispositive negative answer to the former kind of question ('*Is* there life on some other planet?'), or a dispositive positive answer to the latter kind ('Are *all* Xs Ys?').

That being said, however, we can at least say that the methods for determining answers are, in both Mathematics and Science, public and accessible. And the answers are continually tested and applied.

3.5 Philosophical questions (by contrast)

Philosophy is different. Philosophy differs by posing questions that are *essentially controversial*. These questions are important and of long standing; yet they continue to invite speculative answers, or even answers backed by arguments, that vary widely across the spectrum. Given any philosophical question, one can always find thinkers responding to it from *opposing extremes*. Moreover, they do not simply assert their views dogmatically; rather, they tend to be able to offer detailed, complex, and substantive reasons and arguments for them. That is where, in Philosophy, critical acumen is at a premium: when one needs to find whatever flaws one can in a case presented by an opponent with a diametrically opposed view to one's own.

Philosophical questions are often *reflexive*, and especially so when, as *meta*-questions, they challenge philosophical positions themselves. So let us go reflexive on the very characterization that we have just given of the supposed contrast between scientific and mathematical knowledge, on the one hand, and philosophical 'knowledge', on the other.

3.6 Realism v. Anti-realism

Is it really the case that every scientific or mathematical question has a definite, correct answer?

The *realist* will answer 'Yes'. The realist holds that every scientific question, and every mathematical question, admits in principle of a definite correct answer – whether or not we could ever discover it. Either there are black holes, or there aren't. Either every even number greater than 2 is the sum of two prime numbers, or some even number greater than 2 is not the sum of two prime numbers. The realist says that the truth is 'out there', even if we do not know it, and even if we could never, in principle, come to know it. That is to say, the truth can *transcend* our knowledge of it, and indeed our means of ever coming to know what it might be.

By contrast, the *anti-realist* holds that *all truths are knowable*. If there really are black holes, then there must be a way for us to find out that there are. Likewise, if there are no black holes, then we must be able to find out that this is so. If every even number greater than 2 is the sum of two prime numbers, then we must be able one day to prove this; otherwise, we must be able to disprove it.

So we see already that there is a huge disagreement between two philosophical positions, concerning truth itself and our possible means of coming to know it. The realist, if she thinks that Philosophy uncovers truths, will regard the essentially controversial nature of certain philosophical questions as explained by the *intellectual inaccessibility of whatever answer happens to be the right answer*. She will think that such questions, like scientific and mathematical ones, *do* have definite answers, but that those answers can elude even our best efforts to discover them. So the realist can suffer a certain kind of intellectual frustration, or disappointment, or humiliation, in not being able to discover what is supposedly a settled answer to her question.

The anti-realist, by contrast, will regard the essentially controversial nature of certain philosophical questions as reflecting the open-ended but so far inconclusive nature of our investigations. Certain philosophical questions, like any number of sufficiently deep and difficult scientific and/or mathematical questions, simply cannot, at any given stage of inquiry, be settled one way or the other. When there is no outright proof or disproof, and no preponderance of evidence either way, the anti-realist is resigned to neither asserting nor denying *p*, in response to the question whether it is the case that *p*. The anti-realist can remain intrigued, deeply interested, and puzzled; but will not think it appropriate to react to the current state of indecision and controversy the way the realist does.

Let us have a look, now, at one of the greatest and most controversial of all philosophical questions.

3.7 Example of a philosophical question: *does God exist?*

This is a philosophical question. At one extreme, the *theist* will answer 'Yes', and offer all manner of arguments and considerations in support of that answer. At the other extreme, the *atheist* will anwer 'No', and likewise offer all manner of arguments and considerations in support of that answer. We shall be examining all these arguments later, in Part III.

By way of foreshadowing: in Part III we shall find that two of the famous arguments that a theist might offer *for* the existence of God – Anselm's Ontological Argument, and Aquinas's Cosmological Argument – are presented as conceptual, *a priori* pieces of reasoning. They are comparable in their logical structure to mathematical proofs, which set out to establish *theorems* on the basis of axioms that are accepted as self-evident. By contrast, another argument for the existence of God, namely the Argument from Design, is comparable in its logical structure to a scientific explanation, in which an hypothesis is invoked in order to explain certain observational evidence.

Finally, the atheist's main argument *against* the existence of God, known as the Argument from Evil, is an attempt to employ *a priori* reasoning in order to reduce to absurdity the *assumption* that God exists. The argument's premises are statements of the usual powers that religious tradition vests in the Deity, along with the premise – accepted by both sides of the debate – that there is much evil and suffering in the universe. (Hence the name of the argument: the Argument *from Evil*.)

In between the atheist and the theist is the *agnostic*. The agnostic remains uncommitted to any particular answer. The agnostic is not persuaded one way or the other by the respective arguments and considerations. The agnostic, however, keeps an *open mind*. She is prepared to be swayed either way, provided only that a sufficiently persuasive argument can be presented to her. It is just that as of now – so she claims – she has yet to be presented with a conclusive argument either way.

The term 'agnostic' has come to be closely associated with the undecided position in response to the question of God's existence. But the term can have wider application. In response to any philosophical question – *Is mind distinct from body? Can we be sure that the future will resemble the past? Are there moral facts? Could truth transcend what we could possibly know?* – there is room for the agnostic answer: 'I don't know. I cannot make up my mind. The currently available evidence and arguments are not compelling either way.'

3.8 Adopting a philosophical position

If philosophical questions are essentially controversial, why shouldn't one simply be an agnostic in response to all of them? In theory, one could; perhaps, even, *should*. But even the most sophisticated and open-minded thinkers are not inclined to agnosticism in response to every philosophical question. Instead, they become *committal* with respect to at least some such questions, if not to all of them. That is, they take a definite stand; they make up their minds. In so doing, they adopt what is sometimes called a *Weltanschauung*, or way of looking at the world. They do so, however, while yet keeping very open minds about the possibility of encountering new evidence and new arguments that might make them change their point of view. They do so, moreover, only after *thoroughly thinking through all the alternatives*, so that they truly know where they stand.

3.9 Undergoing a philosophical education

The purpose of a philosophical education is to enable one to find *reasons to commit oneself* one way or another in response to important philosophical questions. What is important is not so much the particular set of answers one arrives at by way of reflective equilibration (the process of reaching equilibrium). Rather, what is important is the *process of rational reflection* that one has undergone in order to arrive at such equilibrium. One needs to *open one's mind* to the possibility that one has premised one's personal and intellectual life thus far on *unexamined assumptions* about God, self, life, personhood, purpose, meaning, rationality, value, thought, language, the future, free will, morality, causation, space, time, the physical universe, and our place in it. And not only that; *some* of those assumptions (or indeed many of them, or perhaps even *all* of them) might, upon being more consciously considered, wilt in the light of critical scrutiny. One may need to suspend them or abandon them; indeed, one might even need to reject them. This is an extreme, and often emotionally unsettling, case of rational belief revision.

  Part of the excitement of doing Philosophy seriously comes from taking on the huge issues, and examining even widely held assumptions critically, and from scratch, as it were. The philosopher is always looking for the precise *reasons* for which one might hold *any* view on any important matter. For many a beginning student, this process of rational examination can be challenging, disorienting, at times even upsetting. But by embarking on the intellectual journey, and uncovering one's own reasons for ending up at whatever reflective equilibrium one eventually reaches, one occupies that position with deeper understanding, deeper commitment, and deeper justification. One acquires, shall we say, one's moral and intellectual compass.

  One needs to become familiar with the *space of alternative viewpoints* that can importantly differ from one's own. This is the great hallmark of *invisible diversity*, perhaps the most important kind of diversity to appreciate, foster, and respect. This is the diversity of *deep intellectual conviction* about how 'everything hangs together' – or perhaps doesn't. It is a diversity that transcends race, religion, gender, sexual orientation, socio-economic class, and the various other dimensions on which variation makes up the diversity that politicians (and higher educators) like to stress.

The invisible diversity of deep and well-thought-out intellectual conviction is, to this author's mind, humanity's greatest asset. It is also the asset that is the easiest to squander, to neglect, to allow to fall into disrepair, if institutional forces for conformity seek to limit it, constrain it, or undervalue it. Those institutional forces can be 'higher'-educational; political; theocratic; or plutocratic. Usually they emanate from the decisions, influence and actions of individuals who themselves are bereft of any sense of the intrinsic value of that which they are neglecting, or undernourishing, or dismantling, or vandalizing, or rendering inaccessible to persons of ordinary means. Philosophy is that discipline *best positioned*, from reflecting on its own turbulent history – and, thereby, *uniquely obliged* – to sound the alarm, whenever necessary, about barbarians at the gate.

3.10 The need to avoid dogmatism

A first requirement on undertaking this intellectual journey is that one should free oneself of dogmatic commitments to any particular answers in response to philosophical questions. This might entail *internal conflict* of high order. The God-fearing synagogue-, church-, mosque-, or temple-goer might be seriously conflicted in trying to 'suspend belief' in the existence of God. Yet such suspension of belief is required in order to undertake a critical examination both of the evidence and arguments *for* the existence of God, and of the evidence and arguments *against* the existence of God. Likewise, the atheist scientist might be seriously conflicted in trying to 'suspend disbelief' in the existence of God. Yet suspension of *dis*belief is required for that critical examination just as much as suspension of *belief* is required.

There are many other fundamental beliefs, besides belief in the existence of God, that are prone to being held dogmatically, with insufficient critical examination. Some of the most important of these are the following:

- one's mind, or soul, is immaterial, and is distinct from one's body;
- one's mind, or soul, is immortal;
- we have free will;
- certain central beliefs have to be held *on faith*, and not in response to total available evidence and one's exercise of reason and understanding;
- there are fundamental mysteries – but with factual answers – that lie beyond all human comprehension;
- one's good or bad conduct in life will be rewarded or punished in the afterlife;
- moral laws are 'God-given';

- certain kinds of testimony, deriving from divine revelation, have to be taken on trust, and never subjected to rational criticism on the basis of the total evidence.

3.11 The need to avoid fallacious thinking

A second requirement on undertaking this intellectual journey is that one should free oneself of all habits of sloppy thinking or argumentation. There is no better introduction than a grounding in Philosophy, to the topic of 'Critical Thinking' (often taught – quite unnecessarily, in the author's view – as a separate course from Introduction to Philosophy). Immunization against the most important of these intellectual contagions is so important that we devote an appropriate measure of attention to them here.

We shall in later chapters engage in some quite refined examination of some subtle logical matters. Here we seek to prepare the beginner for the required level of rigor. The intention in this early section is wholly *prophylactic*: we are concerned to identify various crass errors in argumentation, of kinds that reveal the arguer to be very *il*logical. In order to learn logic thoroughly, the student must make the acquaintance not only of patterns of thinking that are good, but also of some that are bad, and indeed with some that are downright ugly. The rest of this section furnishes a sort of chamber of horrors for the logical acolyte. The examples on display here might not have the same harrowing effect on the logical sensibilities of impressionable young minds as would medieval instruments of torture on their moral sensibilities; but they should come close.

Fallacies are *invalid arguments or inferences*. There are infinitely many of them. But there are a few forms of fallacy that crop up quite frequently, and for which one must be vigilant. They should be avoided in one's own argumentation, and exposed and criticized in one's opponent's argumentation. As already explained, an argument is an attempt to move in thought *from* certain premises *to* a sought conclusion, in such a way as to transmit truth. A fallacy in an argument will undermine the guarantee (deductive or inductive) that truth is being transmitted from the premises to the conclusion.

One can also, with a fallacy, botch an attempt to show that a set of assumptions is inconsistent. A fallacious *reductio ad absurdum* argument will lead one to the over-hasty conclusion that the premises form an inconsistent set. But perhaps they form a consistent set after all, and it is only the fallacious step that produces a mistaken impression of inconsistency.

Logical fallacies, then, are mistaken steps in reasoning – reasoning in which the propositions involved are correctly identified, but in which the attempted inferential transitions among those propositions are not properly made. Here we have space to mention only a select several of the most prominent logical fallacies.

We turn now to the logical fallacies, which are less gross than the rhetorical ones, and therefore at times harder to detect. They turn on incorrect attention to the logical forms of the statements involved, while masquerading as logically correct.

The fallacy of equivocation.

Example:

> All knowledge is power. All power corrupts. Therefore all knowledge corrupts.

Here, the word 'power' is the source of equivocation. In the first premise, it alludes to increased understanding, an ability to work things out for oneself (a power for self-improvement, if you like). In the second premiss the kind of 'power' in question is political power, power over people's lives, power to influence governmental decision-making, both legislative and executive. *Obviously*, the conclusion does not follow from the premises once one has distinguished the two very distinct meanings of the word 'power' in question. (Ironically, the more knowledgeable the citizenry, the *less* likely they are to be helpless in the face of political power wielded corruptly.)

The fallacy of composition.

Example:

> Norman Tebbit, the saturnine British Secretary of State for Employment (1981–83) once made a famous remark about how his unemployed Welsh coal-miner father 'got on his bike and looked for work'. This was by way of comment on British unemployment in 1981. He was trying to persuade his audience at the Conservative Party Conference that it would be possible for the British population to achieve full employment if only each worker had the same determination as his father.

Tebbit was exploiting (implicitly) the following inference pattern:

> Any person who tries hard enough can find work.
> So, it is possible for everyone to find work if they try hard enough.

The logical form of this fallacy is:

> For every *x*: it is possible that *Fx*.
> So, it is possible for it to be the case that: for every *x*, *Fx*.

In symbols:

$$\frac{\forall x \lozenge F(x)}{\lozenge \forall x F(x)} \, ,$$

where $\lozenge$ represents 'it is possible that' and $\forall$ is to be read as 'for every'.

The conclusion, thus analyzed, simply does not follow from the premise. There is the depressing phenomenon of so-called 'structural' unemployment: no matter how hard a society tries, it cannot attain full employment. Granted, in ordinary circumstances, when *not* everyone is making a tremendous effort to find a job, the go-getters like Tebbit Senior can land a job by making a special effort. But, if *everyone* got on their bikes to look for work, the relatively few available jobs would quickly be filled, and, after the traffic jam had died down, there would still be many willing workers unemployed.

The fallacy of quantifier-switch.

Example:

> St. Thomas Aquinas's 'Second Way', also known as the Cosmological Argument for the Existence of God, contains the following essential but fallacious step:
>
> > Every thing or event is caused, or brought into being, by some other thing or event.
> > So, some thing or event caused, or brought into being, all other things and events.

Aquinas thought that this Prime Mover was God. This questionable step has the same logical form as the following:

> Every number is greater than some other number.
> So, some number is less than all other numbers.

The latter inference is clearly invalid: the premise is true of the real numbers (negative and positive), while the conclusion is false. (There is no least number; they keep on going back infinitely far 'to the left'.) Another argument of the same form, which is clearly invalid, is the following:

> Everyone is fathered by someone else.
> So, someone fathered everyone else.

The fallacy of affirming the consequent.

Example:

> If it rains, then the ground gets wet. The ground is wet. So, it's raining.

This has the form:

> If A then B.
> B.
> So, A.

The 'if-then' claim is generally true. But the ground might be wet because the sprinklers have been on, not because it is raining.

The fallacy of denying the antecedent.

Example:

> If it rains, then the ground gets wet. It's not raining. So, the ground isn't wet.

This has the form:

> If A then B.
> Not-A.
> So, not-B.

Again, it may not be raining, but what if the sprinklers are on?

The fallacy of over-hasty generalization.

Example:

> 3 is prime; 5 is prime; 7 is prime. So, all odd numbers are prime.

The arguer has not looked at *all* odd numbers; indeed, the very next odd number, 9, is *not* prime. The mathematician needs special methods for proving universal claims about natural numbers. She cannot simply enumerate instances, because there are too many of them (i.e., infinitely many). Instead, she has to show that the property in question is possessed by 0, and that if any number n has the property, then so too does $n + 1$. This is the so-called Principle of Mathematical Induction.

There can also be over-hasty generalization in *inductive* reasoning (the kind of reasoning that is concerned to reveal regularities in the behavior of objects in the external world). Unless one has a large enough sample of a given population, it would be unwise to extrapolate trends that you think you have found in the sample. For example, if you were to choose five people at random coming out of the election booths, and ask them how they voted, and were told 'Republican' by three of them, and 'Democrat' by the other two, you would be unwise to conclude that the Republicans would win with three-fifths of the vote. There is a significant chance that your sample might be very unrepresentative: perhaps, even, the Democrats are on their way to a landslide victory. Even with much larger samples of a few hundred or so, there is still a margin of error of a few percentage points either way. (This, in a 'first past the post' voting system, makes psephology a precarious science.)

The fallacy of post hoc, ergo propter hoc.

Example:

> Lots of migraine sufferers used to believe, before we were all better informed by the relevant science, that eating chocolate would bring on a migraine. They believed this because almost every time they ate chocolate, they would shortly thereafter suffer a migraine. Their reasoning was that, since the migraines followed upon eating chocolate, the chocolate was causing the migraine.

This is mistaken. When a migraine is about to come on, the brain is in a state that results in your craving chocolate. So, usually, you eat chocolate – and, as luck would have it, manage to do so just before the onset of the migraine. Both the (craving for, hence) eating of chocolate, and the migraine, have a *common cause*. It is not the chocolate that is causing the migraine, it is whatever state is behind your craving the chocolate in the first place.

This brings to a conclusion our prophylactic account of some of the worst logical fallacies to which untrained thinkers can be prone. (We shall, however, identify an excruciating new one in Chapter 17.) The beginner in Philosophy must be on guard against them. And one of the most effective ways to ensure that one's thinking is free of such fallacies is to study the essentials of Logic. That is why an introductory course in Logic is so often a prerequisiste for more advanced courses in Philosophy.

3.12 The need for dispassionate contemplation

Another requirement on undertaking this intellectual journey, especially in the company of others, is that one conduct it as a *civilized conversation*. The best way to do this is to regard the questions, the evidence one way or the other, and the arguments one way or the other, as *impersonal, abstract objects* that are not the personal property of any one thinker, but are rather *communal* property, and the subject of *dispassionate contemplation*. Although it is important to attribute original ideas, insights, lines of argument, etc., to the thinkers who first thought of them, their contribution is nevertheless to what is sometimes called 'The Great Conversation'. It engages all minds willing to communicate about these issues, regardless of their own convictions, or 'where they are coming from'.

The best way to prevent philosophical differences from developing into hostile personal conflicts is to *de-personalize* the issues. Talk about 'the concept C', or 'the theory T', or 'the argument A', or 'the refutation R', as an *intellectual object* that can be dispassionately scrutinized. Never let any argument of yours be an attack on a thinker; make it an attack only on certain propositions or theories. Make it impersonal and objective. In intellectual migration, avoid personal denigration. One can venerate a great thinker, and still beg to differ. Many a great thinker has held a false belief; or developed a vague or incoherent or trivial or platitudinous theory; or given a fallacious argument; or deployed a confused concept. Refute the false belief; criticize the theory; diagnose the weak spots in the argument; and reveal the confusion in that concept. But do not denigrate the thinker in doing so.

Even more crass than *logical* fallacies are *rhetorical* ones – and these must be avoided at all costs in The Great Conversation. Rhetorical fallacies don't even correctly identify the propositions on which the argument at hand should be concentrating. When someone commits a rhetorical fallacy, it is because they are trying to deceive the audience over what is at issue, or over what their opponent believes, or over the relevance of their own claims to the matter at hand. Here we have space to mention only three of the most important rhetorical fallacies.

The fallacy of Argumentum ad baculam.

Example:

> The Pope appealed to the leaders of the Allied forces, Roosevelt, Churchill, and Stalin, to avoid a certain course of military action that might have endangered some great European ecclesiastical architecture. Roosevelt and Churchill wanted to accede to the Pope's request, and reiterated the reasons for restraint to Stalin. Stalin refused to be moved. He leaned forward and asked 'Exactly how many divisions does the Pope have?'

'Bacula' is the Latin word for 'club', as in the kind of thing that would have been used, in the old days, to clobber an enemy's head. So *Argumentum ad baculam* is argument that appeals to the implied threat of force – force by means of which one will ensure that one's own view (or decision) will prevail. *It has absolutely nothing to do with intellectual reasons or justifications. It is simply a method of intimidation.*

The fallacy of arguing against a straw person.

Example:

> So you're an *atheist*, eh?! You Godless swine! Look at what those atheist Commies did in Cambodia! No doubt you condone that. You think it's OK to blow prisoners' heads off when they're eating apples …

The atheist in question might be the most moral person you will ever meet. She might have more refined ethical sensibilities, and a much deeper understanding of South-East Asian politics, than the Bible-thumping interlocutor who would have the audience believe that she was Pol Pot's spokeswoman. Her views are being misrepresented. By constructing a 'straw person' – a set of opinions mistakenly or dishonestly attributed to one's opponent – the arguer tries to win a cheap victory. It is usually much easier to refute an absurd or exaggerated or ill-informed view *not* held by one's opponent, than to find out exactly what one's opponent really believes, and why, and then to criticize her for her genuinely held views.

The fallacy of Argumentum ad hominem.

Example:

> A: I believe there should be universal health care. I believe that every child has a right, regardless of parental income, to receive free preventive and curative care whenever she needs it. I believe that senior citizens should be completely relieved of the anxiety over how to pay for their medications in their old age. Our society is rich enough to do this; and we're lagging behind all the other major industrialized nations in this regard. We can equip our army with nuclear weapons, but we can't even ensure the health of our children and grandparents.
>
> B: You're saying all this only because you've got five runny-nosed kids whom you don't feed properly, four sick grandparents whom you've been neglecting, and have just moved all your aggressive-growth stock out of health funds and into telecommunications funds.

Here, B is trying to discredit A (and his views) by making a personal attack on A that has nothing to do with the principled issues (concerning universal health care), or with the reasons that A might offer for his views on them. You don't refute a proposition by discrediting the character or credentials of the person stating it. You have to argue against the proposition by giving grounds for rejecting *it*. You need to lead appropriate and relevant evidence, marshaled in a logical way that will persuade a bystander who knows nothing about anyone who might assert the proposition in question.

At the end of the road, one who lives 'the examined life' might well have the same fundamental beliefs as they held before this intellectual journey was embarked upon and completed. The newly won advantage, however, is that those beliefs will be held with a much deeper understanding of all the relevant issues involved – and, one hopes, greater respect and tolerance for those who beg to differ.

3.13 Abilities demanded by Philosophy

The beginner in Philosophy does not need much by way of preparation. It usually suffices to have a healthy respect for intellectual pursuits of all kinds. There are certain abilities, however, which will stand the beginner in good stead. These are the abilities to:

1 spot hidden assumptions;
2 find fallacies in arguments;
3 think up unusual situations in order to test the applicability of concepts;
4 argue rigorously;
5 anticipate objections; and
6 express oneself in clear, simple, and precise terms.

With that basic intellectual equipment, and a willingness to consider challenges to even the most firmly held beliefs, the beginner can enjoy a promising future in the discipline.

Problems

1 Do you think that the ability to pose distinctively philosophical questions is a gift enjoyed by relatively few? What questions can you recall ever raising at a very early age which could properly be called *philosophical* questions?
2 Which of the abilities listed in §3.13 do you think you have, and which do you think you lack? How would you set about making good those lacks?
3 Do you think that a person's religious convictions rule out the possibility that they might be seriously reconsidered from a philosophical standpoint?
4 Why, do you think, are so many thinkers prone to commiting serious fallacies in their thinking? Is not fallacious reasoning counterproductive? Should not that tendency have been eliminated by natural selection?
5 What do you think is the source of the realist's belief that every declarative sentence has a determinate truth-value?
6 If a mathematical conjecture is provably unprovable from our current axioms, and also provably irrefutable on the basis of those axioms, does it follow that the conjecture must be false if those axioms are true?

4   Important Concepts and Distinctions

Despite its readiness to engage with all the various scientific disciplines on matters metaphysical, epistemological, ethical, and foundational, it is likely that Philosophy will remain centrally concerned with perennially important conceptual distinctions. These distinctions are formulated by means of certain important philosophical concepts. Mastery of those concepts requires one to understand and be able to apply the distinctions involving them. So these philosophically important concepts and distinctions really go hand in hand.

Those who challenge the value of Philosophy often point to how its fundamental problems appear to remain unsolved; or, worse, are completely insoluble; and how they tend to re-surface, in perhaps different guises, at every important juncture in the history of ideas. If Philosophy, *contra* these detractors, can claim any kind of *progress* at all, then it is in large measure owing to its accumulation of the important distinctions to be discussed in this chapter. Once drawn and grasped by practicing philosophers, these distinctions re-shape the discussion of any topic to which they are relevant. They can never subsequently be ignored or neglected, without vigorous argument in support of doing so. (On this point, see the Introduction to Kenny (2004).) An understanding of these distinctions is a major aim of any contemporary philosophical education. Philosophical naïveté on any topic is by and large attributed in proportion to ignorance of the relevant distinctions that the preceding philosophical tradition has drawn.

Successive generations of philosophers might come (i) to wield certain conceptual distinctions slightly differently than intended by their originators; or they may even come (ii) to reject them as untenable, or intellectually fruitless. Still, *familiarity* with these distinctions, and with the concepts they involve, is absolutely essential for a fully developed understanding of Philosophy as a discipline. The beginner needs at least a rudimentary understanding of these distinctions at the very outset, since so much of philosophical theorizing and controversy involves their application. (An example of (i) is how Kant's delineation of analytic, as opposed to synthetic, truths was amended after the adoption of Frege's logic in place of Aristotle's syllogistic.)

Here is a summary list of the most important distinctions that we shall be covering in this chapter:

appearance/reality; mind/body; objective/subjective;
abstract/concrete; descriptive/normative;
empirical knowledge v. rational knowledge;
necessary/true/false/impossible; and theory/evidence.

Chapter 5 is devoted to the two famous distinctions whose importance was heavily stressed by Kant: *a priori/a posteriori*, and analytic/synthetic.

Let us take these distinctions in order, so as to impart some preliminary sense of how they can be brought to bear on matters that interest the contemporary philosopher.

4.1 The appearance/reality distinction

The appearance/reality distinction is motivated by (i) *perceptual illusions*, and (ii) *disagreements arising from limitation of point of view, or unusual conditions*.

Let us consider perceptual illusions first. There is the well-known and widely experienced illusion of sticks looking bent when half-submerged in water. Our pre-historic ancestors almost certainly knew about that illusion, and that it was indeed illusory. More recently, cognitive psychology has given us the *Müller-Lyer illusion*. The upper horizontal line in the following diagram looks longer than the lower one, but in fact it is exactly as long:

Now let us consider disagreements arising from limitation of point of view, or unusual conditions. You and I see different aspects of the same scene: was that object obliquely glimpsed really square, or was it just a rhombus? was that object presented almost on edge really circular, or just elliptical? is that object really yellow, or is it just this sodium lighting making it look that way?

In the case of disruptive illusions, or perceptual circumstances known to be compromised, the reasonably reflective observer is all too keenly aware of the gap between appearance and reality. One would be preaching to the choir to stress it to him. But what about when the gap *is* there, but *escapes the observer's notice*? The need to be mindful of the appearance/reality distinction, for the fully reflective thinker, never goes on vacation.

Thus a certain kind of philosopher (an extreme skeptic, or irrealist) may draw to the attention of a moral agent who is happily reconciled to the duties and obligations of her moral code the disquieting (or potentially liberating?) thought that perhaps she is not *really* under any of those obligations, or beholden to discharge those duties, after all. Perhaps the appearance, to the 'moral intellect', of the *bindingness* of those moral norms is purely fictitious. Perhaps *there are no moral facts at all. That* would be a gap between appearance and reality, if ever there was one. Unprompted by any intimations of illusion, or of occupying a severely limiting vantage point, the thinker is confronted by a possibility that had never even occurred to her before: that her whole way of 'taking the world' – here, its moral dimension – is, as it were, founded upon a *global illusion*. This kind of 'irrealism' can be radically unsettling. The suggestion is that all appearance is *mere*, and that there is no underlying reality of the kind she thought she had been perceiving, or attuned to.

Whether or not we wish to side with any irrealist by entertaining such radical misgivings, we nevertheless have to acknowledge that our senses can give us the *mistaken* impression that things are thus-and-so. Appearances can be *misleading*. Perceptual judgments – those judgments that are most sensitively attuned to the sensory data – can be *in error*. We learn, however, to correct the mistaken deliverances of one sensory modality, such as vision, when it is prone to error, by attending to another sensory modality, such as touch. This stratagem will work, for example, with the illusion of bent sticks in water. The stick might *look* bent, but it certainly does not *feel* bent. We also learn to correct for the limitations of our point of view. This includes distance from the perceived object(s), angle or color of lighting, spatial orientation, employment of extra senses, etc. When we get different 'takes' on a situation in this way, and attend to all the different kinds of sensory information that they might afford us, and employ methods of measurement and other more objective criteria, we are able to form cognitive representations of how things *actually* are, as opposed to how they might misleadingly, 'at first glance' as it were, *appear* to be.

But that is not all there is to the appearance/reality distinction. Thus far, it seems, the prospect is held out of attaining a correct representation of how things are by simply acquiring a richer range of sensory impressions, and processing them more carefully. But surely, the naïve thought might go, getting a proper grip on reality involves more than just piling up perceptions, in the hope that errors will largely cancel one another out, and a consensus across sensory channels will emerge? Surely we need to get a deeper grip on how things *really* are – in *themselves*, as it were? Surely we should be able to do so quite independently of how things might appear to us, or indeed to any other kind of rational agent that is able to perceive the world in some fashion, and represent it in thought?

This is a yearning for the 'real' as something more than just a superposition and integration of sensory impressions from the different sensory modalities. This is a longing to be able to grasp, intellectually, how things are in *themselves*, quite independently of how they might *appear to be* to any observers. It was a major feature of Kant's critical philosophy that he argued that this is an unrequitable yearning or longing, and one that is deeply irrational. The appearance/reality distinction is important. It needs to be drawn. But in drawing the distinction we do not need to resort to the philosophical extravagance of postulating *things in themselves* whose true nature cannot be revealed by perception augmented by explanatory hypotheses based thereon.

4.2 The mind/body distinction

We are aware of our own bodies in two importantly different ways.

The *first* way is the 'merely mechanical'. We realize that our bodies are physical objects, subject to the laws of energy and motion in the inanimate world. We are most acutely aware of this when we are at the mercy of physical forces that we cannot resist – tumbled by crashing waves in rough surf; falling out of a tree; losing one's footing on a steep slope …

The *second* way, however, is that our bodies will, within certain limits, 'do our bidding'. We can struggle to surface from the undertow; grab at branches as we fall; spreadeagle ourselves to exert friction on the screed …In trying to move our own bodies, we are aware of our own exertion of will (as well as of our spontaneous reflexes). We realize we do things *for good reasons*, such as avoiding injury and death. We are *mindful* of the extent to which we can *will* our own movements – movements, however, that are possible only within the constraints of the physical laws that govern our anatomies, and all other bodies, animate or inanimate. These laws we cannot change.

One can be, then, in a state of heightened awareness as a result of immediate physical dangers. Paradoxically one can be in a state of heightened awareness at the other extreme – comfortably ensconced in a safe and tranquil retreat, with one's eyes closed, not distracted by any extremes of heat or cold, or sounds, smells or aftertastes. In such circumstances one can become acutely aware of one's trains of thoughts, memories, reflections; pangs and plans; joys and regrets. One can engage in abstract contemplation of prime numbers, computable functions and infinite sets.

Comfortably thus ensconced, one might entertain the conceptual possibility of *zombies* – creatures supposedly like us in all observable respects, but strangely devoid of the kind of inner life we are currently discussing. One might wonder whether zombies are *metaphysically* possible (Chalmers (1996) argues that they are).

At the other extreme, one might entertain the possibility of a locus of awareness such as we take ourselves, under those congenial circumstances, to be, that is *no more than that* – just a locus of awareness, *without* a body to do its bidding. Such a locus of awareness would, presumably, spend a great deal of its time thinking about numbers, functions and sets, since there would be precious little else it *could* think about, given that, *ex hypothesi*, it has no body, hence no sensory organs or brain, that might have accumulated any memories, suffered any pangs, executed any plans, experienced any bodily joys, and committed any acts that it would later regret.

The experience of *being conscious* curiously presents itself, then, as possible without having a material body. Such a locus of awareness is what philosophers nowadays call a *disembodied Cartesian soul*. One does *not*, however, need to believe in the metaphysical possibility of disembodied Cartesian souls in order to grasp the important qualitative difference between mind and body. It is enough to acknowledge a rudimentary 'pre-reflective awareness' that accompanies any sensations one enjoys – for these are always experienced as sensations *of one's own*.

We have hinted that we might not really be able to make sense of being disembodied but conscious beings. And zombies might just be a philosopher's fancy – a conceptual possibility, but a metaphysical impossibility. Prescinding from questions about zombies and disembodied Cartesian souls, however, we can still sensibly ask 'What is fundamental to a person's identity?' – her 'stream of consciousness', regardless of potential body-hopping; or the identity of her body itself, regardless of how disease, or injury to, or operations on it might impair or change her personality, memory, preferences, values, aspirations and chosen life-projects? What *is* a person, ultimately – her *mind*, or her *body*? Note how *this* major problem about personal identity could not even be posed without our grasping the distinction between mind and body. And, with that distinction grasped, one can also ask: What is the relationship *between* a person's mind and her body? *That* is what is known as the 'mind–body problem'. We devote the greater part of Part IV to it.

4.3 The objective/subjective distinction

It is difficult to isolate a fixed sense in which philosophers understand the 'subjective' and the 'objective', even though they are agreed that there is a sharp contrast between them. This leads to a certain looseness of understanding of the distinction itself. One has to be careful, in philosophical discussion and debate, to make clear the exact sense in which one is intending the notions of 'subjective' and the 'objective' to be understood, in the context at hand.

The objective/subjective distinction is best motivated or illustrated by a few main independent contrasts that can be intuitively drawn. These contrasts are as follows:

(i)   The contrast between so-called *secondary* qualities (such as color) and *primary* qualities (such as shape, size and mass).

(ii) The contrast between an isolated agent's perspectivally limited, and perhaps biased, perceptions and opinions; and those beliefs that arise as the consensus of a group of individuals who are able to communicate with, hence are able also to criticize, one another.

(iii) The contrast between rational agents' subjective assessments of probabilities (often called *credences*); and the supposedly independent, objective *chances* that are thought to be built into the physical world.

(iv) The contrast between, on the one hand, thinking of ethical or moral qualities as 'projected' by the mind onto the world; and, on the other hand, thinking of them as properties of agents' characters and actions and of situations *in* the world, which can be discovered, represented and reflected in ethical or moral judgments.

(v) The contrast between the 'first-person' perspective on experience, on the part of the perceiving subject – how things seem to me, how things feel to me; and the 'third-person' perspective on the world that results from observers' shared experience of things outside of themselves.

The first contrast (i) we owe to John Locke. He highlighted the intuitive difference between the *shapes* and the *colors* of physical objects. Shapes we take to be independent of our perceiving them; colors, we realize, depend on our perceiving them. Science, Locke thought, could address only the problem of describing the primary qualities of objects, and the laws governing them. The primary qualities are shape, size, mass and location of physical bodies, in the case of the science of mechanics. There are also, of course, the forces of interaction, such as gravitational and electromagnetic forces; but these relational properties are also primary, or (metaphorically speaking) 'colorless'. They are 'there in the world' independently of any perceiving subjects. Objective truth, on this view, is to be had only about primary qualities. The rest – all secondary qualities included – is at best subjective. (Secondary qualities have recently been re-named within the analytic tradition: they are now called 'response-dependent concepts'.)

Another feature of Science, stressed to a greater extent by figures later than Locke (and especially by Popper), is its independent and objective *testability*. Here is where the second contrast (ii) is important. Scientific hypotheses, unlike mere subjective opinions, earn their status as attempts to get at the *objective* truth about the world because they can be *tested* and *criticized* and possibly even *refuted* through the investigations of others.

The third contrast (iii) between subjective and objective is in the modern theory of probability. There are different accounts of what probabilities *are*. At the 'subjective' end, they are taken to be degrees of belief (credences) of rational agents. At the 'objective' end, probabilities are thought of as long-run frequencies, or as determined by certain objective features in the physical world (such as the uniform composition and geometric symmetries of a die). Interestingly, despite the apparent gulf between these two conceptions of probability, they both satisfy the mathematical laws of probability theory due to Andrey Kolmogorov (1903–87).

The fourth contrast (iv) between subjective and objective underlies the opposing meta-ethical views of *emotivism* and *projectivism*, on the one hand, and *cognitivism* and *realism*, on the other. The issue at stake is whether ethical and moral judgments are mere expressions of emotion, desire or sentiment, which are not fact-stating; or are genuine judgments of fact that can be evaluated as true or false.

The fifth contrast (v) between subjective and objective is the one explored in greatest depth by the area of Philosophy known as Phenomenology. It has ramifications for Metaphysics, Epistemology, and Ethics, as well as for theories of personal identity and socio-political relations. Varieties of Phenomenology are professed by philosophers in the Continental tradition, such as Franz Brentano (1838–1917), Edmund Husserl (1859–1938), Martin Heidegger (1889–1976), Jacques Lacan (1901–81), Jean-Paul Sartre (1905–80), Simone de Beauvoir (1908–86), and Maurice Merleau-Ponty (1908–61). Vestiges of the phenomeno-logical way of thinking are arguably to be found even in the epistemologies of the analytical philosophers Bertrand Russell and Rudolf Carnap, both of whom began with the sensory data of a perceiving subject as basic or given, and sought to 'construct' the objects of the exernal world out of those data (exploiting the various similarities and continuities to be descried among the data). More recently, Thomas Nagel (b. 1937) has advanced an extreme realist phenomenological thesis: that there is *something that it is like* to be a bat (say), or any other creature that senses things and acts within the world. The inner nature of that 'being-for-itself' (as Sartre might have put it) is in principle inaccessible to us human beings; but, for all that, says Nagel, *there is* something that it is like to be a radically different life-form that perceives and acts.

   If, after these five very different examples, the reader still wishes to have univocal senses for 'subjective' and the 'objective', and the distinction between them, it would appear that the best one can offer is something along the following lines. If one thinks of an axis joining a rational agent to an external world that contains both other agents and objects of other kinds, the rule of thumb is that those features that are located at the agent's end (especially within the agent's mind) are subjective; while those located at the other end, 'in the world', are objective. But of course as soon as one takes a naturalizing view of the agent – regarding her as a complex physical object, interacting with other objects in a shared world – the dual prospect arises of *objectivity about subjectivity*, and *subjectivity about objectivity*.

4.4 The abstract/concrete distinction

The abstract/concrete distinction is motivated by this prime example: numbers are abstract; physical objects are concrete. These are the reasons why:

1   Numbers have no causal role; physical objects do.
2   Numbers lie 'outside' space-time; physical objects do not.
3   Numbers are not sensed; physical objects are.
4   There are infinitely many numbers, and necessarily so; but there could well be only finitely many physical objects.
5   Finally, there are systematic logical differences in the way we learn to talk about numbers and the way we learn to talk about physical things.

But if numbers are abstract, and knowledge is the result of how our brains are affected by things in the real world, how can we ever come to *know* (with *certainty*) facts about numbers?

Numbers serve here as a *paradigm example* of abstract objects. Note that we did not even specify whether we were thinking of *natural*, or *whole* numbers; or of *integers* (negative and positive); or of *rationals* (fractions); or of *reals*. There are, of course, yet other mathematical objects, and they are *all* abstract. *Sets*, for example, are abstract, even ones whose *members* are concrete.

Even outside Mathematics, we have occasion to deal with abstract objects. In grammar, for example, we distinguish between *types* and *tokens* of linguistic expressions. *Tokens* are *physical* things or events: typically, utterances or inscriptions. But different tokens can be of the same *type*. And types are abstract things. For example, if I say that there are two tokens of the word 'one' in the following sentence-token:

One plus one equals two

then I am thinking of the word 'one' as an abstract expression-*type*. If I think of the *type* of the sentence just displayed, I realize that it contains two *occurrences* of the *word-type* 'one'. These distinct (and still abstract) type-occurrences of the word 'one' within the sentence-type become two corresponding and distinct *tokens* of that word-type when the sentence-type is tokened. Sentence-types are sequences of word-types; and sequences of words can of course have repetitions of words within them. When speaking of types, we call these repetitions *occurrences*. When sentence-types (i.e., abstract sequences of word-types) are tokened, distinct occurrences (of word-types) become distinct tokens (of the same word-type). The notion of an occurrence finds application also when *words* are construed as sequences of *letters*. The word-type 'deed' contains two occurrences of the letter 'd', and two occurrence of the letter 'e'. The token of the word-type that you have just read between the quote marks contains, correspondingly, two distinct tokens of the letter 'd' and two distinct tokens of the letter 'e'.

Carefully distinguishing types from tokens, and tokens from occurrences, is not a captious exercise. It is very important for an understanding of certain major philosophical positions, such as the type-type- and token-token-identity theories of the relationship between mind and body. More on these anon.

Some theorists hold that *colors* are abstract objects. The color red, or the universal *redness*, they maintain, is the abstract thing or attribute that is instantiated by, or 'partaken in', all and only red things. This is supposedly the case even though redness inheres only in concrete, observable objects.

Philosophers tend to agree that we have a reasonably firm understanding of the distinction between abstract and concrete. They tend to disagree, however, over whether there actually are any abstract objects, and, if so, which ones these really are. A *nominalist* is someone who denies the existence of *any* abstract objects, maintaining that to believe in them is to be in the grip of an intellectual illusion. We label as a *Platonist* someone who (especially in Mathematics) believes in the existence of abstract objects.

4.5 The descriptive/normative distinction

Think of the word 'ought' here as expressing a *moral* 'ought', as in 'One ought not to kill innocents'. We are acutely aware that, all too frequently, what *is* the case *ought not to be* the case; and that what *was* the case *ought not to have been* the case. Examples would be otiose for those with reasonably normal moral sensibilities; and would be useless for those without them. So we shall refrain from the usual list that ends with the Holocaust.

Put another way:

> The *deontic* operator 'It ought to be the case that …' (O) is *non-factive*. That is to say, the *inference* 'Op, therefore p' is *invalid*, or *fallacious*.

Contrast this with the *factive* operators 'It is known that …' (K) and 'It is necessary that …' (□). The inferences '*Kp*, therefore *p*' and '□*p*, therefore *p*' are both valid.

Statements of the form O*p* are *normative*. In fact, statements of the form O*p* are most frequently made when *p* is *not* the case – their role being to draw attention to the latter fact as a source of moral concern or even outrage, and as grounds for reforming or retributive action. By contrast, the statement *p* in question, especially when it is devoid of any operators like O, is a *descriptive* statement, possessed of truth-conditions that can be verified as obtaining, when they do obtain, by straightforwardly mathematical and empirical investigation – in the broadest sense, by the natural sciences.

Now, the *distinction* between the descriptive and the normative is a genuine distinction only if the grounds for the truth or assertability of normative statements are not themselves part of the reality that can be investigated by the natural sciences. The distinction is useful, and worth making, mainly to a theorist who is *not* committed to the view that the normative is 'naturalizable'.

Many theorists of the normative, indeed, think of normative statements as *not* making factual claims whose truth (in the best cases) can be discovered by the usual methods of scientific investigation. They are *non-cognitivists* or *quasi-realists* or *irrealists* about the normative. Non-cognitivists think of normative statements as expressing the preferences or pro-attitudes of the speaker; or evincing certain emotions on her part. Their leading idea is that what appear to be *statements* (of fact) in the case of morals are no such thing; rather, they *express* or *project* a speaker-attitude. Quasi-realists, by contrast, do not go so far. They still take seriously one's making of what appear to be moral statements, in an assertoric mode; but they propose that we should suitably revise our understanding of such statements' role in discourse, so as to (i) cordon them off from the genuinely descriptive statements that science is supposed to deliver, but also (ii) earn us the right to continue speaking in moral terms, as though we were indeed making genuine statement in doing so. They seek, as it were, to 'save the appearances' of moral assertions while re-construing them as not about genuinely factual matters.

Irrealists go much further, grabbing the bull by the horns. They say that moral assertions are uniformly *false*, for want of a real subject matter.

It is to theorists such as these that Hume appealed (since he was one of them) when he drew attention, in his famous *Treatise on Human Nature* (Hume (1738)) to what is now known as the 'is–ought' fallacy, or, after Moore (1903), the 'naturalistic fallacy'. According to Hume and Moore, no conclusion of the form Op may be validly derived from descriptive premises (no matter how numerous) of the form 'It *is* the case that q_1, ..., It *is* the case that q_n'.

The descriptive/normative distinction is sometimes referred to as the 'fact/value' distinction. Clearly, the value-theorist who insists on it, and who believes, with Hume, that all 'is–ought' transitions are fallacious, cannot allow that evaluative statements are statements *of fact*. For that would undermine the very framing of the problem highlighted by the 'is–ought' fallacy (assuming that it is indeed a fallacy).

4.6 The empirical/rational distinction

Empirical knowledge depends for its justification on the operation of our five senses (sight, hearing, touch, taste, smell; possibly also proprioception, and 'internal' sensing, such as is involved with pain and nausea). Examples of propositions known (or believed) on the basis of empirical evidence are:

> Grass is green.
> All ravens are black.
> All emeralds are green.
> All metal bars, when heated, expand.
> Any two bodies attract each other with a gravitational force.
> This lectern is made of wood.
> Water is H_2O.
> She's feeling queasy.
> I have a toothache now.

Rational knowledge is knowledge that can be acquired and justified *without* appealing to sensory evidence. It derives solely from the exercise of reason and understanding.

A *logical* example of rational knowledge would be the *Law of Non-Contradiction*:

> It is not the case that both P and not-P.

(For 'P' here substitute any proposition you wish.)

Conceptual examples of rational knowledge are:

> Every red thing is colored. Nothing can be both red and green simultane-
> ously all over. It is possible that there could be a transparent white object,

even if one does not actually exist. All horses' tails are animals' tails. Every physical object is extended. Every bachelor is an unmarried man. Persons in pain know they are. I am here now. (A *priori* true for the author, when he wrote it down. A *priori* true for you, dear reader, as you read it for yourself.)

Arithmetical examples of rational knowledge are:

Zero is the first natural number. Every natural number has a successor. No two distinct natural numbers have the same successor. There is no last (i.e., greatest) natural number. $2 + 3 = 5$.

For those readers unfamiliar with this terminology: the successor of a natural number n is the natural number that comes immediately after n, i.e., $n + 1$.

In any account of rational knowledge, the subject of *Logic* looms large. Logic is that branch of Philosophy that studies *valid argument*, or the 'laws of thought'. These laws are *normative* or *prescriptive*, not descriptive. They tell us how we *ought* to reason. Logic is the purest means by which we can generate newer knowledge from knowledge we already have.

The most basic valid forms of reasoning may be stated as *rules of inference*, such as

$$\frac{P \qquad Q}{P \, and \, Q} \qquad \frac{P \quad if \, P \, then \, Q}{Q} \qquad \frac{F(a) \qquad a = b}{F(b)} \, .$$

You may think of these rules as templates for truth-preserving transition in thought *downwards* (on the page). The first rule assures you that if you have already shown that P is true, and have shown that Q is true, then you may immediately infer (i.e., make the deductive transition to) their conjunction 'P and Q'. The second rule assures you that if you have already shown that P is true, and have shown that the conditional statement 'If P then Q' is true, then you may immediately infer the conclusion Q. Finally, the third rule is one we use all the time when reasoning in mathematics with equations: if you have shown that some object a has the property F, and have shown that a is identical to b, then you may immediately infer that b has the property F. Example: from '7 is prime' and '$7 = 3 + 4$', you may immediately infer '$3 + 4$ is prime'.

The adverb 'immediately' here (in the phrase 'immediately infer') is very significant. It means that these rules are utterly *primitive*, and cannot be derived from other rules. If you cannot grasp the validity of the rule

$$\frac{P \qquad Q}{P \, and \, Q}$$

then you cannot be credited with an understanding of the word 'and'. If you cannot grasp the validity of the rule

$$\frac{P \quad if\,P\,then\,Q}{Q}$$

then you cannot be credited with an understanding of the conditional construction 'if …then ___'. And if you cannot grasp the validity of the rule

$$\frac{F(a) \quad a=b}{F(b)}$$

then you cannot be credited with an understanding of the logical relation of identity (represented by '=').

Chains or, more generally, tree-like arrays of (instances of) such basic steps of inference are called *proofs*. Logical proofs show what conclusions are *logically implied*, or *entailed* by given assumptions. Proofs establish valid arguments. Validity turns on logical *form*; it depends only on the meanings of the *logical constants* such as 'not', 'and', 'or', 'if …then …', 'some', 'all', 'is identical to'; and on the *repetitions* of non-logical expressions within the sentences concerned. The logical constants we have mentioned are the ones whose inferential powers are characterized by the modern system of *first-order logic*.

Logic can also provide proofs of *inconsistency* of systems of belief that are inherently *contradictory*. Our scientific theories, for example, can be found to contradict what we observe. For predictions are *logically deduced* from those theories taken in combination with statements of initial or boundary conditions. These predictions may conflict with what we observe when we perform an experiment satisfying the initial conditions. When this happens, we may regard the scientific theory as *refuted*. So Logic plays a crucial role in *testing* scientific theories against the observable evidence. That is why even the most extreme empiricist has to concede that *rational* knowledge of 'relations among ideas' is involved in choosing from among competing scientific theories that have been constructed on the basis of the empirical data.

Mathematicians use Logic to prove mathematical *theorems* from mathematical *axioms*. The axioms are usually obvious, self-evident, certain. Logical proofs draw out from the axioms deep, elegant, and arresting theorems. This poses an interesting problem: how can logic produce arresting theorems from obvious axioms when all its primitive steps are obvious and necessarily truth-preserving? Many of those theorems subsequently find application in the natural and social sciences. This poses another interesting problem: how can Mathematics, which is all about *abstract* objects, be brought to bear on an external world of *concrete* objects, in such a way as to enable us to anticipate their behavior, and perhaps even control it? What explains, in the memorable phrase of Eugene Wigner (1902–95), the 'unreasonable effectiveness of mathematics'?

4.7 The distinctions between the necessary and the true, and between the false and the impossible

Think of the rectangle below as containing all propositions, or all statements in one's language. The usual picture is that it is partitioned into the *true* and the *false*; and that among the former are the *necessary* propositions, and among the latter are the *impossible* ones:

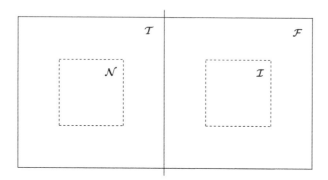

The way we explain the difference between the 'merely' true and the necessarily true is by invoking the notion of a *possible world*, due to Leibniz. Possible worlds were belatedly exploited by Saul Kripke (b. 1940) in the first formal semantics for formal languages containing symbols representing the notions 'it is necessary that …' and 'it is possible that …'. These are the two main operators in so-called *modal* logic. The formal notation $\Box p$ represents 'It is necessary that p', and the notation $\Diamond p$ represents 'It is possible that p'.

'Mere' truth is truth in the *actual* world. *Necessary* truth, by contrast, is truth in *every possible world*. Possible worlds are coherent alternatives to the actual world, embodying how the contingent facts might otherwise have been. The explanation of the difference between the 'merely' false and the impossible is exactly the same, but with 'true' replaced by 'false' throughout.

Here are some examples to help fix ideas.

Necessarily true ($\mathcal{N}$):

Not(*P* and not *P*).	[Logical]
$2 + 3 = 5$.	[Mathematical]
All red things are colored.	[Conceptual]

True but not necessarily so ($\mathcal{T}$):

Grass is green.	[Empirical]
All metal bars, when heated, expand.	[Empirical]
There are eight planets in our solar system.	[Empirical]

False but not impossible ($\mathcal{F}$*):*

Grass is purple.	[Empirical]
Some metal bars, when heated, contract.	[Empirical]
There are only seven planets in our solar system.	[Empirical]

Impossible ($\mathcal{I}$*):*

P and not-P.	[Logical]
$2 + 3 = 7$.	[Mathematical]
This ball is red all over and green all over.	[Conceptual]

Now, the astute reader will have noticed a threat of circularity in our explanation above of possible worlds. In our characterization of them, we used the notions 'coherent' and 'contingent'. The former might just be a synonym for 'possible', and the latter means 'neither necessary nor impossible'. So have we really made any progress in explaining the concepts of necessity and possibility with the required level of generality, as opposed to gesturing at the concepts via the illustrative instances that we have provided?

First, let us relate the two modal concepts to one another. The necessity of a proposition *p* may be equated with the impossibility of its negation, not-*p*:

It is necessary that *p* if and only if it is not possible that not-*p*.

Or, in symbols:

$$\Box p \leftrightarrow \neg \Diamond \neg p.$$

Given that we understand negation ($\neg$), we can focus our clarificatory efforts on possibility ($\Diamond$). The challenge is to specify senses in which one world is a possible alternative to another. From our vantage point in the actual world, which alternative worlds can we countenance as (i) *logically or conceptually* possible? (ii) *metaphysically* possible? (iii) *nomologically* possible?

Ad (i). Logical or conceptual possibilities include those that are the furthest-fetched. In this sense we can regard as possible certain worlds where the weirdest things might be the case, provided only that no logical or mathematical contradiction is involved in imagining them. These could include the imaginary worlds of hallucinating acid-heads.

Ad (ii). More tightly constrained are the *metaphysical* possibilities. An example of such a constraint is that no metaphysically possible world W can contain *you* as an inhabitant unless W contains also the very same egg and sperm from whose union *you* actually resulted in the actual world, and in W *you* result from that same union. It is not just a matter of finding for you, in the other world W, a *Doppelgänger* who is passingly similar to you in outward appearance or is called by the same name. The identity has to be more thorough than that; it has to be much more 'intrinsic'. On the other hand, there are metaphysically possible worlds W' in which your parents exist, *but did not produce you or your siblings*, even though they produced *other* children in W'. This is an interesting metaphysical asymmetry: our parents are essential to us – they are necessary for our own existence – but not conversely.

The reader might have seen those strange 'worlds' depicted in the ingenious drawings of M. C. Esher. A particularly famous one involves weird convolutions of ever-ascending but back-looping stairways. This is a spatially, hence metaphysically, *im*possible world.

Ad (iii). Most tightly constrained of all are the *nomological* possibilities. As the adjective suggests (*nomos* in Greek means *law*), these are possible worlds in which the same laws of nature govern what goes on as govern what goes on in the actual world. An alternative, nomologically possible world might be one where, say, the Sun happens to have fewer planets than it actually does; or the Milky Way galaxy happens to contain more habitable planets than it actually does; or the furniture in your living room has been rearranged. But all these alternative facts are contemplated as obtaining in a world in which the laws of general relativity and quantum mechanics (say) still hold.

Recall the following important distinction from Chapter 1, which we shall be discussing at greater length in Chapter 5. *A posteriori* truths are ones we can know only on the basis of sensory experience; by contrast, *a priori* truths are those that are knowable without recourse to any sensory experience. (We set aside here any sensory experience that might be needed in order to acquire grasp of any of the constituent concepts involved. The point is just that, once those concepts are mastered, no further sensory experience would be relevant to the determination of the truth of the *a priori* proposition involved.)

For a long time, philosophers thought it was obvious that

(i)   all necessary truths are knowable *a priori*,

and that the following corollary of (i) is also obvious:

(ii) all truths knowable only *a posteriori* must be contingent,
        i.e., not necessary (and obviously also not impossible).

Many, however, have now been persuaded by some resourceful examples from Kripke that these two principles are mistaken. Counterexamples to (i) and (ii) appear below.

Necessarily true ($\mathcal{N}$):

Water is H_2O.   [Empirical; knowable only *a posteriori*]

True but not necessarily so (T):

The standard meter rod is one meter long.   [Conceptual; knowable *a priori*]

4.8 The theory/evidence distinction

Our discussion of this distinction has been saved for the very end of this chapter because of the significantly increased demands that §4.8.2 makes on the reader's attention. The considerations, however, are laid out as clearly and accessibly as the intrinsic difficulty of the material permits. The slow and careful reader will be rewarded for patient effort.

The theory/evidence distinction is important for our understanding of how our systems of knowledge are organized, and how the various items of knowledge that they contain are justified. It is important to understand, at the outset, that evidence for a theory is not necessarily what 'ultimately justifies' all the statements of the theory. We need to distinguish between *evidence for* a theory, and any *foundational basis* that the theory might enjoy. All that is required, logically, of the evidence for a theory is that the theory should *logically imply* the evidence. But it would be the exception rather than the rule that the evidence would logically imply any theory that explains it. Evidence itself is, in general terms, comprised of statements that are evidently true to well-positioned and competent observers (in the empirical case), or are evident upon suitable intellectual reflection (in the mathematical case, or in the area of *a priori* normative theorizing).

4.8.1 The empirical case

In the case of empirical knowledge, the evidence should consist of very basic, observable matters of particular fact, about which one can expect different observers' agreement to be reliable. We should be aware of how other statements not directly included in the evidence are 'inferred' from it. Frequently, so-called *inductive* inferences will be involved. These are inferences that *go beyond* the singular bits of evidence that prompt them (the premises for the inference), by arriving at conclusions that are logically stronger than the premises, taken collectively. For this reason such inferences are sometimes called *amplifying* or *ampliative*. An ampliative inference is, by definition, *logically fallacious* from the point of view of *deductive* logic. But with *inductive* reasoning about the external world, matters are different. Such inferences can and often do strike one as 'sound', in so far as world is concerned. 'What does one mean here by "sound"?', the reader might ask. Quick answer: the truth of the premises provides some sort of guarantee that the conclusion is *highly likely* to be true. Here are some examples of inductive inferences that are sound in this informal sense:

1   Raven #1 is black; Raven #2 is black; …; Raven #n is black;
     so, all ravens are black.

2 Emerald #1 is green; Emerald #2 is green; ...; Emerald #*n* is green; so, all emeralds are green.
3 Metal bar #1 expanded when heated; Metal bar #2 expanded when heated; ...; Metal bar #*n* expanded when heated;
   so, all metal bars expand when heated.
4 Every otherwise unsupported object of which anyone has let go has dropped to the ground;
   so, every otherwise unsupported object of which anyone lets go drops to the ground.
5 Every lump of sugar that has been dropped into boiling water has dissolved;
   so, every lump of sugar that is dropped into boiling water dissolves.

The conclusions of these inductive inferences are not logically implied by the immediately preceding data (their premises); rather, the logical implication is the other way round.

To what extent does the evidence really support, or confirm, or make more likely, a theory built upon it? Does the theory integrate and explain the evidence? Does the theory generate new predictions that can be put to evidential or experimental test? These are questions that are to be raised about any theory put forward on the basis of the evidence.

The important thing about a good empirical theory that is 'based' on a certain body of observational evidence is that it is not just a summary of the evidence; logically, it *goes beyond* the evidence, by implying observation statements that have yet to be verified or falsified. It is a major problem for the articulation of good scientific method to explain how theories *ought* to be constructed on the basis of given evidence. (Philosophical observation: this is a methodological 'ought', not a moral one. Metaphilosophical question: *Really?* Might not the first kind of 'ought', upon deeper analysis, turn out to be a special case of the second one?)

4.8.2 The mathematical case

The beginner who has had no experience of university-level Pure Mathematics might wish to skim this subsection, but should not neglect it altogether. It contains explanations of some terminology that will be used again later.

It is important to consider an *a priori* case such as Mathematics, when seeking a fuller understanding of how any theory relates to the possible evidence for it.

Matters are slightly different in the case of mathematical knowledge from what has just been explained for the case of empirical knowledge. Consider, as an instructive example, the theory of natural numbers (the familiar 'whole numbers'). This theory is what foundationalists call 'arithmetic'. The natural numbers form the infinite *progression*

$$0, 1, 2, 3, \ldots \text{ ad infinitum.}$$

(A progression can also be characterized, more long-windedly, as a *discrete linear ordering in which exactly one element is not immediately preceded by any element.*)

We have an infinite supply of 'particular' or 'singular' facts about these numbers (the 'numerical data', so to speak). A hackneyed example is '2 + 2 = 4'. A less hackneyed one is Kant's famous '7 + 5 = 12'. These two examples concern addition. But we would wish also to consider multiplication. Particular (true) statements of the forms '$n + m = p$' or '$i \times j = k$' comprise what we are here calling the 'numerical data'. These are the simple arithmetical truths (the 'basic equations') that one could take to be the direct analogues of observational statements in the case of empirical knowledge – in spite of the fact that there are infinitely many of these simple truths. We are going to examine the relationship between the 'numerical data' and the arithmetical theory that seeks to capture *all the truths* about the natural numbers, i.e., all the true sentences in the language of arithmetic, no matter how complex they might be, grammatically. Among such statements are those of more general but still readily understandable forms, such as 'Every number is less than some prime number'.

The notion 'n is prime', it is worth pointing out, can be explicitly defined in terms of the primitive notions we shall be using:

for all m, for all k, if $m \times k = n$, then either $m = s0$ or $k = s0$.

In symbols:

$\forall m \forall k(m \times k = n \rightarrow (m = s0 \vee k = s0))$.

Likewise, the notion 'n is less than m' can be so defined:

for some k, $k \neq 0$ and $n + k = m$.

In symbols:

$\exists k(\neg k = 0 \wedge n + k = m)$.

The standard theory about the natural numbers uses the name 0 and the successor-function symbol s, to re-designate the infinite progression as

$0, s0, ss0, sss0, \ldots$ *ad infinitum.*

To repeat: we are interested in the behavior of these numbers under addition ($+$) and multiplication ($\times$). We want to know not only the 'computational' facts (the true *equations*), but also all the true *generalizations* about numbers. We have suggested that we take the *basic equations* as the *data* for the theory of arithmetic.

But now we must address the following question:

Can those data form a sufficient *foundation* for the theory of arithmetic?

The data can be arranged in the following two infinite tables. (Here we revert to standard decimal notation, for obvious reasons of economy of display.)

+	0	1	2	3	4	5	...
0	0	1	2	3	4	5	...
1	1	2	3	4	5	6	...
2	2	3	4	5	6	7	...
3	3	4	5	6	7	8	...
4	4	5	6	7	8	9	...
5	5	6	7	8	9	10	...
⋮	⋮	⋮	⋮	⋮	⋮	⋮	⋱

×	0	1	2	3	4	5	...
0	0	0	0	0	0	0	...
1	0	1	2	3	4	5	...
2	0	2	4	6	8	10	...
3	0	3	6	9	12	15	...
4	0	4	8	12	16	20	...
5	0	5	10	15	20	25	...
⋮	⋮	⋮	⋮	⋮	⋮	⋮	⋱

Each table contains, in its *i*-th row and *j*-th column, the sum, or product, respectively, of *i* and *j*, in that order. The addition and multiplication tables contain the basic information about the two operations + and × that the logician or mathematician would have to express by means of infinitely many equations:

$$0+0=0 \qquad 0 \times 0 = 0$$
$$1+0=1 \qquad 1 \times 0 = 0$$
$$0+1=1 \qquad 0 \times 1 = 0$$
$$0+2=2 \qquad 0 \times 2 = 0$$
$$1+1=2 \qquad 1 \times 1 = 1$$
$$2+0=2 \qquad 2 \times 0 = 0$$
$$3+0=3 \qquad 3 \times 0 = 0$$
$$2+1=3 \qquad 2 \times 1 = 2$$
$$1+2=3 \qquad 1 \times 2 = 2$$
$$0+3=3 \qquad 0 \times 3 = 0$$
$$\vdots \qquad\qquad \vdots$$

The result of any (finite) addition or multiplication problem, of whatever complexity of nestings of operations, can be worked out by developing each table just (finitely) far enough. Answers to these computational problems are given by *equations*. The part already on display in the tables above suffices, for example, to 'verify by look-up' the equation

$$(2+3) \times (1+2) = 15$$

and the equation

$$2 + ((3 \times 1) + 2) = 7.$$

Look-up operations, however, fall short of theoretical insight. In particular, they do not afford any awareness of *generalities*, such as

for all n, $n + 0 = n$

(in symbols: $\forall n\, n + 0 = n$)

and

for all n, $n \times 0 = 0$

(in symbols: $\forall n\, n \times 0 = 0$).

From now on, we shall give the full symbolizations immediately after the sentences in 'logician's English'. This will help the logically unversed reader to acquire a sense of the logical syntax of formal languages.

Standing 'outside' the tables, and imagining them rotated about their diagonal axes from top left to bottom right, we can 'see' that the *laws of commutativity* hold for the two operations of addition and multiplication:

for all n, for all m, $n + m = m + n$

$\forall n \forall m\, n + m = m + n$

and

for all n, for all m, $n \times m = m \times n$

$\forall n \forall m\, n \times m = m \times n$.

It is harder, however, to 'see' in similar fashion that the *laws of associativity* hold:

for all n, for all m, for all k, $(n + m) + k = n + (m + k)$

$\forall n \forall m \forall k\, (n + m) + k = n + (m + k)$

and

for all n, for all m, for all k, $(n \times m) \times k = n \times (m \times k)$

$\forall n \forall m \forall k\, (n \times m) \times k = n \times (m \times k)$,

let alone that the *law of distributivity* holds:

for all n, for all m, for all k, $n \times (m + k) = (n \times m) + (n \times k)$

$\forall n \forall m \forall k\, n \times (m + k) = (n \times m) + (n \times k)$.

Here is the basic conundrum for the theorist about numbers. The tables above, or the infinite lists that spell out their information as basic equations, *determine all* the computational (or equational) facts about addition and multiplication on the natural numbers. So, in an intuitively obvious sense, they should fix also the truth-value (*True* or *False*) of *any statement in the language of arithmetic*, no matter how logically complex that statement might be. But the infinite set of true basic equations above (the 'basic computations') fails to entail any *generalities* about numbers. Indeed, not even the set of *all* true equations entails any generalities about numbers. As is the case with ordinary scientific induction, we confront here the hard logical fact that *no amount of evidence in the form of 'particularities', not even an infinite amount, can collectively entail a statement of universally generalized form about the infinite domain of things in question* (here: the natural numbers).

The mathematician is therefore forced to lay down *at least some* generalities as *first principles*, to be used as starting points in proofs of generalizations about the numbers. In a triumph of distillation, Richard Dedekind (1831–1916) and Giuseppe Peano (1858–1932) between them did two things. First, Dedekind laid down two axioms (first principles) to fix the idea of the progression

$$0, s0, ss0, sss0, \ldots ad\ infinitum.$$

The axioms in question were

for all n, $sn \neq 0$

$\forall n \, \neg sn = 0;$

and

for all n, for all m, if $sn = sm$ then $n = m$

$\forall n \forall m (sn = sm \rightarrow n = m).$

These say, respectively, '0 is initial' and 'The successor relation never branches backwards'.

Secondly, Peano laid down what are now known as the *recursion equations* for addition and multiplication:

Logician's English:	Fully formal logical notation:
for all n, $n + 0 = n$	$\forall n \; n + 0 = n$
for all n, for all m, $n + sm = s(m + n)$	$\forall n \forall m \; n + sm = s(m + n)$
for all n, $n \times 0 = 0$	$\forall n \; n \times 0 = 0$
for all n, for all m, $n \times sm = (n \times m) + n.$	$\forall n \forall m \; n \times sm = (n \times m) + n.$

All by themselves, the recursion equations logically imply *every true equation of arithmetic*. They encapsulate the total content of the addition and multiplication tables above, as well as all results of their iterated applications. *But* – and this is a significant 'but' – they do not, by themselves, entail the theoretically interesting generalities mentioned above (commutativity, associativity, distributivity).

In order to capture these and other generalities as logical consequences of our first principles, we need one more first principle of overriding importance: the Principle of Mathematical Induction. The aim behind the postulation of this principle is to capture the idea that the progression

0, s0, ss0, sss0, ... *ad infinitum*

contains *all* the natural numbers. It does this by stipulating that any property *P* holds of all numbers provided that *P* holds of 0, and *P* holds of the successor of any number of which it holds:

if (*P*0 and for all *n*, if *Pn* then *Psn*), then for all *m*, *Pm*

$(P0 \wedge \forall n(Pn \rightarrow Psn)) \rightarrow \forall m Pm.$

Here, now, is the rub. If we want the Principle of Mathematical Induction to be a single statement, we need to include in it the explicit *second-order* prefix 'For all *P*':

For all *P*, if (*P*0 and for all *n*, if *Pn* then *Psn*), then for all *m*, *Pm*

$\forall P((P0 \wedge \forall n(Pn \rightarrow Psn)) \rightarrow \forall m Pm).$

That, however, makes our language a so-called *second-order* language, because it allows one to express generalizations not only about individuals (here, the numbers) but also about *properties of* individuals. And the problem with a second-order language is that it has *no complete proof-system* (see §1.2.3).

One can seek to avoid that limitation by insisting, instead, on regarding '*P*' in

if (*P*0 and for all *n*, if *Pn* then *Psn*), then for all *m*, *Pm*

not as a second-order variable with a universal reading, but rather as a schematic 'placeholder' for all the infinitely many formulae of the *first-order* language that could be substituted for those occurrences of '*P*' in what is now the (first-order) *Axiom Scheme* of Mathematical Induction. This brings with it the reassurance that we have a complete proof-system for the first-order language we are working with; and we also know that every important result that mathematicians have already proved by appeal to Mathematical Induction can have its proof formalized at first order by choosing suitable substituends for '*P*' in the uses the proof makes of Mathematical Induction.

The aforementioned Dedekind–Peano axioms, along with the Axiom Scheme of Mathematical Induction, form what is now known as the theory PA (for 'Peano Arithmetic' – Dedekind, sadly, losing thereby the credit he richly deserved for his own pioneering contributions).

But now we face another, quite extraordinary, problem. It turns out that there is no *unique* consistent theory in the first-order language of arithmetic that contains *all the true numerical equations*. Put another way: within the confines of a first-order language, anyone who takes the set of *true numerical equations* as the sole 'data' that need to be explained (i.e., logically implied) by their theory of arithmetic has to choose somehow from among *infinitely many* different theories when seeking to capture *all the truths* about numbers. These competing theories, we repeat, *all agree* on *the true numerical equations*.

It turns out, for reasons too deep and technical to broach here, that the guiding methodological principle governing choices of ever-stronger theoretical principles for arithmetic has to be to ensure that the standard progression of numbers captures *all the numbers there are*. This is remarkably like applying 'Occam's Razor', which in the natural sciences is the admonition not to 'multiply entities beyond necessity'. Occam's Razor, it turns out, applies just as sharply in the foundations of arithmetic. We have to do everything we can to avoid being obliged to acknowledge the existence of so-called 'non-standard' natural numbers – those shadowy entities that lie 'beyond' all the whole numbers, in any so-called 'non-standard model' for arithmetic. The only way to avoid commitment to them is by making the right choices of new theoretical principles. And this process, ironically, takes us way beyond the numerical 'data'. The data concern *what is*. The arithmetical principles we need (beyond instances of Mathematical Induction) seek to tell us *what is not*. These principles come from a much deeper source – from Logic, or from *a priori* intuitions – than the 'numerical evidence' itself.

Problems

1 You have almost certainly heard the dismissive comment (about a certain set of beliefs or assertions) that it is 'just a theory'. Under what conditions would such a comment actually succeed in being dismissive or critical?
2 Do you think that the alleged 'naturalistic fallacy' is an impediment to bringing any scientific findings or hypotheses to bear on the question of how we ought to conduct ourselves?
3 Is it at all important for the pursuit of science that we resolve the question whether numbers exist?
4 In light of the distinction between primary and secondary qualities, in what sense would a 'science of color (vision)' be possible?
5 Do any of the distinctions listed and discussed in this chapter strike you as unclear in principle? insufficiently motivated? unlikely to serve any useful intellectual purpose? a 'distinction without a difference'? *undermined* or *made obsolete* by more recent scientific findings?
6 Choose a simple phenomenon or regularity in nature whose scientific explanation you understand. Can you clearly distinguish the respective contributions, to that explanation, of *empirical statements* and of *mathematical statements*?

5   Kant's Two Distinctions

The previous chapter covered the following distinctions:

1   appearance/reality
2   mind/body
3   objective/subjective
4   abstract/concrete
5   descriptive/normative
6   empirical knowledge v. rational knowledge
7   necessary/true/false/impossible
8   theory/evidence.

This chapter is devoted to the two famous distinctions whose importance was heavily stressed by Kant:

1   *a priori/a posteriori*
2   analytic/synthetic.

5.1 The distinction between *a priori* and *a posteriori* knowledge

We have already, in §1.1, provided some brief remarks about this distinction and about the distinction to be discussed in §5.2 (between analytic and synthetic truth). The logical, conceptual and arithmetical examples of rationally knowable truths given above are also fine examples of *a priori* knowledge. One can come to appreciate that they are true merely by exercising one's reason and understanding. One does not need to undertake any empirical investigations in order to establish them as true. No observations are needed; no compilations or analyses of observational data; no experimental set-ups; no field work.

By contrast, the propositions in the earlier list in §4.6, beginning with the jaded example 'Grass is green', are said to be *a posteriori*: that is, they are knowable only *after* taking in the relevant sensory evidence for their truth.

Many *a priori* truths of the conceptual kind are generated by the relations of *subordination* and *superordination* of concepts or attributes. Thus:

Human beings are rational animals.
All red things are colored.

One can think of concepts as arranged in a tree-like structure. A portion of the tree might be:

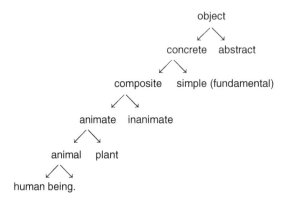

Let us be clear about how the indicated relations of subordination are to be understood. Look, for example, at the subordination of *animate* to *composite*. We are saying that it is *a priori* that all animate things are composite. If someone questions whether this is so, the answer is affirmative: given that we already deploy the concepts *animate* and *composite*, as these have been developed in the appropriate regions of our language and our theorizing, we can, without needing any further recourse to sensory experience, respond with a confident 'Yes' to the question 'Are all animate things composite?' The only non-composite things are (whatever turn out to be the *absolutely*) fundamental particles. So the only way to falsify the claim that all animate things are composite would be to describe a possible case, without insult or injury to the *concepts* involved, of an animate *fundamental particle*. But this cannot be done. For suppose the critic proffers α as a would-be animate fundamental particle. *Qua* fundamental particle, α would be governed by the laws of fundamental particle physics. Yet, *qua* supposedly animate thing, α would have to behave in ways characteristic of animate things. It would have to respire; take in nutrients; grow; and potentially reproduce after its own kind. All that is behavior incompatible with the behavior allowed (on α's part) by the laws of fundamental particle physics.

The branch of Philosophy known as *ontology* is concerned with the fundamental 'branchings' that one would want to make within the 'tree of being'. It would be concerned with whether the distinctions involved get at an independent fact of the matter, or merely reflect human interests, be these the accidental results of our biological make-up or of our social and linguistic conditioning.

It is a matter of controversy whether all the relations of subordination and superordination represented by the arrows in such a 'tree of being' are purely conceptual, or whether they incorporate empirical findings. The conceptualist contends that sensory experience might well be needed in order to *acquire a grasp* of the concepts involved in the tree; but that, once the concepts are grasped, or understood, it is *by virtue of that understanding alone – by virtue of the exercise of that grasp* – that one can appreciate that certain subordinations and superordinations obtain. Thus rational knowledge of the conceptual variety is possible. (For example, from the tree fragment above: 'All human beings are animals.')

5.2 The analytic/synthetic distinction

Logical and conceptual truths are often called *analytic.* They are supposed to be true *by virtue of their meanings alone.* Statements that depend for their truth not only on their meanings but also on 'the way the world is' are called *synthetic.*

One of the major controversies of post-Kantian philosophy is over the question:

Are there any synthetic a priori truths?

This is why 'synthetic' cannot be equated with 'empirical'. Kant maintained there were important synthetic *a priori* truths, and that among these were the fundamental principles of natural science (such as the principle of causation: *Every event has a cause*) and mathematical truths (both arithmetical and Euclidean-geometrical). In inventing the analytic–synthetic distinction in the first place, Kant had wanted to show that mathematics was (wholly) synthetic *a priori*, arising out of the pure forms of intuition of space and time. (Cf. Kant (1781), tr. Norman Kemp Smith.) Arithmetic arose out of the pure form of

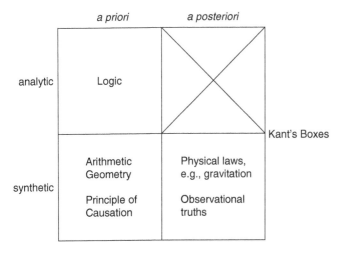

intuition of time, and Euclidean geometry out of the pure form of intuition of space. So for Kant the arrangement of truths was as in the diagram just given. Note that everyone is agreed that the top box on the right, for 'analytic *a posteriori*', has to be empty.

It is worth devoting some space to tracing the subsequent re-arrangements of truths among the three boxes of interest that were effected by later philosphers. That there could be so many forms of disagreement over the classification of truths among the three available boxes speaks to the pervasive hold that the two distinctions (analytic/synthetic, *a priori/a posteriori*) have had on the thinking of almost all of Kant's successors.

Before embarking on an historical account of the most important classificatory vacillations, let us point out that the following assignments of truths to boxes remained untouched. This enables us to omit, for the time being, further mention of them.

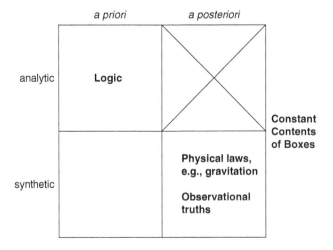

From now on the reader will not see these particular boldface entries any more, until they re-enter the philosophical action.

Frege, while agreeing with Kant that geometry was synthetic, nevertheless sought to argue that arithmetic, on the contrary, was wholly analytic (hence still *a priori*), by virtue of reductive definitions to, and derivations within, pure logic. (Cf. Frege (1884; reprinted 1961), tr. J. L. Austin.)

The founding father of Logical Positivism, and patron of the Vienna Circle, Moritz Schlick (1882–1936), agreed with Frege's views on arithmetic, as developed further by Russell and Whitehead in *Principia Mathematica*.

But Schlick dealt with geometry somewhat differently from Frege, given the success of the axiomatizations of Euclidean and various non-Euclidean geometries by David Hilbert (1862–1943), and the use of non-Euclidean

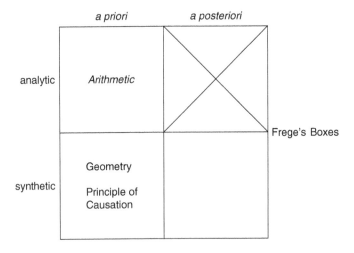

Frege's Boxes

geometries in the theory of general relativity of Albert Einstein (1879–1955). Schlick distinguished between pure (or formal) geometry, and applied (or physical) geometry. On Schlick's view, the geometry of physical space (that is, *applied* geometry) was indeed synthetic, as both Kant and Frege had maintained; but, moreover, was *a posteriori*. *Pure* geometry, by contrast, followed logically (hence: analytically) from axioms that were conventions, or implicit definitions of the concepts involved in them. Thus the *a priori* status of pure geometry is compromised by its being analytic. Either way, geometry is not both synthetic and *a priori*. (Cf. Schlick (1918); revised edn. of 1925 translated (by A. E. Blumberg) as *General Theory of Knowledge*, Open Court, La Salle, 1985. See especially §II.C.38: 'Is there a Pure Intuition?', pp. 348–58.)

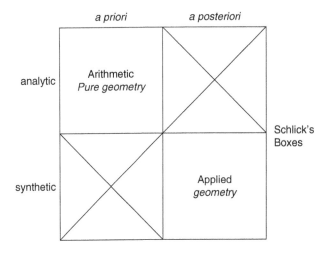

Schlick's Boxes

Moreover, Schlick and others maintained further that the principle of causation is actually *false*. This was because they took seriously the quantum mechanical account of the *uncaused* and *random* nature of radioactive decay of fundamental particles. According to quantum mechanics, individual micro-events are not caused, and are accordingly unpredictable. All that quantum mechanics allows is that statistical frequencies of such events within large ensembles can be predicted.

Carnap wrote his *Habilitationsschrift* under Schlick's direction in Vienna, after studying with Frege in Jena. In this work (Carnap (1922)) Carnap took a slightly different line from Schlick on geometry. For Carnap the *topological* core of applied geometry (common to projective, affine, Euclidean and various non-Euclidean geometries) was *a priori*. Topology was the only part of the science of space that was still a transcendental precondition for our being able to think about things in space at all. Only the metrical part of applied geometry was *a posteriori*. The correct choice of axioms for the geometry of physical space, in so far as the measurement of distances and angles was concerned, could only be made *a posteriori*.

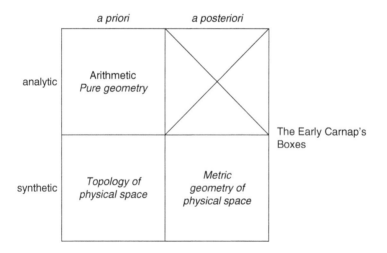

The Early Carnap's Boxes

The later Carnap, however, as the main representative of mature Logical Positivism, eventually abandoned that slight resuscitation of the synthetic *a priori*. For the Logical Positivists, natural science took care of the synthetic *a posteriori* truths; logicians, mathematicians, and 'analytical' philosophers took care of the analytic *a priori* truths; and those were all the truths there were. So mature Logical Positivism reverted to Schlick's Boxes. We restore here, as a reminder, the truths in boldface of which we have been making no mention. Logical Positivism famously *evacuated* the synthetic *a priori*. According to Logical

Positivism, there were no synthetic *a priori* truths *at all*. If this is so, then the two distinctions analytic/synthetic and *a priori/a posteriori* coincide:

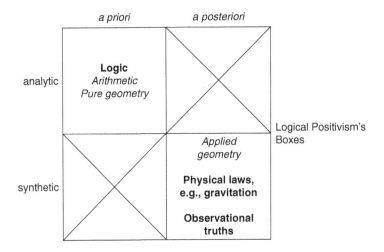

Logical Positivism's Boxes

Later, with Gödel's proof of the incompleteness of arithmetic (Gödel (1931)), it was thought that the logicist reduction of arithmetic must fail, and that arithmetic was after all synthetic (albeit still, of course, *a priori*):

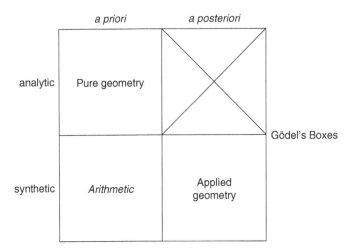

Gödel's Boxes

Behind the classification of arithmetic as synthetic is Gödel's Platonism. He regarded arithmetical knowledge as knowledge of facts concerning an abstract structure, the progression of natural numbers, to which we had intellectual access by means of a faculty of intuition akin to perception. So our arithmetical statements were about an aspect of our world, albeit a wholly abstract one.

It should come as no surprise that a distinction that had led to such vacillating classifications of these important areas of human knowledge should eventually come under attack. After all, if one couldn't classify major areas of human knowledge uncontentiously by using the distinction, the distinction itself must be at best unclear and at worst useless. So, according to Quine (see Quine (1951)), we should dismantle both distinctions – analytic/synthetic and *a priori/a posteriori* – and think at best in terms of the *degrees of entrenchment* of our knowledge-claims (or, better: our *beliefs*) in their collective confrontation with sensory experience. This essay of Quine's is one of the most famous and influential essays in twentieth-century Analytical Philosophy. It was Hilary Putnam (b. 1926) who pointed out that Quine's attack on the analytic/synthetic distinction was just as much an attack on the *a priori/a posteriori* distinction. (See Putnam (1983).) For a retrospect 'forty years on', see Quine (1991). Quine's alternative picture is as follows.

> Sensory experience
> – Periphery –
> Observation sentences
> Standing sentences
> Low-level generalizations   Quine's Bolus
> Scientific hypotheses
> Mathematics
> Logic
> – Core –

Those claims that lay nearer to the core were, for Quine, more immune to revision than those that lay nearer to the periphery. But, in principle, every statement was liable to revision, including even laws of logic.

These last two claims can be construed within boxes rather than a bolus if we like. If the distinctions were still in play, and not jettisoned as groundless, or hopelessly vague, or nonsensical, we could picture the latest position as follows:

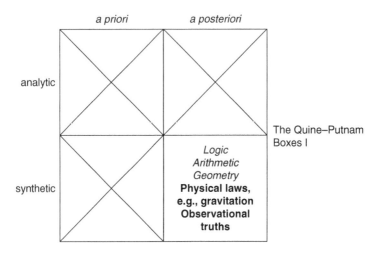

The Quine–Putnam Boxes I

One begins to appreciate, however, the futility of maintaining the two distinctions when the boxes look like *that*.

One well-known criticism of the Quinean position of radical revisability is that there still have to be some constraints on how truth-values are to be reassigned to statements in the light of sensory experience. (See Priest (1979).) And these constraints must surely belong to Logic, and be *a priori*. Moreover, the only explanation for their being *a priori* is that they are legitimated by the very meanings of the logical operators involved. Thus they (that is, their sentential renderings) are also analytic. (Ideally one would wish to treat inferences on a par with statements, and apply the distinctions in play to inferences as well. But the weight of convention limits discussion to the status of statements, or sentences, thereby excluding transitions among sentences.)

The foregoing considerations imply that the boxes, in just the relevant regards, should really look like this:

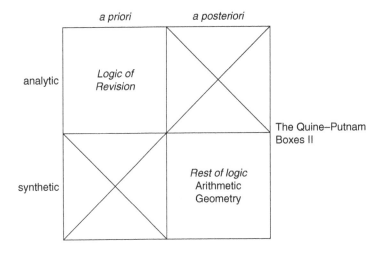

Against the background of such a variety of competing classifications of logic, arithmetic, and geometry based on the two distinctions, and of Quine's attack on the distinctions themselves, it might seem futile:

1. to invoke or rely upon the distinctions, and
2. to offer a classification of logical and mathematical knowledge using them.

But the two distinctions just will not die. In late twentieth-century Analytical Philosophy the notions of analyticity and *apriority* were vigorously rehabilitated, in a predictable rearguard action against Quine. Whatever one's stand on the two distinctions, as either intelligible or useful, one simply cannot do Philosophy competently without grasping how the distinctions have been both formulated and applied.

Problems

1   Do you think that the analytic/synthetic and *a priori/a posteriori* distinctions coincide? Give detailed reasons for your answer.

2   Konrad Lorenz, the famous ethologist, suggested that what is known *a priori* by an individual is so by virtue of the fact that, for the individual's *species*, the knowledge in question is *a posteriori*. So the *a priori* is what natural selection has caused to be innate. What do you make of this suggestion? (The original source is Lorenz (1941).)

3   Does Quine's 'Two dogmas of empiricism' (1951) make a convincing case against the clarity and value of Kant's distinction between analytic and synthetic truths?

4   Do you think that one can distinguish clearly between the sensory experience required in order to acquire mastery of various concepts or word-meanings, and the sensory experience (or lack of it) that is required in order to verify a sentence involving the words in question?

5   A neo-Kantian offers the following argument. 'Logical truths are true by virtue of proofs from the empty set of assumptions. Proofs are abstract objects whose study forms a branch of combinatorial mathematics. So, knowledge of logical truth is attained only through acquaintance with (quite complicated) abstract objects. Logical truth cannot, therefore, be analytic. At best it is *a priori*; but, like mathematical truth in general, it is *synthetic*.' Discuss.

6   Could the analytic/synthetic distinction be drawn in such a way that some parts of Mathematics count as analytic, while other parts count as synthetic?

7   The realist about truth (see §6.1) maintains that there could be truths that transcend all possible means of verifying, or coming to know them. *A priori* truths are ones that *can be known* without recourse to sensory experience. Does this entail that the realist's verification-transcendent truths cannot be classified as *a priori*?

6   Important Opposing '-Isms'

Most philosophical debate takes place between representatives of extremely opposing viewpoints. Through the long history of the discipline, these opposing positions have become quite well defined, even if somewhat loosely in certain cases. Part of the interest of contemporary philosophy derives from trying to state certain positions more clearly, using more recent methods or concepts. That is why so often, in the writings of contemporary philosophers, one detects an element of reprise, a hint of variation-on-a-well-known-theme, in the ideas being put forward. In broad terms, what they are claiming might well have been anticipated by some ancient, medieval, or early modern philosopher. The contemporary philosopher can plead, in mitigation, that there is somehow some new energy or interest in the view, given the more recently created conceptual materials being used to express it.

The following pairs of polar opposites are examples of conflicting philosophical outlooks/temperaments/world-views. It is difficult to give succinct definitions of each of them. They are best explained by giving a short list of their major theses and preferred methods. That they are substantive positions, however, is borne out by the fact that when one is confronted with a new topic of philosophical interest, one can 'extrapolate' each of the opposing views so as to make a good guess about what proponents of each of them would say about the new topic in question.

Sometimes we have to specify an '-ism' as being *about* some property or kind of thing. Examples:

realism about truth;
skepticism about meaning;
individualism about mental content;
Platonism about mathematical entities;
foundationalism about morals;
objectivism about logic;
dualism about mind;
subjectivism about color;
innatism about grammar;
evolutionism about language.

6.1 Realism v. [Anti-realism, Idealism, Irrealism, Instrumentalism, Eliminativism, Solipsism]

There is *realism about truth*; and there are *realisms about different kinds* of entities.

Realism about truth is the view that propositions are determinately true or false, independently of us, and whether or not we could ever come to know their truth-values. Thus truth is thought of as potentially *verification-transcendent*. 'Coming to know' is thought of as *discovering* what the facts are, rather than as *constituting or creating* those facts.

Anti-realism about truth is the view that truth is in principle knowable: there can be no facts of the matter transcending our ability, in principle, to establish what they are. On this view, truth is *epistemically constrained*.

Realism (or anti-realism) about truth is often called *semantic* realism (or anti-realism).

Then there is *realism about different kinds of entities*. One can take a realist view, for example, of the *theoretical entities of science*: molecules, atoms, protons, neutrons, electrons, …, hadrons, leptons. These things (if they exist) would be too small to see or feel or perceive in any (instrumentally unaided) way. But the realist claims that they exist, they are real, for all that. Similarly, a realist view can be taken of the *abstract entities* that mathematicians seem to be talking about: numbers (natural; integral; rational; real; complex; …); points, lines and planes; functors and categories; sets and classes; groups, rings, fields, lattices, Boolean algebras; vector spaces, topological spaces, etc. Realism about mathematical entities is also called *Platonism*. The anti-realist about mathematical entities is called a *nominalist*. Nominalism, in general, is the view that there are no abstract entities: they are just convenient fictions, or figments of our imagination.

Idealism is the view that the ultimate reality is mental (the contents of our own minds, or perhaps the contents of all minds); and the so-called 'external' world of physical objects is nothing more than some sort of logical construction out of sensory states. Our minds do not mirror nature; they make it up. The most extreme form of this already extreme doctrine is *solipsism*: the view that the only reality is one's own mental reality. According to the solipsist, even other *minds* are logical constructs out of the contents of one's own mind.

Irrealism about Xs is the view that there are no independent, objective, substantive facts about Xs; indeed, Xs might not exist at all. Thus our assertions about Xs, if we wish to keep making them in order to communicate with one another and coordinate our social actions, would have to be construed as not really representing how Xs are. Either these assertions are uniformly in error (there being no Xs, really); or they are not really assertions at all. If the latter, then the speech act of apparently 'asserting' a claim about Xs would have to be re-construed as a use of language to do something else. If for X here we take 'moral value', then we see that irrealism is very like projectivism, subjectivism, and emotivism. When one asserts that *it is good to help the poor*, the irrealist about moral value might well re-construe this as not really an asssertion about matters of fact, but rather an exhortation: *Help the poor!*; or an *interjection*: *Helping the poor? Hurrah!*

Instrumentalism is an anti-realist view about theoretical 'entities' in science (the scare quotes here are supplied by the instrumentalist). The instrumentalist sees no reason to believe in these entities; rather, they are no more than convenient fictions that we 'posit' in order to be able to make predictions about our observations of medium-sized observable entities – which, for the instrumentalist, are the only real things there are.

Eliminativism about Xs is the view that there are no Xs, and we should not even engage in the convenient fiction of theorizing as if there were any Xs. Rather, we should commit ourselves to there being no Xs, eschew all (apparent) reference to them, and talk about only such things as really exist, and are genuinely explanatory of our observational data. Eliminativism is the correct attitude about witches, goblins, elves and fairies. It is the correct attitude to the misguided scientific posits of phlogiston and the ether. And some philosphers of mind (called eliminative materialists) even go so far as to claim that it is the correct attitude towards mental states such as beliefs and desires. There aren't really any such states, they say, in a completed and perfected scientific account of the world and everything in it. There are only complicated physical states of the brain and central nervous system. Unable to cope with the complicated details, they say, we make do with simplistic, but ultimately false, mentalistic accounts of the causal springs of human behavior.

6.2 Substantialism v. Deflationism about Truth

One of the age-old questions in Philosophy, going back to Plato, is '*What is truth?*'. There is a kind of opposition among answers to this question that is not neatly classifiable as a contrast between Realism and any of the versions of Anti-realism discussed in §6.1 – even though the latter contrast is characterized in terms of divergent views about the nature of truth.

The divergence of view between the Substantialist, on the one hand, and the Deflationist, on the other hand, is of a quite different kind. For the semantic Realist and the semantic Anti-realist of §6.1 are both Substantialists. Each of them holds that truth is a substantial property of our thoughts, or of declarative sentences of our language. They differ only in whether they regard truthmakers, or states of affairs, or realizations of truth-conditions, or grounds-for-truth, as always *epistemically accessible*. For the Realist, substantial truth can consist in states of affairs that transcend our capacities for verification; whereas for the Anti-realist, a proposition *p*'s being true consists in *there being a proof of p*, or *there being a warrant for asserting that p* – an intrinsically knowable matter.

The Deflationist about truth holds that truth is a very *insubstantial* notion. Here we use the modern label 'Deflationist' for the position most simply and directly opposed to substantialism about truth. Most Deflationists regard their position as directly descended from the so-called Redundancy Theory of Truth of Frank Ramsey (1903–30). According to the Deflationist, there is nothing more to a proposition p's being true than ... p, or its being the case that p. The Deflationist claims that to assert 'It is true that p' is to do no more, and no less, than to assert that p. Thus the claim 'It is true that p' is no more, and no less, than the claim that p. *The talk of truth adds nothing*, so the Deflationist maintains; and, in a more extreme mood, some Deflationists even conclude that there cannot therefore be any such *property* as truth for the truth-operator or truth-predicate to stand for. If you wish to continue with your talk about truth, the Deflationist says, then you can capture everything there is to know about it by simply postulating the infinite flock of biconditionals of the form 'p if and only if it is true that p' – one for each sentence p in the language. Now of course whether p itself can be allowed to contain occurrences of 'it is true that ...' is a deep and difficult question. The reader is referred to Chapter 28 for a discussion of some of the difficulties that arise from allowing languages to contain their own truth-operators or truth-predicates.

6.3 Descriptivism v. Projectivism

Descriptivism about a given area of discourse – say, morality – is the view that one's declarative statements really can succeed in representing things the way they are. And the way they are is independent of our thus representing them. Things would be that way even if we were not here to represent them as being that way, or were here but represented them as being some other way. The opposing view of *projectivism* maintains that we are merely projecting our sentiments or attitudes onto states of affairs that do not genuinely involve any of the projected qualities or properties.

Thus, the descriptivist will say that a true claim of the form 'X is morally good' registers the genuine possession, by the action X, of the moral property of goodness. By contrast, the projectivist will say that that 'property' of goodness is chimerical; at best we are projecting our attitude of commendation, thereby trying to get other people to act in X-like ways. But in no way, according to the projectivist, are we registering a genuine property of X that inheres in X, independently of our human moral sensibility.

Similar moves would be made by the descriptivist and the projectivist about ascriptions of color to physical objects. Indeed, that is why Hume famously characterized projectivism in general as involving 'the gilding and staining' of things with 'the colors of our internal sentiments'.

6.4 Transcendentalism v. Positivism

Transcendentalism is a view that comes from the critical philosophy of Immanuel Kant, according to which the mind makes an essential contribution to the constitution of what we take to be external reality. Transcendentalism incorporates, importantly, the claim that because of the way the mind is structured and operates, certain kinds of knowledge are available without recourse to any sensory experience. Moreover, these kinds of knowledge significantly constrain the way the world is or can be; it is knowledge going beyond what one could 'read off' from the meanings of the words involved in its expression. Such knowledge is called *synthetic a priori*. Here, 'synthetic' means 'not analytic', i.e., not attainable simply by analysis of the meanings of the words involved in the expression of that knowledge. And '*a priori*' means – as has already been explained in §1.1 and §5.1 – that the knowledge can be attained without any recourse to sensory experience. For Kant, both mathematics (i.e., arithmetic and [Euclidean] geometry) and the metaphysical foundations of science (involving principles of substance, causation, and reciprocal interaction) were examples of synthetic *a priori* knowledge.

Positivism, by contrast, is the view that there simply are no synthetic *a priori* truths. No proposition can be true simply because of the way the mind 'makes the world have to be' in order for any knowledge of the world to be possible. Rather, the only propositions that can be known to be true are either analytic (true by virtue of the meanings of the words involved in them) or *a posteriori* (knowable only on the basis of sensory experience). And analytic truths, remember, are knowable without recourse to sensory experience, hence are *a priori*.

6.5 Absolutism v. Relativism

Again, moral values provide a good illustration for this pair of polar opposites. The *moral absolutist* claims that there is a fixed, independent, culturally invariant, and eventually attainable, 'right' system of morality. This system would provide a vantage point from which deficient systems could rightly be criticized. This system is the one we are heading towards when we talk of making 'moral progress'.

Presumably this system would label as immoral such past or present practices or social traditions as: human sacrifice to appease the gods; incest; forced child labor; slavery; rape and pillage; genocide; the infliction of pain on, or killing of, innocents; cannibalism; religious persecution; terrorist assaults on civilians when doing battle for a political cause; rites of *unwilling* passage, such as forced genital mutilation; performance of medical procedures without the patient's informed consent; oppression of women; drunk driving; child pornography; and statutory apartheid for the different racial or ethnic groups in a multicultural nation, etc. Interestingly, Chrysippus (d. 206 BC) argued for the permissibility of both incest and cannibalism. More controversial items for inclusion on the list of immoral practices would be: systems of polygamy; the use of addictive substances; abortion; suicide; euthanasia; revolutionary violence against politically oppressive regimes; and capital punishment. But one would hesitate to go so far as to add adult pornography, prostitution, fervent displays of religiosity, gambling, punk rock, heavy metal, or body-piercing.

Against this, the *moral relativist* claims that what counts as a moral code within any human group at any time and place is a wholly conventional matter. They could have chosen different moral norms, but happened to choose the ones they did. Only those within that group are bound by them. But, importantly: *there is, in principle, no external moral vantage point from which one could say that* one system of norms is inferior to some other. Inter-systematic comparisons are impossible. Every moral judgment has to be made from within one historically conditioned (and conventional) system. That system will be but one from among the many out there. It cannot (without being disagreeably chauvinistic) provide an absolute vantage point from which competing systems could rightly be condemned as 'primitive' or 'barbaric' or 'evil' or what have you. Ultimately, says the relativist, there is no such thing as absolute right or wrong. There are only historically changing opinions as to what is right or wrong; and there is no reason to believe that these evolving opinions would ever converge on one final, stable, perfected system on which no further improvements could be made.

6.6 Objectivism v. [Subjectivism/Psychologism]

We shall illustrate this contrast with the topic of logical inference. *Objectivism about logic* maintains that certain patterns of inference really are the right ones. They are *objective norms* that should govern our thought processes when we work out predictions of scientific theories (say), or consequences of sets of mathematical axioms. An example of such a pattern of inference is *Modus Ponens*:

P. If P then Q. Therefore, Q.

In symbols: $\dfrac{P \quad P \to Q}{Q}$.

This pattern will preserve truth from its premises to its conclusion, whatever propositions one has in place of P and Q. Many a beginning student of logic, however, will reason fallaciously with the pattern called *Modus Morons* (or 'affirming the consequent'):

P. If Q then P. Therefore Q.

In symbols: $\dfrac{P \quad Q \to P}{Q}$.

Now, what if a majority of people reasoned this silly way? Would that make *Modus Morons* a 'law of thought', worthy of inclusion in the science known as Logic? Of course not, replies the objectivist. No amount of incorrect human thinking can alter how we *ought* to think.

Psychologism in logic, by contrast, is the view that Logic is (or should be?) simply the codification of the 'actual' laws of thought, in the sense of 'statistically average patterns of actual reasoning'. It also involves the view that meaning-phenomena have only to do with the mental ideas and images that people carry in their heads. Psychologism does not admit the existence of independently graspable senses, or meanings, that could be the common intellectual property of communicating thinkers. Psychologism, rather, sees all meaning as essentially tinged with mental imagery, which of course could vary greatly from one thinker to the next, and would make it puzzling how, and that, thinkers do succeed in communicating objective thoughts to one another.

6.7 Cognitivism (in ethics) v. Emotivism

Cognitivism in ethics is closely connected with descriptivism. It is the view that moral truths are knowable, by appeal to certain kinds of relevant evidence, and by the exercise of the right parts of our cognitive equipment and sensibilities. For the cognitivist, one's moral convictions are *beliefs*, which are capable of being true or false. There are moral facts 'out there', and we can correctly register them, or even come to know them. We *discover* them. We cannot just make up our moral rules as we go along, exercising only arbitrary whim or selfish desires. For in doing so we will in all likelihood be failing to track the moral facts.

Emotivism, by contrast, holds that when we make our moral judgments we cannot be aiming at any knowable truths, and sometimes hitting them; rather, we are not expressing truth-apt beliefs at all. When we make moral judgments we are just registering our *emotional reactions* to action X or personality trait Y or policy Z or whatever it is that has evoked that reaction. Emotivism has been called the 'Boo-Hurrah' theory. The proposition *Killing the innocent is morally wrong* means, according to the emotivist, no more than:

> *Killing the innocent? Boo!*

The proposition *It is morally right to keep your promises* means, according to the emotivist, no more than:

> *You intend to keep your promises? Hurrah!*

6.8 Theism v. [Atheism/Naturalism]

(Mono)theism is the view that God exists. It is the essential kernel common to the three main religious traditions historically emanating from the ancient cultures of the Middle East: Judaism, Islam, and Christianity. Each of these traditions differs only in the 'extra' propositions attached to the proposition that God exists. These extra propositions will concern God's possession of certain perfections (omniscience, omnipotence, omnibenevolence); God's role in the creation of the universe; God's being both the source of moral law and the dispenser of reward or retribution in the afterlife; God's interventions in human history, etc.

Atheism is the view that there is no God. Students raised in God-fearing families often need to be reassured that atheists are every bit as likely as followers of an established religion to be morally principled people. The commonest kind of atheism is *naturalism*: the view that everything about the natural world and human existence within it can be explained in purely naturalistic terms, without recourse to God as creator, designer, intervener or sustainer.

In Part III we shall examine all the main arguments for or against the existence of God. Chapter 17, in particular, addresses the creationist's case against naturalistic atheism. It examines the book-length argument provided by the creationist Philip Johnson, who holds naturalists responsible for the moral and political decay that he believes afflicts the USA.

6.9 Determinism v. Libertarianism

Determinism is the metaphysical thesis that every event taking place at any given instant of time is fixed, or determined, by earlier events. 'Event' is to be construed broadly, so as to include *physical* events like volcanic eruptions, *psychic* events like falling in love, and *political* events like the tearing down of the Berlin Wall, or a declaration of war, or the making of an international treaty. Also included are human decisions – including any decision to try to refute the thesis of determinism. So it would seem, at first blush, that the determinist denies the possibility of any exercise of so-called 'free will' by human beings. To be more precise, the determinist maintains that every *caused* event (including those directly caused by human 'choices' or 'decisions' – note the scare quotes here) is determined by antecedent physical events. Uncaused events (such as the random radioactive decay of radium atoms) are not determined.

Libertarianism in metaphysics is the *prima facie* contrary thesis that human beings are able to make free, unconstrained and unforced choices, especially ones that will have a significant effect on their future lives. These include such choices as whom to take as a romantic partner; what major to study in college; *whether to attend college at all*; what career to embark upon; whom to marry; whether to have children; whether to write a book attempting to refute determinism, etc. (Not all metaphysical libertarians are libertarians in the sense of that word in the political domain. Political libertarians advocate minimal government regulation or intervention in the lives of citizens. It would not be a contradiction in terms for a political libertarian to say, in gloomy metaphysical terms, that it was predetermined by her unhappy childhood at the hands of aggressively over-attentive parents that she would end up being a political libertarian.)

Uncaused events offer no succor to the person who believes in free will. For random micro-level sputterings in brain cells are hardly the sort of event that the libertarian would wish to hold up as evidence that one has freely made up one's mind to do something. The libertarian believes – even while conceding that there might be quantum-mechanically random firings in brain cells – that human choices really are free, and that in making them we are the genuine authors of our own destiny. For the libertarian, we cannot be wholly in the grip of unfolding physical forces operating independently of our exercises of will. The exercise of free will cannot be an illusion; we *must* be making a difference to our own lives when we freely choose to act one way rather than another.

Compatibilism is the view that physical determinism can be reconciled with libertarianism. The compatibilist seeks somehow to make sense of the phenomenology of our free exercise of will, and of its felt importance to the moral evaluation of human actions, while yet subscribing to a thoroughly 'physical-causal' account of all the happenings in the universe. In Chapter 25 we examine the debate over free will in greater detail, and commend for consideration a personal version of compatibilism, based on evolutionary considerations.

6.10 Rationalism v. Empiricism

In a nutshell: *Rationalism* is the view that all worthwhile knowledge is produced solely by the exercise of reason, without recourse to sensory experience. By contrast, *Empiricism* is the view that all knowledge (including even mathematical knowledge) is the product of reasoning in various ways *from the data of sensory experience*. There is no knowledge to be had completely independently of any sensory experience.

Rationalism faces the challenge of how knowers could come to know both mundane facts about the observable world, and higher-level regularities within it, without any recourse to sensory experience. Empiricism, by contrast, faces the challenge of how to account for our logical and mathematical knowledge, which appears to be gained in a completely *a priori* fashion, by means of proofs employing principles and rules that appear to be intuitively self-evident, and at times even analytically so.

6.11 Foundationalism v. [Anti-foundationalism/Coherentism]

Consider any region of knowledge: scientific; mathematical; moral; or theological. The *foundationalist* about that region says that its known propositions can all be organized in a structure involving logical dependencies on some ultimate 'immediately or directly' knowable basis.

For empirical Science, this basis might consist of sensory experience (perceptual reports), and the dependencies would be those that could be articulated by some inductive logic or abductive logic or logic of discovery.

For Mathematics, the basis would consist of axioms (such as Euclid's axioms for geometry), and the dependencies would be those of deductive logic, whereby theorems are derived from the axioms.

For morality, the basis might be some simple principle such as (i) the Utilitarian claim that the good is to be determined by what maximizes happiness, and minimizes suffering, for the greatest number; or (ii) the Kantian claim that the right action is to be determined by asking oneself whether one could consistently will the maxim describing the action to become a universal law of human nature. One would then have to account for how the more derivative moral assessments would be derived, either within Utilitarianism or within Kantianism. Utilitarianism, certainly, will require ancillary premises of an empirical kind, about the ways in which various contemplated actions or policies would actually increase the happiness, or the suffering, of those affected by them.

By contrast, the *anti-foundationalist* maintains that there are no privileged or especially secure starting points upon which we can build our edifice of knowledge by inferential means. Rather, different propositions can be taken as immune to doubt, or given, or basic, or provisionally unquestioned, depending on the purposes at hand. All our knowledge is a logically interwoven fabric of propositions lending one another mutual support. No proposition ever receives absolutely preferential treatment, either by virtue of the kind of concepts it involves, or by virtue of its logical structure. Every proposition is liable to be revised (disbelieved rather than believed) on the basis of possible future courses of sensory experience.

6.12   Dualism v. [Monism/Materialism]

In the philosophy of mind, *dualism* (usually attributed to Descartes) is the doctrine that minds are distinct entities (or substances) from physical bodies. Although each mind has its own human body, and each human body its own mind, they are nevertheless distinct kinds of entities. Minds are in time but not in space; whereas human bodies are in both time and space. Bodies are extended; minds are not. Minds can also (according to Descartes) be disembodied; they can survive the destruction of the body, and might even be immortal. Yet, somehow, minds interact with the living bodies that they inhabit. Thus physical influences on the body, interpreted as sensations, can induce within the mind various beliefs, desires, fears, hopes, etc. Conversely, mental processes (such as deliberating about what to do) can induce the body to move in various way. The 'twoness' implicit in the term 'dualism' is that of two distinct kinds of entities: minds and bodies; as well as two distinct kinds of causation: mental and physical.

Monism, by contrast, is the view that there is only one kind of entity, broadly speaking: physical bodies. Galaxies, stars, planets, organisms, cells, chromosomes, genes, codons – these are all very different kinds of physical entities, but at least they are all just that: *physical*. They are all subject, ultimately, to the laws of physics. For the monist, there are no such 'things' as minds; there are only organisms behaving in such complicated ways that we find it natural and compelling to think of them as occupying various mental states and undergoing various mental processes: sensing, perceiving, believing, desiring, intending, deciding, acting …

This is monism about *things*. They are all physical things. But some physical things – these organisms – can be thought of as having mental *attributes*. And, if we do not think that these attributes are definable in physical terms, then we might be drawn to what is called *attribute-dualism*, even while holding entity-monism. *Attribute-dualism* is the view that physical things, while being the only kind of things there are, can nevertheless possess radically different, mutually irreducible, kinds of attributes (or properties). First, there are the things' *physical* properties, whose distribution across matter in space and time is the subject of the physical sciences. Secondly, there are (on the part of at least some of those things) their *mental* properties, whose possession by organisms would be the subject of an independent, irreducible science of psychology.

It is this way of looking at the relationship between the physical and the mental that allows one to insist that the level of psychological explanation is *autonomous*. It serves purposes and achieves explanatory insights that cannot be replicated within the confines of a purely physicalistic theory.

Another way of putting this is to say that the psychological theory cannot be *reduced to* the physical theory. In due course we shall go into the question of reductionism in greater detail. We shall see that there is theoretical room for one to agree that the physical facts 'fix' what the mental facts might be, but that nevertheless the theory of the mental facts cannot be reduced to any theory about the physical facts. This 'fixing' of one level of facts by another level of facts is called *supervenience* – for more on which, see §6.13 and §14.2.

6.13 Reductionism v. Anti-reductionism

The attribute dualism described in §6.12 is a species of *anti-reductionism* (concerning mental attributes).

Reductionism (concerning mental attributes), by contrast, is the view that all mentalistic properties (such as 'x has a toothache', 'x believes that snow is white', 'x wants blue skies', etc.) can be reduced to, or expressed in, purely physical terms: 'x's brain (and nervous system) is in such-and-such a neurochemical/electro-physiological state'.

Reductionism can be assessed by two criteria, one more demanding than the other. The less demanding question to ask is this:

> Would it be possible, **in principle**, to reduce the higher-level theory to the lower-level theory?

In posing this question, it is very important to understand how the qualifier 'in principle' governs our considerations. It means that any prospect of reduction on offer from the reductionist need be no more than *logically* and *conceptually* possible. That reductionism *is* possible in this weak sense has been maintained by certain foundationalists and methodologists apprised of the deep and intriguing implications of a result in mathematical logic known to its practitioners as 'Beth's Definability Theorem'. We cannot go into these implications at this stage, but shall reserve that important discussion for §14.2.1.

A permissible case for reduction in the weaker sense under consideration here could be made even if the 'reducing definitions' and the resulting 'reduced sentences' standing in for higher-level sentences of manageable length were super-exponentially longer than their higher-level counterparts. They might need, say, as many symbols as there are fundamental particles in the universe. Just as Russell once tartly remarked that our human inability to complete an infinite task is a 'merely medical' impossibility, so too could we offer here the observation that reductions of this kind would be 'merely cosmic' impossibilities. *And it would be the kind of impossibility which, by the rules of this particular game – adjudicating answers to the question posed – one is allowed to ignore.*

This is a much easier standard to meet than the one implicit in the more demanding question:

> *Would it be **practically** possible, or **feasible**, to reduce the higher-level theory to the lower-level theory?*

The reductionist who proposes an affirmative answer to *this* question is, by the prevailing consensus, both overly ambitious and highly implausible. No one knows remotely how one might carry out a full theoretical reduction both feasibly and in detail, in the case of mental states and brain states.

Some reductionists might take their inspiration from the mathematical case, where we have a successful paradigm of reduction. Every mathematical theory, about any kind of mathematical structure, can be reduced to purely set-theoretic terms. One can define one's chosen mathematical structure as a complicated kind of set, and, using that definition, derive as theorems of set theory all the axioms (or, more accurately, their translations into the language of set theory) of the mathematical theory in question.

Reductionism (of the mental to the physical) is not at all like the reduction of, say, number theory to set theory. There are no clean definitions of mental states in terms of physical states; and the physical theory is nowhere near being formulated as definitively as set theory is today. Hence there is no immediate prospect of ever deriving principles of psychology, via still-to-be-formulated definitions of mental states in terms of physical states, from the basic principles of physics (or of chemistry or neurobiology).

Nevertheless, there is an implicit metaphysical article of faith behind the yearning for reduction that affects some materialists. This is that we somehow owe our mental states to the physical states of our brains (and nervous systems). Surely, the thought goes, it is the physical states that somehow 'fix' what our mental states are, rather than the other way round?

Another way of putting this idea is as follows. Imagine that you occupy mental state M (holding a particular belief, say) by virtue of occupying (on this occasion, at least) the physical state P. Then: if you were, counterfactually, *not* in mental state M, then you would have had to be in some physical state *other* than P. The slogan would be: 'No difference in mental state without a corresponding difference in physical state'. Another way of putting it would be: 'The physical determines the mental', or 'The mental depends on the physical'. This kind of determination or dependency is not *causal*. It is an acausal, synchronous covariance. Philosophers have a name for this welcome, if rather mysterious kind of determination or dependency: *supervenience* of the mental on the physical. The mental *supervenes on* the physical. Literally, from the Latin roots: 'comes down (on it) from above'. That is why one speaks metaphorically of a *higher* level of facts supervening on a *lower* level of facts. The physical is also called the *supervenience basis* for the mental. (The word 'basis' often carries the connotation of being something determinative, located, metaphorically, lower down.)

The advantage of thinking in terms of supervenience is that one need not go so far as to claim that reductionism must be true. The physical *might* determine the mental (i.e., the mental could supervene on the physical) without it being the case that our *theorizing* about the mental is reducible, *even if only 'in principle'*, to our theorizing about the physical. As some philosophers also like to say: psychology is an *autonomous* discipline. It is irreducible *in principle* to any 'lower-level' physical theorizing. It uses its own basic concepts that cannot, even in principle, be defined in physical terms. By means of these mentalistic concepts, it explains and rationalizes human behavior. It makes human actions intelligible. It represents human beings as capable of being in various cognitive and appetitive states, and acting in purposive ways to achieve understandable goals. It represents us as occupying *intentional states*: states of mind that are 'about' things and events in the external world. These intentional states, says the supervenience theorist, will never be reducible to purely physical terms – certainly not reducible in any *feasible* way, and possibly even irreducible *in principle*. States of mind are *sui generis*, and indispensable for fully explanatory theorizing about the behavior of human beings. This is especially the case when the behavior is *conduct* – that is, social behavior regulated by norms of morality, the law, institutional rituals, protocol, and etiquette.

The same broad considerations concerning the relationship between two 'levels' of wordly facts arise at other interfaces besides that of neurophysiology with psychology. For each pair of neighboring levels, the same question of reducibility (of theorizing at the higher level to theorizing at the lower level) can be raised, in both the weaker and the stronger forms explained above. Further examples of such pairs (of levels of fact appropriately describable by the given disciplines) are: fundamental particle physics, interfacing with chemistry; organic chemistry, interfacing with molecular biology; individual psychology, interfacing with sociology/anthropology/economics. We omit mention of many other similar pairings here; the general idea is clear enough. This theme will be re-visited in §14.1; and the discussion of reductionism will be resumed in §14.2.

6.14 Innatism v. [Behaviorism/Environmentalism]

Innatism is the view that there are important structures already in the new-born or infant mind/brain, which do not require sensory experience in order to be instilled. They are inborn (hard-wired) or at least 'wet-wared'. Sensory experience might be required in order to activate or trigger them, and to stimulate their full development. The triggered growth, however, will be rapid. It will outpace any developments that would result from simple learning by an 'unstructured' mind/brain. (The philosopher's favorite phrase for the unstructured mind/brain is *tabula rasa* – the Latin for 'blank slate'.) The various structures involved tend to be domain-specific. They enable categorization of objects, perception of spatio-temporal arrangements and processes, diagnosis of causal sequences and interactions, development of linguistic vocabulary and grammar, etc.

With such rich structure already in place, and making for sophisticated intellectual processes, it becomes less likely that all that is in the mind/brain can be revealed in gross bodily behavior – the externally observable movements of the whole organism. This is where the tension arises with the doctrine of *behaviorism*.

According to the behaviorist, one should avoid attributing too much internal, cognitive structure to the mind/brain. The aim of psychology, or the science of the mind, is simply to explain the relationship between sensory stimuli and behavioral responses. The behaviorist couples this 'stimulus-response' doctrine with the methodological principle that one should not posit more entities (or structures) than are needed in order to generate the explanations that one is seeking. If the correlations between sensory input and motor output can be accounted for by postulating more meager structure, then that is well and good. Thus the behaviorist seeks first to model the mind/brain as no more than a 'general problem-solving device', a 'black box' mediating efficiently between perception and action.

The big question, of course, is whether behaviorism can accomplish its aims without having to resort to the richer postulations of the innatist. How should the behaviorist account for, and exploit, the known 'modularity' of the mind/brain? And how should the behaviorist account for the child being able to learn the rich grammar of a natural language on the basis of relatively meager amounts of evidence (in the form of utterances heard, and utterances produced and corrected)? This is known as the innatist's *poverty of stimulus* argument against behaviorism. It is owed to the theoretical linguist Noam Chomsky (b. 1928).

6.15 Essentialism and Necessitarianism v. Anti-essentialism and Accidentalism

Essentialism is the view that individual objects have certain properties essentially, in the sense that if they lacked such properties, they would not *be* the objects they are. For example, membership of a natural kind might be essential to any given organism. Take an individual horse. If it were not a horse, then it would not *be* that individual. By contrast, that it was grazing in such-and-such a field at noon on January 1, 2015 is an *accidental* (non-essential) property of this horse. It may well be that it was so grazing. But we can make sense of the thought that it *might not have been* so grazing. We can keep hold of the very same horse in thought, as it were, while ringing the changes on those properties that are not essential to it. Such properties are called *accidental* properties of the horse.

An even more exigent natural property that has been suggested (by Saul Kripke) as essential for the individual horse is that it should have been the result of the union of exactly the very sperm and the very egg that did, in fact, unite to bring it into existence. Had the sperm or the egg been different, the resulting creature (although a horse) would not have been *that very* horse.

Accidentalism simply denies essentialism. On this view there is no reason to regard *any* property of any thing as essential to its identity (and existence). Our ability to think of an individual in counterfactual circumstances, where some of its properties are imagined as being different than they actually are, is very robust, according to the accidentalist: we need only preserve some sensible cluster of properties in order to be able to keep on thinking of the individual thus varied as *one and the the same* individual.

6.16 Philosophy as *a priori* ('first philosophy') v. Philosophy as continuous with science and common sense

Earlier, we described Philosophy as a conceptual discipline, implying that it could be pursued without any regard for empirical facts. This is the conception of *'first philosophy'*: a discipline of thought, involving analysis and clarification of both methods and concepts, that would be prior to any scientific investigations of how the world happens to be. 'First philosophy' held sway until the twentieth century, when a counter-movement began, with the aim of *naturalizing* philosophy.

The naturalizing philosopher takes science seriously, and as not in need of preparatory foundations of the kind that the 'First philosopher' thought had to be provided. Science and Mathematics together serve as our best model of truthful theorizing; philosophical insights should be attained by integrating and synthesizing what the various branches of modern science tell us about the fundamental features of the world, and the place of humankind within it.

The main problem to be faced by any naturalizing philosophy is to provide an account of the special status of the *norms* that govern our thinking. Why do logically correct steps of inference have the necessity and cogency that they do? How can the naturalizer account for the 'hardness of the logical *must*', and for Kant's 'moral law within me'?

6.17 Individualism v. Communitarianism

Individualism (about meaning) is the view that the facts about what an individual might mean by his or her words – the conditions that make it the case that *this* is meant, as opposed to *that* – are entirely within the individual's mind/brain (or, as one might say, are *hide-bound*). Only the internal states of the speaker can contribute to the determination of what the speaker means by any word, phrase or sentence.

Communitarianism holds, by contrast, that no individual could mean anything by a sequence of words or gestures or written marks unless there were other individuals (forming a linguistic community) helping to determine the linguistic norms in virtue of which any word or gesture or mark could have its meaning. And even in the case where the speaker is doing something entirely unprecedented, and relying on having his innovative sounds or marks be interpreted as intended to communicate a new meaning in context, we still require an audience to appreciate these meaningful innovations. In the absence of any audience, the innovating would-be communicator would not be meaning anything at all.

6.18 Skepticism and Revisionism v. Quietism

Skepticism comes in many varieties. There is skepticism about divine beings; about the external world of physical objects; about other minds; about causation; about abstract objects; and about values, norms and meaning. The skeptic denies that we really know the reality of the things or properties or relations in question. Typically this involves making out that the seemings to the contrary are just that: mere seemings. The 'knowledge' that we *think* we have is not really knowledge at all. Not only is it not justified or certain; it is *false*. Skepticism is a philosophically valuable *provocation*: it makes us try to get clear about *why* we hold the beliefs that we do about certain kinds of thing, property, or relation. It challenges us to *justify* those beliefs. If ever it succeeds, it forces us to re-assess the role, in our previous thought, of our apparent commitment to whatever has been subjected to the skeptical challenge.

Quietism is the frame of mind in which one refuses to be disturbed or provoked by skeptical worries. Its rule of thumb is that what *appears*, to common sense, to be in order *is* in order. At best the quietist will try to diagnose the source of the skeptic's worry, and reveal it as somehow wrong-headed or pathological. The quietist sees the right task of philosophy as that of providing the necessary *therapies* to help philosophically confused thinkers get back on an even keel.

A good rule of thumb is that one has to pick and choose carefully those things about which one will entertain skepticism, and those things about which one will be quietist. What *appears* to common sense to be in order might very well not be, on closer examination. On the other hand, some skeptical worries might be ridiculously far-fetched, made up in a fit of philosophical cleverness, and not worth taking at all seriously. Naturally, the skeptics in question would not agree with such an assessment; and that is why skeptical debates rage on indefinitely, once they are launched. Skepticisms *never go away*.

In Part IV we go to the most famous source, in modern philosophy, for skepticism about the external world: Descartes. We examine the radically skeptical case he raised, and the way he sought to resist its conclusion.

6.19 Evolutionism v. Saltationism

The hallmark of *evolutionism* is its claim that complex structures (such as the mind/brain, or human languages) have evolved from less complex pre-cursors. Each of the precursor stages would have arisen randomly, and conferred some advantage on those that possessed it. They would, consequently, have left more descendants enjoying the (heritable) structures in question.

The next round of improvement or further development would then have been able to build on the previous ones, since these would have become widespread.

The process of changes over long periods of time and across many generations can be thought of as 'incremental' or 'gradual'. These metaphors, however, have to be qualified in view of the obvious possibility of eras of very rapid change under strongly directed selection pressures for particularly advantageous innovations. Also, precursor components of some systems might be assembled for purposes of their own; and only later, when they suddenly find themselves able to interact, will a new function emerge for the ensemble of those previously independent components. (This is what evolutionary biologists call 'exaptation'.) The ensemble can have features never before selected for; which, once in place, will be the target of strong selection pressures.

Two challenging areas for the application of such evolutionism are the development (over thousands of generations) of (i) human language and (ii) human consciousness.

What might the primitive precursors of today's natural languages have been? How might language have acquired its logical and grammatical complexity? It is tempting to think of human language as having had its evolutionary origins in the simple gestures or grunts of hominid ancestors. These could have acquired reliable meanings, and even become stylized and conventional. But how does one get from a system of 'atomic' grunts to a system of grammatically complex utterances? Surely there is a richly detailed story to be told, even if (alas) there is, in the nature of things, not much accessible evidence on which it could be based or tested. (After all, our more tongue-tied evolutionary ancestors have all died out.) Such, anyway, is the evolutionist's supposition.

The famous linguist Noam Chomsky is rather notorious for having insisted on a conflicting *saltationist* view: that language came onto the evolutionary stage all in one piece (or all in one go), as a result of some catastrophic mutation event.

Likewise, the philosopher Colin McGinn (b. 1950) has a saltationist view of consciousness: that consciousness must have come onto the evolutionary stage suddenly and all in one go, the way a light gets switched on. But why should it be so? Why should there not be, as it were, dim precursors of consciousness, all the way down the phylogenetic order? Little twinges of pain or pleasure, glimmerings of visible light (via primitive eyes), etc.? Why shouldn't McGinn's metaphorical light switch have been equipped with a rheostat?

Another saltationist about consciousness is the psychologist Julian Jaynes (1920–97), whose theory is even more radical. Jaynes maintains that our present-day consciousness, as human agents, of our own beliefs, desires and willings – a consciousness that 'unites' these mental states as states of one undivided mind – is something that postdates the ancient Greeks. In early Greek literature, Jaynes claims to find evidence for the claim that human beings' minds were 'bicameral'.

6.20 Mentalism v. Linguisticism (concerning relative priority of thought and language)

Mentalism is the doctrine that thought can be complete, complex, yet essentially silent – *languageless*. According to the mentalist, one could entertain propositions, or hold beliefs, or harbor desires, without having any linguistic means for articulating them. In acquiring language, one would only be acquiring a medium for the public communication of what one already had, privately, in one's mind.

For the *linguisticist*, nothing could be further from the truth. Language is essential to thought. It is only through language, in fact, that we can *have* thoughts. There is no thought without talk. Linguisticism has dominated recent analytical philosophy as a widely held dogma. It is a dogma, however, that is beginning to crumble at the edges, as we learn more about the richness of pre-lingistic infants' conceptual repertoires, and about the richness of social interactions in species that have only rudimentary systems of communication.

Problem

Choose any one of the distinctions discussed above. Go to a respectable resource such as the online *Standford Encyclopedia of Philosophy*, and find out the following:

1 the original source(s), in the literature, of the distinction in question;
2 the most influential and canonical statements of the opposing '-isms' on each side of the distinction;
3 the most important objections that have been raised against the same;
4 how each '-ism' responds to the objections in question;
5 whether you yourself have your mind made up as to which of the '-isms' you favor.

Note that this is a question template with twenty instances.

Part II
Philosophy and Method

7 What is Logic?

Logic is the science or art of *good reasoning*. *Informal logic* is concerned with reasoning expressed in ordinary language, with a minimum of symbolism. *Formal logic* is a more precise and systematic study of reasoning that employs symbolism for the purposes of brevity, clarity, generality and abstraction.

7.1 The basics of symbolizing sentences in logical notation

One needs only a modicum of symbolism in order to formalize arguments of considerable logical complexity, such as are found in Mathematics. Typically we need formal symbolic analogues of *names*, and *predicates*. Predicates come in various *arities* – indicating how many names would need to be supplied in order to form a simple sentence from the predicate in question.

Thus, with a one-place predicate $F(\ )$ (symbolizing, say, '... is fat') one need only supply one name, say j (symbolizing, say, 'John') in order to form the simple sentence $F(j)$ (symbolizing 'John is fat'). With a two-place predicate $L(\ ,\ )$ (symbolizing, say, '... loves ...') one needs to supply two names, say j and m (symbolizing, say, 'John' and 'Mary') in order to form the simple sentence $L(j, m)$ (symbolizing 'John loves Mary').

In order to symbolize 'Someone loves Mary', one uses a variable-binding expression called the *existential quantifier*: $\exists x L(x, m)$. This formal sentence is rendered in logician's English as 'for some x, x loves Mary'. Likewise, 'Everyone loves someone' would be symbolized as $\forall x \exists y L(x, y)$; and 'Someone is loved by everyone' by $\exists y \forall x L(x, y)$. Here, the *universal quantifier* $\forall x$ is to be read as 'for every x'.

It is easy to see that in order to form these symbolic sentences in a step-by-step fashion, one needs to build up *formulae*, containing *free occurrences of variables*. Thus the last formal sentence was built up as follows. First, form $L(x, y)$ from the two-place predicate L and the variables x and y. These two variables are *free* at their occurrences in $L(x, y)$. Because x enjoys a free occurrence in $L(x, y)$, one may append the quantifier prefix $\forall x$, so as to obtain the formula $\forall x L(x, y)$, in which the occurrences of x are now *bound* (hence, no longer free), but the occurrence of y is still free. So one can now append the quantifier prefix $\exists y$ so as to obtain the formula $\exists y \forall x L(x, y)$, in which y is likewise bound. The result of the two bindings is that the *well-formed formula* just formed contains no free occurrences of variables. And that, for the logician, is what turns it into a formal *sentence*, capable of being true or false; and capable of serving as a premise in an argument, or as a conclusion. Formulae without free variables are called *closed* formulae, or sentences; and formulae *with* at least one free occurrence of a variable are called *open sentences*.

We aim here to keep symbolism to a minimum. But saving students from being exposed to logical symbols is a form of cognitive neglect. It dumbs the curriculum down to a point of intellectual deprivation. Those trying to save Humanities students from the sheer joy and exhilaration of symbol-mastery are being both patronizing and discriminatory. But that is a wider issue, to do with the politics of pedagogy, into which we cannot here be drawn.

7.2 Arguments

In reasoning, we produce *arguments*. An *argument* is made up of *premises* and a *conclusion*. The premises are the 'starting points' of the argument, and the conclusion is its 'endpoint'. The argument seeks to *establish* its conclusion *on the basis of* its premises. Viewed another way, the argument seeks to show that the premises would, if believed to be true, provide *adequate reason* to believe in the truth of the conclusion. So, if one believed, or was willing to assert, all the premises, then one should believe, or be willing to assert, the conclusion.

But it is not necessary that one believe all the premises. An argument can be good even if its premises, taken jointly, constitute a quite incredible story. Indeed, the whole point of the argument might be to bring out the utter incredibility of the set of premises involved. The argument might establish an obviously false conclusion on the basis of those premises, thereby showing that it would be unwise to believe all the premises. The most extreme case of this is the form of argument known as *reductio ad absurdum*, where the conclusion is a patent contradiction (something of the form '*P* and not-*P*'; or, just as bad, a primitive *contrariety* such as 'It's green all over and it's red all over (at the same time)'. A *reductio-ad-absurdum* argument shows that the premises precipitating the contradiction *cannot all be true*. This is for the simple reason that *no contradiction or contrariety can be true*.

If the premises are true, *then* the conclusion is true ... that, at least, is what a *good* argument would show.

The logician has a special word for 'good' when talking about arguments. Good arguments are said to be *valid*.

Definition 1. An *argument of the form*

> *Premise no. 1, Premise no. 2, ...; therefore, Conclusion*

*is valid just in case the following holds: under **any** interpretation according to which Premise no. 1, Premise no. 2, ... are all true, the Conclusion is true also.*

This definition calls for premises and conclusions of argument to be capable of being *true* or *false*. Thus they must be *propositions*, or *statements*, or *declarative sentences* in some mutually understood language. Such things are called *truth-bearers*. Truth-bearers are what can be *asserted* (or *denied*).

Truth-bearers also serve as the 'core' of other so-called 'speech acts', such as asking a question, issuing an order, or expressing a wish. In the question *Is the door shut?*, we have no assertion, but rather a request for information. The request can be met by making an appropriate assertion: *The door is shut* or *The door is not shut*. Likewise, in the order *Shut the door!*, we have no assertion, but rather a contextually sanctioned command that the door be shut. The order can be obeyed by shutting the door. Then it will be true to say *The door is shut*. Finally, in the wish *Would that the door were shut!*, we have no assertion, but rather an expression of preference. The wish can be fulfilled by shutting the door. Then it will be true to say *The door is shut*.

Note how in all these non-assertoric speech acts, the core proposition *The door is shut* features essentially in explaining the nature of the act, and the conditions for its success. There is something primitive in the notion of assertion, or fact-stating. Truth-bearers are at the heart of all communication, and are presupposed in all the uses that we make of our language. And Logic focuses, in the first instance, on truth-bearers. In Logic we week to account for how the truth of certain truth-bearers would *guarantee* the truth of certain others.

Now of course, guarantees vary in their strength or reliability. If you want an *absolute* guarantee, whereby it is *necessary* that, if the premises are true then the conclusion is true also, then you need to engage in *deductive* logic. If, however, you will be satisfied by a non-absolute, but still pretty reliable guarantee, given how things in the world tend to behave, then you will be able to engage in *inductive* logic.

Let us illustrate this with two examples, one from deductive logic, the other from inductive logic. Each is a good example of its kind. The logician's or methodologist's aim, in each case, is to explain *why* they are good.

Deductive example.

> Premise 1: All Armenians are Bolsheviks
> Premise 2: All Bolsheviks are Communists
> *therefore*
> Conclusion: All Armenians are Communists

Inductive example.

> Premise 1: Emerald no. 1 is green
> Premise 2: Emerald no. 2 is green
> ⋮
>
> Premise N: Emerald no. N is green
> *therefore*
> Conclusion: All emeralds are green

The first argument is *deductively* valid. The truth of its premises provides an absolute guarantee for the truth of its conclusion. It is impossible – no matter even if one were to change the laws of nature, or any of the contingent facts about our world – for the premises to be true and the conclusion to be false.

The second argument, about the emeralds, is by contrast not deductively valid; but it is *inductively* valid. It is not deductively valid because it *could possibly be the case* that emerald no. $N + 1$ turns out not to be green. We know, however, especially when N is large enough, that for a 'natural kind' of things like emeralds this is highly unlikely. Natural kinds are precisely the sorts of things whose observable properties (or certain important ones, at least) are reliably *projectible*, when possessed by sufficiently many members in a sample within the kind, to *all* members of the kind in question. Natural science relies on such inductive reasoning all the time, when arriving at general 'laws of nature'. Let us re-visit our earlier definition of validity of arguments:

> An argument of the form
>
> > Premise no. 1
> > Premise no. 2
> > ⋮
> >
> > *therefore*
> > Conclusion

is *valid* just in case the following holds: under *any* interpretation according to which Premise no. 1, Premise no. 2, …are all true, the Conclusion is true also.

We see now that the difference between deductive and inductive logic is really a difference over how generously (or permissively) to interpret the word 'interpretation' in this definition. The deductive logician wants to give 'interpretation' the *widest possible* interpretation. She is willing to consider as admissible interpretations the most bizarre stories or situations, provided only that we do not change the meanings of the *logical* words like 'all', 'some', 'not', 'and', 'or', 'only if', etc. Provided that one keeps *those* words' interpretations fixed, one is at liberty to *re-interpret* all the other, *non-logical*, words as one pleases. In the example above, these would be the words 'Armenian', 'Bolshevik' and 'Communist'. Thus the *deductive* logician's notion of validity ends up being very demanding: truth must be preserved from premises to conclusion in a vast host of situations, covering normal, not-so-normal and even downright bizarre ones.

By contrast, the *inductive* logician is willing to countenance only those interpretations that conform to the broad *uniformity of nature* that is presupposed by our inductive practices. We believe that the future will be, in certain important respects, like the past; that the deep regularities in nature hold in all places and at all times; that like causes produce like effects; that members of a given natural kind resemble each other in important respects; etc. This is what is involved in believing in 'the uniformity of nature'. Now, if we insist that any admissible interpretation of our language must be one that respects these uniformities, then (when assessing validity) one will have a much *narrower* class of interpretations to consider than is the case in deductive logic. Accordingly, the notion of inductive validity will be more liberal, or lax: it will be *easier* for an argument to be *inductively* valid than it will be for it to be *deductively* valid. For, only a restricted collection of situations or interpretations need be considered, when asking (in the inductive case) whether the truth of the premises will secure the truth of the conclusion. If we are considering only the orderly, uniform worlds of the inductivist, truth will transmit *more easily* from premises to conclusion. Nevertheless, there are still many examples of inductively *in*valid arguments. And one needs to be on one's intellectual guard against them.

Both kinds of logician – deductive and inductive – are concerned to characterize the good arguments (by their standards) and the bad arguments (by those same standards). It is just that their standards differ. It is much harder for an argument to be deductively valid. There is, however, a compensation: it is much easier to *characterize* which arguments are deductively valid. This is because every argument that is deductively valid is inductively valid, but not vice versa. It is easier to generate the class of deductively valid arguments than it is to generate the class of inductively valid ones. In fact, some philosophers have expressed pessimism over the prospect of ever formulating an 'inductive logic'. So far, no such thing has been produced. All we have are various rag-bag methods for inductive reasoning in specific kinds of situation. We do not yet have a 'canon of induction' that would apply uniformly in all cases of (inductive) reasoning presupposing only the most general uniformity of nature.

So, although most of our everyday reasoning aspires only to be inductively valid rather than deductively valid, we have the irony that, when we study Logic, we tend to concentrate on deductive validity rather than inductive validity. This is for the simple reason that deductive validity is better understood, and more successfully systematized, than inductive validity.

Indeed, deductive validity has become a science of logico-linguistic *form*, which is why deductive logic is sometimes also called *formal logic*.

The most important property of a deductive argument, as already stressed, is its *validity*:

$$\frac{P_1,\ldots,P_n}{Q} \text{ is valid}$$
if and only if
whenever $P_1,\ldots,P_n$ are all true, Q is true also.

That is, deductively valid arguments are truth-preserving.

From now on, unless indicated otherwise, we shall mean deductive argument by 'argument', and deductively valid by 'valid'.

The best arguments, of course, are ones with true premises validly implying true conclusions. But note that a valid argument may have false premises and a true conclusion:

$$\frac{\text{Dubya is a liberal}}{\text{Either Dubya is a liberal or snow is white}};$$

and it may have false premises and a false conclusion:

$$\frac{\text{Reagan is immortal}}{\text{Someone is immortal}}.$$

What a valid argument cannot do, however, is take one from true premises to a false conclusion. Hence their importance.

Valid arguments, ideally, can be *proved*; invalid arguments can be *counterexemplified*.

A *proof* is a piece of discourse from which one can read off the premises and the conclusion, and in which steps are arranged from the main premises to intermediate conclusions, which then become intermediate premises for further steps, which …finally terminate with the main conclusion. Each step should be convincing, obviously valid, easy to understand. An example of such a step would be so-called 'and-Introduction':

$$P, Q; \text{ therefore } (P \text{ and } Q). \text{ In symbols: } \frac{P \quad Q}{P \wedge Q}.$$

Anyone who doubts the validity of this step does not understand the logical connective 'and'.

A *counterexample* to an invalid argument is a 'possible world' (an imaginary or actual state of affairs) in which its premises are true but its conclusion is false.

Example 1. The invalid argument

> Someone is fat
> Someone is bald
> Someone is fat and bald

has many counterexamples, one of them being:

> John – fat but not bald;
> Mary – bald but not fat;
> John distinct from Mary;
> John and Mary the only two individuals in existence.

Example 2. The invalid argument

> Someone loves everyone else
> People who are loved by anyone love themselves
> Someone loves him/herself

has only one counterexample: a world in which there is only one person, who does not love him/herself. In this world the premises are (vacuously) true – for what counterinstances could there be? – and the conclusion is obviously false. *The argument would become valid if we supply an extra premise such as 'There are at least two people' or 'Someone loves someone'. The first of these has the advantage that, when adding it, one still needs both the original premises to secure the conclusion.* (Italics added here for later reference.)

Arguments that are invalid as strictly stated, but which become valid by adding explicitly an extra premise that is tacitly assumed (and which is most likely true, in the context of the discussion) are called *enthymemes*.

Sometimes arguments have as their conclusions a contradiction, or an absurdity. Such arguments are to the effect that their premises form an inconsistent set. They cannot all be true together in any possible world. An argument of this kind is also called a *reductio ad absurdum*. They are used to show that an opponent's position is internally contradictory, or incoherent. The solution to Problem (3) below is an example in point, in that it brings out the (possibly unexpected) incoherence of a set of four principles concerning truth and knowledge.

If an argument is valid, then its premises together with the negation of its conclusion form an inconsistent set. Conversely (for the classical logician) if the premises together with the negation of the conclusion of an argument form an inconsistent set then the argument is valid. This conceptual fact is exploited by the so-called 'resolution-method theorem-provers' in computing science.

Most 'arguments' in everyday life fall far short of the ideal of logical validity. They do not state all the premises that would be needed in order to secure the conclusion; they are almost all enthymemes. But the worst ones involve various more serious fallacies, or use cheap debating tricks – as we saw in §3.11.

7.3 Philosophical notions employed in the study of logic and language

The study of valid argumentation leads one to consider many other notions of philosophical importance. They are directly relevant to our understanding of the structure and content of our linguistic expressions. Arguments consist of premises and conclusions. These are sentences (or statements, or propositions, or assertions) that have meaning and truth-conditions. They may involve reference to objects, by means of names, such as 'John', and definite descriptions, such as 'the integral of the real-valued function $y = 2x$ from $x = 3$ to $x = 5$' – in the mathematician's usual symbolism,

$$\int_3^5 2x\,dx.$$

We predicate properties of the things to which we refer: John is bald; 7 is prime. Our declarative statements may also involve generalization or quantification: existential, as in 'There are milestones on the road to Dover', or universal, as in 'All prime numbers are odd'. They may involve identity: the Morning Star is the Evening Star; the logarithmic base e raised to the exponent πi, plus 1, is equal to (that is, is identical to) 0:

$$e^{\pi i} + 1 = 0.$$

These notions are involved in the first rudimentary investigations of the logico-linguistic skeleton of our language. All the bones and joints are reasonably well understood now, and a course in first-order logic with identity is the standard way to learn what philosophers, logicians, and mathematicians have clarified and systematised in this connection. For an introduction to the system of first-order logic with identity, and an exposition of the major completeness and incompleteness results for logic and arithmetic, see Tennant (1978).

Full-blown natural languages such as English harbor many sources of difficulty for logicians, however, and the closer study of these has given rise to areas of philosophy known as philosophical logic, philosophy of logic, and philosophy of language. A few words are in order about the most important problematic features of natural language, from the logician's pont of view.

7.3.1 *Token-reflexiveness*

Words such as 'I', 'you', 'here', 'now' depend on the token of the sentence used for their reference in context. (A *token* is an utterance or an inscription.) Natural language owes its flexibility and utility largely to these 'all-purpose' words that require the context to be specified before one understands the full import of what is being said by means of them. See Barwise and Perry (1984).

7.3.2 Semantic closure

A language is semantically closed if it is able to 'talk about itself' and about the relation between itself and the world. Semantic closure gives rise to the well-known semantic paradoxes, of which perhaps the most famous is the Liar Paradox: 'This sentence is false'. If it is true, it is false; if it is false, it is true. The workings of semantically closed languages are very mysterious, and modern logicians are developing some very complicated and sophisticated theories to deal with them. For a good exposition of the paradoxes, see the titular essay in Quine (1966), and Sainsbury (1987).

7.3.3 Vacuous terms

Names like 'Pegasus' and descriptive phrases like 'The King of France' do not denote. Frege thought they represented a logical imperfection; logically perfect languages, according to Frege, would not contain vacuous terms like these. All terms would denote. But modern logicians have given up this overly restrictive view. Logics that recognise such possibilities for the singular terms of the language are called *free* logics. They are free of the implicit default assumption, in standard logic, that every singular term of the language denotes.

Special care is needed when reasoning with free logics. For an account of the ways in which the standard rules of deductive logic need to be qualified and amended in order to obtain free logic, see Tennant (1978), Chapter 7. These amendments involve judicious use of so-called *existential presuppositions*, which are sentences of the form 't exists', where t is a singular term. In symbols: $\exists x\, x = t$. Sentences of this form are commonly abbreviated to $\exists! t$.

Examples of sentences enjoying this logical form would be 'Pegasus exists' (false); 'Santa Claus exists' (false); 'The King of France exists' (false – see Russell (1905); this is the famous example used by Russell when setting out his theory of definite descriptions); '0 exists' (true); 'for all numbers m and n, their product $m.n$ exists' (true); '$\{x|\neg x = x\}$ exists' (true); '$\{x|x = x\}$ exists' (false – see the brief explanation of the fundamentals of set theory given in §28.4.3 and §28.4.5); 'for all numbers m and n, $\frac{m}{n}$ exists' (false, because this quotient is undefined for $n = 0$); 'God exists' (jury out – see Part III).

7.3.4 Vagueness and ambiguity

Predicates like 'bald' and 'rich' are *vague*, in that they have borderline cases, for which it is not determinate whether the predicate applies. Sentences can be *ambiguous* (that is, have more than one meaning) because of ambiguous words or ambiguous structure. Examples are 'He was hiding near the bank' and 'Visiting relatives can be boring'.

The idea behind finding the logical form of a sentence (in a given use) is to specify exactly how it is constructed from its constituent words, so that there is no problem of structural ambiguity. Word ambiguity has simply to be legislated out of a logically possible language. Vague predicates present another problem, put into focus by the Sorites Paradox: if one has a heap of sand, it remains a heap upon removal of one grain of sand. By iteration of this principle, 'it' is still a heap when every grain has been removed. Do we have to surrender transitivity of deduction if the language contains vague predicates? (The transitivity principle is that if A implies B, and B implies C, then A implies C.) For an exploration of the issues raised by vagueness, see Keefe (2000).

7.3.5 Referential opacity

The *Principle of Substitutivity of Identicals* is the following rule of inference:

From $P(a)$ and $a = b$, one may infer $P(b)$.

Symbolically:

$$\frac{P(a) \qquad a = b}{P(b)} \ .$$

Example:

7 is prime; $7 = 5 + 2$; therefore, $5 + 2$ is prime.

Another example:

The Morning Star has nitrogen in its atmosphere; the Morning Star is the Evening Star; therefore, the Evening Star has nitrogen in its atmosphere.

The Principle of Substitutivity of Identicals runs into difficulties, however, in contexts of propositional attitude (such as belief) and in contexts of modality (such as necessity). For example, are the following two inferences valid?:

The Propositional-Attitude Inference:
Hegel believed that 8 is greater than 7; the number of planets is 8; therefore, Hegel believed that the number of planets is greater than 7.

(For the record, Hegel believed there were exactly seven planets.)

The Modal Inference:
It is necessary that 8 is greater than 7; 8 is the number of planets; therefore, it is necessary that the number of planets is greater than 7.

(It is a logical possibility that there might have been only seven planets.)

Speakers of English with fine-tuned grammatical sensibilities will object to the foregoing rendering of the modal inference: more precisely, to the rendering of its conclusion 'It is necessary that the number of planets is greater than 7'. They will insist that the conclusion ought rather to be expressed in one or other of the following two ways:

1 It is necessary that the number of planets be greater than 7.
2 The number of planets is necessarily greater than 7.

These two forms of English sentence are more discerning. The first uses the subjunctive mood; the second makes the modal operator adverbial. They serve to mark an important contrast: that between necessity *de dicto* and necessity *de re*. '*De dicto*' means *about the proposition (the thing said)*. The *dictum* in question is the proposition

The number of planets is greater than 7,

which can be symbolized as

$\#xP(x) > 7.$

'*De re*' means *about the thing* (that is under discussion). The thing in question here is that number which, in the actual world, is the number of planets. That happens to be the number 8 (now that the International Astronomers' Union has demoted Pluto from being a planet). We are dealing with necessity *de dicto* when we make the necessity operator dominant, as in the following rather lumpen form:

It is necessary that (the number of planets is greater than 7),

which we may symbolize as

$\square(\#xP(x) > 7).$

We are dealing, by contrast, with necessity *de re* when we make the singular term (referring to the number of planets) dominant:

The number of planets is such that *it* is necessarily greater than 7,

which we can re-write as

The number of planets is such that (it is necessary that (*it* is greater than 7)).

This we may symbolize as

$(\#xP(x))_y \square (y > 7).$

Here, we are treating *singular-term insertion* as a logical operation that has *scope*. The insertion of a singular term is understood as occurring at a certain stage in the logico-grammatical construction of a sentence. To illustrate, using the examples at hand: we can take the predicate

$$\ldots > 7$$

and apply the necessity operator to it:

$$\Box(\ldots > 7)$$

and only thereafter insert the term $\#xP(x)$ into the gap indicated by the dots. In order to indicate this, the logician uses a 'bound variable' (here, y) once again:

$$(\#xP(x))_y\Box(y > 7).$$

The singular-term occurrence is now said to have *wide scope*. The displayed occurrence of the operator $\Box$ is said to be within the scope of the singular term. This gives us the *de re* reading of the (structurally ambiguous) English sentence 'It is necessary that the number of planets is greater than 7'.

The *de dicto* reading is obtained by reversing the order of the two construction-steps just identified. Start once again with the predicate

$$\ldots > 7,$$

but this time insert the term first:

$$(\#xP(x))_y(y > 7).$$

Since no other operator intervenes between the term $\#xP(x)$ and its insertion point, this can be simplified to

$$\#xP(x) > 7.$$

Then apply the modal operator:

$$\Box(\#xP(x) > 7).$$

Now we have the promised formalization that captures the *de dicto* reading.

The availability of alternative logical forms, for different 'readings' of what might appear to be a single English sentence, is crucial to resolving the issues surrounding referential opacity. The two symbolic forms above are to be evaluated differently, because of the different ways they are composed from their constituent expressions. Let us explain.

In order for the *de dicto* claim

$$\Box(\#xP(x) > 7)$$

to be true, the subordinate sentence #xP(x) > 7 needs to be true not only in the actual world, but also in every possible world that is an alternative to the actual world. But there are, presumably, alternative possible worlds in which there are fewer than seven planets, and in such worlds the sentence #xP(x) > 7 is false. We see that the *denotation* of the complex singular term #xP(x) ('the number of planets') depends on the world one is in. In the actual world, this denotation is the number 8. But in certain alternative possible worlds, the denotation of the term #xP(x) might be (say) the number 6. It is false that 6 > 7. Hence, in such a world, it would be false that #xP(x) > 7. Hence, in the actual world (to which such a world is a possible alternative), it is false that □(#xP(x) > 7). So, on its *de dicto* reading, the conclusion of the modal inference is false, even though its premises are true – whence the modal inference is invalid.

Consider now the *de re* reading of the conclusion, given by the symbolization

$$(\#xP(x))_y\Box(y > 7).$$

What is the status of the modal inference on *this* reading of its conclusion? In order for the *de re* claim to be true, we start by latching onto the denotation of the 'wide-scope' singular term #xP(x), this denotation being determined by the facts in the *actual* world. So the denotation in question is the number 8. We now 'hold onto' that number as the *mathematical object* that it is, and consider it in each possible world, 'in place of' y within the formula y > 7. In each possible world, that is, we are evaluating the claim 8 > 7. This claim is true in every world – it is a *mathematical truth*, and mathematical truths are true of necessity. So the formula □(y > 7) is made true by 'plugging in' the value 8 for y. And 8 is the denotation, in the actual world, of the singular term #xP(x). Hence the sentence (#xP(x))_y□(y > 7) is true. So, on its *de re* reading, the conclusion of the modal inference is true, and the modal inference is valid.

The *de re/de dicto* distinction can be applied also in the case of propositional attitudes. There are two ways of reading the conclusion of the propositional-attitude inference (concerning Hegel's beliefs):

De dicto reading: Hegel believed that the number of planets is greater than 7. In symbols:

$$h\mathcal{B}(\#xP(x) > 7).$$

De re reading: Hegel believed, of the number that happens to be the number of planets, that *it* is greater than 7. In symbols:

$$(\#xP(x))_yh\mathcal{B}(y > 7).$$

On the *de dicto* reading of its conclusion, the propositional-attitude inference is invalid. Not so, however, on the *de re* reading.

One of the intellectual tasks that philosophers willingly undertake is this kind of disambiguation of grammatically ambiguous claims, in order to obtain a more precise understanding of both the truth-conditions of speakers' assertions and the validity of the various inferences they may draw. The study of the logic(s) governing the so-called 'modalities' of necessity and possibility is known as *modal logic*. The study of the logic governing the propositional attitude '*x* knows that *p*' is known as *epistemic* logic. The study of the logic governing the propositional attitude '*x* believes that *p*' is known as *doxastic* logic.

Modal operators, and verbs of propositional attitude, as we have seen above, create *referentially opaque* contexts. Referential opacity reveals itself in the failure of the Principle of Substitutivity of Identicals:

$$\frac{P(a) \qquad a = b}{P(b)} \quad ,$$

whose validity is a centerpiece of the standard, *extensional*, first-order logic governing the logical operators *not* ($\neg$), *and* ($\wedge$), *or* ($\vee$), *only if* ($\rightarrow$), *some* ($\exists$), *all* ($\forall$), and *is identical to* ($=$), which suffice for the logical formalization of Mathematics. With an extensional language, the truth or falsity of a sentence depends only on *what the objects are* and *how they are related*. Truth-values of sentences of an extensional language do *not* depend on *the way in which an object is denoted*. That is why Substitutivity of Identicals holds. This, however (as we have seen), is *not* the case with languages containing modal operators or verbs of propositional attitude. In the extended languages containing those sorts of expression, it can make a great deal of difference to the truth-value of a sentence to have a particular object denoted in one way rather than in another. Languages for which this is the case are called *intensional* languages, by contrast with the extensional language of Mathematics.

For classic essays on the problem of referential opacity, and intensionality more generally, see Linsky (1971).

7.3.6 *Paradoxes of relevance*

At its inception in the hands of Aristotle, formal logic employed a notion of 'following from' that involved the premises being *relevant to* any conclusion that follows from them. The two premises of any valid Aristotelian syllogism, moreover, are always consistent with each other. One can always supply an interpretation of their predicate-terms that makes them true.

By the early twentieth century, logicians had broadened the scope of their inquiries, so as to include arguments whose premises form an *inconsistent* set. With such a set of premises, no possible interpretation of their predicate terms makes all of them true. Clearly, a good system of logical proof ought to be able to *reveal* any inconsistency lurking within a given set of premises. That is, we need to be able to *disprove* such a set of premises, taken together, by deducing absurdity (symbolized by '⊥') from them.

The question then arises: how is one to understand the possibility of *anything other than* ⊥ itself 'following from' an inconsistent set of premises?

Modern logic has settled for an intuitively startling answer: *every proposition whatsoever* is held to follow logically from *any* inconsistent set of premises. Distilled to its simplest form, modern logic has nailed to its mast the following principle of inference:

A; not-A; *therefore,* B

– or, symbolically:

$$\frac{A \quad \neg A}{B} \; ,$$

where A and B may be utterly unrelated propositions that are completely irrelevant to one another. The latter has become known as *Lewis's First Paradox* of irrelevance (in modern logic). It meets with tremendous resistance from almost all acolytes and a significant number of experts alike. The simple thought is: Why should the blatantly inconsistent set $\{A, \neg A\}$ logically imply any *wholly disconnected, unrelated, irrelevant* conclusion B?

Modern logicians regard the 'simple thought' in question as overly naïve, and as symptomatic of a beginner's failure to appreciate the alleged advantages of 'rounding out' and 'simplifying' our formal system of logic. A great deal of pedagogical energy is expended on getting students to accept that the apparently paradoxical principle is one that earns its keep. Students are assured that the principle can come to be accepted with equanimity as one masters the system, and that indeed it is *necessary* as a part of the system if that system is to serve our deductive needs adequately.

Trained logicians who 'buy this line' have clearly reached a reflective equilibrium about the workings of thought and language in which certain high-level principles are allowed to outweigh the nagging counterintuitiveness (at the level of 'logical phenomena') of Lewis's First Paradox.

Other logicians, known as *relevantists* – the ones who beg to differ with the 'standard line' on the Lewis Paradox – are anxious to 'clean up' modern logic by expunging the paradoxes of relevance. They wish to *respect* those intuitions about the 'logical phenomena' – the intuition, for example, that it is manifestly silly to say that the pair of premises $\{2 + 2 = 4, \; 2 + 2 \neq 4\}$ logically implies that the moon is made of green cheese. Relevantists wish to eschew such silliness while yet retaining as many proofs, or valid arguments, as are needed in order to serve the methodological needs of Mathematics, Science and common sense.

At the time of this writing, there is ongoing debate over relevance – over whether, and, if so, how, one ought to ensure relevance between the premises and the conclusions of good arguments. The main manifesto for relevantists is Anderson and Belnap (1975). These authors, however, favor an approach on which classical logic's missing ingredient of relevance has to be restored to the *connective* 'if … then … ', while all the usual properties of deducibility are preserved. The present author advocates an alternative approach, on which the major reforms are to be made to the structural properties of proofs, hence also of deducibility. For further details, see Tennant (2005). It is a good thing for the beginning student of Philosophy to know that, even in matters this deeply foundational for rationality at large, philosophers and logicians have not yet arrived at a universal consensus.

Problems

1 Why is the validity of an argument in formal logic, as the adjective implies, said to be a matter of form, and not content?
2 How has modern logic improved upon Aristotle's system of syllogistic?
3 Do these principles form a consistent set?

> Every known proposition is true.
> If $(P \wedge Q)$ is known then P is known and Q is known.
> Some true proposition is not known to be true.
> Every true proposition can in principle be known.

4 The Absurdity Rule in classical logic allows one to derive *any* proposition from a contradiction. (Example: $2 + 2 = 4$; $2 + 2 \neq 4$; therefore, the moon is made of green cheese.) Consider how one might preserve all the logic one reasonably needs, while giving up this rule.
5 Verify the italicized claim in the discussion of **Example 2** above.
6 What is free logic? How exactly does it differ from standard logic?

8 Inductive Reasoning

8.1 The structure of arguments

Any *argument*, as we have seen, has premises, an inference marker, and a conclusion:

$$\frac{P_1,\ldots,P_n}{Q}.$$

See Copi *et al.* (2010) for a wealth of examples of arguments from Economics, Politics, Philosophy, etc. The reader can use these to practice identifying the premises, the conclusions, and the inference markers in various prose passages purporting to be arguments.

In Chapter 7 we contrasted two importantly different types of argument: *inductive* and *deductive*. So far we have laid stress on the latter. These are arguments that are logically guaranteed to preserve truth from their premises to their conclusions. Deductive arguments can be systematically characterized.

8.2 Inductive arguments

There are, however, other arguments that pass as convincing to various degrees, in that their premises render their conclusions *probable* or *likely*, without necessarily entitling one to be as confident about the conclusions as one might be about the premises. These are the *inductively valid* arguments.

The problem with inductive arguments is that no one has yet come up with a satisfactory systematic theory about them, and a formal logical system that would allow one to construct all and only the inductively valid arguments. Indeed, some philosophers believe that the very notion of inductive validity is a chimera. They maintain that what passes for inductively valid reasoning is simply the process of making a conjecture on the basis of evidence. There is no way that the evidence can justify the conjecture. All one can require is that the conjecture explain the evidence; and make new predictions. Future failure of these predictions would justify the jettisoning of the conjecture.

This, however, is an extreme view (associated with the name of Popper). It calls on us to relinquish all intuitions about inductive validity. But surely we have *some* such intuitions? A more moderate view would hold that we do indeed have strong intuitions about inductive support. These intuitions are to the effect that certain kinds of evidence provide strong grounds for certain kinds of conclusions. On this view it may be our intellectual inadequacy as analysts and theorists and system-builders that explains our failure, thus far at least, to formulate a satisfactory formal system of inductive reasoning. C. D. Broad (1887–1971) did, after all, call the failure to solve the problem of induction 'the scandal of Philosophy'.

Some arguments combine both deductive and inductive elements. A good example would be legal arguments. In legal arguments one reasons (often in an inductive fashion) to a verdict; then one reasons (deductively) to the passing of sentence (imposition of a jail term; instruction to pay damages, etc.).

8.3 A *Leitmotif*

We now introduce what will be a *Leitmotif* for much of what follows. This simple diagram encapsulates a fundamental distinction between two kinds of statement, within a deductive context: those that can be *proved*, and those that can be *refuted* (or *disproved*):

On the left is our generic symbol for a *proof* of a statement *P*: an isosceles triangle with *P* at its bottom vertex, and with the triangle's base at the top representing the premises (here, not mentioned) on which the conclusion *P* rests. On the right is our generic symbol for a *refutation* of a statement *P*. The symbol ⊥ stands for *absurdity*. We make a point of mentioning *P* as one of the premises on which the conclusion ⊥ rests, because we wish to draw attention to the fact that *P* has been *refuted*, possibly with the assistance of premises that are not explicitly mentioned alongside *P*.

Both a proof and a refutation would in general have fine structure – that is, would contain other sentences appropriately arranged to effect the logical passage towards *P* (in the case of the proof) or from *P* – along, perhaps, with some side-assumptions – to absurdity (in the case of the refutation).

In Mathematics, one is primarily interested in proofs of theorems *P*. These proofs would make the conclusion *P* rest ultimately on simple, indubitable axioms. (That is why we have the horizontal line at the top of the proof schema. It represents the secure foundation for the inverted pyramid that is the proof.)

In Natural Science, by contrast, one is primarily interested in testing hypotheses *P* by trying to construct refutations of them. These refutations will make the absurd conclusion ⊥ rest ultimately on P along with other statements about which one is more certain than one is about P. These other statements likewise are not shown explicitly on the horizontal line at the top of the refutation schema; for we want to pinpoint our interest in P. It is important to bear in mind, however, that both proofs and refutations can have those extra assumptions.

In Mathematics we go for outright assertions (theorems) backed by proofs. Once proved, a theorem remains proved. It is every bit as certain as are the axioms on which it rests. The proof gives us a guarantee that if the axioms are true, then the theorem proved from them is true also.

In Science, by contrast, we set up hypotheses and then test them against the evidence, alongside other (less tentative) hypotheses. The evidential statements and these other hypotheses are the extra assumptions not indicated explicitly in the refutation schema above.

Now there is of course an interplay between proofs and refutations. In Mathematics, for example, one may wish to prove a statement of the form 'not-P'. (A good example would be: *it is not the case that the square root of 2 is the ratio of two whole numbers.*) One would prove not-P by assuming P and constructing a refutation of it (that is, a proof of ⊥ from the assumption P). Then one would take one more step to conclude to not-P, getting rid of the assumption P in the process. So one would end up with a proof of not-P, with not-P standing as the final sentence at the very bottom.

In Science, likewise, one might construct a refutation of an hypothesis P by invoking, among other results, some theorems Q of (applied) Mathematics. These would have their place as conclusions of subproofs on the way to constructing the overall proof of absurdity from P plus all the other extra assumptions that may be involved.

So we see that proof and refutations can depend on one another; can indeed form parts of one another. It is only the overall end-result which we have distinguished by means of our schemata above. In Mathematics, one wants, ultimately, proofs of theorems P; in Science, all one can get, ultimately, is a refutation of an hypothesis P.

Note that general hypotheses in Science – hypotheses of the form 'All Fs are Gs' – can never be proved outright, the way that a mathematical theorem can. Experience can only lead to their *refutation*. All our general scientific theories are, in effect, tentative conjectures that have survived a wide range of testing against experience. We gain confidence in them the more such tests they pass without succumbing to refutation. But we can never have the same confidence in them that we have in a mathematical theorem once possessed of an outright proof of it.

Now both proofs and refutations, in Mathematics and in Science, are rigorous. They can in principle be formalized so that every step is correct and unquestionable, leading inexorably to the result claimed. There is a trade-off, however, between the need to convince and the time available to do so. We typically fill in only as much deductive detail as is needed in order to satisfy a critical interlocutor. If the interlocutor is skilled at filling in missing details, and can 'see' how the proof would go without having every step explicitly filled in, then one can get on with the job more quickly, emphasizing in one's presentation only the most salient points that signpost the rigorous deductive route. This can be done, for example, when writing a technical paper for a learned journal, whose readers will all be experts in the discipline.

But one has to bear in mind that whatever argument one gives, *it should be possible in principle to spell out every step in full detail if pressed to do so by someone who does not follow, or who is not persuaded by, the compressed version.* It might not be enough simply to say 'It is obvious that ... ' (which is the mathematician's favorite way of masking a potential error when the going gets tough or indeed impossible). The italicized principle is one that applies also to *philosophical* argumentation. We shall have occasion, in Chapter 15, to apply this principle with a vengeance, in order to see whether the famous 'Ontological Argument' for the existence of God can be made logically convincing.

When criticizing or appraising philosophical arguments – whether one's own, with hindsight, or those of another – one should likewise be prepared to attend constantly to the structure of argument. In so far as that structure is lacking, one has a defective piece of philosophical theorizing.

Now there are some brands of philosophy that find argumentative rigor and depth a kind of intellectual anathema. These opposing brands of philosophy extol instead the virtues of loosely connected aphorisms and insights. But in the absence of any tighter organisation of these insights, one is left with a loose jumble, a mélange, a farrago of half-baked inspirations. The theses, such as they are, will only intersect by sharing a notion or two. They will be as unrelated as are two words that have only a letter in common. Philosophical theory requires organisation of a deeper kind than would be found in a conceptual crossword puzzle.

8.4 Inductive arguments (resumed): Hume's 'old riddle' of induction

We began above by representing the structure of arguments in general in terms of premises $P_1, \ldots, P_n$ and conclusions Q:

$$\frac{P_1, \ldots, P_n}{Q} \ .$$

When the argument is deductive, this is fine. But when the argument is *inductive*, we must be very careful to appreciate the exact relationship such an argument would bear to appropriate deductive arguments.

To put it simply: inductive 'arguments' try to bridge the gap between evidence and explanatory hypothesis. Recall how we said earlier that there is no logic of scientific discovery; there is only a logic of scientific testing. The creative leap from evidence to hypothesis was left mysterious and unexplained. But the return passage from hypothesis to evidence had to be a deductive one. Inductive logic would be an attempt to systematise and codify the means whereby one can make that leap from evidence E to hypotheses H that would explain E. We have been accustomed to representing the hypotheses as 'above' the evidence in our pictures so far:

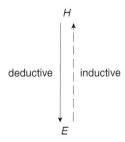

What we must now note is that the passage 'upwards' in these diagrams from the evidence E to the hypothesis H would be turned upside down when representing it as an inductive argument. For in the inductive argument the premises would be the bits of evidence, and the conclusion would be the hypothesis induced:

$$\frac{E_1,\ldots,E_n}{H} \quad (=E) \quad .$$

The commonest examples of inductive arguments involve extrapolation of observed properties of members of natural kinds: so-called *enumerative* induction. Natural kinds are the categories appropriate for scientific generalizations; indeed, the notions of induction and of natural kind are co-eval. Induction is justified on natural kinds; natural kinds are what induction applies to best.

Take, for example, the natural kind *emerald*. Suppose $e_1,\ldots,e_n$ are all the emeralds we have seen so far. Suppose moreover that each of them has turned out to be green. Then the evidence is

   $\{G(e_1),\ldots,G(e_n),\ e_1$ is an emerald, $\ldots,\ e_n$ is an emerald$\}$.

We then make the inductive leap to the conclusion that *every* emerald is green: for every emerald e, $G(e)$. This leap can be displayed as

$$\frac{G(e_1),\ldots,G(e_n),\ e_1 \text{ is an emerald}, \ldots, e_n \text{ is an emerald}}{\text{for every emerald } e, \ G(e)} \quad .$$

The inductive step takes us from the particular to the general. If it is reliable, then it is *inductively* valid. But the step is not *deductively* valid. That is, the evidence $\{G(e_1),\ldots,G(e_n),\ e_1$ is an emerald $, \ldots, e_n$ is an emerald$\}$ cannot *logically guarantee* the conclusion 'for every emerald e, $G(e)$'. For it is logically possible for the evidence to hold while yet not all emeralds be green. Some as-yet-*un*examined emerald might turn out not to be green.

This is Hume's famous skeptical point about induction. The truth of the evidence does not *logically guarantee* the truth of the induced conclusion. This is what makes induction so distinctively (and disturbingly) different from deduction. Hume's point makes clear what might be called the *old* riddle of induction. It can be given many illustrations.

Suppose that whenever we have, in the past, hit a cue ball in snooker at a red ball, accurately enough to make the cue ball collide with the sitting red ball, the red ball has moved off from where it was sitting before the collision. Unfortunately, there is no *logical* reason at all why, despite this regularity in the past, it should be manifest when next we strike the cue ball so as to put it on course to hit the red ball. The red ball could simply sit still despite the collision, as though fixed to the table, deflecting the cue ball. That is a logically possible state of affairs. Or it could spontaneously 'dodge' the approaching cue ball. This too is a logically possible state of affairs. In fact, there are myriad possibilities, logically speaking: the red ball might levitate just high and long enough for the cue ball to pass underneath it. Or the collision could take place alright, but with the unusual result that the two balls just sit there, at rest, in continuing contact with each other. Yet another logical possibility is that the cue ball (or the red ball) could, at the moment of collision, simply *vanish* before our eyes.

Suppose that the Sun has risen above the eastern horizon every morning in the history of the human species. Unfortunately, there is no *logical* reason why it should rise there tomorrow, or indeed rise at all. The Earth could suddenly stop rotating, and roast one of its sides. Indeed, the side nearest the Sun could even turn to ice, rather than roast. Or the Earth could start rotating in the other direction around its axis. That is a logically possible state of affairs.

Suppose that every raven we have examined has turned out to be black. Unfortunately, there is no *logical* reason why the next raven to be examined should turn out to be black. It might be white. That is a logically possible state of affairs.

Suppose that every swan we have examined has turned out to be white. Unfortunately, there is no *logical* reason why the next swan to be examined should turn out to be white. It might be black. That is a logically possible state of affairs. (Indeed, it is actual: there are black swans in Western Australia.)

Suppose that every emerald we have examined has turned out to be green. Unfortunately, there is no *logical* reason why the next emerald to be examined should turn out to be green. It might be *blue*. That is a logically possible state of affairs. Indeed, it might even be *grue*. (For an explanation of 'grue', see §28.1.2.)

Suppose that for as far as we have been able to determine by means of our telescopes, the speed of light has a particular constant value c. Unfortunately, there is no *logical* reason why in some galaxy so distant that its light since its formation has not yet reached us, the speed of light should be c. It might be some other value c'. That is a logically possible state of affairs.

How can we be sure that the future will be like the past? How can we rely on the uniformity of Nature? Why should like causes produce like effects? Why should things of a kind all have particular properties (such as color) in common?

There are many ways of posing the riddle; and no satisfactory way of answering it. It remains, as Broad once said, the scandal of Philosophy that no one has yet answered the riddle satisfactorily.

The riddle rests simply on the following logical observations, of which we have just given examples above:

1 no past observations can logically imply any future observations (predictions);
2 no observations about states of affairs close by can logically imply any observations (predictions) about distant states of affairs;
3 no observations about *some* things of a kind can logically imply any observations (predictions) about *all* things of that kind.

Note that what we are calling predictions here are the would-be conclusions of inductive inference. The notion of prediction does not essentially involve future time. It involves only the notion of projection to cases not covered by the evidence at hand. Our negative logical observations can be summed up by saying that neither time nor space nor kindredness can provide the logical glue that would make the predictions stick. That is the old riddle of induction.

By contrast – in the case of the emeralds, for example – the hypothesis we have induced ('for every emerald e, $G(e)$') will deductively imply each bit of evidence $G(e_i)$. That is, each argument of the form

$$\frac{\text{for every emerald } e,\ G(e) \qquad e_i \text{ is an emerald}}{G(e_i)}$$

will be deductively valid. This is a minimal adequacy condition in induction: namely, that the conclusion induced from the evidence should deductively imply the evidence.

Compatibly with this minimal adequacy condition, however, there will in general be many conclusions that could be induced. Remember, each such induced conclusion is to serve as an hypothesis that both explains the observational evidence obtained under boundary conditions BC, say, and also allows us to make predictions about further observations that might be obtained under yet other conditions. Each such hypothesis will explain the evidence by deductively implying it; and will generate predictions by deductively implying them. In each of the deductions, the statement BC of boundary conditions may be taken as another premise alongside the hypothesis concerned.

But there will in general be more than one hypothesis that will do this, no matter how extensive the evidence E may be. This is the problem of *rival hypotheses*. It is also known as the problem of *underdetermination of theory by evidence*. It is what makes scientific controversy possible. It is what underlies the claim that all our scientific theorizing, however successful it has been to date, is really no more than *conjecture*. For the evidence does not dictate exactly which hypothesis is justified as the explanation of the evidence. A good inductive logic would constrain as narrowly as possible the set of rival hypotheses that can be induced from the evidence *E* under given conditions *BC*. It would then leave to other methodological considerations (such as simplicity) the final choice of just one among the set of rivals.

Let us make clear with a picture what is involved in there being rival hypotheses with regard to evidence *E* under conditions *BC*. We shall deal with the simplest case, where there are ony two rivals. The treatment will generalize in an obvious way to any number of rivals. They just have to be pairwise rivals in the sense about to be explained for hypotheses H_1 and H_2. We are supposing that each of H_1, H_2 can be induced from the evidence *E* that was obtained under conditions *BC*. Thus the deductive picture is that each of the hypotheses, by itself, explains the evidence by deductively implying it, with the help of *BC* as another premise:

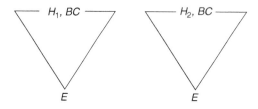

So far so good. But H_1 and H_2 are supposed to be rivals. How so? The rivalry arises with respect to the predictions they generate (by deductively implying them). The predictions will be (observational) statements *P* not yet 'in' the evidence *E*. That is, *E* will not deductively imply *P*. The rivalry will lie in the fact that H_1, in conjunction with some description *BC′* of boundary conditions (not necessarily the same conditions as *BC* above), will deductively imply some such *P*; while H_2, along with the same boundary conditions *BC′*, will deductively imply not-*P* – or vice versa. Let us look at the former case. We have H_1 and *BC′* deductively implying *P*, but H_2 and *BC′* with *P* leading deductively to absurdity:

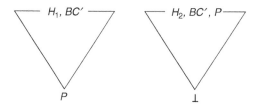

This gives us an idea as to what scientific testing aims to establish. Suppose we wish to adjudicate experimentally between two rival hypotheses, each of which explains the evidence *E*. What the scientist needs to do is identify some 'crucial' observational statement *P* for certain experimentally contrivable conditions *BC′*. The logical situation should then be that *P* is deductively implied by one of the hypotheses H_1 in conjunction with *BC′*; but that *P* is contradicted by the other hypothesis H_2 in conjunction with BC'. The diagram above once again makes this clear. The creativity of the experimental scientist (as already remarked) lies in the ability to contrive the conditions BC', and to identify the crucial observational statement P. When the experiment is performed – that is, when the conditions BC' are realized – then 'Nature takes its course', leading either to the observation P or to the observation not-P. Whichever it is decides the fate of one of the hypotheses. Only one of H_1 and H_2 will survive the test; the other will have to be discarded.

The great problem for inductive logic is that there is in general too bewildering a variety of rival hypotheses that explain the evidence E. Remember our minimal adequacy condition in induction: namely, that the hypothesis H induced as conclusion from the evidence E, under given conditions BC', should deductively imply the evidence E. There is one obvious and trivial 'hypothesis' that meets this minimal adequacy condition: namely, the statement 'if BC' then E'. Conjoined with BC', this hypothesis immediately yields E. But does it yield anything else? That is, does it allow us to make new predictions? It would appear not. The hypothesis 'if BC' then E' amounts to no more than a statement of the evidence under the stipulated conditions. The hypothesis is as certain as the evidence, because it does not venture beyond it. 'If BC' then E' tells us nothing about what to expect under other conditions BC^*.

But we know that we need more than this from a good hypothesis H: it is both to explain all the evidence E to date, and to predict new observations P not already implied by E. The requirement of 'predictive power' works against the otherwise comforting fact that the hypothesis is no less certain than the evidence for it.

So there are two requirements in tension with one another here. The first requirement is that the hypothesis should be supported as strongly as possible by the evidence E. This requirement inclines us to the likes of 'if BC then E' in hypothesis choice. But the second requirement is that the hypothesis should tell us more about the world than we have already observed to be the case. This requirement inclines us to an hypothesis H that ventures beyond the evidence, implying predictions that are no part of the evidence E to date. In this way the hypothesis acquires predictive power. It thereby becomes less certain than the evidence E, but it becomes open to test.

At no stage of our investigations does the total evidence acquired suffice for the *truth* of our scientific hypotheses, in the way that mathematical axioms suffice for the truth of mathematical theorems. As already noted, hypotheses in Natural Science venture *beyond* the available evidence. These hypotheses venture to say something about *all* objects or events of a particular natural kind, even when only a limited sample of these might have been observed when gathering the evidence from which the hypothesis is induced. Such universal claims are both *stronger* and *simpler* than the detailed statement of the particular evidence on which they are 'based'. The price paid for *logical strength* and *simplicity* is *uncertainty*. The truth of the evidence cannot logically guarantee the truth of those strong and simple hypotheses.

It would appear, then, that the task is to optimize between the conflicting requirements of evidential support and predictive power. The question is: is there an inductive logic that can do this? We might feel confident that there is, since it seems that we manage it (albeit inchoately) ourselves. That is, we make successful inductions. Surely, the optimist would say, we should be able to systematize what it is that we do as scientists when thinking up hypotheses *H* to explain evidence *E* under conditions *BC*? After all, haven't we successfully done the same thing with mathematical reasoning? Have we not succeeded in analyzing all the logical moves that we make in Mathematics, so as to have now a complete system of rules of deductive inference according to which all good mathematical arguments can be proved rigorously?

The answer of course is 'yes' – we have done this for Mathematics, and with resounding success. We even have as a result some deep metatheorems about the formal logical systems we have set up and about the mathematical theories that can be developed within these systems. We know a great deal about the power, both expressive and deductive, of such systems and theories. We know how that power is limited in various ways; but a detailed exposition of these insights would be out of place here. (The interested reader can look forward to Part V.) It is enough to concede to our optimistic questioner the success of *deductive* systematization. But when it comes to systematization of *inductive* reasoning, there does not appear to be much ground for the optimism just expressed.

Since we never establish the truth of any scientific hypothesis as certain, what is the value of our science? A reasonable answer here is that we use science to *guide our actions*. And our actions are based on (what we take to be) *our most reliable beliefs*. We are fully aware that our actions cannot always be based on certainties. The best beliefs we have are, by default, those which have saved *all* appearances, including the appearances involved in critical tests. If anyone does not wish, with this explanation, to trust science as a guide to life, that person is invited to show what *other* sorts of beliefs would fare better, in the sense that they would make *us* fare better. What *other* sorts of beliefs would enable us to anticipate the future course of events, build our technologies, devise our therapies, and explain why the world appears the way it does?

8.5 How probability figures in scientific reasoning: Reichenbach's straight rule

It would be a mistake to think that the problem with inductive inferences is that they are confined to examples like the one above, concerning the color of emeralds (or, in other oft-cited examples, the color of swans, or of ravens). The unusual feature of *that* example was that *100 percent* of the emeralds 'sampled' thus far had been observed to be green. It is a reasonable default assumption that the sample of actually observed emeralds had not been selected with any *biased intention* (conscious or unconscious) in favor of getting this 100 percent rate of observed greenness. It is not as though the observers who are scientifically interested in the color of emeralds could have been hoodwinked by the suppliers in the long supply chain originating with the workers who actually dug the emeralds out of the ground. It is not as though the diggers or the middlemen found significant numbers of non-green emeralds (purple ones, perhaps? or cerise?) and surreptitiously disposed of them so that they did not end up in the 'sample' to be viewed by those with scientific interests.

The inductive inference concerning the emeralds can be re-written in a slightly different, interesting form:

> In the sample of observed emeralds, 100 percent of them were green.
> The sample was fair.
> *Therefore*, among all emeralds at large, 100 percent of them are green.

It is immediately seen that this is but a special case of a more general rule of inductive-statistical reasoning, where $0 \leq X \leq 100$:

> In the sample of observed instances of natural kind K, $X\%$ of them had property P.
> The sample was fair.
> *Therefore*, among all instances at large of natural kind K, $X\%$ of them have property P.

This more general rule is (a simple form of) what statisticians call *Reichenbach's straight rule*. It admits of more sophisticated tweakings, in which the sample size is taken into account:

> In the sample of N observed instances of natural kind K, M of them had property P.
> The sample was fair.
> *Therefore*, among all instances at large of natural kind K, $\frac{M}{N}$ of them have property P.

In this form, the rule is still vulnerable to the same kind of inductive skepticism as was directed against it when X took the value 100 (or, in the notation of this last version of the rule, when $M = N$). Any value for the actual at-large frequency *distinct* from X or $\frac{M}{N}$ affords, technically, a *falsification* of the conclusion of the rule. Yet we do not commonly think of our reasoning as in serious error if we discover, in the fullness of time, that the true at-large frequency of P-type Ks is only *slightly* different from X or $\frac{M}{N}$. We happily allow, that is, for *margins of error* in our predictions of frequencies.

A more acceptable form of the 'straight rule', therefore (which the reader might think is becoming more crooked by the minute) is as follows:

> In the sample of N observed instances of natural kind K, M of them had property P.
> The sample was fair.

Therefore, the probability-density function of the actual frequency of *P*s among all instances at large of natural kind *K* is centered on the value $\frac{M}{N}$, and quite tightly clumped around it.

We shall spare the reader the mathematics involved in making more precise what is meant by 'centering' here, and being 'tightly clumped'. The looser intuitive formulation is quite adequate for the philosophical point to be made.

Which is this: by invoking the notion of probability, and long-run frequencies within large populations, we can make habitual forms of inductive reasoning appear more intelligible and less vulnerable to skeptical doubts about its validity (in the newly explicated sense).

8.6 How probability figures in scientific reasoning: making hypotheses more probable

[**Note:** This section presupposes the reader's familiarity with the notion of a logical consequence relation, denoted here as $\vdash$. If readers read this symbol as 'logically implies', with a not-yet-fully-explicated grasp of what this notion amounts to, they will still get the important gist of what is being laid out in this section. But readers who find themselves at sea with these technical notions can return to this section after learning a little more about logic in later chapters of the book.]

8.6.1 *The various interpretations of the notion of probability*

The notion of probability is subject to various interpretations. The probability of an event (alternatively, of the proposition that the event in question occurs) might be thought of as:

- the *objective chance* that it occurs; or
- the *physical propensity* of the physical system to produce events of that kind, or to bring about the truth of that kind of proposition; or
- a human subject's (hopefully rational) *degree of belief* that it occurs; or
- the *long-run frequency* of occurrence of events of that kind with respect to some suitably chosen reference class (such as the long-run frequency of a coin landing heads, within the reference class of tosses of the coin).

Probability can also be thought of as:

- the *degree of confirmation*

of the proposition concerned.

Degrees of belief (see the third interpretation of probabilities above) might be operationalized, or measured, by the *odds in a wager* that the agent is prepared to accept. One requirement of rationality – a normative requirement that is not always met by actual people – is that the odds on various bets that the agent would accept should 'cohere', in the sense of satisfying the axioms of the probability calculus. If they do not satisfy those axioms, it will be possible for a bookmaker to make out a so-called 'Dutch book' of judiciously chosen bets, so that the bettor is bound to lose money in the long run. That is, the bettor's expected return, given his incoherent odds, will be negative.

Despite the foregoing variety of interpretations of the real-valued function $p(A)$ of events or propositions A, there is widespread agreement on the mathematical properties of the function. Let us suppose that its domain of definition is a set or class of propositions, and that these propositions form the field of a logical consequence relation $\vdash$.

8.6.2 *The axioms of the theory of probability*

We begin our discussion by stating four utterly basic axioms for any real-valued probability function $p(\ )$ defined on propositions A. The first axiom limits the range of possible numerical values for probability. The other three axioms impose logical constraints on the probability assignment, as it collapses the partial ordering of logical consequence among the propositions involved to the linear ordering of their probability values (i.e., the linear ordering that they enjoy as real numbers).

In plain English, the axioms are as follows:

1   Probabilities lie between 0 and 1 inclusive.
2   Logical truths have probability 1.
3   Logical falsehoods have probability 0.
4   The probability of any proposition is at least as great as that of any proposition that logically implies it.

We can express these axioms slightly more formally as follows. Axioms (1)–(3) hold for all propositions A. Axiom (4) holds for all propositions A and all propositions B.

1   $0 \le p(A) \le 1$.
2   If $\vdash A$ (i.e., A is logically true), then $p(A) = 1$.
3   If $A \vdash \perp$ (i.e., A is logically false), then $p(A) = 0$.
4   If $A \vdash B$ (i.e., A logically implies B), then $p(A) \le p(B)$.

Intuitively, the simple thing one needs to understand about probability is this: assigning probabilities to propositions effects a *linearization* of the *partial* ordering already imposed on the propositions by the relation of logical consequence or deducibility. Before dealing with probabilities, we have the relation $\vdash$, which *partially orders* the sentences of the language. Upon introducing probabilities subject to the foregoing axioms, one goes further and *linearizes* this ordering of the propositions (that the sentences express). The main constraints are really quite minimal: logical falsehoods must be assigned probability 0; logical truths must be assigned probability 1; and 'in between', as it were, the probability assignments on contingent propositions must 'respect' the relation ⊢ that is already in place. Axiom (4) requires only that if $A \vdash B$, then $p(A) \leq p(B)$.

Thus far we have introduced only the notion of *absolute* probability. There is a companion notion of *conditional* probability, $p(A|B)$, to be read as 'the probability of A, given B'. The latter notion is defined as follows. Note that it is admissible only when $0 < p(B)$. The reader is reminded that the connective $\wedge$ means 'and'.

Definition 2. *If* $0 < p(B)$ *then*

$$p(A|B) =_{df} \frac{p(A \wedge B)}{p(B)}.$$

8.6.3 A theorem about probability that is philosophically significant

We now employ the notions of absolute and conditional probability to state a theorem in the theory of probability that has important philosophical consequences. Explanation of our choice of symbols (H, S, K, and E) will emerge in due course.

Theorem 1. *Suppose*

1 $H, S, K \vdash E$;
2 $0 < p(H \wedge (S \wedge K))$;
3 $p(H|S \wedge K) = p(H|K)$; *and*
4 $p(E|S \wedge K) < 1$.

Then

$$p(H|E \wedge (S \wedge K)) > p(H|K).$$

The proof of Theorem 1 will be found in Appendix B.

The reader is asked to take on trust that careful inspection of the formal proofs given there reveals that the only probability axiom used in the proof of Theorem 1 is Axiom (4).

Philosophical comment on Theorem 1

We shall describe the import of each of the four assumptions of Theorem 1, in the context of experimental testing of a scientific theory. Think of S as describing the initial- and boundary-conditions of some experimental set-up, devised against the background of our knowledge K to date. The hypothesis H to be tested is used as an assumption, along with K and S, to logically deduce some prediction E (an evidential statement whose truth we can eventually determine by running the experiment). Thus assumption (1) of Theorem 1 is satisfied, namely $H, S, K \vdash E$.

So too is assumption (2), namely $0 < p(H \wedge (S \wedge K))$, since otherwise we would not, as rational agents, even be considering the hypothesis H.

Assumption (3), namely $p(H|S \wedge K) = p(H|K)$, tells us that, against the background of our knowledge K to date, simply setting up the experimental apparatus (thereby making S true, and known) cannot change the conditional probability of the hypothesis H, given what is known. Setting up the apparatus cannot *increase* that conditional probability; nor can doing so *decrease* it. This is because the truth of the hypothesis H (should H be true) is supposed to transcend, and not depend in any way on, the observable truths that may come to be known as a result of human beings' experimental intervention in the natural order. (H will be a suitably 'high-level' hypothesis.)

Finally, assumption (4), namely $p(E|S \wedge K) < 1$, tells us that without the help of H as an assumption, we are less than fully certain that E will turn out to be true, even given the conjunction of our background knowledge K with the knowledge S that the experimental set-up is in place (but without the experiment yet having been run).

When the experiment is run, however, and E is discovered to be the case, the epistemic result (as stated by the consequent of Theorem 1) is that the conditional probability of H (given all that is now known) has been raised:

$$p(H|E \wedge (S \wedge K)) > p(H|K) = p(H|S \wedge K).$$

That is, the 'posterior' conditional probability $p(H|E \wedge (S \wedge K))$ is greater than the 'prior' conditional probability $p(H|K)$. Moreover, there is an important intermediate result within the proof of Theorem 1 (as the reader will see in Appendix B):

$$p(H|E \wedge (S \wedge K)).p(E|S \wedge K) = p(H|K).$$

From this it follows that the posterior conditional probability $p(H|E \wedge (S \wedge K))$ will be all the greater the smaller the value of $p(E|S \wedge K)$. That is, if E is a very surprising result – corresponding to a very low value for $p(E|S \wedge K)$ – it will lend more confirmation to the hypothesis, in the sense that the posterior conditional probability $p(H|E \wedge (S \wedge K))$ will be all the greater than the prior conditional probability $p(H|K)$.

Thus we have a *probabilistic* vindication of our tendency to be more confident about an hypothesis whose predictions E, on the basis of initial- and boundary-conditions S, are borne out by experiment.

Perhaps the correct response to the extreme inductive skeptic, then, is to inquire respectfully whether the founding figure for the skepticism being pressed was one of those great and admirable philosophers who did their work *before* the advent of probability and statistics, or at least before they could have been expected to take it into account in their own work. To put matters in perspective: Jacob Bernouilli (1654–1705) proved his (Weak) Law of Large Numbers in 1689, but his *Ars Conjectandi* was published only in 1713, eight years after he died. Abraham de Moivre (1667–1754) published *The Doctrine of Chances*, the first textbook on probability theory, in 1718. The great inductive skeptic David Hume (1711–76) wrote his *Treatise of Human Nature* in 1739–40. But Hume was not a mathematician, and was probably not influenced deeply enough by the work of de Moivre and of Bernouilli and other Continental probability theorists. Hacking (2001), at pp. 251–52, conjectures 'I think [Hume] had read Abraham de Moivre's book ... but probability theory had hardly begun when Hume proposed the problem of induction'.

Pace Hume, the quietist about induction appears to gain *some* support, at least, from developments in the modern theory of conditional probabilities and statistical inference. (This line of thought can be found in Carnap (1947). In Hacking (2001), Chapters 20–22 are very useful for a more detailed defense of this view.)

Problems

1 Does our habit of using induction to form beliefs about the external world stand in need of any *a priori* justification?
2 How, do you think, did our species acquire the habit of inductive reasoning?
3 Does inductive reasoning require the use of language, or do even languageless creatures engage in certain forms of inductive reasoning?
4 Explain the connections among empirical support for a theory, the theory's predictive power, and its simplicity.
5 Describe the role of Mathematics, as you understand it, within scientific explanation and prediction.
6 How does the reliability of Reichenbach's Straight Rule relate to sample size?

9 The Method of Conceptual Analysis

Analytical philosophers, as the designation suggests, set great store by possible *analyses* of concepts of philosophical importance. This does not mean that analytical philosophy is concerned solely with such matters. Rather, analytical philosophy is Philosophy conducted with a readiness to require and provide conceptual analyses when this is called for; and to challenge and criticize conceptual analyses that may be defective.

9.1 Conceptual analysis as provision of necessary and sufficient conditions

Conceptual analysis is an important means to an end. The means is clarificatory; the end is the pursuit of truth and understanding. Introspection on our concepts enables us to clarify them, and enables us thereby to reach a more perfect understanding of them: of how they hang together, and of how they apply to things and events in the world. The standard way of trying to clarify a given concept is to provide an *analysis* for it: that is, a statement of the *individually necessary* and *jointly sufficient* conditions for its application. The statement of such conditions usually involves other concepts, taken to be better understood or previously clarified.

But such attempts at conceptual analysis might be faulty; and philosophers have to police themselves, and be on the lookout for inadequate analyses. Philosophically sharpened intuitions are involved in the attempt to demonstrate the inadequacy of particular attempts to clarify our concepts. These intuitions lead to the construction of thought-experimental *counterexamples* to faulty conceptual analyses on offer; on which, more below.

The beginner in Philosophy needs to be informed that a great deal of contemporary philosophical discussion in the journals is concerned with providing counterexamples to proposed conceptual analyses. It is part of what philosophers call 'negative critique'. This is to be contrasted with (allegedly) *positive* contributions, such as: offering a newer, better analysis of the given concept; or offering a new philosophical system; or providing newer and better arguments for the main theses of an existing philosophical system. Despite the negative connotations of the word 'negative' in the context 'negative critique', however, a great deal of positive fame accrues to those who excel at such critique.

Philosophers who engage in conceptual analysis are concerned with the *modal* features of relationships among concepts. Thus we find them considering such questions as whether it is *necessary* to have a language in order to have thoughts; or whether it is *necessary* to be embodied in order to be a locus of consciousness; or whether it is *possible* that there be a true proposition that is in principle *unknowable*. A metaphysician might inquire whether any of one's properties is *essential* to one's identity. An epistemologist might inquire whether *there could be* a justified true belief that did not amount to knowledge. And a moral philosopher might inquire whether the moral qualities of an act *necessarily involve* the agent's intentions.

In all these examples, the modal element is crucial. Words like 'necessary', 'possible', and 'essential' are clues to the philosophical nature of the concern. Note that even modern philosophers like Quine and Donald Davidson (1917–2003), who are opposed to any purported distinction between truths of fact and truths of meaning, nevertheless display considerable expertise as *analytical* philosophers in the way they treat the *conceptual* issues posed by questions with the modal flavor of the examples just given.

Let us now explain in schematic detail the technique of conceptual analysis. It involves stating *individually necessary* and *jointly sufficient* conditions for the application of the concept in question. Accordingly, suppose one is dealing with an intuitively understood relational (two-place) concept of the form

$$\mathcal{C}(x,y).$$

Take this as the *analysandum* (i.e., that which is to be analyzed). We want to understand the exact conditions under which this relationship actually holds. To this end, we need to state an *analysis*, in the biconditional form

$\mathcal{C}(x,y)$
   if and only if
(Condition$_1(x,y)$ **and** Condition$_2(x,y)$ **and** ... **and** Condition$_n(x,y)$).

Here, Condition$_1$, ..., Condition$_n$ are the so-called *individually necessary* and *jointly sufficent* conditions on x and y that we are seeking. They are *individually necessary* because each of them has to hold in order for the analysandum $\mathcal{C}(x,y)$ to hold; and they are *jointly sufficient* because if they all hold together, then the analysandum holds. The n-fold conjunction of these conditions on the so-called 'right-hand side' of the above biconditional is called the *analysans*. (That is, the analysans is the n-fold conjunction of the n actual conditions that we might try to specify, in order to give the sought analysis.)

Moreover, the analysis is supposed to hold as a matter of *necessity*:

> **It is necessarily the case that:**
> **for all** x, y
> $\quad [\mathcal{C}(x,y)$
> **if and only if**
> $\quad (\text{Condition}_1(x,y) \text{ and } \text{Condition}_2(x,y) \text{ and } \dots \text{ and } \text{Condition}_n(x,y))].$

More often than not, however, this explicit modal prefix is omitted. Everyone involved knows that, by the rules of the game, it implicitly governs the biconditional on offer.

We begin with the most famous example of conceptual analysis in the history of the subject.

9.2 X knows that p

9.2.1 Plato's analysis

Consider, for example, the (relational) concept

> X knows that p,

where X is a rational agent and p is a proposition. What does it *mean* to say this, for particular values of X and of p?

The traditional analysis of knowledge, which goes back to Plato (in the *Theaetetus*), and which was not seriously challenged until the twentieth century, is as follows:

> X knows that p
> $\qquad$ **if and only if**
> $[X$ believes that p
> $\quad$ **and**
> p is true
> $\quad$ **and**
> X is *justified* in believing that $p].$

Knowledge, in short, is *justified true belief*. The three conditions in the analysans are *individually necessary*:

> X knows that p **only if** X believes that p;
> X knows that p **only if** p is true; and
> X knows that p **only if** X is justified in believing that p.

And the three conditions are *jointly sufficient*:

> **if** [X believes that p
>> **and**
>> p is true
>> **and**
>> X is justified in believing that p],
> **then** X knows that p.

9.2.2 Gettier counterexamples to Plato's analysis

A serious problem for the traditional analysis of knowledge came from Edmund Gettier (b. 1927), who described what are nowadays known as 'Gettier cases'. These are cleverly thought-up situations involving a particular agent X and a particular proposition p, described in such a way that they plausibly satisfy the three conditions of the foregoing analysans, but in which, intuitively, one does *not* want to say that X really knows that p. A Gettier case challenges the *joint sufficiency* of the three conditions in the traditional analysis. (See Gettier (1963); and Nozick (1981).)

Here is a Gettier case.

> Smith and Jones have both applied for a certain job, and are being interviewed for it. While Jones is interviewing, and before Smith goes in for his own interview, two things happen. First, Smith carefully counts the coins in Jones's jacket pocket (Jones having left his jacket hanging over a chair in the waiting room). There are ten such coins. Secondly, the company president drops by and tells Smith that Jones will get the job. Normally such an assurance would justify the resulting belief, namely the belief that *Jones is the man who will get the job*. So too would it justify any logical consequence of *that* belief and *other* justified ones, such as the belief that Jones has ten coins in his pocket. One such logical consequence is the belief p that the disappointed Smith now happens to infer:
>
> > p: The man who will get the job has ten coins in his pocket.
>
> It later turns out that the company president's assurance was wrong. The job is offered to Smith. As it happens, unknown to the nosey Smith, he also has ten coins in *his* own pocket. So Smith's belief p is *both true* and *justified*. We would not, however, wish to count it as *knowledge* on Smith's part.

Gettier's challenge to the analysis of knowledge as justified true belief has had a significant impact on recent Epistemology. Reactions have ranged from the optimistic to the pessimistic. Optimists have attempted to tighten the requirement of justification; and the results have been mixed. Pessimists have urged that we should give up altogether on what, they maintain, is a misguided attempt to analyze knowledge as a special kind of belief. Rather, they claim, knowledge is a more primitive notion than had hitherto been appreciated. It cannot be fashioned from the notion of belief by simply supplying suitable extra constraints on what *kind* of belief is in question.

There are other analyses, too, of philosophically important notions that have likewise been challenged by philosophical dissenters. Some have concerned the notion of *causation*; others have concerned the notion of *meaning*; yet others have concerned the notion of *free will*; and so on. The aim of such analyses is to establish important connections among concepts, some of which are perhaps simpler to grasp than others, and which may therefore be used, in an analysans, to cast light on an analysandum. The aim of the critics is to show that a given analysis is in error, and does not establish the conceptual connections that its proponent thinks it does. The critic can either challenge the alleged joint sufficiency of the conditions in the analysans; or challenge the alleged necessity of any one of them. Those engaged in such negative critique of philosophical analyses have generated some highly imaginative counterexamples, in which the ranges of application of our concepts are tested to their limits. This is all in an attempt to get clear about what exactly we mean when we use philosophically important terms (like 'knows', 'causes', 'person', 'freely chooses', ...). These terms are important not least because of the role they can play in our determinations of moral and legal guilt and responsibility.

9.3 The Paradox of Analysis

The *Paradox of Analysis* is this: for an analysis to be correct, it has to preserve the meaning of the concept or claim being analysed. How then can an analysis ever be informative?

Sometimes it is not possible to ensure that only more familar or more basic and less problematic notions appear in the analysans. Nevertheless, the analysis might be of interest. Where it is not possible, the analysis might still be of interest because of the way it links the truth of

$$Analysandum(x_1, \ldots, x_n)$$

in general to the truth of

$$Analysans(x_1, \ldots, x_n),$$

where '$Analysans(x_1, \ldots, x_n)$' involves other, so-called *co-eval*, concepts.

Co-eval concepts are ones which have to be mastered together, because of the way they depend on each other. They are just as obscure, elusive, important, fundamental, problematic, ... as one another. Thus it is open to one who opposes the claim that Plato's analysis of knowledge is a reductive analysis to point out that, even if the necessary equivalence holds, nevertheless the concept of knowledge is just as basic as the concept of belief, and that (perhaps) the notion of truth is on a par with that of belief: truth can attach only to beliefs, and the only thing that matters about a belief is whether it is true.

What is interesting about co-eval concepts is how they might have to interanimate: that is, they might have to come all together in one package, as it were, in order for any of them ever to have any purchase. In such circumstances philosophical analysis is still important, in bringing out precisely this 'keystone arch' principle in the architecture of our conceptual apparatus. Our conceptual apparatus may be less like a pyramid, and more like a geodesic dome made of interlocking struts.

9.4 The analysis of the notion of valid argument

The modern analysis of validity of argument owes much to Frege, Bernard Bolzano (1781–1848), Tarski, and Gerhard Gentzen (1909–45). It is dealt with in Chapter 7.

9.5 Russell's analysis of the truth-conditions of sentences of the form 'The F is G'

Russell (1905) gave an analysis of definite descriptions in order to clarify the logical forms of various statements in mathematics, and in order to provide his theory of knowledge-by-acquaintance and knowledge-by-description. Frank Ramsey once called it a 'paradigm of analytical philosophy'.

The problem Russell addressed was that of how to understand descriptive phrases that did not denote. Russell offered the following analysis of the truth-conditions of any sentence of the form 'The F is G':

There is exactly one F and it is G,

or, equivalently,

The F (exists and) is G.

In symbols:

$$\exists x (\forall y (y = x \leftrightarrow Fy) \wedge Gx).$$

Note that Russell's analysis, on this account of it, does not really involve the provision of an analysans consisting of various individually necessary and jointly sufficient conditions for the truth of 'The F is G'. Rather, it involves *providing a perspicuous logical form* for the analysandum, and exploiting formal logical symbolism to that end. One could, of course, 'bash it into' the shape of a conventional analysis by providing an analysans of the more roundabout form

there is at least one F
and
there is at most one F
and
every F is G.

But this is not nearly as elegant as the single logical form that we furnished above.

On Russell's analysis, 'The King of France is bald' is *false*, because there is no King of France. (See Russell (1910).) The analysis also affords a useful distinction between two kinds of negation, which one can call *internal* and *external*:

Internal negation	$\exists x (\forall y (y = x \leftrightarrow Fy) \wedge \neg Gx)$	The F (exists and) is not G.
External negation	$\neg\exists x (\forall y (y = x \leftrightarrow Fy) \wedge Gx)$	It is not the case that the F (exists and) is G.

Here once again we see the different expressive possibilities that are opened up by allowing different operator-occurrences to fall within one another's scopes in different ways. (See the discussion in §7.3.5.) With the necessity operator, we can distinguish the *de re* and *de dicto* readings of 'It is necessary that the F is G':

De re	$\exists x (\forall y (y = x \leftrightarrow Fy) \wedge \Box Gx)$	The F (exists and) is necessarily G.
De dicto	$\Box\exists x (\forall y (y = x \leftrightarrow Fy) \wedge Gx)$	It is necessarily the case that the F (exists and) is G.

Russell's analysis can be effected in two other notationally different, but expressively equivalent ways. First, one can introduce the term-forming operator ι, corresponding to the definite article 'the', so that the English descriptive phrase 'the F' can be translated as

$$\iota x F(x).$$

For obvious reasons, this ι is called a *variable-binding term-forming operator*. With ι-terms one can proceed to employ the 'term insertion' operation explained in §7.3.5. Thus we would have the following pithier formalizations:

De re	$(\iota x F(x))_y \Box Gy$	The F (exists and) is necessarily G.
De dicto	$\Box G(\iota x F(x))$	It is necessarily the case that the F (exists and) is G.

Secondly, one could treat ι not as a variable-binding term-forming operator, but rather as a *binary quantifier*. On this treatment, ι is regarded as taking two predicates to form a sentence. With ι in this capacity, the formal sentence

$$\iota x(F(x), G(x))$$

symbolizes the English sentence 'The F is G'. Once again, we are afforded the expressive nuances of *de re* and *de dicto*:

De re	$\iota x(F(x), \Box G(x))$	The F (exists and) is necessarily G.
De dicto	$\Box \iota x(F(x), G(x))$	It is necessarily the case that the F (exists and) is G.

9.6 Grice's analysis of meaning in terms of belief and intention

This analysis is important in that it attempts to reduce the notoriously problematic notion of (linguistic) meaning to others that are supposedly easier to understand. The reader should be aware that the term 'intensional', as used by philosophers, means 'having to do with meaning'.

No claim is made by Grice or any of his followers to the effect that his analysis of meaning would enable one to 'break out' of the so-called 'intensional circle'; rather, one is exploring conceptual relations *within it*. The concepts involved are co-eval, to use the terminology introduced earlier. To break out of the intensional circle, one would have to provide analyses of meaning, belief, desire, intention, etc., that involved only physicalistic (e.g., biochemical or neurological) vocabulary. It is hardly likely that such reductions of one domain of discourse (here, the psychological or intensional) to another (here, the physicalistic) would ever preserve meaning – which it is the task of analysis to do.

Grice's analysis of 'X means p by S', very roughly, is as follows:

X intends that his use of S should get the audience to believe that p;
    and
X intends the audience to recognise this intention;
    and
X intends that his audience's recognition of that intention should be part of the reason why they come to believe that p (if they do not already believe that p).

For the original analysis, see Grice (1957), and for further developments and refinements, see Grice (1969).

9.7 Mackie's analysis of 'event A caused event B'

Event A can cause event B without A's being *necessary* in order for B to occur. For example, Adolf might shoot someone and kill them an instant before a 10-ton rock crushes them. Adolf's shot caused the death, but was not necessary for it.

Likewise, event A can cause event B without A's being *sufficient* for B to occur. For example, Guy's striking the match might cause the explosion, without being sufficient by itself. For, there might not have been enough oxygen; in which case, Guy's striking the match would *not* have caused the explosion. Also, the matchbox might have been wet; in which case, Guy's striking the match would have been similarly ineffectual.

Mackie gives the following analysis of the cause–effect relation:

> A causes B
> > **if and only if**
> A is an insufficient but necessary part of an unnecessary but sufficient condition for B to occur.

There are also many rival analyses to Mackie's. See Mackie (1974).

9.8 Frege's analysis of the notion of number

For Frege, numbers were concepts of concepts. When we say 'The number of apples is 2' we are invited to think of numbers being referred to on a par with apples. But what we have said is equivalent to 'There are two apples', and this involves merely predicating *twoness* of the concept 'x is an apple', without commitment to numbers as objects.

Objects (like apples) fall under first-order concepts (like 'x is an apple'). First-order concepts in turn fall under second-order concepts (like 'There are two …' or 'There exist some …'). This last expression is worth noting: existence, for Frege, is not a first-order concept. It is not a property of individuals. Rather, like number, it is a concept of concepts (or, if one prefers: a property of properties) of individuals. (See Frege (1884; reprinted 1961). With this analysis of number and existence one can fault the Ontological Argument for God's existence. See §15.1.6.)

There has to be a linkage, however, between saying 'The number of apples is 2' (which involves the *substantival* use of the expression '2') and saying 'There are exactly two apples' (which involves the *adjectival* use of the word 'two'). Indeed there is: the two ways of expressing oneself are *necessarily equivalent*. We may offer the following (schematic) analysis of number-attributions:

> The number of Fs = $\underline{n}$
> > **if and only if**
> there are exactly n Fs.

Instances of this scheme involve, on their *left-hand sides*, identity statements in which there occur the *abstractive term* 'The number of Fs', and the *numeral* $\underline{n}$.

The numeral $\underline{n}$ is the canonical name for the number n itself, considered as an object of pure-mathematical interest. Thus, in the standard notation of Peano arithmetic:

$\underline{0}$ is the numeral '0';
$\underline{1}$ is the numeral 's0';
$\underline{2}$ is the numeral 'ss0';
$\underline{3}$ is the numeral 'sss0'; ... and so on.

The abstractive term 'The number of Fs' is what gives the abstract world of numbers its purchase on the world of ordinary things. It makes clear how numbers can find application in our thought about things of any kind. The Fs can be physical things. By *counting* them, one attains a *number* (the number of Fs), which is an abstract thing. One can also, of course, count abstract things. One can say, for example, that the number of **prime numbers** between 2 and 20 is 7:

2 **3** 4 **5** 6 **7** 8 9 10 **11** 12 **13** 14 15 16 **17** 18 **19** 20.

Instances of the scheme above involve, on their *right-hand sides*, numerosity-quantifications of the form 'there are exactly n Fs'; in symbols: $\exists_n xF(x)$. These can be defined in the obvious inductive way, without reference to, or quantification over, numbers as objects. The first few definitions in the series are as follows:

$\exists_0 xFx =_{df} \neg \exists xFx;$
$\exists_1 xFx =_{df} \exists x(Fx \wedge \forall y(Fy \rightarrow y = x));$
$\exists_2 xFx =_{df} \exists x_1 \exists_2 (Fx_1 \wedge Fx_2 \wedge \forall y(Fy \rightarrow (y = x_1 \vee y = x_2)));$
$\exists_3 xFx =_{df} \exists x_1 \exists_2 \exists x_3 (Fx_1 \wedge Fx_2 \wedge Fx_3 \wedge \forall y(Fy \rightarrow (y = x_1 \vee y = x_2 \vee y = x_3)));$
...

In general, we have *Schema N* for natural numbers (see Tennant (1987), at p. 234):

$\exists_n xFx =_{df} \exists x_1 ... \exists x_n (Fx_1 \wedge ... \wedge Fx_n \wedge \forall y(Fy \rightarrow (y = x_1 \vee ... \vee y = x_n))).$

The biconditional scheme above can now be seen to be a deep *logico-mathematical* principle governing all our thought about the whole numbers 0, 1, 2, 3, ... By this we mean thought about the numbers themselves (mathematical thought) and thought about other things, in which we *apply* the numbers, when counting finite collections of those things.

9.9 Lewis's analysis of conventions

Any analysis of conventions faces the following problem. The analysis must be consistent with the claim that the words of our language have the meanings that they do as a matter of convention. This immediately implies that the conventions that bestow meanings on words cannot be conventions in that sense of the word that conjures up images of people convening, to hammer out an agreement, using language to do so. For the question would immediately arise: *How did the expressions of **that** language acquire their meanings?* – and we would be off on a vicious infinite regress.

David Lewis (1969), however, gave an ingenious analysis of conventions (especially linguistic ones) that avoids this pervasive problem. His analysis proceeds in terms of the reciprocal beliefs and expectations concerning other people's coordinated behavior when they face a recurring communal problem, and are aware of past salient solutions. The solutions can arise, in the first instance, as quite arbitrary or accidental choices to deal with a coordination problem.

Imagine, for example, people newly possessed of self-propelled vehicles, who make their way about the countryside on paths that just happen to be a little wider than two of these vehicles side by side. On the first occasion that two drivers appear to be on course for a head-on collision, they might happen to avoid it by veering slightly to the left, and passing each other safely by. The next time they encounter each other in a similar situation, they both recall the way they dealt with the problem the first time round. Once again, they veer to the left, and avoid colliding. In due course, they come to expect each other to stick to this 'discovered' solution to their coordination problem. In this little community of two drivers, veering to the left becomes the *conventional* way to avoid colliding. One can imagine how the convention can spread to yet other drivers, until it becomes fixed as the community-wide solution to that particular recurring coordination problem. I expect you to veer to the left; and I expect you to expect me, likewise, to veer to the left. In due course, the convention might become formalized and explicit, as in a written code of rules of the road. But at its inception, the convention had no need for language. It was born of the mutual expectations of the different parties to it. All the while, there was the alternative: *veer to the right.* But history and happenstance never lit on it. The conventional solution to the recurring coordination problem was *arbitrary.* It didn't have to be that way; it might have been some other way. But it wasn't.

Lewis, in his book *Convention* (1969), begins with a first pass at a definition of what a convention is, and proceeds to refine it further on the basis of objections or problems that he raises for his own account. His settled offering comes on p. 78:

A regularity R in the behavior of members of a population P when they are agents in a recurrent situation S is a *convention*

if and only if

it is true that, and it is common knowledge in P that, in almost any instance of S among members of P,

1   almost everyone [in *P*] conforms to *R* [in *S*];
2   almost everyone [in *P*] expects almost everyone else [in *P*] to conform to *R* [in *S*];
3   almost everyone [in *P*] has approximately the same preferences regarding all possible combinations of actions [in *S*];
4   almost everyone [in *P*] prefers that any one [in *P*] more conform to *R* [in *S*], on condition that almost everyone [in *P*] conform to *R* [in *S*];
5   almost everyone [in *P*] would prefer that any one [in *P*] more conform to *R'* [in *S*], on condition that any one [in *P*] more conform to *R'* [in *S*],

where *R'* is some possible regularity in the behavior of members of *P* in *S*, such that almost no one [in *P*] in almost any instance of *S* among members of *P* could conform to both *R'* and *R*.

Condition (5) is what shows that the chosen conventional form of behavior *R* is *arbitrary* in the appropriate sense – namely, that there are possible alternatives *R'* that *might have been chosen instead*, but which happened not to be (when the convention to behave in way *R* in situations *S* was established.) Thus in our imagined community of beginning drivers, *veering to the left* in order to avoid collisions on narrow paths became the conventional behavior *R*; while the alternative *R'*, of *veering to the right*, did not get a foothold.

That is the breakthrough thought behind the success of Lewis's treatment of another very important set of conventions, namely the conventions governing *the use of linguistic expressions themselves* within a linguistic community. The required *linguistic* conventions can get established *without any need for language in which to express them, and agree upon them*. There need not be any convening in order for a convention to take hold within a community.

At the dawn of language, one tribesman might have warned another of the presence of a venomous snake, say, by improvising a wave of his hand with a hissing noise. *In situ* it does not take a lot of *noûs* to work out what the warner is 'getting at'. (The reader will be able to provide a rudimentary Gricean account of the reciprocal beliefs and intentions of the parties to this communicative exchange on this occasion. See §9.6.) The beneficiary of this warning might, the next day, find himself in a situation where the roles are reversed. *He* then warns the *other* of that same sort of danger, by using the very same form of expression of which, the day before, he had been the beneficiary. For that form of expression is *salient*, as a solution to this kind of coordination problem. Long story short: eventually, merely hissing to one another can come to have the conventional meaning 'Watch out, there's a poisonous snake nearby that right now you cannot see!'

Something along these lines, writ large, must be behind the emergence of human languages with their large but idiosyncratic vocabularies and varied but (at a deeper level) commonly structured grammars. One of the fascinating problems that accompanies such an account is whether the linguistically structured expression of thought is subject to *conventionally invariant logical rules* governing the logical operators. Languages vary, of course, in the sounds they use to express a logical operation like negation. But is the operation of negation itself something inevitable, something transcendental, something *independent of any particular language*, something that must behave *the same logical way* in any and all languages? Similar questions can be raised for all the other logical operators that have already been mentioned: conjunction, disjunction, implication, and both existential and universal quantification. Is the logical skeleton (of inferential necessities) that these operators afford something that must be built into any language, notwithstanding the fact that any given language may have its own uniquely quirky ways of actually expressing these operators?

9.9.1 An afterword on the form of Lewis's analysis of conventions

The attentive reader might be wondering how it is that Lewis's analysis given above displays the general form of analyses that we gave earlier. We said that for an *analysandum* $C(x,y)$ we would be looking for a biconditional of the form

$C(x,y)$
> **if and only if**
> (Condition$_1(x,y)$ **and** Condition$_2(x,y)$ **and** ... **and** Condition$_n(x,y)$)

where Condition$_1$, ..., Condition$_n$ are the so-called *individually necessary* and *jointly sufficent* conditions on x and y that we are seeking.

In Lewis's case, the *analysandum* is $C(R,P,S)$ – 'A regularity R in the behavior of members of a population P when they are agents in a recurrent situation S is a *convention*'.

In his foregoing *analysans*, however, the conjunction signs linking the five conditions that Lewis states are not dominant. Instead, the conjunction of Lewis's five conditions is prefixed with 'it is true that, and it is common knowledge in P that, in almost any instance of S among members of P, ...'. But this is no great drawback, for this prefix can be distributed across the five conditions. Let us call those conditions Condition$_1(R,P,S)$, ..., Condition$_5(R,P,S)$. Note that 'it is true that, and it is common knowledge in P that' boil down to 'it is common knowledge in P that', since (common) knowledge is *factive*: knowledge implies truth. Moreover, knowledge distributes across conjunctions:

$$K(\varphi_1 \wedge ... \wedge \varphi_n) \leftrightarrow (K(\varphi_1) \wedge ... \wedge K(\varphi_n)).$$

Problems

1 Is the Paradox of Analysis a good reason to abandon the project of conceptual analysis?
2 What is the difference between providing conceptual analyses and writing a dictionary?

3 Choose one of the well-known examples of analysis described above, and conduct research on the original source and the critical secondary literature in response to it. Let Google be your guide ...

4 Would you be prepared to say that a person who is unable to provide even a rudimentary analysis of some concept has not properly mastered it?

5 Why, in your opinion, did philosophers get involved in the project of providing conceptual analyses?

6 Do Gettier-type examples convince you that Plato's analysis of knowledge as justified true belief is defective?

10 The Method of Conceptual Explication

In Chapter 9 we examined the method of conceptual analysis, which is concerned with providing individually necessary and jointly sufficient conditions for the application of certain important concepts.

There is another, related, treatment of important concepts that needs to be explained and discussed. This is the slightly different project of conceptual *explication*.

10.1 Conceptual explication provides a precise theoretical substitute for an informal concept

Explication is a matter of replacing an intuitively grasped, but pre-theoretical, concept with a more exactly characterized one. This characterization will be within a *formal* theory of the subject matter within whose *informal* description the intuitive concept (the *explicandum*) has been deployed. So, explication is typically called for when one is seeking to make an informal theory or description of a subject matter more formal and precise.

The formal theory can furnish an *explicans* in two possible ways. First, it might provide an explicit definition of the explicandum. It will define the explicandum in terms of simpler concepts already characterized by the formal theory. Secondly, and alternatively, the explicans may be embedded in theoretical postulates. These will show exactly how it relates to other concepts already characterized by the theory in question.

Perhaps the best example of conceptual explication is that developed in the 1930s, of the intuitive notion of *computable function* on the natural numbers. We shall devote some space to this example, since it is such a paradigm instance of explication – indeed, perhaps the 'founding instance' of the method. It is an example so good that all subsequent explications of other concepts may be measured against it, when assessing their degree of success.

10.2 The intuitive notion of a computable function

Intuitively, a function f from natural numbers to natural numbers is *computable* just in case there is an *explicit set of instructions*, which is *finitely long*, and which enables one, for any given input n, to *compute* the output f(n), if such output is defined. When the output *is* defined, such a computation will involve only finitely many steps, and will take a finite period of time to carry out. The method of computation will be mechanical and deterministic. Carrying out the instructions will require no creativity or ingenuity or insight.

Some examples of computable functions on the naturals are: adding two numbers; multiplying the same; finding the highest common factor of two numbers; finding their least common multiple; finding whether a given number is the square of another number (yielding 0 if it isn't, but yielding the latter if it is). All these examples involve at least two numbers as inputs. For the rest of the discussion, we shall confine ourselves to functions involving only one input. A good example of this kind is the function taking the value 1 on prime numbers, and taking the value 0 on composite ones. How many such functions might there be?

By well-known combinatorial considerations, there can be at most *countably* many finitely long sets of instructions. The so-called 'diagonal argument' in §10.2.2 establishes that there are *uncountably* many functions from ℕ to ℕ. So: among the *uncountably* many functions in general (computable or not) from ℕ to ℕ, there are only *countably* (infinitely) many *computable* ones. The notion of a *computable function from ℕ to ℕ* is therefore a tightly constraining one. Moreover, it appears, intuitively, to be a stable and robust notion, at least to mathematicians and computer scientists. More evidence to vindicate this appearance will emerge in due course.

A very similar diagonal argument in §10.2.3 establishes that among the (countably many) computable functions there must be *partial* functions. Not every computable function is everywhere defined.

We proceed now to examine these two diagonal arguments.

10.2.1 The diagonal argument: preliminaries

A *total* function f from ℕ into ℕ determines, for every natural number n as 'input', a natural number f(n) as 'output'. A *partial* function g from ℕ into ℕ, by contrast, might have, for certain numbers n as input, no number g(n) as output. For such input n, the function g would be *undefined*. And if g were moreover a computable function, we would say that the computation 'of' g(n) *does not terminate*.

Take the simplest case of one-place functions (not necessarily computable ones) mapping the set ℕ of natural numbers into ℕ. As already indicated, a simple so-called 'diagonal argument' (set out in §10.2.2) shows that there are *uncountably many* such functions that are *total* (that is, strictly more of them than there are natural numbers). It is therefore obvious that there are uncountably many functions from ℕ into ℕ *tout court*, total or partial.

The diagonal argument is a *reductio ad absurdum* argument. The two main assumptions which, jointly, precipitate the absurdity, are the following:

1 The functions under discussion are all total.
2 The diagonal function whose construction the argument describes belongs to the very class of functions that are under discussion.

Since the diagonal argument, as we have indicated, reduces this pair of assumptions to absurdity, there are (at least) two rational reactions in response to it, respectively contradicting each of the foregoing assumptions. It would be rational to react by drawing one or other of the following conclusions.

1 The diagonal function whose construction the argument describes is not total.
2 The diagonal function whose construction the argument describes does not belong to the very class of functions that are under discussion.

Whether we opt for conclusion (1) or conclusion (2) will depend on whether we wish to hold on to assumption (1) or to assumption (2).

Let us now proceed to the diagonal argument itself.

10.2.2 The diagonal argument, first version

Suppose for *reductio ad absurdum* that there is a countable list of total functions from $\mathbb{N}$ into $\mathbb{N}$:

$$f_0, f_1, f_2, \ldots .$$

Consider now the following infinite array, in which the *i*-th row represents the respective outputs of the particular function f_i on the inputs 0, 1, 2, 3, 4, …:

$$
\begin{array}{ccccccc}
\mathbf{f_0(0)} & f_0(1) & f_0(2) & f_0(3) & f_0(4) & \cdots \\
f_1(0) & \mathbf{f_1(1)} & f_1(2) & f_1(3) & f_1(4) & \cdots \\
f_2(0) & f_2(1) & \mathbf{f_2(2)} & f_2(3) & f_2(4) & \cdots \\
f_3(0) & f_3(1) & f_3(2) & \mathbf{f_3(3)} & f_3(4) & \cdots \\
f_4(0) & f_4(1) & f_4(2) & f_4(3) & \mathbf{f_4(4)} & \cdots \\
\vdots & \vdots & \vdots & \vdots & \vdots
\end{array}
$$

Consider now the 'diagonal' function f defined as follows:

$$\text{for all } n, \ f(n) = f_n(n) + 1.$$

Note how the function f is defined by altering the values on the *diagonal* of the array above, indicated in boldface. (This is why the function f is called 'diagonal', and why the present form of argument is called a 'diagonal' one.)

Since each f_i is total, the diagonal function f is total.

The diagonal function $f : \mathbb{N} \mapsto \mathbb{N}$ will therefore be on our imagined list of *all* total functions as f_k, for some k. Thus for this k we have

$$\text{for all } n, \ f(n) = f_k(n).$$

But now, instantiating our two displayed generalizations above with respect to k, we have

$$f(k) = f_k(k) + 1$$

and

$$f(k) = f_k(k).$$

Hence

$$f_k(k) = f_k(k) + 1.$$

Contradiction.

Conclusion: There are uncountably many total functions from $\mathbb{N}$ into $\mathbb{N}$.

10.2.3 *The diagonal argument, second version*

The second version of the diagonal argument is governed by the assumption (into whose justification we can subsequently inquire) that, if one were to be presented with a finite list of instructions (in English) for the 'computation' of an output for any given number as input, *one would be able to tell* whether the function in question is guaranteed to be a computable function. Call this the Governing Assumption.

On the Governing Assumption it follows that there is an effectively enumerable list of the respective methods of computation for all the computable functions from $\mathbb{N}$ into $\mathbb{N}$:

$$f_0, f_1, f_2, \ldots .$$

To see this, enumerate first, in any infinite list, all the finite sets of English instructions for 'computation' of outputs on arbitrary numbers as inputs. By the Governing Assumption one can go down this list, deleting any set of instructions that one can tell does *not* offer a guarantee that the function being 'computed' is really a computable function. The undeleted members of the list, we shall assume, are those finite sets of English instructions that *do* offer the guarantee of genuine computability.

Here is a finite list of instructions in English for the 'computation' of a number as output, from any given number n is input, that does *not* offer the guarantee of genuine computability:

> Take n as input. Wait for the beginning of the Third World War. If your side wins, return the output $2n$. Otherwise, return the output 2^n.

Suppose now, for *reductio ad absurdum*, that every one of the *genuinely* computable functions f_i is total.

Consider the infinite array

$$
\begin{array}{llllll}
f_0(0) & f_0(1) & f_0(2) & f_0(3) & f_0(4) & \cdots \\
f_1(0) & \mathbf{f_1(1)} & f_1(2) & f_1(3) & f_1(4) & \cdots \\
f_2(0) & f_2(1) & \mathbf{f_2(2)} & f_2(3) & f_2(4) & \cdots \\
f_3(0) & f_3(1) & f_3(2) & \mathbf{f_3(3)} & f_3(4) & \cdots \\
f_4(0) & f_4(1) & f_4(2) & f_4(3) & \mathbf{f_4(4)} & \cdots \\
\vdots & \vdots & \vdots & \vdots & \vdots
\end{array}
$$

as we did in §10.2.2, and define the 'diagonal' function f once again as follows:

for all n, $f(n) = \mathbf{f_n(n)} + 1$.

Since (by assumption for *reductio*) each f_i is total, the diagonal function f is total.

Each f_i is computable, and (by the Governing Assumption) the list of the respective methods of computation for $f_0, f_1, \ldots$ is effectively enumerable. We shall now show that the diagonal function f is therefore computable. For, take any given input n. In order to compute the value $f(n)$, proceed mechanically as follows. Effectively enumerate the finite descriptions of the respective methods of computation for the functions on the list until you arrive at the one for f_n. Use it to compute the value $f_n(n)$. Then add 1. Clearly we have just given a finite description of a method of computation for the diagonal function f. And *one can tell* that this method of computation is genuine (given the Governing Assumption).

The diagonal function $f : \mathbb{N} \mapsto \mathbb{N}$ will therefore be on our imagined list of *all* total computable functions as f_k, for some k. Thus for this k we have

for all n, $f(n) = f_k(n)$.

But now, instantiating our two displayed generalizations above with respect to k, we have

$f(k) = f_k(k) + 1$

and

$f(k) = f_k(k)$.

Hence

$f_k(k) = f_k(k) + 1$.

Contradiction.

Conclusion: Not every computable function is total (provided that the Governing Assumption holds).

10.3 Explicating the notion of computable function

With *explication* we take an intuitive, pre-formal notion (the explicandum) and 'firm it up' by means of a precisely defined one (the explicans), which henceforth does duty for it. In the early 1930s, the intuitive, pre-formal notion of a computable function was crying out for explication. It was serendipitous – or was it? – that the Allied nations' dire need for high-speed cryptography was looming on the historical horizon.

The class of (intuitively) *computable functions* from natural numbers to natural numbers began to engage mathematicians' interest in the 1920s. Once logicians' and mathematicians' interest was focused on the notion of computability, there soon emerged several different formal explications of the notion '*f* is a computable function'. These were owed to various famous figures, among them Kurt Gödel, Alan Turing, Alonzo Church (1903–95), Emil Post (1897–1954), and Stephen Kleene (1909–94). Each of them furnished a different formal definition intended to explicate the notion of computable function. All these definitions were in due course shown (mathematically) to characterize exactly the same functions. This was strong evidence that the intuitive concept of a computable function was stable and significant. Here we shall provide details for only two of these explications, due to Gödel and to Turing respectively.

On the one hand, Gödel's explication (Gödel (1986)) provided an ideal basis for metamathematical proofs of the famous *limitative* results, in particular his First and Second Incompleteness Theorems for formal arithmetic.

On the other hand, Turing's explication (Turing (1937), Turing (1938)) really stands out because of the way it treats the process of mechanical computation as abstractly as possible, with amazing conceptual economy.

We shall now examine each of these two explications in turn.

10.3.1 *Gödel's general recursive functions*

Gödel offered the precise concept of a *general recursive* function, taking as basic certain 'easy' and familiar functions like addition and multiplication, and providing ways of combining recursive functions that one has already specified, so that one can form new ones. Gödel's recipe for generating recursive functions was a very natural 'mathematical' one, working from the most familiar arithmetical operations through to more complicated computable ones, by employing an incisive analysis of the various means by which mathematicians build up those more complicated, but still computable, functions.

Remember that computable functions are functions defined on the natural numbers, and taking natural numbers as values.

The *basic* recursive functions to which Gödel helped himself were fourfold. First, he took as basic the functions of addition and multiplication (both of which are so familiar to the reader as not to need any explanation). Secondly, he took as basic two other less familiar functions. The first of these less familiar basic functions was the 'characteristic function for identity' for which we shall use the notation $c_=(m,n)$. It is a two-place function. It takes the value 1 if $m = n$, and takes the value 0 if $m \neq n$. If one thinks of the value 1 as the answer 'Yes', and the value 0 as the answer 'No', then the characteristic function of identity provides truthful answers to the question 'Is the number m identical to the number n?'. The second less familiar kind of function that Gödel took as basic was actually a family of similar functions: the 'coordinate projection' functions. Coordinate projection functions take the form id_k^m, for varying values of m and k. Given an m-tuple of numbers $n_1,\ldots,n_m$, the value $id_k^m(n_1,\ldots,n_m)$ is n_k. Using the projection function id_k^m is just a matter of picking the k-th member of the m-tuple in question.

It is intuitively clear that all these basic recursive functions are computable.

Next Gödel provided some means of building up more complicated recursive functions, using operations which, intuitively, preserve the property of computability. Think, for example, of the four-place function $(m + n).(j + k)$. We know we can compute the two sums $m + n$ and $j + k$; and that we can then multiply together the outputs of these two computations as inputs for a final computation of the product $(m + n).(j + k)$. Thus the outputs of the more deeply embedded functions (the additions in question) become the inputs to the function 'on the surface', so to speak (the multiplication in question). This feature can be generalized; it becomes the *principle of composition* of recursive functions:

> If f is an n-place recursive function, and $g_1,\ldots,g_n$ are m-place functions, then $f(g_1,\ldots,g_n)$ is an $(n.m)$-place recursive function.

Composition is not the only operation for building recursive functions that intuitively preserves the property of computability. There was one other such operation that Gödel invoked, call *minimization of regular functions*. This calls for some explanation; but every part of it is very clear. First, we have to explain what is meant by a 'regular' function.

Definition 3. *Suppose f is an $(n + 1)$-place function. Then f is a regular function just in case*

> *for all $m_1,\ldots m_n$ there is some p such that $f(m_1,\ldots m_n,p) = 0$.*

Now we are in a position to define the operation of minimization mentioned above.

Definition 4. *Suppose f is a regular function in the sense of Definition 3. Then the n-place function g is said to be obtained from f by* **minimization** *just in case for all $m_1,\ldots m_n$, $g(m_1,\ldots m_n)$ is the* **least** *number p such that $f(m_1,\ldots m_n,p) = 0$.*

That completes Gödel's recipe for constructing recursive functions in general. Any such function can be built up from the four basic functions (addition, multiplication, the characteristic function of identity, and projection of the k-th member of an n-tuple), using only the two computability-preserving operations of composition, and minimization of recursive functions.

This elegant mathematical explication takes the form of what a logician calls an *inductive definition*. There are *base* clauses, dealing with the simplest of the entities being defined. Then there are *inductive* clauses, dealing with the means by which more complex entities of the kind in question can be built up. Finally, there is a *closure* clause to the effect that any entity of the kind in question can be built up according to the basis clauses and inductive clauses already stated. This kind of definition permits the mathematician to prove results of the form 'All entities of the kind in question have property Φ'. First, one proves that the basic entities enjoy the property Φ. Next, one shows, for each entity-building operation, that if the building blocks enjoy property Φ, then the result of operating on them to produce a more complex entity also enjoys property Φ. Having done that, one is justified (by the closure clause) in concluding that all entities of the kind in question have property Φ.

10.3.2 *Turing machines*

We shall explain here, at preferential length, the concept of a Turing machine. This is because it finds an important application in the Functionalist philosophy of mind (see Chapter 24).

Turing, by contrast with Gödel, offered a *prima facie* wholly different kind of explication of the notion of computable function, in terms of idealized finite-state machines. Such a 'computing machine' scans a tape on which it can read one cell at a time. Each cell contains a '1' or is blank. That is all that the machine can register. The machine is equipped with a 'program' that tells it unerringly what to do next, given the state it is currently in and the condition of the cell that it is currently scanning. The possible actions that the machine can perform are: delete the '1'; inscribe a '1'; move one cell to the left; move one cell to the right; or halt (and signal that you have done so). These utterly basic mechanical operations, astonishingly, prove to be sufficient unto all the demands of computation in general. Indeed, the laptop computer on which this is being written is, in a straightforward sense, no more than a glorified Turing machine. (Well ... *almost*. Unlike a Turing machine, a laptop does not have an infinite tape, for storage of the intermediate results of sub-computations. But one could, in principle, add arbitrarily many hard drives.)

With computable functions, the dependency of output on input can be spelled out as a mechanical, or rule-governed, way of actually *calculating* the output for any given input. Take the example of the two-place function + of addition on the natural numbers. Given any two natural numbers x and y, their sum $(x + y)$ is not only uniquely determined – as befits functions in general – but also *mechanically determinable*. Take, for example, the inputs 5 and 7. The output $(5 + 7)$ is mechanically determinable as 12. One can give an explicit recipe for finding the answer 12 from the inputs 5 and 7. One can spell out the steps of calculation that need to be undertaken in order to arrive at this answer.

These steps are exhaustive, exact, and unambiguous. They leave nothing to the creativity or imagination or inspired insight of the mathematician. They are 'rote', or *algorithmic*. And in any computation, only finitely many steps are involved, before the computation terminates with a definite answer.

We are so familiar with addition that we lose sight of the fact that it is special in this way, especially when small inputs are involved. But even if you learn off by heart that $7 + 5 = 12$, this does not undermine the fact that addition is computable. Indeed, all it underscores is that the 'computation', in such a case, is trivial – in the case of 7 and 5 as inputs, one simply takes one look at a 'look-up' table stored in memory. The recipe is as simple as that.

A more interesting case, involving more complex computation, would be to compute, for highish inputs like 1,000, outputs of the function that maps each natural number n to the n-th prime number. A prime number is a natural number greater than 1 that cannot be divided without remainder by any natural numbers besides itself and 1. The first few prime numbers in the infinite series of primes are 2, 3, 5, 7, 11, 13, 17, 19, 23, 29, 31, ... What is the 1,000-th number in this series? No doubt, very large – but you could in principle *compute* it by following a fixed recipe of explicit rules.

A Turing machine is understood as a device capable of occupying only *finitely many* physical *states* (at least, in so far as these states are to have any computational or informational significance). One of these states is designated as the *initial state* for any computation that the machine is to perform. The *inputs and outputs* to a Turing machine are written on the *cells* on a *linear tape*, which is potentially infinite in both directions. The machine has a 'scanning head' that can read the conditions of these cells one at a time. To keep matters as austere as possible, Turing allowed for each cell to have only one of *two conditions*: marked v. unmarked, full v. empty, 0 v. 1, black v. white, magnetized v. demagnetized, or what you will. That is, the machine will use a *binary alphabet*. (It can be shown that we get the same class of possible machines this way as we would if we allowed, in general, any *finite* alphabet. This is important for the philosophical application of the notion to be made below.) The machine is capable of a limited range of *actions* in response to the condition of the scanned cell. It can move one cell to the right; or one cell to the left; or change the condition of the cell; or halt.

(Remember that all this quasi-mathematical discussion will eventually assume philosophical significance. The concept of a Turing machine is centrally involved in the Functionalist philosophy of mind – perhaps the most influential contemporary conception of the nature of mind.)

How does a Turing machine 'know' what to do when computing a particular function? Answer: it has a *program*, which is nothing more or less than a *finite set of instructions*. And what is an instruction? It is a command of the form

If you are in such-and-such state, and the cell you are scanning is in such-and-such condition, then perform such-and-such action, and thereafter enter such-and-such state.

For example, the instruction

(131, 0, 1, 17)

will mean

> If you are in state #131, and the cell you are scanning has a 0 in it, then
> change it to a 1, and enter state #17.

The way a Turing machine M computes an output $M(k)$ for a given natural
number k is as follows:

- Set up the machine in its initial state.
- Feed the (otherwise empty) tape into the machine from the left, with just k
  successive cells inscribed with 1. That is, the tape will have the overall form

  $\ldots /0/0/0/1/1/1/1/\ldots$ (k occurrences of 1)$\ldots /1/1/1//0/0/0/\ldots$

- Wait for the machine to halt. (We can assume that a light on top of the
  machine starts flashing when, and only when, the machine halts.)
- Read off the tape on the right of the machine. The output $M(k)$ is n just in
  case there are exactly n successive occurrences of 1 inscribed on the tape.

10.3.3 Other explications of computable functions

Church, Post, and Kleene also provided their own signature formal explications
of the notion of a computable function, using their own special conceptual
resources. Church furnished what is now known as the λ-calculus; Post defined
what are now known as 'production systems'; and Kleene defined a class of
functions in terms of his so-called 'equational systems'. Suffice it to say that
these different explications really do look different, to the untrained eye. Each
results from addressing the problem of how to explicate the notion of computable
function by using an idiosyncratic, but suitably powerful, set of conceptual
materials and methods.

10.3.4 The Turing–Church Thesis

Here is the amazing result that emerged after a few years of foundational
foment, as these pioneers of the computing age started comparing notes: *all
the different formal explications turned out to be **provably co-extensive***. That is
to say, any function definable in any one of the senses characterized turns
out to be definable also in each of the other senses characterized. Moreover,
the background mathematics that is needed in order to establish that these
different kinds of function are co-extensive is very weak indeed: the system of
so-called Exponential Function Arithmetic suffices. So there is absolutely no
epistemological problem in taking their coextensiveness as an *a priori* certitude.

Various independently motivated attempts were made, then, using different formal conceptual materials, to characterize precisely a certain class of abstract objects – here, the intuitively computable functions. The formal explications all *coincide in extension*, and this is a matter of *a priori* certitude. They all agree on which functions may be characterized as computable. We know, then, that we are dealing with a stable and robust pre-theoretical notion. Accordingly, the *Turing–Church Thesis* says that

> *a function is computable if and only if it is definable in any one (hence, in each) of these various, provably equivalent, formal ways.*

Computability, then, is a paradigm example of an informal, pre-theoretical concept that has been satisfactorily *explicated* – in this case, by the formal concept of a recursive function, or a function computable by a Turing machine (to name the two most famous formal explications, due to Gödel and Turing respectively).

One of the benefits of (the presumed truth of) the Turing–Church Thesis is that we can re-visit the diagonal argument given above, which rested on what we called the Governing Assumption. We can now *re-prove* the claim that not all computable functions are total, *no longer making any use of the Governing Assumption*. This is because, courtesy of the Turing–Church Thesis, we can effectively enumerate the computable functions by effectively enumerating, 'instead', the *Turing-Machine computable* ones. The latter task can be accomplished with absolute precision, with no hostages to fortune in judging, intuitively, whether a given finite set of English instructions really does guarantee that the function in question is genuinely computable. This is because Turing machines themselves can be effectively coded *as numbers*, and, given any such number, one can effectively determine *whether* it encodes a Turing machine, and, if so, exactly *which* Turing machine it encodes. This removes all doubt from the claim, in the proof above, that *one can effectively enumerate all and only the* (Turing-machine)-*computable functions*. The diagonal argument in question now goes through as before. Not all computable functions are total.

Another significant benefit of the Turing–Church Thesis is that it affords an exceptionally simple proof of Gödel's famous result that first-order arithmetical truth is not axiomatizable. We shall be exploiting the Turing–Church Thesis to this effect in Chapter 30. The argument to be presented there will involve yet another application of the diagonal method.

Explicating the informal concept of a computable function was a magnificent achievement by the logicians and foundationalists of the 1930s. One of the services that philosophers can render is to emulate this achievement in yet other conceptual domains. That, for example, was what Carnap took himself to be doing in his monumental work on the foundations of the theory of probability (Carnap (1950)), in which he explicitly introduced, for the first time, the very idea of explication.

10.4 Explication of the notion of cognitive significance

The search for a criterion (or definition, or explication) of cognitive significance is of long standing. Unfortunately, for a very long time it was of dubious success. The challenge is to analyze or explicate the notion of cognitive significance, so as to reveal just how the empirical content of the theoretical sentences of science is acquired from the logical relationships they bear, within the scientific theory in question, to the observation sentences by means of which the theory can be tested. This tradition started with Ayer (1946), and continued through the swan-song of Carnap (1956), although it began to peter out with the famously pessimistic paper Hempel (1950). It has been revived again more recently in various efforts by, among others, Wright (1986) and Tennant (1997), Chapter 11.

Ayer sought to define the notion of cognitive significance under the label 'indirect verifiability', in the second edition (1946) of his influential manifesto *Language, Truth and Logic*, in which the main doctrines of Logical Positivism were brought to the attention of the English-speaking world. The most difficult challenge now facing any attempted account of cognitive significance is to ensure that it is not vulnerable to the embarrassing sort of 'collapse proof' that was visited by Church (1949) on Ayer's misguided attempt to define the notion. A collapse proof is one that reveals a really serious defect in the proposed definition (or explication) of an intuitive notion. Such a proof shows (as Church's proof did in Ayer's case) that the proposed *definiens* turns out, quite unexpectedly, to apply to *all* the sentences of the language (or to all but a negligible subclass), and not just to those sentences satisfying the target notion (here, 'being cognitively significant'). In the terminology of statistics, a collapse proof reveals that there are too many 'false positives' for the definiens in question. There could also be too many 'false negatives' – that would be a definitional collapse of a different kind.

A 'false positive' for a definition seeking to capture the notion of cognitive significance would be 'The Absolute is perfect'. A 'false negative' would be 'Snow is white' (or, indeed, 'Snow is black'). At the every least one wishes, with one's definition of cognitive significance, to *rule in* obvious cases such as observation statements, and widely used and accepted scientific hypotheses such as Newton's Law of Gravitation, or the Maxwell–Faraday laws of electromagnetism. One also wishes to *rule in* certain less obvious cases, such as now-discarded hypotheses that ended up being falsified by experience but which, at the time they were proposed, were not known to generate any false predictions. For that is the hallmark of a good (i.e., cognitively significant) scientific generalization: it admits, in principle, of falsification by experience.

Since there is no widely agreed definition of cognitive significance, we shall end this discussion without giving the details of any particular definition. It is enough to mark, for the beginner, the fact that, of all the fraught notions that philosophers have tried their hardest to explain and understand over the last several decades, that of cognitive significance appeared to be both significant and cognitively accessible. Once a question mark was placed over its accessibility (to our analytical and explicatory efforts), the reaction of many philosophers, unfortunately, was to abandon the intuitive notion as not so significant after all – indeed, perhaps, as at best confused, and at worst incoherent and useless. That is not the considered view of the present author, however, who regards the notion as vital and important for the 'science wars'. It is a notion still deserving of a satisfactory analysis, and worthy of serious further consideration by young minds entering the Philosophy profession. There just has to be something importantly different between, on the one hand, the hysterical drivel one hears spouted on evangelical TV channels, and, on the other hand, the sober-minded discourse of Science. The former is not cognitively significant; the latter is. And we need to get clear about the deep reasons why.

Problems

1 Sketch an algorithm to compute the n-th prime number.
2 The Turing–Church Thesis says that all intuitively computable functions are recursive (equivalently, can be computed by a Turing machine). Have you thought about the converse claim: that all recursive (Turing-machine computable) functions are intuitively computable? Make sure you understand why this is so.
3 Why is the Turing–Church Thesis plausible?
4 (More advanced) Read around in the literature on recursive functions (Rogers (1967) would be a good place to start) to find the proof of the famous result that the Halting Problem for Turing machines is undecidable. Make sure that you can explain to a non-mathematician what the Halting Problem is. (Note that the proof of this problem's undecidability is yet another example of a beautiful diagonal argument.)
5 Examine Hempel (1950) carefully in order to determine whether Hempel *proves* anywhere in that paper that the notion of cognitive significance cannot be satisfactorily explicated.
6 What informal notions, besides those of computable function, probability and cognitive significance, do you think deserve to be properly explicated?
7 'Axiomatic geometry is an explication of our intuitive concept of space.' Discuss.

11 The Method of Thought-Experiment

11.1 The role of thought-experiments in philosophical critique

Philosophical reasoning (like mathematical reasoning) can be criticized in either one of two ways: (1) one can object to the assumed truth of a basic assumption made in the course of the argument, and taken for granted for the purposes of that argument; or (2) one can object to the validity or suasive power of a particular step or transition made in the course of the argument.

In meeting a criticism of kind (1), the proponent of the argument has to beware of the dangers of (a) infinite regress, (b) circularity, and (c) inconsistency or incoherence of the set of premises eventually taken as 'ultimate'.

In Mathematics, criticisms of kind (2) (i.e., criticisms of fallacies in deductive reasoning) can be backed up by displaying a 'counterexample'. This will be some model or construction that satisfies the immediate premises for the questionable step, but falsifies its conclusion. Any good teacher of Mathematics will have considerable experience doing this for students. If a student, for example, makes a step from 'f is continuous on $(0,1)$' to 'f is *uniformly* continuous on $(0,1)$', the teacher will no doubt say something like

> No, no! Consider the function $f(x) = 1/x$. This is continuous on $(0,1)$ but, because it gets ever steeper as x tends to 0, one's choice of δ to take care of every choice of tolerance ϵ is going to depend on the point x in question . . .

So too in Philosophy. When someone draws a questionable (i.e., fallacious) inference in philosophical argumentation, the way we criticize it effectively is to engage in a *thought-experiment* – one which reveals that the premises *could be true* while yet the conclusion *would turn out false*. The literature of contemporary analytical philosophy is replete with superbly inventive, ingenious and creative thought-experiments of this kind. (In fact, it sometimes seems to this author that philosophers acquire greater reputations for their ability to construct counterexamples than for their ability to prosecute long trains of valid reasoning.)

Other cases of the exercise of introspective intuition are to be found in the thought-experiments of metaphysicians, epistemologists and philosophers of mind and language. In these thought-experiments, one tests to the limit the application of concepts of philosophical importance. One imagines wildly different 'possible worlds' or bizarre situations which serve to bring out distinctions among concepts that might otherwise be taken to be the 'same', by virtue of applying to the same objects under normal circumstances.

One can represent what is happening in a thought-experiment by means of a pair of diagrams. In normal circumstances, two concepts F and G (for example, 'human being' and 'rational animal'; or, more suggestively, 'fat' and 'greedy') might coincide in extension. That is, they may apply to exactly the same things. Let us represent things (or objects, or individuals, or particulars, or entities) as dots within a rectangle, which represents the limits of the world. Let us represent the extension of concept F within that world by a solid boundary, and the extension of concept G by a dotted boundary. The co-extensiveness of concepts F and G in the actual world may be represented like this:

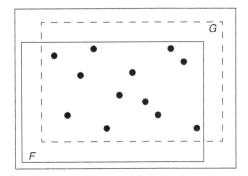

If normal circumstances were all that ever came under consideration, one might be led to conflate the two concepts F and G: that is, to identify them as concepts simply because they happen to apply to the same things. But the identity of concepts is not owed to happenstance. It is owed to their *necessarily* applying to the same things. For F to be the same concept as G, it is *necessary* that anything that is F, is G; and it is *necessary* that anything that is G, is F.

So suppose now that it is a mistake to conflate the concepts F and G. That means that either it is not necessary that every F is G; or, it is not necessary that every G is F. To bring out the failure of either of these necessities, it is enough to describe (or imagine, or construct) a possible world or different set of circumstances in which something is F but not G; or is G but not F:

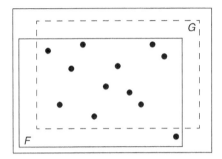 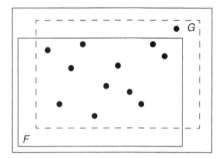

These two diagrams illustrate the respective possibilities. Of these different possible worlds one intuits that the concepts would, therein, apply to different things, thereby bringing out the difference between those concepts. Of course the force of the intuition depends on the way the details of the imagined 'possible world' are fleshed out.

Now in examining any analysis of a concept F on offer, a critically minded philosopher often has recourse to the method of thought-experiment: the construction, even in wild imagination, of a possible world in which there is an object or situation to which the *analysandum* concept F applies, but the *analysans* G does not (as illustrated in the diagram on the left above); or vice versa (as illustrated in the diagram on the right above). Criticism of a proffered analysis is an act of de-conflation. One imaginatively prises two concepts apart: the one to be analyzed, and the (usually complex) one that has been offered by way of analysis. One brings out a potential mismatch in their ranges of application (their extensions).

Whenever conceptual analyses of important concepts are offered, the race is on to find counterexamples that will force a refinement of the analysis, or even the eventual abandonment of the analytical project in question. This is when philosophical energies become focused on the search for ingenious counterexamples. In this exercise one sees the philosophical imagination at work, at times with inspiration, subtlety, genius. It is an intellectually creative exercise. A training in logic is invaluable both for those who wish to engage in the analysis or explication of concepts of philosophical importance, and for those who wish to demonstrate that a proffered analysis is defective.

Someone outside academic philosophical circles may not be aware of just what a staple the far-fetched thought-experiment has become. In no particular order, we enumerate below some of the thought-experiments to be found in the late nineteenth- and twentieth-century philosophical literature. They have become a standard part of the analytical philosopher's intellectual tool-kit.

Almost all thought-experiments involve absurdly improbable scenarios; but that does not detract at all from their dialectical potency. When students learn Philosophy they learn, among other things, how to open their minds to the most far-fetched, bizarre possibilities – situations which stretch certain concepts to their limits, in order to explore the conceptual connections among the concepts themselves. In acquiring this intellectual skill, they have to learn to put aside their beliefs concerning the *probability* or *likelihood* or *feasibility* of the imagined scenarios. Convictions about how remote these possibilities may be, given one's everyday experience (or even given one's scientific knowledge as well) will actually *detract* from the student's ability to gain increased *philosophical* understanding of what is at issue. All that is necessary is that the thought experiment should be conducted in such clear and simple terms that certain 'truths within it' will be granted intuitively, or upon appropriate reflection. Skillfully arranged, the right scenario will make the premises of the challenged inference true, and make its conclusion false.

For the analytical philosopher, misunderstanding of the analytical method is a recurrent risk when pursuing exchanges with scholars in other disciplines. The present author once engaged in such an exchange with the well-known mathematical popularizer Reuben Hersh, co-author, with Philip J. Davis, of the best-selling book *The Mathematical Experience* (Hersh and Davis (1981)).

Hersh had alleged that numbers are non-abstract and humanity-dependent. The present author sought to elicit certain conclusions from this view, and then construct (perfectly licitly) certain thought-experiments that would confound those conclusions. One of the thought experiments involved inviting Hersh to consider the *conceptual possibility* of extraterrestrial intelligent beings who are capable of mathematical thought and its linguistic communication. (It was not even required that one maintain such ETI as a *physical* possibility *modulo* our current best physical theories.) Another thought-experiment invited Hersh to consider the possible extinction of all intelligent beings, followed by their serendipitous evolutionary recapitulation, to the point of re-developing number theory in the same form that it had had with their cosmic precursors.

The purpose of these two thought-experiments was to create difficulty for the view that the natural numbers would cease to exist if human beings ceased to exist; and for the view that human intellects would have a total monopoly on intellectual access to the natural numbers. Both of these views were explicit, or clearly implicit, in what Hersh had maintained.

Hersh expressed disbelief in the likelihood of such beings or sequences of events. He failed to appreciate that such an objection would be *entirely beside the point* in such a conceptual exercise. Among professional philosophers at least, a certain erudite delight is sometimes to be had from making a well-known thought-experiment *even more preposterous and far-fetched* than the original, in order to establish yet another conceptual point not made by the original. The perverse intellectual delight stems from making the needed 'intuitively evident' truths in the weird situation intuitively evident *despite* the utterly far-fetched nature of the imagined scenario.

The famous Cambridge mathematician John Littlewood (1885–1977) once related a story of his visit to his old high school, to give an invited talk to the sixth form (= senior year, for those in the USA). He was giving them a simple proof, in the course of which he said 'Suppose now that x is a real number'. A hand went up in the back of the room. 'But Sir, suppose x *isn't* a real number!'

Clearly the young objector had failed to grasp what was going on with 'Let ...'-clauses in the kinds of quantified reasoning so essential to modern mathematics. These forms of reasoning are now perfectly well understood, and are codified exactly in highly developed systems of natural deduction.

In the same way, anyone who scoffs at a thought-experiment on the grounds that the envisaged situation is hugely unlikely, or irrelevant to daily human concerns, has simply failed to grasp what is going on with the 'Let's imagine a case where ...' clauses in the kinds of thought-experimental reasoning so essential to contemporary Philosophy. These forms of reasoning are perfectly well understood, and are a core component of highly developed forms of philosophical argumentation. Naturally, being more discursive and open-ended, they have not been codified in the precise way that first-order logical reasoning has been. But that is not the crucial issue at stake in this analogy.

11.2 Some famous thought-experiments in analytical philosophy

Two excellent sources providing accounts of thought experiments in much greater depth than can be managed here are Sorensen (1992) and Gendler (2000).

11.2.1 The ship of Theseus

Plutarch (AD 75) is the oldest extant source for the famous example of the ship of Theseus, which is re-built plank by plank, until none of the original pieces of wood remains. Is it still the same ship? To make the question more pressing: suppose that the removed planks are reassembled to make another (?) ... or the original (?) ... ship. Which one *is* the original ship? This is one of the oldest thought experiments concerning the interplay among matter, form, persistence and identity.

11.2.2 Descartes's evil demon

This celebrated thought-experiment in Meditation I in Descartes (1641a) is perhaps the progenitor of them all. Descartes's evil demon is supposed to be able systematically to deceive him in all his thinking about the external world. Descartes's aim was to thereby cast doubt on any inference roughly like 'I (appear to myself directly to) perceive that p, and that perceptual impression coheres with all my other impressions; therefore, it is true that p'.

11.2.3 Putnam's brain-in-a-vat

Putnam (1981), Chapter 1, imagined an alternative scenario of a 'brain in a vat', whose sensory stimulations are supplied by a mad scientist, and whose afferent nerve signals are monitored by said scientist. Putnam's aim was to make the problem of skepticism about the external world more compelling.

11.2.4 Putnam's Twin-Earth

Putnam (1973) undertakes a thought-experiment involving 'Twin Earth', where everyone and everything on Earth has a molecule-for-molecule *Doppelgänger*, except that what appears to be water on Twin Earth has the chemical constitution XYZ rather than H_2O. The purpose of this thought-experiment was to challenge the assumption that 'meanings are in the head'.

11.2.5 Gettier-type examples

We saw above that one of the most famous of philosophical analyses holds that knowledge is justified true belief. Gettier-type examples seek to challenge this analysis in its right-to-left direction. That is, they involve situations where one would intuitively be prepared to say that a person is justified in holding a particular belief, and that the belief in question is true; but where one would nevertheless not be prepared to say that the person *knew* the truth of the proposition in question. Gettier's example was of a fellow who had a red Ford, which gets stolen but is promptly replaced with an exact replica.

11.2.6 Williams's example of 'character and memory switch'

Williams (1970) gave an example of two people who are offered the prospect of the 'character and memory switch', followed by reward to one and punishment to the other. The purpose of this thought-experiment was to raise doubts about whether bodily continuity is sufficient for personal identity.

11.2.7 The problem of the inverted spectrum

The problem of the inverted spectrum was given in Locke (1689), in the chapter 'Of True and False Ideas'. Modern philosophers have resuscitated Locke's problem (where, say, one's impressions of red and green get switched), in order to challenge the functionalist in the philosophy of mind (*see* Chapter 24). For the functionalist claims that every mental state is characterized by the logical role it plays as a state in the 'program' that 'is' the human mind. This, in the light of the example of the inverted spectrum, would appear to underdetermine the phenomenal reality of particular color-impressions on the part of a conscious subject.

11.2.8 Jackson's scientist Mary

Jackson (1982) gave an example involving the scientist Mary, who knows everything there is to know about neurochemistry, etc., but who sees everything in black, white, and grays. The purpose of this thought-experiment is to challenge the notion that materialism could hold all the truth there is to know about mental experience. (That is why it has earned the label 'the knowledge argument'.)

11.2.9 Kripke's standard meter-rod

Kripke (1980), at pp. 54ff., gives the example of the standard meter-rod in Paris, in order to challenge the inference from 'proposition P is known *a priori*' to 'proposition P is necessary'. For, one knows *a priori* that the standard meter-rod is 1 meter long; yet, for all that, it is possible that that very rod *not* be exactly 1 meter long. Its contingent length in the actual world happens to fix for us the precise length of 1 meter. But, with that precise length fixed, we can then imagine that very rod being of a different length in another possible world.

11.2.10 Ayer's universe of sounds

Ayer (1963), at p. 34, gave an example of a universe consisting of four sounds, repeated *ad infinitum*, in a series with no beginning and no end:

... , A, B, C, D, A, B, C, D, ...

It was intended as a counterexample to the famous and contentious Principle of Identity of Indiscernibles – the Leibnizian principle that maintains that any 'two' things possessed of exactly the same properties, and standing in exactly the same relations to 'other things', are identical, i.e., are one and the same thing. Hacking (1975), at pp. 254–55, turned Ayer's example on its head. He points out that

> [Leibniz]'s reply is to query whether this Ayerial world has anything except the sounds A, B,C, and D, each occurring just once. We know that, if there is absolute space-time serving as a receptacle for objects or sounds, then [the Principle of Identity of Indiscernibles] is false. ... But if time is defined in terms of relations between objects, then we cannot use the temporal position of the objects or sounds to show that, for example, there are two (or infinitely many) occurrences of A. ... *There is not enough structure in Ayer's universe to guarantee a linear order to time.* (Emphasis added.)

11.2.11 Searle's 'Chinese room' argument

Searle (1980) advanced the famous *Chinese room argument* against any func-tionalist or computationalist account of mind. He asks one to imagine a monoglot English-speaker (such as himself) sitting in a locked room all by himself (presumably with an 'in' slot and an 'out' slot in one of its walls), using a manual (written in English) to produce responses, written in Chinese characters, to input-batches that are also written in Chinese characters. When he gets really efficient at it, any outside observer would think that the person inside the room was a Chinese speaker (and reader). But, *ex hypothesi*, he is not. The English manual that he is using contains the functionalist's proposed 'set of rules' for manipulating symbols on the basis of their form alone (which is the essence of a computer program). Searle thereby challenges the notion that all that is involved in linguistic understanding is mechanical, 'symbolic' computation. See §24.3.5 for further discussion.

11.2.12 Block's 'China brain'

Block (1978) popularized the following thought-experiment. Imagine every person in China having a walkie-talkie radio, so that the whole population is like a neural network, each Chinese person receiving and sending signals like a neuron, with the walkie-talkie connections mimicking the pattern of axons and dendrites in a human brain. The whole Chinese population would therefore instantiate a functionalist's program of supposedly mental states. Would this macro-entity be conscious, the way a human brain is?

11.2.13 Zombies as a possible refutation of physicalism

Physicalists in the Philosophy of Mind form a category that includes, among others, behaviorists, psycho-physical identity theorists, and functionalists. These are all theorists who believe that the physical facts fix all the mental facts; so they are not denying the reality of the mental itself. All of them hold in common that conscious mental states and processes arise somehow from the physical workings of the brain and central nervous system. The most problematic imaginary counterexample that these physicalists have to wrestle with is the possibility of *zombies* – creatures that are constituted, and behave, like human beings, but who (if a personal pronoun is appropriate here), we are invited to imagine, have no inner experiences at all. The first question to confront is whether zombies really are metaphysically possible. (Not every imaginable type of thing need be metaphysically possible.) Then, if they are held to be metaphysically possible, the second question to confront is whether that possibility refutes the philosophical thesis of physicalism about mind. The reader can gain good access to the debate through Campbell (1970); Kirk (1974); Block (1980); Chalmers (1996); Kirk (2005); and Kirk (2008).

Problems

Acquaint yourself, using the cited sources, with the following thought-experiments in the contemporary philosophical literature. In each case, decide whether the thought-experiment in question achieves its inventor's stated aim.

1 The 'deviant causal chains' that are intended to create problems for any attempt to give a causal analysis of knowledge. (Peacocke (1979))

2 Runaway trolley-car examples and doomsday machine examples, which are intended to raise problems for various Utilitarian accounts of what the right thing to do is. (Foot (1967))

3 The 'Cretan translation manual', which was invoked in an attempt to give a clinching example of the necessarily indeterminate character of translation. (Massey (1978))

4 The telecloning and split-brain examples that are intended to create problems for various accounts of personal identity. (Dennett's Introduction to Hofstadter and Dennett (1981))

5 The 'quadder', who interprets '$x + y$' in such a way as to get the sum of x and y if they are both less than 57, but to get 5 otherwise. The quadder poses problems for the view that what a speaker means by a certain expression must be determined by past and present facts concerning the speaker. (Kripke (1982))

6 *Swampman* – the being who is created by a bolt of lightning hitting an old tree stump in a swamp; and is a molecule-for-molecule replica of the thought-experimenter in question, who (in the thought experiment) had been killed by another lightning bolt nearby, just moments before. The example is best understood as a challenge to an insufficiently sophisticated materialism about the mind, according to which current mental states are wholly determined by *current* physical states. (Davidson (1987))

7 The *'lifelong' Robinson-Crusoe example*, raised as a challenge to the view that thought and language are necessarily social. (Ayer (1954))

8 The Makropulos case: adduced to disabuse one of what might otherwise *seem* to be a rational longing for immortality. (Williams (1973b))

9 Languageless but obviously rational creatures: thought up as a counterexample to the analytical dogma that thought requires talk. (Kirk (1967))

12   Intellectual Creativity and Rigor

12.1 Creativity and rigor in intellectual pursuits

From what has been said thus far about mathematical proof, scientific discovery and testing, and philosophical analysis and criticism, one is in a position to venture a general claim about creativity and accomplishment in all three of those areas. This is an attempt to 'get to the bottom' of what is involved in such creativity.

It is analogous to the way theoretical linguists try to 'get to the bottom' of the various natural languages spoken by the peoples of this planet. Despite their surface dissimilarities, these languages have yielded, upon investigation, similarities at a deeper level. They appear to be cut to a common pattern, which it is the task of theoretical linguistics to make clear. The linguist is after the common pattern in these different systems of communication. This modern approach to linguistics began with Chomsky (1965).

In a similar way, we are now after the common pattern in creative thinking in the different areas of Mathematics, Science and Philosophy.

A great *mathematician* is one who can identify a statement of deep interest and importance; (i) prove it, if it is true; and (ii) construct a counterexample (a mathematical 'possible world'), if it is false. The proof will be from a given set of axioms. The counterexample will also be constrained by those axioms: it must be a possible situation (a 'model', in the parlance of mathematicians) in which the axioms are true but the conjecture turns out false. One of the classic statements about mathematical creativity is Poincaré (1913), Book I, Chapter III: 'Mathematical Creation'.

A great *scientist* is one who can identify a sweeping generalization H of great predictive power. The scientist can then test it against available evidence E, and reject H if it fails to explain E. The failure can be of two kinds: E may not be deducible from H; or, worse, one may be able to deduce absurdity from the conjunction of H and E. The first kind of failure involves the ability to find a counterexample. The second kind of failure involves the ability to construct a (dis)proof. The scientist must be able to find the counterexample, or the (dis)proof, as the case may be. (A *disproof* is a special kind of proof – one whose *conclusion* is absurdity. A disproof shows that the set of assumptions that it used to derive absurdity cannot all be true, in *any* possible world.)

If, however, the hypothesis H succeeds in explaining the evidence E (that is, if there is a proof *of evidence E* as conclusion, from hypothesis H), then the scientisit will go further. He or she will try to *deduce* from H new predictions P concerning experimentally contrivable circumstances (scientifically 'possible worlds'). In thinking up the experimental situations that would provide a good test of an hypothesis, the scientist is once more devising models: possible worlds in which certain boundary conditions hold true. The idea is that, if the hypothesis is true, then the observations ought to bear out the new predictions P that have been deduced from the hypothesis in conjunction with the statement of the boundary conditions. The new predictions P, that is, can then be tested against further evidence E' that comes to light once those experimental circumstances have been contrived. Once again, this testing by E' has the logical structure just described. So we see that the scientist has to be involved in (i) finding proofs and (ii) constructing models, or possible worlds.

A great *philosopher*, likewise, is one who can identify concepts and fundamental beliefs of great importance; offer interesting, illuminating analyses of those concepts, or necessary and sufficient conditions for the truth of those beliefs; and construct imaginative counterexamples to defective rival analyses. Once again, the thinker is (i) finding proofs, or (ii) constructing counterexamples.

In all three cases – mathematician, scientist and philosopher – creativity is patterned, *logically*, in the same way. It involves a search for order and system; a high degree of logical or deductive insight, involved in the discovery of proofs; and a fertility of imagination, involved in the discovery of counterexamplary models. The mathematician can construct counterexamples within a framework of given axioms; the scientist can think up experiments to perform in the real world; the philosopher can think up a possible, perhaps even bizarrely different, world to bring out the distinction between two concepts or beliefs.

Behind these kinds of creativity, centrally at work in its exercise, is the ability to construct a line of argument, a train of reasoning, a chain of inferences, a proof. Note how with these metaphors – line, train, and chain – one has the impression of thought being shackled, or manacled, or inexorably driven. It is what Wittgenstein called the *hardness of the logical must*. Mathematical conjectures, scientific hypotheses, and philosophical analyses have to be put in leg-irons, and brought to the fatal shores of observation and introspective intuition.

Moreover, *finding* a proof or a counterexample to a given conjecture is no rote matter, contrary to the hope and expectation that Leibniz expressed with his famous injunction *Calculemus!* For we now know, by Church's undecidability theorem for first-order logic (see Church (1936a), Church (1936b)), that there is no effective method for deciding whether there is a proof of a given conclusion from given premises.

12.2 General principles, rules and methods

In Science we count, measure, take readings, pick random samples, note maxima and minima, calculate means and standard deviations and coefficients of correlation. We postulate that various measurable magnitudes are governed, in their change over time, by certain differential equations; it is then a mathematical task to find out what sorts of function satisfy those differential equations. When we feed in boundary conditions we determine constants of integration; when we want a prediction for time t we compute the value of the integrated function for time t. Science appears to be totally reliant on the mathematics of number and probability.

Moreover, scientific breakthroughs tend increasingly to be associated with the use of a new kind of mathematical theory, or a new use of an existing one. (This is another justification that can be offered for doing 'pure' mathematics: one can never predict with certainty that it will forever remain 'pure'.) Early in the twentieth century we had Einstein's theory of relativity, based on non-Euclidean geometry; and the theory of quantum mechanics, due to Max Planck (1858–1947), Niels Bohr (1885–1962), Werner Heisenberg (1901–76), and Erwin Schrödinger (1887–1961), applying the mathematics of Hilbert spaces and Hermitian operators. More recently, we have seen catastrophe theory, invented by René Thom (1923–2002), applied to the description of sudden changes – 'threshold phenomena' – of complex dynamical systems, in which it is difficult to trace out lines of local causal influence; and we have seen the theory of chaos and fractals developed by Benoit Mandelbrot (1924–2010) applied to describe the behavior of systems obeying non-linear equations. A new form of Mathematics can bring with it a new 'mind-set', a new way of seeing phenomena, a new way of conceptualizing cause and change in the domain to which it is applied. So the role of Mathematics in Science is not just confined to counting and measuring and doing arithmetical or statistical calculations with the results. It can provide instead part of the very language and conceptual apparatus for our description of the world.

So: Science makes extensive, and apparently indispensable, use of Mathematics. In the rest of this chapter we shall examine Philosophy's perennial fascination with Mathematics. In the next chapter we shall show how Mathematics needs Logic.

12.3 Philosophy's perennial fascination with Mathematics

Plato, Descartes, Leibniz, Berkeley, Hume, Kant, Frege, Russell, Wittgenstein, Carnap, and Quine are just a few of the great philosophers who have wrestled with the nature of Mathematics. Mathematics raises problems in both ontology (the study of what there is) and epistemology (the theory of knowledge). What are mathematical objects? And what is the nature of mathematical knowledge?

Thought about these two main issues has been deeply influenced by the following features of Mathematics. (These features are stated here in the way majority opinion among philosophers and mathematicians would have them. For each such opinion there are always some dissidents.)

12.3.1 Mathematical truths are necessarily true

Another way of putting this is to say that mathematical truths are true in all possible worlds. It would not matter how bizarrely different another world might be. It could be the weirdest creation of science fiction; or a figment of the creative metaphysician's thought-experiments. In any such world it would still be true that (for example) $7 + 5 = 12$; and that for no whole number $n > 2$ can one find positive whole numbers a, b, and c such that $a^n + b^n = c^n$.

12.3.2 Mathematical truth seems to rest on a few primitive, self-evident truths (so-called 'axioms')

From these axioms the remaining truths can be logically derived. This was the great intellectual discovery of the ancient Greeks – specifically, Euclid. From just a few basic postulates Euclid derived all of the then known geometry.

12.3.3 Mathematical truth is knowable without sensory experience

Another way of putting this is to say that mathematical truth is *a priori*. To come to know a mathematical truth, it *suffices* to have a proof. It is also *necessary* to have a proof. We have to be careful to discount the sensory experience possibly needed in order to *acquire* the concepts involved in formulating the truth in question. Once one has mastered these concepts, one can come to know the truth simply by reasoning – one does not have to observe the external world, or carry out experiments within it. The proof is a purely intellectual construction, which can be communicated to other mathematicians. That this involves processes in the external world, such as writing symbols on a board or in the sand or on a piece of paper, is neither here nor there. The existence of the proof *type* transcends these physical manifestations or 'tokenings', as philosophers call them. The proof type is indeed another mathematical object, in the same realm as the objects talked about in the statements that occur in the proof itself. (One contemporary problem has arisen for the idea that a mathematical proof does not require sensory experience, or in general experience of the external world. The problem is that nowadays we can use computers to carry through details of proofs that would take us far too long. Here we seem to be relying on the correct functioning of physical machines in arriving at mathematical knowledge.)

12.3.4 Mathematical objects are in an eternal realm other than that of space-time

Where exactly is the number 0? If you point to any empty region and say 'there', then answer this question: where exactly is 'the' square root of -1? (There are actually two of them; and no way to tell which is which. See Shapiro (2012).) Where exactly is the power set of the set of natural numbers? Are there any straight lines in physical space? Mathematical objects would appear to be *sui generis* – of their own kind. They are abstract as opposed to concrete objects. They do not inhabit space-time. They are not part of the causal order. Yet the structures they form are invariant, immutable, and eternal, giving rise to necessary truths about them. They seem to be accessible only to intellectual intuition, or to thought 'with one's eyes closed', as it were.

12.3.5 *Mathematics begins with very simple concepts, and builds up much more complicated ones by means of definitions*

The first kind of definition is *explicit definition*. Here, the concept to be defined is expressed as a logical compound of concepts already available and understood.

Take, for example, the concept '*x* is a prime number'. This can be defined as '*x* is a natural number divisible without remainder only by itself and 1'. The latter definition involves the concepts of divisibility and of remainder. These can in turn be defined in terms of multiplication and addition, two of the simple concepts that one takes as primitive when doing the arithmetic of whole numbers.

Another example of explicit definition would be the concept of a triangle. In a geometry using as basic the concepts of point, line and plane, a triangle can be defined as consisting of three non-concurrent lines each pair of which intersects. Alternatively, it could be defined as consisting of any three distinct points, along with the lines joining each pair of them.

A final example of explicit definition is that of the derivative $f'(a)$ of a real-valued function $f(x)$ defined on the reals, at the argument $x = a$:

$$\lim_{\delta \to 0} \frac{f(a+\delta) - f(a)}{\delta}.$$

This in turn requires an explicit definition of the notion

$$\lim_{\delta \to 0} g(\delta),$$

which may be given thus:

$$\iota y (\forall \epsilon > 0 \exists \gamma > 0 \forall x (|x| < \gamma \to |g(x) - y| < \epsilon)$$

(the unique real number y such that for every positive tolerance ϵ one can find a positive bound γ such that for every real number x within the bound γ of 0, $g(x)$ is within the tolerance ϵ of y).

Next there is the method of *inductive definition*. This is the kind of definition that 'stratifies' the instances of the concept C into levels $C_0, C_1, \ldots$ *ad infinitum*. Level C_0 consists of the simplest instances of the concept C, which can be specified directly. Then at each subsequent level C_{n+1} one includes instances that can be 'constructed out of' instances at any one of the preceding levels $C_0, \ldots, C_n$. The means of construction can be specified clearly. Something is an instance of the concept C only if it appears at some level C_n.

A simple example of an inductive definition is that of the function called '*n* factorial' (written *n*!):

$$0! =_{df} 1$$

$$(n+1)! =_{df} (n+1).(n!).$$

Another example of an inductive definition is that of a formula of a logical language. Here the simplest formulae are specified directly (as A, B, C,... or what have you; so-called *atoms*, or *propositional variables*); and the means of construction are the connectives of negation ($\neg$), conjunction ($\wedge$), disjunction ($\vee$) and implication (if $\rightarrow$). These connectives allow one to form, respectively, formulae of the compound forms

$$\neg \varphi, \; (\varphi \wedge \psi), \; (\varphi \vee \psi), \; (\varphi \rightarrow \psi)$$

from formulae φ and ψ that have already been formed.

The final method of definition to be mentioned here is that of *implicit definition*. This is the method whereby one 'fixes the meanings' of terms by using them in a set of basic principles. This, in effect, is how the notions of point, line and plane are 'defined' in geometrical theorizing. One can give informal hints, such as that a point is that which has no length or breadth, a line is that which has length but no breadth, etc. But these hints are not part of the theory itself. Rather, the theory implicitly defines what counts as points, lines and planes by spelling out all the structural interrelationships that obtain among such entities. Any interpretation of the language that makes the theory true will then contain its versions of points, lines and planes.

12.3.6 Mathematical concepts are the most 'ideal' types in science

Bishop Berkeley was exercised by the puzzle of how it is that we can prove results quite generally for all triangles by thinking about 'only one triangle', namely the one we happen to draw on the page when doing the proof. The modern logician's answer is that we use only such information about the drawn triangle as would be available for any triangle whatsoever. All triangles have exactly the same features in common in so far as their triangularity is concerned. The same cannot be said about, say, horses (or could it?).

12.3.7 Mathematics is full of vivid metaphor at the informal level; but can be treated in a rigorous, symbolic, fully formalized way as well

When communicating mathematical ideas and results informally, we use language rich in visual and spatial metaphor, and metaphors of motion and touch: impact, taking apart, putting together, constructing, choosing, finding, selecting, ... Yet when a proof is completely refined as a mathematical object itself, it is simply a partial ordering of occurrences of formulae in a completely formal language. Only the shapes of the symbols and the patterns of their occurrences within the proof are relevant to determining whether the arrangement is indeed a proof. The proof is completely purged of metaphor. Informal mathematical creativity can involve the exercise of an almost poetic power of intellect; and yet the ultimate object produced – the formal proof – is utterly devoid of any traces of such origins. This polarity of discovery and presentation is hardly equalled in any other branch of intellectual endeavor.

12.3.8 *Really powerful mathematical intuition or insight appears to be a gift of genius granted to but a few*

Think of Carl Friedrich Gauss (1777–1855), who worked out, at the age of five, how to add every number from 1 to 1,000: $1,001 \times 500 = 500,500$. Think of Srinivasa Ramanujan (1887–1920), writing down the results on infinite series summations that (so he claimed) an angel had done for him on a tablet in his dreams, while he was asleep. (See Kanigel (1991), a fascinating biography of Ramunajan.) Think of Henri Poincaré (1854–1912) boarding the Sunday charabanc after drinking thrice-boiled coffee, and being hit in a flash by the series of Fuchsian functions. Think of Saul Kripke, who at the age of sixteen invented possible worlds semantics for intuitionistic and modal logics. (See Kripke (1963).) Think of Harvey Friedman (b. 1948), who at the age of sixteen proved that if intuitionistic Zermelo–Fraenkel set theory is consistent, then so is classical Zermelo–Fraenkel set theory. Western and Eastern culture has long had a deep reverence for such astonishing talent. Its products enter our cultural heritage, and serve to elevate, edify, and enrich the lives of those who come after.

Mathematics is used to mediate in disputes. It was the measurement of land on the Egyptian flood plains that led to the birth of geometry. Mathematics is used to whisk people from one place to another. It was the invention of the differential and integral calculus that put the technology of aeronautics, rocketry and ballistics within reach. Mathematics is used to store and process information on any topic. The information-processing revolution would not have got under way without the pioneering efforts of philosophers, mathematicians and logicians in the 1920s and 1930s on the notion of computable function. Of course, all these uses have their 'downsides'. We have airplanes helping to destroy the ozone layer, Scud missiles, nuclear weapons, the danger of Big Brother, and computer crime.

12.3.9 *Mathematical knowledge is one of the best available examples of objective knowledge*

Even you and the computer criminal could agree on whether the computation was mathematically correct. The scientists of one superpower can check the mathematical calculations of defecting scientists from another superpower.

12.3.10 *Mathematical knowledge is one of the best examples of knowledge that can be accommodated in an increasingly generalized conceptual framework*

Ever since Euclid, the process of axiomatization has led to the choice of more basic concepts in various branches of Mathematics. The last century has also seen the development of various theories aiming for the utmost generality, in which all of extant mathematics could be developed. Such theories are type theory, set theory and category theory.

12.3.11 *Mathematics is curiously applicable to reality*

Witness applied mathematics, and its 'unreasonable effectiveness' (Wigner (1960)). The first great physicist of the experimental age, Galileo Galilei (1564–1642), wrote that

> Philosophy is written in this grand book – I mean the universe – which stands continually open to our gaze, but it cannot be understood unless one first learns to comprehend the language in which it is written. It is written in the language of mathematics, and its characters are triangles, circles, and other geometric figures, without which it is humanly impossible to understand a single word of it; without these, one is wandering about in a dark labyrinth.
>
> (Translated in Popkin (1966), p. 65)

12.3.12 *Mathematics, at times of conceptual convulsion, can produce paradoxes*

The most famous example is Russell's Paradox. Frege had tried to lay the foundations of a set theory which had principles of such generality that (he hoped) it could really be regarded as a branch of logic. In this theory all of mathematics was to be derived by defining numbers as suitable sets. Hence the title of Frege's program: Logicism.

Frege included in his theory the very general principle that any property determined a set: the set of all and only those objects that possess the property in question. This is nowadays known as the Principle of Naïve Comprehension. Its naïveté was revealed as follows.

> Russell asked Frege to consider the property 'not being a member of oneself'. According to Frege's principle, this property must determine a set. Let R be such a set. R is the set of all and only those things that are not members of themselves. Now comes Russell's question: is R a member of R (i.e., of itself)? If it is, then it has the defining property of R, namely that it is not a member of itself. So R is *not* a member of itself. But now, since R is not a

member of itself, it must belong to the set of all and only those things that are not members of themselves – that is, to R. So, after all, R *is* a member of itself.

Russell's Paradox brings out the hubris involved in thinking that we can conceive of the universe as a finished totality: that we can grasp as one thing all that there is. For the Russell set is, in effect, the set consisting of everything. This is because nothing is a member of itself. Thus the defining property of the Russell set – non-self-membership – applies to everything.

The 'paradox' can be understood now as a *reductio ad absurdum* of the assumption that there is such a thing as the Russell set. This assumption is lurking in the background, and implicitly used, when we 'instantiate' the general claim that any thing is a member of the Russell set if and only if that thing has that set's defining property, i.e., non-self-membership. The instantiation is to the particular claim that the Russell set is a member of the Russell set if and only if the Russell set has the defining condition of non-self-membership. Indeed, the unwarranted existence assumption is invoked even earlier, in the initial passage to the general claim itself. For that general claim was derived from the Naïve Comprehension Principle according to which for every property (in particular, non-self-membership) there exists a set of things having that property. So the proof of Russell's Paradox is knee-deep (both knees) in commitment to the existence of the Russell set.

The correct response to Russell's Paradox is to get clear about the conditions under which sets of different kinds exist. Frege's principle was too naïve in its generality. It was replaced by a family of principles that licensed the existence of various less ambitious sets much more cautiously. Thus it was that modern set theory was born, and came to be appreciated as a part of Mathematics rather than of Logic.

12.4 How Mathematics needs Logic

Much of Mathematics is based on intuition, especially of a spatial or visual kind. But even when doing something as vividly visualizable as plane geometry, the rigorous development of any branch of Mathematics requires us to be able to write down in an exact language the first principles that we regard as self-evident and true. We ask ourselves what the basic notions are; and what the basic truths concerning them may be. The basic notions concern kinds of mathematical entities, their primitive properties, and the primitive relations among them.

When doing geometry, for example, we may take the primitive kinds of entity to be points, lines and planes; or, alternatively, take as primitive entities points and sets, thereby treating lines and planes as sets of points. Once having chosen our primitive entities we have to specify their primitive properties and relations. In geometry, these will include the relations of identity, coincidence and betweenness. We may also specify a distance function, or metric, whose job it is to say how far apart from each other any two points are. Then we advance to lay down axioms or postulates or first principles governing these entities and their functions, properties and relations. In geometry, we say that any two points coincide with exactly one line; that for any three points x, y, z the distance between x and y plus the distance between y and z exceeds or equals the distance between x and z... and so on.

We must not postulate *too much*. For some truths (such as Pythagoras's Theorem) lack that immediate self-evidence that one demands of a postulate. Such truths have to be uncovered *as* truths, by logically deducing them from the postulates.

Nor may we postulate *too little*. For otherwise we shall fail logically to deduce some of those truths. We deduce deep and interesting theorems from the postulates or axioms by means of proof. A proof is simply an arrangement of sentences, with dependencies among them clearly marked, that starts with the axioms and ends with the theorem desired. The dependencies have to conform to certain rules of inference, in order to ensure the preservation of truth. Examples of such rules of inference (which we have already seen before) are:

A; if A then B; so, B.
a has property F; a is identical to b; so, b has property F.

Logic is the study of simple rules of inference such as these, and of the structural properties of proofs that can be constructed in accordance with the rules.

In Logic we study rules of inference for the so-called *logical* words: 'and', 'or', 'not', 'if ...then ___', '... is identical to ___', 'some', 'all'. The rules of inference spell out patterns, or forms, of correct reasoning. An important branch of Logic, known as proof theory, studies how these small or local patterns can best be put together to form large or global patterns, called proofs. The genius of a great mathematician lies in being able to start with simple axioms and fill in the steps, in one of these global patterns, that lead one to a deep theorem as a conclusion.

Proofs preserve truth. This is because all the rules of inference do, and proofs are made up of steps of inference in accordance with those rules. So when we have a proof of a theorem from certain axioms, we have a cast-iron, logical guarantee that if those axioms are true, then the theorem is true also. Proofs can (ideally, in principle) be checked. This is because proofs are finite pieces of discourse, every step of which has to conform to one of only finitely many permissible patterns. Each of these steps can be checked, *mechanically*, for correctness. Mathematics, ideally, can be developed as a branch of abstract knowledge by employing the method of logical proof from mathematical axioms. A mathematical theorem is simply a statement that can be proved from those axioms. So: Logic lies at the heart of Mathematics; and Mathematics lies at the heart of Science. We therefore see how vital Logic is to Science.

12.5 Logical reasoning v. creative or inventive insight

We speak here of an ideal Science, a Science in which every step of explanation or prediction can be spelled out explicitly so as to pass logical scrutiny. But actual scientific reasoning is not always like that. Even scientists reason unconsciously and intuitively, and are not necessarily able to be rigorously explicit about how they do it. Nevertheless, *in principle, there should be a logical re-construction of the train of reasoning that they have employed.* We have encountered this dictum before (towards the end of §8.3); and we are willing to reiterate it at every pertinent opportunity.

We make this claim only in so far as we are considering how a scientist might apply a given theory in order to explain or predict particular phenomena. This explanation or prediction involves deducing a statement of particular fact from general theoretical hypotheses and statements of boundary conditions, etc. We are assuming that the hypotheses are already at hand; and that, using them as logical starting points, the scientist then reasons towards the statement of particular fact that has to be explained or predicted. We are claiming only that this process of reasoning is a logical one, which can in principle be spelled out in every detail, and formalized as a proof.

An entirely different matter is how a scientist arrives at a theory, or system of hypotheses, in the first place. This would, in a vivid sense, be the logical reverse of what we have just been describing. If the inexorable steps of logical progression are like heavy breakers impelling one towards the beach of experiential test, how does the scientist ever head the board out from a known stretch of beach, to get to the breakers farthest out? How does the scientist go against the flow, and tap into the deep swell? How does he or she ever get to 'hang ten'?

Good scientists know which wave to choose; and then ride it for all it is worth. The choice is deeply intuitive and creative. There is no 'logic' of scientific discovery. There is only the logic of testing theories once they have been discovered. This ironically, is the essential message of Popper's great book on scientific methodology, whose English title was, inappropriately, *The Logic of Scientific Discovery*. The German title, *Logik der Forschung*, would have been better translated as *The Logic of Scientific Research*.

12.6 Rigor

The message so far has been that deep thought, historically, has required rigor. We speak here of the kind of conceptual and logical rigor that has been displayed in the development of mathematics and modern science. This requirement of conceptual and logical rigor entails the following.

1 A desire to penetrate to the heart of the matter when choosing basic concepts. Examples: the concept of set in modern mathematics; the concepts of point, line and plane in ancient geometry; the concepts of person and free will in

metaphysics and moral philosophy; the concepts of space, time and causation in the metaphysical foundations of Science.

2   A desire to isolate the most logically fruitful and yet self-evident truths involving those concepts. Examples: Euclid's and Hilbert's axioms for geometry; the Dedekind–Peano axioms for number theory; the Zermelo–Fraenkel axioms for set theory.

3   An intellectual honesty that involved respect for the demands of consistency. Example: Frege's response to Russell's Paradox.

This last example is worth embellishing. Frege's Afterword to volume II of his *Grundgesetze der Arithmetik*, written in October 1902, begins with the heart-breaking admission:

> Hardly anything more undesirable can befall a scientific writer than to have, at the completion of his work, one of the foundation-stones of his edifice shattered.
>
> (Frege (1903; reprinted 1962), p. 253; author's translation)

Our next message concerning deep thought is that as we move away from the most technical areas like logic, mathematics and theoretical physics, and address other deep problems, especially philosophical ones – *we still need rigor*. We need rigor to isolate fundamental concepts; to identify fruitful and self-evident truths involving them; to maintain consistency in our theorizing; and to push for a unified framework of thought and understanding in which all the pieces of the jigsaw can fall into place.

These are central and essential features of any system of concepts, thought and reasoning whose goal is knowledge of truths and effective communication of those truths. Even if we believe that the history of Philosophy shows us that it is arrogant to think that we could ever arrive at the definitive or self-evident truth about any deep philosophical matter, we can insist at least on the following requirements for openness and for critical mindedness. (Note that these are all requirements on the formulation or presentation of theories *once we have found them*. They are not guidelines for invention, or recipes for creation, or methods of discovering theories.)

1   We should be prepared to put our theories forward in the clearest possible terms. We should be prepared to explain our terminology. This might be by ostension (pointing) or any of the various methods of definition. These explanations come to an end when the audience understands all the terms used in the definitions.

2   We should be prepared to meet arguments that reveal inconsistencies in our theories. We must either be able to show that the arguments are somehow defective (for example, by involving a misunderstanding of a term) or be able to revise our theory in the light of the inconsistency revealed. This second course of action may involve some sort of 'entrenchment' ordering of the

different statements of the theory. The entrenchment ordering would reflect our relative preparedness to give up the statements. (The theory of 'theory dynamics', or 'belief revision', is a relatively recent addendum to the canon of deductive logic. Ordinary deductive logic can be thought of as 'logical statics', by contrast with the dynamics of theory change. For the author's contribution to the latter field, with critical coverage of earlier approaches, see Tennant (2012b).)

3 We should leave our audience in no two minds as to whether we have taken a stand on any important issue, and, if so, what the stand is. That is, we should spell out the consequences of our theory for all the important areas of evidence, previously unsolved questions, etc., that prompted the search for the theory in the first place.

4 We should try to be honest in our presentation of our theories. We should give our audience the best possible understanding of how we ourselves see the logical priorities and interdependencies of different theses within our system. That way one can help one's own audience find the weak spots, the mistakes, the implausibilities, the internal contradictions.

5 We should interpret criticism of our theories as just that; not as personal criticism of ourselves. We should take heart from the evolutionary epistemologist who said that one of the great leaps in the evolution of our species came when we were able to let our theories die in our stead.

6 We should hold our theories sincerely: that is, be prepared to act upon them. This further entails (7):

7 We should so formulate our theories that it is evident what their 'cash value' in terms of human action might be. This is a demand of the school of thought known as pragmatism. It is not the philistine claim that higher thinking has to yield advantages for the taxpayer (that notion is of rather recent vintage in nations with fine university traditions). The claim of pragmatism is older, and more profound. It is at root a claim about the possibility of meaningful theorizing on any topic. Such theorizing, if true, must be such that its truth makes a difference to the potentialities of human action and flourishing (however remote). Otherwise, there is no way for the 'content' of the theory to manifest itself; no way even for anyone who puts the theory forward to show that they themselves actually grasp what the theory says.

This last requirement evolved historically into the Logical Positivists' demand for a criterion of 'cognitive significance'. The implicit contrast here is between *cognitive* and *appetitive*. 'Appetitive' means having do do with felt needs, wants, and desires. 'Cognitive' means having to do with the ways in which we come to know or believe. A sentence is cognitively significant just in case it has a truth-value (true or false) that we could in principle come to know; or, rather more carefully, just in case (i) it can be understood as possibly endowed with such a truth-value, and (ii) in understanding the sentence, we have a clear idea of what would lead us to regard it as true, or as false.

A *criterion of cognitive significance* – once a Holy Grail for twentieth-century empiricists – would separate sensible scientific discourse from the rest. In particular, it would rule out meaningless and untestable metaphysical speculations. The metaphysical speculations rife at the time of the emergence of Logical Positivism did not seem to make any 'connection' with even the possibility of distinctively confirming or disconfirming sensory evidence. They could not be used as a rational guide to decision, choice, and action. The demand that a good (scientific) theory should make such a connection seems eminently reasonable, if its truth is to matter. We do not free ourselves from this demand simply by showing that various attempts in the past explicitly to formulate an exact criterion of cognitive significance have, for one internal reason or another, failed. The formulation of such a criterion, as pointed out at the end of Chapter 10, is simply unfinished analytical (or explicatory) business.

Philosophical analysis, as shown in Chapter 9, is the task of getting clear about meanings of terms in our language. Such analysis involves tracing conceptual dependencies and presuppositions, formulating necessary and sufficient conditions of various concepts, or, where such conditions cannot be found, indicating criteria for the application of those concepts.

12.7 The nature of dialectic

The kind of reasoning in which skill needs to be acquired when doing Philosophy is commonly called 'dialectic'. The term derives from a dialogic conception of the search for truth. Two interlocutors put forward ideas to one another, and either rebut or accept critical amendments. Under the impetus of mutual criticism, the hope is, one will be impelled towards the truth of the matter.

But one may object to this claim. The usual purpose of debate is to persuade or browbeat, by foul means as well as fair. Consensus reached is therefore simply an agreement in opinions, which are no likelier to be true for having been arrived at by eventual unison.

This pessimism, however, is exaggerated. Provided both parties to the debate are equally skilled in criticism, the truth is much more likely to emerge from the give-and-take between them, than from their working in isolation. Each can keep the other on his or her toes in the check for continuing consistency in what one says. Each can alert the other to relevant considerations, observational evidence, and intuitions that bear one way or another on the matter under discussion. Remember here that we are talking about the ideal conditions of joint intellectual inquiry. We are not seeking to justify aggressive, argumentative habits of discussion.

The dialectical pattern of philosophical presentation has its roots in the dialogues of Plato. (One canonical translation of Plato's dialogues into English is Hamilton and Cairns (1989).) In these dialogues Socrates and other discussants get to grips with topics such as virtue, the soul, innate knowledge, etc., and advance to enlightenment with Socrates always one step ahead. This dialectical mode can be internalized when a single philosopher commits thoughts to paper when constructing a philosophical argument. There is no general prescription for successful style when writing philosophy. But one always does well to attend to the dialectical format in any piece of philosophical prose.

The format should make it clear what the main ideas and issues at stake are. The author's own thesis should emerge clearly. It can be contrasted with well-known opposed theses of other writers. One can explore common ground with them and then seek to justify one's diverging line. One should anticipate the main possible objections to one's argument, and provide rejoinders. Since each rejoinder usually involves more collateral argument, this process can potentially be repeated.

When one speaks of the *dialectical depth* of an author's argued position, one has in mind the extent to which he or she has developed in the text this to-ing and fro-ing between the author's claims and those of all imaginable opponents. Being able to imagine certain objections – particularly ones that no opponent has yet raised – and rebut them in advance is a sign of intellectual creativity and suppleness. Someone who can do this skillfully is clearly not so dogmatically wedded to their view as to have blinkers on. The to-ing and fro-ing, or dialectical deepening, should serve to make clear what basic assumptions the author's overall claims ultimately rest upon; and how those assumptions have been marshaled in support of them.

Consistency is a prerequisite for truth; it is necessary for truth. So it is especially important that the assumptions appealed to should be mutually consistent. But consistency is not a guarantee of truth; it is not sufficient for truth. Consistency simply means freedom from internal contradiction. There are many deranged and false stories that are free from internal contradiction. So consistency is not enough for truth.

The only guarantees or quality-indicators of truth lie in the axioms; the evidence; and in the correctness of the logical passages hence and thence respectively. Another quality-indicator, one might add, is the simplicity and unity of one's theory.

Maintained truth has to begin somewhere. One cannot construct informative truth out of nothing. The mathematician must appeal to axioms. The natural scientist is answerable to the evidence of intersubjective reports of observation. The philosopher relies on shared intuitions as starting points.

And therein lies the problem with much philosophical disagreement. First, the intuitions are not always shared. Secondly, it is not always clear whether the contestable philosophical thesis is one which is being derived from the intuitions, like a mathematical theorem from the axioms; or whether the contestable thesis is being put forward as an explanation of the intuitions, the way a scientific hypothesis is put forward to explain the observational evidence.

In response to both these problems, part of the task in doing Philosophy is to be able to reform the intuitions of one's interlocutor. This is only possible by creating a system of philosophical thought that does a great deal of justice to central intuitions. One then sensitively extends it to the more problematic areas where the disagreement may lie. The hope is that here, as in Science generally, systematicity and simplicity will be marks of truth. Thus it emerges that a contestable philosophical thesis is more like a scientific hypothesis than a mathematical theorem. The thesis gets tested against intuitions, in the way that an hypothesis gets tested against its evidence. Seldom does one derive a philosophical thesis from intuitions in the way that one derives a mathematical theorem from axioms.

Problems

1   What did Leibniz mean by his injunction 'Calculemus!'? Find out where in his writings it appeared, and what he was concerned to explain and recommend to his reader.
2   We said at the end of §12.2 that Science makes extensive, and apparently indispensable, use of Mathematics. But does Science *need* Mathematics, *in principle* (even conceding that it does so *in practice*)? (For a way into considerations relevant to this question, see Field (1980).)
3   Explain the logical structure of a scientific explanation of a particular phenomenon or regularity. What are the marks of creativity in the search for such an explanation? What are the marks of rigor?
4   Why, in your view, is so much that is passed off as Philosophy very much lacking in rigor? What do you think accounts for the survival, within the corpus of much-cited works, of philosophical treatises that *lack* rigor?
5   In §12.3 we listed a dozen special features of mathematics 'in the way majority opinion among philosophers and mathematicians would have them'. And we remarked 'For each such opinion there are always some dissidents'. Formulate a clear and thorough account of any such dissident views about mathematics that you hold, either as a mathematician or as someone who is interested in the nature of the subject quite generally.
6   In §12.7 we wrote 'consistency is not enough for truth'. In mathematics, however, ensuring the consistency of one's theory is a major preoccupation. Mathematicians seem to think that a theory's consistency *does* ensure its truth. Is there a contradiction lurking here?

13 Deduction in Mathematics and Science

In Chapter 8 we were concerned with the contrasts between deductive and inductive validity, and to that end we needed to give some account of deductive proof and disproof. In this chapter, the focus is exclusively on deduction; and we take the liberty of repeating some of the earlier parts of our exposition of the basics of logic, since they are so important, and can never suffer from repetition. It also means that this chapter can be read independently of Chapter 8.

13.1 Proof, truth and falsity

Mathematics and natural science both aim at the truth. Mathematics aims at necessary truths about abstract structures and objects. Natural science, by contrast, aims at law-like truths about the various natural kinds of physical objects and events forming the causal order in space and time. It is a matter of contemporary debate whether these laws are *metaphysically necessary*, even though not *logically necessary*; and it is a problem for contemporary philosophers to explain whether, and if so how, truths differ from truths. We cannot go into these issues here.

Logic serves both mathematics and natural science. Logic does not itself aim at the truth. Rather, it merely *transmits* truth. It transmits truth from the premises to the conclusion of any logically valid argument. It also re-transmits falsity. That is, it re-transmits falsity from the conclusion to the premises of any logically valid argument. Logic provides *proofs* of logically valid arguments. We shall continue to represent a proof schematically as a triangle, with its premises at the top and its conclusion at the bottom:

It is the task of logic to provide means of constructing such proofs for any valid argument.

This is done by means of *rules of inference* that govern the so-called *logical words* (words like *not, and, or, if ... then ..., some, all, ... is identical to ...*) in the premises and conclusion of the argument. The formal symbols often used for these logical words are as follows:

not	¬
and	∧
or	∨
if ... then ...	→
some	∃
all	∀
is identical to	=.

There are of course alternative notational conventions allowing the use of different symbols than those displayed above. (Exactly what it is about a word or phrase that makes it a *logical* one is a topic of considerable controversy among philosophers of logic.)

When an argument is valid – that is, when it transmits truth from its premises to its conclusion – we say that the premises *logically imply* the conclusion, or that the conclusion is a *logical consequence* of the premises.

A proof is a finite piece of discourse that *shows* that a particular argument is valid. Proofs are made up of various steps that are in accordance with the *rules of inference* that govern the aforementioned logical words in the premises and conclusion of the argument. An essential feature of a proof is that one can *tell* (by inspection) that it is indeed a proof, and one can *read off from it* in a straightforward way both the premises and the conclusion of the argument that it establishes as valid.

When we have a proof of the conclusion from the premises, we say that we have *inferred* or *deduced* the conclusion from the premises. In that case we shall write the 'turnstile statement':

Premises ⊢ *Conclusion.*

Recall from Chapter 1 that the symbol ⊢ is called the *turnstile*, and is used to claim the *existence of a proof* showing that the conclusion follows from the premises. The turnstile statement is not itself a proof. It merely asserts the existence of a proof. (In general such a proof would be *much* longer than the turnstile statement.)

The orthodox view is that *whether* an argument is logically valid depends only on the structure of its premises and its conclusion, and *not* on the existence of a proof making clear that it is indeed valid. Thus one could give an argument consisting barely of its premises and conclusion, with no hint as to how to negotiate the route from the former to the latter; and assume that there is a fact of the matter as to whether truth really is transmitted from the premises to the conclusion. A proof would be welcome in *establishing* that fact, and making it evident or certain; but, on this view, the proof would play no role in *constituting* the fact that the argument was valid.

A less orthodox, opposed view is that the validity of any argument is indeed *constituted* by the existence of a proof leading from its premises to its conclusion. So long, however, as we concern ourselves only with systems of logic that do provide proofs for every valid argument, we shall not need to take a stand on this issue for the purposes of the ensuing discussion.

When logicians and philosophers talk about theories, they usually intend the word in an idealized sense: a theory is a set of statements that is *logically closed*, that is, a set already containing all statements that follow logically from it. Thus a theory will contain infinitely many statements, even if only because every statement P logically implies its own double negation: $P \vdash \neg\neg P$. If T is a theory, then a set of axioms for T is any subset of T whose logical closure is T itself. We say that T is *finitely axiomatizable* just in case T has a set of axioms that is finite.

A special case of proof is that of *disproof*: when the conclusion is something absurd. This could either be a contradiction of the form *P and not-P*, or a statement involving *contraries*, such as 'This is solidly green all over now and this is solidly red all over now'. We shall use the so-called *absurdity* symbol ⊥ to register situations of this kind. ⊥ cannot be true. ⊥ is always false. (It is an interesting question whether contrariety is conceptually prior to the notion of sentential negation, and therefore prior also to the formal notion of contradiction afforded by negation and conjunction. Again, however, we cannot pursue this question here.)

When a disproof, or *reductio ad absurdum*, is given:

we know that the premises cannot all be true. At least one of them must be false. We say that they have, collectively, been *reduced to absurdity* by means of the (dis)proof. They have been shown to be *jointly inconsistent*.

Consistency of a theory is *necessary* but not *sufficient* for its truth. A remarkable feature of the deranged stories or world-views of some highly intelligent paranoid schizophrenics is that they are often consistent. As one challenges their statements, they shore them up with more and more bizarre ones. Their story spins on, always coherent, but – the normal observer feels – more and more bizarrely. This should suffice to show that mere consistency, or coherence, is not enough for truth. Not enough for truth in the *actual* world, that is; but that is not to say that *no* possible world could make such a story true. (Problem (6) of Chapter 12 refers.)

13.2 The foundational method in Mathematics

Mathematical proofs proceed from *axioms* that are self-evidently true, via primitively compelling *inferential steps*, to *theorems* as their *conclusions*. The axioms used in a proof are called its *premises*. The conclusions of mathematical proofs can be deep, difficult, elegant and profound results. But – because of their proofs – these conclusions are guaranteed to be true if the axioms are. *Proofs necessarily preserve truth* from their premises to their conclusions.

The proofs themselves provide no guarantee of the truth of the axioms. The axioms have to be intuited as true, or assumed to be true. The proof then gives a logical guarantee that the (assumed) truth of the axioms will *transmit to* the conclusion. This means that the conclusion will be at least as secure as the axioms; but still depends on those axioms for its truth, in the sense that it is the assumed truth of the axioms, plus the logically correct structure of the proof, that furnishes our grounds for believing the conclusion of the proof to be true. Indeed, we are usually *certain* about axioms of Mathematics; that is why we can use them as a foundation for the rest of our mathematical knowledge:

Mathematical Axioms

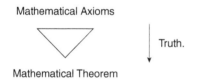 Truth.

Mathematical Theorem

An example of a statement whose truth is not at all obvious, but which can be rendered certain by means of a proof from axioms whose truth *is* obvious, is Pythagoras's Theorem in plane Euclidean geometry. Pythagoras's Theorem states that the area of the square on the hypotenuse (i.e., longest side) of a right-angled triangle is the sum of the squares on the other two sides. This un-obvious claim can be rigorously proved by means of simple logical steps, beginning with those obvious geometrical axioms as starting points.

The geometrical axioms in question are simple claims about points, straight lines and planes, such as that any two points lie on a unique straight line. A full set of such axioms for Euclidean geometry (improving on Euclid himself) was provided by the great mathematical foundationalist David Hilbert. Hilbert's axioms state basic properties of points, lines, incidence, congruence, and betweenness.

So one example of the proof-scheme above would be:

Hilbert's Axioms for Euclidean Geometry

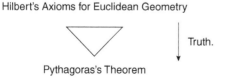 Truth.

Pythagoras's Theorem

This example, like those to follow, points to one of the great puzzles in the philosophy of logic: how can deductive reasoning apparently 'increase information' in this way, if the truth of the conclusion of a deductive proof is *logically guaranteed* by the (assumed) truth of its premises? The logical guarantee is a matter of *necessity*. The increase in information is a matter of *fruitfulness*. The philosophical problem, in a nutshell, is: how can one reconcile the necessity of deduction with its fruitfulness?

Another example of a mathematical theorem, this time one provable from the axioms of number theory, is the statement that every whole number greater than 0 divides into any other whole number a unique whole number of times, and exceeds the (unique) remainder. This is known as the *Remainder Theorem*. In slightly more formal terms, it says:

> For any whole number $n > 0$, and for any whole number m, there is exactly one whole number q, and there is exactly one whole number $r < n$, such that $m = (q \times n) + r$.

The truth of the Remainder Theorem is tacitly assumed whenever we perform 'long division' in order to calculate *the* quotient, and *the* remainder, when one is asked to divide any given whole number (the 'dividend') by a given whole number (the 'divisor') greater than zero.

The axioms of number theory, like the axioms of Euclidean geometry, are simple and self-evident – like the claim that the result of adding 0 to any number is just the number in question: $\forall x\, x + 0 = x$.

The essence of the axiomatic method in Mathematics is that one can start with self-evident claims, and proceed by means of Logic alone to less evident ones. This makes the latter *certain* – because (as is by now becoming our constant refrain) *proofs necessarily preserve truth* from their premises to their conclusions. Here, the premises in question are the mathematical axioms; and the conclusions in question are the theorems proved to follow logically from those axioms.

Correct proof from self-evident axioms always serves to make the conclusion of the proof certain. There are, however, limitations on the potential *scope* of logical-proof-from-axioms. One cannot blithely assume that, given any initially simple-looking mathematical statement, it will be straightforward either to *prove* it or to *disprove* it. An example of a statement that has not yet been been proved true, and has not yet been shown to be false, is Goldbach's Conjecture: *every even number greater than two is the sum of two prime numbers.* Of course, it is quite possible (epistemically speaking) that some clever mathematician will produce a proof of Goldbach's Conjecture tomorrow; or that some computer, busily crunching away at ever-larger even numbers, will in due course find one that is *not* the sum of any two primes preceding it.

Indeed, some writers used to mention 'Fermat's Last Theorem' as their favored example of a simple, interesting general claim about numbers that had been neither proved nor refuted. That example can no longer be used, however, because Andrew Wiles (b. 1953) proved Fermat's Last Theorem at long last, in 1992. It states that for no natural number n greater than 2 can one find non-zero natural numbers a, b and c such that $a^n + b^n = c^n$. Of course, when $n = 2$, we have examples such as $3^2 + 4^2 = 5^2$ – which is why one of the standard illustrations for Pythagoras's Theorem is a right-angled triangle with sides of lengths 3 units and 4 units enclosing the right angle, and a hypotenuse 5 units long. What Fermat's Last Theorem tells us is that there is something very special indeed about that exponent 2, as far as integral multiples of the unit length are concerned.

Another example of our schema for mathematical reasoning would be:

Zermelo's Axioms for Sets

Truth.

Cantor's Theorem

Cantor's Theorem states that every set has strictly more subsets than it has members. (Remarkably, one can prove Cantor's Theorem by appealing only to Zermelo's Axiom Scheme of Separation.) Now the *power set* of any set is the set of all its subsets. So, put another way, Cantor's Theorem says that there is no mapping from any set onto its power set – from which it follows that there is no *one-one* mapping of that kind.

Zermelo's axioms for set theory include simple and obvious-seeming claims such as: given any two sets, one can form a set consisting of just those two sets; given any set, one can form the set of all members of its members, etc. Cantor's Theorem shows how very powerful the *Power Set Axiom* is; that is, the axiom that says that if a set X exists then so does the power set of X. The power set of X will contain strictly more members than X itself. That means that if one postulates the existence of any infinite set such as the set $\{0, 1, 2, \ldots\}$ of natural numbers, then one knows from Cantor's Theorem that its power set will be 'even more infinite'. So, at a stroke, there will be infinitely many infinities – all this from some very innocuous and obvious-seeming axioms about sets. (We discuss this further in §28.4.5.)

Logical proof somehow rearranges the import of the mathematical axioms to reveal surprising, enlightening and profound further results about the mathematical realm being studied. And it does so without going 'beyond' the axioms taken as the starting points of the inquiry. It simply wrings from those axioms new and informative content that was 'already there', so to speak, latent within them. The new truths, arrived at as the conclusions of proofs, are *guaranteed* by the truth of those simple axioms – necessity plus fruitfulness, again.

13.3 Logic and the axiomatic method in Mathematics

So far we have used, as examples, mathematical statements that have been proved. Matters are different with certain other statements that have not been proved *or* refuted – claims whose status as undecided derives from the deeper fact that they are undecid*able* – in the available formal system, assuming it is consistent.

Logicians are involved in the study of statements that may be undecidable on the basis of the axioms at one's disposal. A statement is undecid*able* by a given theory if the theory contains neither the statement nor its negation. (Remember that a theory is logically closed, that is, it contains every statement that it implies.) So an undecidable statement for a given *axiomatized* theory is one that cannot be proved from, nor be proved to be inconsistent with, the axioms of that theory.

Goldbach's Conjecture, as already observed, is at present undecided, but no one knows whether it is undecid*able* (on the basis of our present axioms for number theory).

We do know, however, that arithmetic cannot be completely axiomatized: for any sufficiently strong consistent system A of axioms for arithmetic (number theory), there will be true statements about numbers that cannot be decided by the axioms. This famous result is due to the logician Gödel, and is known as his First Incompleteness Theorem for arithmetic. (Gödel's original proof was given in Gödel (1931).) Gödel's brilliant breakthrough involved constructing a sentence G that was provably equivalent, in the system A, to a sentence which 'said', via arithmetical methods of coding linguistic expressions as numbers, that there is no proof of G in the system A. The First Incompleteness Theorem has been claimed by some philosophers, such as John R. Lucas (b. 1929), to have profound implications for the question whether our minds transcend the limitations in principle on the operation of any machine. (See the anthology Anderson (1964). More recently the 'mind-over-machines' advocates have included Penrose (1989) and McCall (1999). See Tennant (2001) for a rebuttal of McCall.)

Another statement undecidable in A is the number-theoretic codification of the claim *that A is consistent*. This is the humbling impact of Gödel's Second Incompleteness Theorem, which states that no formal system of Mathematics, if both consistent and strong enough to furnish the methods of number-theoretic coding in question, can possibly prove its own consistency-statement. For the system A, this would be the statement to the effect that *there is no proof, in the system A, of the sentence '$0 = 1$'*. The system A cannot prove *that*. It follows from the Second Incompleteness Theorem that we cannot prove the consistency of arithmetic unless we use a system strictly stronger than arithmetic itself.

The Second Incompleteness Theorem also has implications for the foundations of knowledge. It put paid to the so-called Hilbert Program in the foundations of mathematics. Hilbert had aspired to prove the consistency of all mathematics by purely finitary and formalistic means. But the latter means, when codified, yield a theory of numbers strong enough to provide the numerical coding of expressions that Gödel's method exploits. So the finitary theory, if consistent, cannot even prove its *own* consistency, let alone the consistency of a stronger theory such as the Peano–Dedekind theory of arithmetic.

Gödel's original undecidable sentence G was constructed by means of an ingenious, *philosophically informed* recipe of a 'reflexive' kind, inspired by the ancient Liar Paradox 'This sentence is false'. If one assumes this sentence to be false, then one can quickly conclude that it is true. But then what it says is indeed the case – so it is false. Contradiction.

Gödel's inspired variation on the Liar Paradox 'This sentence is false' was to put 'unprovable-in-the-system' in place of 'false', by considering the sentence 'This sentence is unprovable-in-the-system'. If it is provable in the system, then the system is inconsistent. But the system is consistent. So the sentence is unprovable in the system. From this one can quickly conclude that it is true. So all one needs is a way of constructing a sentence G in the language of arithmetic that can be shown, somehow, to 'say of itself' that it is *unprovable* (in the system $\mathcal{A}$). Then G would have to be *true* (provided, of course, that $\mathcal{A}$ is consistent).

It was of course an extremely ingenious and complicated construction that resulted in such a sentence G. Keeping track of what G 'means' (in the reflexive way just explained) involves a great deal of definitional abbreviation. The result is that when G is actually written out in primitive notation, with all the definitions 'unwound', it is an excessively long and complicated sentence in the language of arithmetic, making no readily graspable or intrinsically interesting claim about the numbers themselves. Its *philosophical* interest resides solely in the devilishly clever way in which the aforementioned motivating ideas found their expression through Gödel's pioneering method of coding. Expressions of a formal language can be coded (within the formal arithmetical theory) as numbers, and one can therefore (within that theory) represent grammatical and logical properties of, and relations among, sentences and proofs as properties of, and relations among, their code-numbers. *This* is what enables one to construct a sentence in the formal language of the system that 'says of itself' that it is unprovable within the system.

Since Gödel's original breakthrough, however, mathematical logicians and foundationalists have come up with more 'natural' examples of statements in the language of arithmetic that can be proved to be undecidable in the system consisting of the usual axioms for arithmetic.

In the more powerful and all-embracing system of set theory, as opposed to 'mere' number theory, there have been two celebrated principles whose 'decidability status' (on the basis of other axioms) was of intense and lasting interest dating from the time they were each formulated. We are speaking here of the *Axiom of Choice* and the *Continuum Hypothesis*.

The Axiom of Choice (AC) seems, intuitively, to be true. In order to express it, it is useful to have the concept of a 'choice set' for any set of pairwise disjoint sets.

Definition 5. *Let X be a set of pairwise disjoint sets. Then Y is a choice set for X just in case*

  (i) every member of Y is in a member of X; and (ii) every member Z of X has exactly one member in common with Y.

The Axiom of Choice then says:

  (AC) For every set X of pairwise disjoint sets, there exists a choice set for X.

It is easy to picture the upshot of the Axiom of Choice (see below). The picture makes the Axiom of Choice seem plausible. The distinct horizontal rectangles represent the members of X, and their members are the boldface bullets indicated. The choice set for X is composed by choosing one member from each member of X, so as to form a set like the one represented by the slender vertical rectangle on the right. It 'stands to reason' that, if those chosen bullets had to exist in order to help make up each of the respective members of X, then they should be available for re-arrangement, as chosen, so as to form the choice set displayed. The choice set exists 'at the same level of complexity', as it were, as do the member-sets of the set X itself. By an intuitive 'principle of plenitude' – that we should be able to form as many distinct sets as are logically possible, given the materials for membership already at hand – it seems to us that such a choice set ought, surely, to exist.

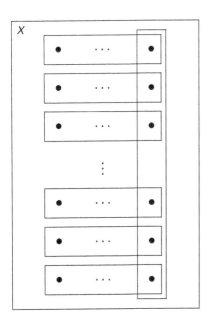

AC has been shown to be undecidable on the basis of the axiom-system ZF of Zermelo–Fraenkel set theory (assuming that ZF is consistent). Gödel himself showed that there is a structure (the so-called 'constructible universe' of sets) that makes all the axioms of ZF true, and makes AC true. (See Gödel (1940) for a full treatment. The results were announced by abstracts in 1938 and 1939.) Later, Paul Cohen (1934–2007) showed that there is also a structure that makes all the axioms of ZF true, but makes AC *false*. (See Cohen (1963), Cohen (1964).) Hence (respectively) there can be neither a disproof nor a proof of AC in ZF.

AC in the context of ZF is therefore similar to Euclid's Parallels Postulate in the context of the remaining axioms of Euclid's geometry. Euclidean space is a structure that makes those remaining axioms true, *and* makes the Parallels Postulate true. But there are also well-defined geometrical structures that make the remaining axioms true, *but* make the Parallels Postulate *false*. The first such structure to be described was that of Beltrami (1868). The straight lines of Lobachevskian geometry were identified with certain curves on three-dimensional, 'pseudospherical' surfaces embedded *within Euclidean space*. Under this interpretation, all the postulates of Lobachevskian geometry were satisfied, including the non-Euclidean postulate to the effect that through any point p off a given line l there are *exactly two* lines, called the *extremals*, that do not meet l in any point, and between which all (the infinitely many) lines passing through p do not meet l either. (In some presentations of Lobachevskian geometry, only the extremals are called parallels of l. See, for example, Kagan (1957), at pp. 37–38.) This furnished a model-theoretic proof of the relative consistency of the two geometries: if three-dimensional Euclidean geometry is consistent, then so too is Lobachevskian plane geometry.

Apprised now of the logical independence of Euclid's Parallels Postulate from the other axioms of Euclidean geometry, the Euclidean geometer is happy to acknowledge that the Parallels Postulate is an explicit 'first principle' of that system of geometry. It is indispensable for the pursuit of truths about Euclidean space.

Likewise, the modern set theorist is now happy to acknowledge that the Axiom of Choice is an explicit 'first principle' of the system of axioms that seeks to uncover the most important truths concerning 'the' set-theoretic universe V. The system ZFC consists of the axioms of Zermelo–Fraenkel set theory along with the Axiom of Choice. Most foundationally aware mathematicians nowadays take ZFC as their working basis.

We turn now to the Continuum Hypothesis (CH). This celebrated conjecture is to the effect that

> every infinite set of real numbers is either countable or in one-one correspondence with the set of all real numbers.

Thus the infinity of real numbers (also known as *the cardinality of the continuum*) is the next-greatest infinity after that of the natural numbers. Put another way: the cardinality of the continuum is the *first* uncountable infinity. CH is therefore to the effect that the real numbers, which, as we know from Cantor's Theorem, are more numerous than the natural numbers, are *minimally* so. They enjoy the very next measure of infinity after that of the natural numbers.

Gödel's constructible universe of sets is one in which not only AC, but also CH is true. Hence one cannot *disprove* CH in ZFC. Cohen's achievement was to construct a universe of sets that makes the axioms of ZFC true, but makes CH *false*. Hence one cannot *prove* CH in ZFC either.

In fact, CH is independent not only of ZFC, but also of various powerful extensions of ZFC that involve postulating the existence of very large cardinal numbers. The independence of CH is proving to be intractably robust. The issue of the 'genuine' cardinality of the continuum is as elusive as it has ever been. The very first problem on Hilbert's famous list of unsolved problems was to settle the question of the cardinality of the continuum. For over a century now, this question has remained unanswered (except in the thinly negative sense supplied by the independence results themselves).

13.4 Logic and scientific method

In §13.2, we have been at pains to stress that deductive reasoning in Mathematics takes one *downwards* from axioms, or first principles, to theorems as conclusions. The axioms are self-evidently true. It is the theorems that are the deep and interesting results.

In the *natural sciences*, the logical direction is reversed. The analogue of a self-evidently true mathematical axiom is an *observation statement* or *datum* (plural: *data*) – a statement that one can tell to be true simply by perceiving things. But observation statements have no generality. They hold only for a particular time and place.

Scientific hypotheses, by contrast, are often deep, elegant, profound – and highly *general*. They make claims about *all* things of a given natural kind, and usually do so with precise mathematical formulations of relationships among various theoretical magnitudes (such as mass, force, acceleration, energy, momentum …). So these hypotheses, from the point of view of interest, generality and the *non-obviousness* of their truth, serve as analogues of mathematical theorems.

Scientific explanations employ important hypotheses as *premises* (*not* as conclusions), along with statements of *boundary conditions* and *initial conditions* (of a given system under observation in a controlled experiment, say). From these statements the scientist deduces, as a conclusion, *either* an observational *prediction* about the behavior of the system in some observable respect (at some time, in some place); *or* some 'lower level' generalization about the objects in the system.

An example of the first type of prediction would be *Halley's Comet will be seen at such-and-such a time on such-and-such date, at such-and-such position in the sky*.

An example of the second type of 'prediction' would be the lower-level generalization *All planets in our solar system have (approximately) elliptical orbits around the sun at one focus of the ellipse*. Notice that what is here called a prediction is not necessarily a statement about the future, whose truth-value has not yet been determined by experience. Rather, it can be a statement that we already take ourselves to have good reason to believe, on the basis of past observational data. The last example was of this kind.

Johannes Kepler (1571–1630) formulated this hypothesis (his so-called First Law of Planetary Motion) – which, despite the label 'Law', is nevertheless *conjectural* – after studying the observational data collected by Tycho Brahe (1546–1601). In such a case, the higher-level scientific hypotheses that imply the law in question will be said to provide an explanation of its (assumed) truth. And failure to imply the lower-level law (in the absence of any independent reason to doubt it) would be a mark held against the higher-level hypotheses, rather than in favor of them.

The triumph of Newton's Laws of Motion and Law of Universal Gravitation was that, in conjunction with certain boundary and initial conditions, they *logically implied* Kepler's three laws of planetary motion:

1 Each planet travels in an elliptical orbit around the sun at one focus.
2 The radius of the orbit sweeps out equal areas in equal times.
3 The square of any planet's 'year' is proportional to the cube of its mean (i.e., average) distance from the sun.

Kepler excogitated these laws from the observational data due to Tycho Brahe.

Brahe took pains not only with his astronomical observations, but also in other areas of his life. Another of his claims to fame was a brass (some say: silver) nose (some say: part of his nose) to replace the one he lost in a duel (some say: to syphilis), not over a woman (some say), but over a mathematical point. The actual cause of Brahe's death is a matter of great speculation and controversy too. On one account, he was too polite to excuse himself from a royal banquet, and his bladder burst, leading to his death shortly afterwards. On another account, he was given mercury (around the time of the banquet) in his nightcap of hot milk by none other than his assistant, *Kepler* – who, so this theory goes, resorted to this desperate measure in order to gain access to Brahe's huge collection of observational data about the positions of stars and planets in the night sky. (See Gilder and Gilder (2004).)

The logical structure of Newton's explanation of Kepler's laws of planetary motion takes the following form, where the direction of logical deduction is downwards:

Mathematical
axioms   Scientific hypotheses
⋮   of great generality
Mathematical   (such as Newton's laws   Boundary and
theorems   ,   of motion and gravitation)   ,   initial conditions

⋮

Lower-level law about a certain class of phenomena
(such as one of Kepler's laws of planetary motion)

The claim that motion under gravitational attraction will trace a conic (the 'lower-level law' in question) was the *conclusion* of a scientific argument, or proof. In the foregoing display, the direction of logical inference is to be understood as *downwards*.

The *premises* for the deduction are, ultimately, the mathematical axioms, the scientific hypotheses, and the statements of boundary and initial conditions. In the case of a planet in an elliptical orbit Newton required only certain *initial* conditions in order to generate predictions as to the future whereabouts of a planet whose present position and velocity are known. Other problem-settings, however, call for statements of *boundary* conditions as well. Such is the case, for example, when one specifies a closed surface in space, with values for various vector fields specified on that surface at time $t = 0$ (or indeed for the duration of the experiment).

The premises mentioned occupy tips of the branches of the foregoing 'proof tree'. The conclusion – say, a lower-level law about motion on conics – is placed at the root. The proof is deductive, hence logically valid. *If* its premises are true, *then* its conclusion is true also. Concerning that inferential transition, there is no possible doubt.

Kepler's second law (that the radius of a planet's orbit sweeps out equal areas in equal times) can be shown to hold just in case whatever force is acting on the planet – be it attractive or repulsive – is on a line *through the center of mass of the Sun*. The fact that the orbits are *closed* (since they are elliptical) means that this force has to be attractive, rather than repulsive. But how big is this force? How does it vary through time? What does it depend on?

Newton's inspired answer was that this centripetal, *gravitational* (i.e., attractive) force was proportional to the product of the two masses (of the Sun and planet), and inversely proportional to the square of the distance between them. Hence it is now called the *inverse-square law of gravitation*. When the mathematical details are deduced, it turns out that the inverse-square form of the force-law nicely accounts for Kepler's first and third laws as well. (Remember, the centripetal nature of the force acting on any planet accounts for the second law.)

When one thinks about the problem in broad qualitative terms, the inverse-square law makes intuitive sense. Given Kepler's second law, the planet would be travelling more and more slowly through space as it moved farther and farther from the Sun. It would be travelling fastest when closest to the Sun; hence the attractive force would have to be greatest at that point, to 'whip the planet round' the tightest part of its orbit. At this point the radius is at its minimum, hence also its square. Thus the inverse of that square is at its greatest – which is what the force needs to be. Similarly, the planet would be slowed down to its lowest speed as it reached the point farthest from the Sun. At that point it would need only a weaker tug of gravity in order to be drawn back nearer the Sun at the more distant of the two foci of the planet's elliptical orbit. And the gravitational force is indeed at its weakest at this point, since that is where the inverse square is at its minimum. So much for rough intuitive sense ... What is needed for the more precise mathematical details concerning the elliptical nature of planetary orbits, and especially for the third law, depends on the very specific mathematical form of the inverse-square law. We cannot broach these details here. The reader will find them in Tennant (2010).

To repeat, so as to drive the point home: by framing his *hypotheses* – his 'source-law' of universal gravitation, along with his hypothetical laws of motion (hypothesizing how it is that forces cause bodies to accelerate) – Newton was able to *deduce* Kepler's laws, which themselves were low-level generalizations extracted from extensive observational data. Here we have a paradigm of hypothetico-deductive explanation.

Newton's dynamical theory held sway until the end of the nineteenth century, when it was eventually discovered that it could not account satisfactorily for the precession of the perihelion of Mercury. It was also discovered that the speed of light appeared to be constant in all inertial frames. This experimental finding (by Michelson and Morley) made it extremely difficult for the combination of Newtonian mechanics and Maxwellian electromagnetism to make sense of all electromagnetic phenomena. Around this time also, investigations of the interior of the atom were uncovering phenomena that could not be explained within the Newtonian theory. Something had to give. Or, rather, something had to *overthrow* or *displace* Newton's so-called 'classical' view of the world, in the small and in the large. The displacing theories were special relativity (Einstein) and quantum mechanics (Einstein, Bohr, Schrödinger, Heisenberg), respectively.

In addition, Newton's hypotheses explained (or correctly predicted) a host of other phenomena, from disparate domains: ocean tides; motions of pendula; motions of vibrating strings; motions of waves in elastic media; motions of projectiles, etc. When a high-level theory like this *unifies* disparate phenomena, it counts heavily in favor of the theory. For then all the different phenomena are understood as manifestations, in different settings, of the same underlying regularities in the world that are given expression in the theory.

As we saw in §8.6, if observation bears out any prediction of our hypotheses, our belief in the hypotheses will be strengthened; but if it contradicts the prediction, our belief might be weakened – even to the point of *dis*belief. Logically, however, we can say that scientific hypotheses whose predictions have not yet been contradicted by experience and observation are nevertheless not conclusively proved. Rather, they are only as-yet-unfalsified. For no finite amount of evidence (which is all we ever have at any stage of our investigations) could ever logically imply the truth of scientific hypotheses that make *universal* claims.

There could always be unexpected instances, or happenings, that would falsify the hypotheses. One cannot rule out this logical possibility. (This principled skepticism, as discussed in §8.4, we owe to David Hume.) So, even though a theory might have passed the test of experience thus far, this affords no logical guarantee that it will continue to do so. It might be falsified some time in the future. Indeed, its potential falsifiability is what some philosophers of science take to be the hallmark of a genuinely *scientific* theory. They say that a theory has no real 'cognitive significance' unless one could specify in advance what consistent, imaginable course of experience would count as *falsifying* the theory.

It was Karl Popper who first clarified this view of the logical role of scientific hypotheses in providing predictions and explanations of phenomena. The main thesis of Popperianism is that no matter how well our scientific theories have fared thus far, they are nevertheless still only *conjectural, hypothetical, speculative,* and potentially *falsifiable.* We only ever *assume* scientific hypotheses, as premises in proofs that provide predictions (observation statements) as their conclusions. No matter how many successful predictions we make, there will be only finitely many of them. And this is not enough to exhaust the logical content of an hypothesis whose logical form is that of a universal generalization. No finite set of data can logically imply a universal conclusion. So our hypotheses cannot themselves be proved from the evidence we have for them, no matter how certain we may be about the evidence itself. Thus we can never attain the same kind of certainty about our hypotheses as we do about those mathematical statements that we have proved as conclusions from self-evident axioms.

Sometimes the theoretical hypotheses invoke theoretical or unobservable entities such as quarks, photons and electrons. We entertain only those hypotheses that are based on or supported by the evidence. It is controversial whether there is any such thing as an inductive logic that would validate the transition from finite bits of evidence to hypotheses of universal form.

The exact nature of this 'support' is a deep problem in the theory of knowledge and the philosophy of science. It is known as the *problem of induction.*

To recapitulate the lesson of Chapter 8: so-called inductive logic (if there is such a thing) would allow us to pass from the bits of evidence, as premises, to our general hypotheses, as conclusions. The pattern would be this:

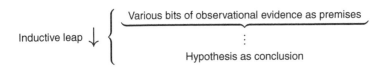

The evidence would at best make the conclusion highly probable; it would not provide a logical guarantee of its truth. The inductive leap is not deductively valid. Good theoretical hypotheses, as we saw above, do not just summarize the evidence and say no more. Rather, they 'go beyond' the evidence on which they are based. For they imply predictions about the behavior of systems, or the distribution of characteristics in a population, or the motions of heavenly bodies, etc., that have not yet been observed or measured. In doing so, they allow us to anticipate the course of our future experience, and to exercise some control over future events.

Note that the predictions are *deductively implied by* the hypotheses. Deductive logic would yield proofs of the downward passages in the following schema:

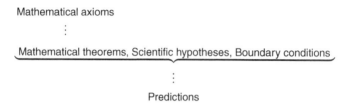

But our observations and measurements may conflict with, or disagree with, or contradict our predictions:

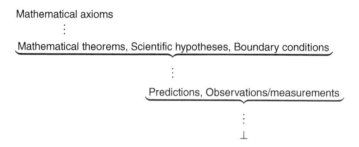

In such a situation we are (rationally) forced to revise our theoretical hypotheses. They have been put to experimental test, and have been found wanting.

13.5 Theory revision

The problem of how to revise one's theories in the light of new conflicting evidence has recently become very important in computing science. So-called expert systems with data bases are programmed to simulate human knowledge and principled understanding of various aspects of the world (oil-drilling; the legal system; automatic piloting; medical diagnosis). They have to up-date their data, and sometimes revise their principles if they are to perform satisfactorily. To do so (that is: for us to be able to make them do so) we have to understand the logic of theory change, or theory dynamics, as it is now known. We may, of course, refuse to revise our theoretical hypotheses in the face of conflicting evidence. We may decide instead to blame our microscopes or our telescopes or our measuring apparatus ('bad data'). Or we may doubt whether the boundary conditions for the experiment were properly controlled ('bad control'). Or we may just hang on to our hypotheses at all costs, because they are the best we have, and choose to disregard the new evidence ('it was a fluke'; 'unrepeatable result').

The problem of where, exactly, to lay the blame in a situation like this – whether to fault the theoretical hypotheses or the 'data' or other auxiliary assumptions – is known as the *Quine–Duhem problem*, after the two philosophers who emphasized its importance for methodology. A few more words about the extent of this problem are in order.

13.5.1 The Quine–Duhem problem

If we make a prediction from tried and tested hypotheses, and subsequent observations *conflict* with, or *contradict* what we predicted, we may cast doubt on *any* of the following.

1 *The new evidence.* Did we *really* make those observations correctly? Were those readings correct? Can we trust our senses in this instance? Might we have been distracted? Did we record incorrectly what we saw?
2 *The boundary conditions.* Did we control them properly during the experiment? Did we monitor them thoroughly enough?
3 *Auxiliary assumptions about our measuring equipment.* Was the equipment properly calibrated? Will it reliably produce the same readings in another situation exactly like the one in the last experiment? Did it malfunction? Was it influenced in some way of which we were unaware, and which would invalidate its readings?
4 *The hypotheses themselves.* Might they *really* have been shown to be false, at long last, in this new experimental situation, after surviving all the tests to which they have been subjected in the past?

It is the whole set of premises, consisting of hypotheses, auxiliary assumptions about measuring equipment, statements of boundary conditions, and experimental observations, which is reduced to falsity or absurdity. The problem now would be: what statement(s) are we to find at fault within that set?

13.6 Desiderata of a scientific theory

1 The theory should *explain all the available evidence.* When the theory is conjoined with suitable statements of initial conditions, boundary conditions, etc., of the system whose behavior it is describing, it should logically imply the observation statements that form the evidence about its behavior through time.
2 The theory should make testable predictions. By conjoining the theory with suitable statements of initial conditions, boundary conditions, etc. (which can be controlled experimentally), it should logically imply observation statements concerning the outcome of those experiments. It should be possible for those observational predictions to be *false*, so that the theory itself is *falsifiable*.

3   The theory should withstand several experimental tests *after* it has been formulated and entertained as good scientific conjecture.
4   The theory should be *economical*. It should not 'multiply entities beyond necessity' (Occam's Razor). The entities that it posits (such as molecules, atoms, electrons...) should be posited only because they enable one to make genuine explanatory and predictive advances.
5   The theory should be *formulated as simply as possible*. This is a requirement partially met by mathematical elegance and tractability, symmetries, level of generality, etc.
6   The theory should *unify disparate ranges of observable phenomena*. It should seek common patterns and mechanisms at the root of the apparent variety in observable phenomena. An example of a good theory in this regard is the Newtonian theory of mass, forces (including gravitational force), and motion. This theory provides good explanations and predictions concerning the following disparate ranges of phenomena:

- the motions of:
    - the planets around the sun
    - a simple pendulum
    - a spinning and precessing top
    - ripples and waves in water
    - a projectile near the Earth's surface
    - falling bodies near the Earth's surface

- the action of the tides;
- the vibrations of a plucked guitar string;
- the altitude of a communications satellite in stationary orbit above the Earth's surface;
- the centripetal force to be exerted by an athlete in the Olympic hammer throw.

13.7 A look ahead to the Argument from Design

The Argument from Design for God's existence (see Chapter 16) is best understood as providing a competing 'scientific' explanation of the observed phenomena of design, complexity, adaptation, etc., that tend to provoke reactions of admiration, wonder, and awe in the observer. *That an all-powerful, purposeful Designer exists* is a high-level hypothesis *from which* one is supposed to be able to deduce the facts of design as we observe them. Thus it is a rival to the naturalist's postulation, instead, of a causal process of random variation and selective retention, which is maintained to have produced the same observed results.

The way to counter the Argument from Design is to judge it on its merits as a proposed scientific explanation; and that is where the criteria listed above would be relevant. The way to criticize the Argument from Design is to contrast its explanatory and predictive power, and its ability to unify disparate ranges of phenomena, with those of alternative naturalistic theories – such as Big Bang cosmology, neo-Darwinian evolutionary theory, and cognitive neuroscience – that attempt to give an account of the origin, evolution and function of complex physical systems.

In this regard the Argument from Design is *unlike* the Ontological Argument and the Cosmological Argument for God's existence (see Chapter 15). The latter two arguments attempt (by philosophical consensus: *fallaciously*) to establish God's existence as a certain conclusion of a 'conceptual' *proof*. This is very different from entertaining God's existence as an *explanatory hypothesis*, as is done by the Argument from Design. The way to criticize the Ontological Argument and the Cosmological Argument is to locate conceptual confusions and/or fallacious moves within the argument, or falsehoods among its premises, so as to show that the argument's conclusion is not secured as true.

Problems

Your responses are best attempted after a careful reading of the chapter, but without returning to the text to recover main ideas or details.

1   Briefly explain Karl Popper's views about the logical character of scientific theories.
2   Briefly explain what the Quine–Duhem Problem is.
3   What are the *desiderata* of a good scientific theory?
4   What is the contrast in logical role between mathematical theorems and scientific hypotheses?
5   How was Gödel's breakthrough idea in proving the incompleteness of arithmetic inspired by the Liar Paradox?
6   Does set theory, with its greater scope and power than arithmetic, manage to decide every sentence of its language?

14 The Methodological Issue of Reductionism

14.1 Levels of reality

The part/whole relation generates a conception of levels of reality. Quarks are parts of protons; protons are parts of atoms; atoms are parts of molecules and macromolecules; macromolecules are parts of cells; cells are parts of bodies; bodies are parts of colonies, herds and societies. Corresponding to these compositional or mereological 'slicings' of the world are the different disciplines that study them: fundamental particle physics; chemistry; molecular biology; histology; anatomy (and individual psychology); sociology, group psychology, economics ...

Or, to take a slightly different route up a different hierarchy of containment: once one reaches molecules, jump to 'physical body' (in the sense of 'lump of stuff'); clusters of physical bodies; clusters of clusters of physical bodies; ... and so on. Then we have the sciences of mechanics and cosmology getting their look-in. Planets with their moons, solar systems, galaxies, and super-galaxies are simply larger and larger clusters of physical objects. There is a bewildering array of levels, and a bewildering array of alternative vocabularies (even in the same language, such as scientific English) tailored to the description of each of these levels. Thus the physicists speak of quarks, leptons, hadrons; the chemists speak of elements, compounds, ions, radicals, valencies, bonds; the molecular biologist speaks of genes, chromosomes, alleles, recombination, replication; the histologist speaks of organelles, mitochondria, membranes, cytoplasm; the anatomist speaks of tissues, organs, etc.; the individual psychologist speaks of memory, perception, learning by trial and error, reinforcement, cross-modal associations; the sociologist speaks of group attitudes, peer group pressure, delinquency, leadership, poverty, exploitation; the economist speaks of income groups, demand, supply, exchange rates, balance of trade, levels of unemployment, capital.

Each one of these theorists makes a choice of systems and their characteristic kinds of behavior, and takes these characteristics as their objects of study. Each one uses basic terms appropriate to the features and behavior of objects discerned as important for and at that chosen level.

Now it may turn out that one discerns important features at any given level by attending to what goes on at a higher level. Thus a molecular biologist is interested in DNA making up genes because of the effects manifested at the organismic or phenotypic level, when the genetic information is expressed. A neurologist might be interested in the effect of pheromone molecules on the brain stem because of how it is implicated in riots at football games.

Each of the theorists is interested *mainly* in what might be called, for his or her discipline, the *centrally leveled* explanations of the behavior of the characteristic objects of study. Such explanations are given at the chosen level. They invoke, or make reference to, only such forces, influences, pressures, powers, etc., as are manifest at that level. Thus the sociologist might seek to explain football riots in terms of totemism, inter-group rivalry, initiation rituals, machismo, betting habits, drunkenness, poverty, disappointment over the team's performance, … All these are states, conditions or forces 'at the same level' as yobbish behavior.

Each theorist in turn is at times forced to look 'downwards' and 'inwards' to come up with explanations that at last marshal the real forces that are doing the work. Thus the sociologist, coming up empty-handed (or with hands only half-full) when looking at all the social forces at work on the football rioters, might have to turn to the neurologist and organic chemist in order to completely explain football riots, by invoking the effects of micromolecules (pheromones) floating in the air. Pheromones are chemical messengers that can have profound effects on animals without their being in any way aware of them. (Sexual attraction is saturated with them.)

There are also practitioners of some of these disciplines who sometimes look 'upwards' to the next level in search of such explanations if they cannot find them at the chosen level or at any lower level. An example would be the practitioners of cybernetics, the science of systems behavior with feedback loops. In the loose hierarchy of scientific disciplines, ranging from hard physics to soft sociology, each discipline can draw on mechanisms characterised by the discipline below, and indeed often does. There is a general tendency, reinforced by past explanatory success, to look downwards and inwards for efficient explanations of behavior of the things in which one is interested. By looking *downwards* we mean looking to the discipline concerned primarily with the behavior of things at the 'next level down'. By looking *inwards* we mean that one looks inside the objects for causal structures and mechanisms mediated by their constituents.

We are thinking here more of animate objects than of inanimate ones. For Newton's theory of gravitation was certainly not arrived at by looking downwards and inwards into apples. He looked, rather, at the planet under his feet and was struck by his idea that way.

Perhaps the most striking success story of the downward- and inward-looking method is that of molecular biology. The discovery of the universal genetic code, and the mechanism of replication, provides a bridge between organic chemistry and evolutionary biology. Perhaps the most exciting – or chilling – prospect is that a downward- and inward-looking methodology will one day furnish a complete account of the psychological workings of the human mind solely in terms of the underlying neurological reality: the network of neurons, joined by axons and dendrites, that form the gray matter of the brain. This would be a triumphant example of reductionism, if ever it could be achieved.

We need, however, to be aware of these chilling prospects *even in the absence* of any genuine, thoroughgoing reduction of psychological theorizing to neurophysiological theorizing in the sense already explained in §6.13. It would be 'enough already' if researchers at some drug company happened upon a robust 'bridge law' connecting (in isolation, as it were) some particular aspect of neurophysiology with some particular aspect of our mental lives. For then they could intervene pharmaceutically to 'treat' certain mental conditions – or to meddle with our minds, depending on one's values. The danger of exploiting bridge laws discovered in isolation, and not formulated within a comprehensive reduction, is that one will begin one's interventions and manipulations at the lower level without fully appreciating the various side-effects they will cause – effects at the higher level at which the symptoms to be allayed arise. Who would wish to calm an energetic, or even rambunctious, child with brain-altering drugs if the unanticipated long-term effect were to be an irreversible erosion of intelligence, or of emotional warmth, or of focus and self-discipline?

14.2 Reductionism

We return to the task (begun in §6.13) of explaining what, in general, is meant by reductionism. As philosophers commonly understand it, reduction is a relation between theories designed to describe different levels of reality. Theories are framed within a chosen vocabulary. When two theories concern different levels, those vocabularies may not have much in common. All the more arresting, then, if one of those theories can be *reduced* to the other, in the following sense:

> T_2 reduces to T_1
>   if and only if
> one can define the terms of T_2 as logical complexes of terms of T_1; and one can use those definitions to derive within T_1 all the statements of T_2 as (suitably re-written) statements of T_1.

This is the strict sense in which reductionism is understood in the philosophy of science. Its explication in the foregoing form is due to one of the visiting members of the Vienna Circle, Ernest Nagel (1901–85) – see Nagel (1961). The claim that T_2 reduces to T_1 implies, but is not implied by, the claim that the second level of reality in question (the one described by the second theory T_2) *supervenes* on the first level of reality (the one described by the first theory T_1).

> One level L_2 (commonly called the 'higher' one) supervenes on another level L_1 (commonly called the 'lower' one)
>   if and only if
> by fixing all the facts (in general, over time) at the level L_1 one thereby fixes all the facts at the level L_2.

A prime example of supervenience, according to the physicalist, is that of mental states (and processes) supervening on brain states (and processes). If we fix all the facts about the brain (in a metaphorical sense of 'fix', of course – suppose, if you will, that God sees to it) then we (or God; or laws of metaphysics perhaps beyond our ken) *ipso facto* fix all the facts about the mental life of the person whose brain it is.

To make the idea vivid, suppose the person in question now believes that p, and does not believe that not-p. His brain is in some total state S. For him to be believing that not-p, his brain would have to be in some different state S'. Fixing the lower-level facts fixes the higher-level facts. The higher-level facts could not be otherwise except in so far as the lower-level facts were permissively and appropriately otherwise too. The inventory of lower-level facts makes possible only one true higher-level story of all that is going on at the higher level.

To claim that a higher level supervenes in this sense on a lower level is a way of having one's metaphysical cake and eating it. One is acknowledging the importance and priority of the lower level, since it determines the higher level. The issue is one-sided: only one level (the lower one, L_1) does the determining, and the other level (the higher one, L_2) is determined. Thus one can maintain, say, the overriding importance of the physical level of reality (L_1) for all of psychology and social science (L_2). The physical facts (L_1) fix the mental, social and economic facts (L_2). But at the same time the supervenience theorist *need not be committed to the claim that the higher-level theory T_2 that describes the level L_2 can be reduced (even if only in principle) to the lower-level theory T_1 describing level L_1*. That is, the supervenience theorist need not seek to undermine the theoretical autonomy of the higher-level disciplines, such as psychology, sociology, and economics. Indeed, those disciplines would retain their utility and autonomy even if reduction-in-principle were possible, provided only that the reduction in question were not *feasible*. (See §6.13 for the contrast between reduction-in-principle and feasible reduction.)

To see that reductionism implies supervenience is easy. The higher-level facts described by the theory T_2 are, by virtue of the reduction, being described by logical complexes in the lower-level vocabulary of the theory T_1. So obviously the lower-level facts are going to fix the 'higher-level' facts. This is because the higher-level facts are, given the reduction, simply lower-level facts in a complex disguise. The reduction provides the disguise for the higher-level facts, as it were, but also, in so doing, reveals them for what they really are.

14.2.1 Does supervenience imply reductionism? An investigation of the philosophical implications of Beth's Definability Theorem

To see that supervenience does not imply reductionism is not at all easy. Indeed, some foundationalists and methodologists might urge that the relevantly qualified jury is still out on this question. It behooves us now to examine in greater detail the nature of the case adverted to in §6.13 – the one that invokes

Beth's Definability Theorem in mathematical logic. (The theorem is due to Beth (1953). The form in which we shall invoke it was proved in Robinson (1956).)

This theorem, which we shall proceed to explain, concerns the so-called *first-order languages* of logic. In such languages, one can generalize about individuals, but one cannot generalize about their properties and relations. One can of course still make statements about any or all individuals having *particular* properties, or standing in *particular* relations – witness 'John is bald', '17 is prime'; 'John loves Mary', '17 is less than 21'; 'Everyone loves someone', 'Every number is less than some number'. But one cannot say such things as 'John is everything but a mentor to Mary', or '17 has all the properties enjoyed by any prime number'.

Despite this apparent expressive limitation, however, first-order languages are the prime choice of both mathematicians and scientists when it comes to expressing their theories' first principles or hypotheses in a rigorous way, and developing their consequences – so much so that Quine, the great regimenter, called first-order languages 'Grade A idiom'. The great advantage of Grade A idiom is that it affords us *total deductive control*, by way of compensating for its occasional expressive limitations. Anything that follows logically from what we say using Grade A idiom can be *proved* from the same, in finite and effectively checkable fashion. (Thus first-order language resolves the Noncompossibility expounded in Chapter 29 in favor of maximizing deductive power, rather than maximizing expressive power.)

So much by way of cautionary stage-setting: Beth's Definability Theorem (which we have yet to state) applies primarily to Grade A idiom (a.k.a. first-order languages). It applies also to sundry infinitary languages, and to certain fragments of second-order languages. There are also languages for which it is known *not* to hold; but these would be unlikely contenders for the title of 'The Formal Language of Ideal Total Science'. So the interesting question that would immediately arise, of course, is whether Beth's Definability Theorem can be proved for such language as is needed in order to express the *combination* of the higher-level theory T_2 and its lower-level counterpart T_1.

The reason why it is so important to know whether Beth's Definability Theorem applies to what ends up being our language of choice for 'total science' is this: *if* the Theorem applies, and *if* the supervenience thesis is true (namely, that the facts at Level 1 fix all the facts at Level 2), *then* reduction-in-principle (of our theory T_2 about Level 2 to our theory T_1 about Level 1) is guaranteed by Beth's Theorem.

How does this work? We offer here some necessarily informal explanation of the terms in which Beth's Definability Theorem is stated, and how these relate to the methodological discussion at hand of levels of fact and levels of theorizing.

The supervenience theorist employs a certain lower-level vocabulary V_1 (consisting of what the logician would call primitive *function symbols* and primitive *predicates*) to describe the lower-level facts about individual things. Remember, this description covers not only particular 'factoids', but also the law-like *regularities* in the behavior and properties of those things – behavior and properties appropriately described *at the lower level*.

The supervenience theorist *also* employs a certain higher-level vocabulary V_2 (consisting, again, of what the logician would call primitive *function symbols* and primitive *predicates*) to describe the higher-level facts about individual things. Once again, this description covers not only particular 'factoids', but also the law-like *regularities* in the behavior and properties of those things – behavior and properties appropriately described *at the higher level*.

These two levels of theorizing do not, in general, pass each other by like ships in the night, making no connection with each other. On the contrary, within the picture of 'total science' there will also be various connections made 'between the levels'. A simple example will make the point. Damage to certain localized regions of the brain is known to impair or destroy various cognitive faculties – memory, or aspects of linguistic competence, or impulse control. Any adequate 'total theory' combining our descriptions of both the mental facts and the neurophysiological facts would have to postulate these basic connections between parts of the brain (when functioning normally) and possession of the relevant cognitive capacities by the person whose brain it is. (These are examples of what are called 'φ-ψ correlations' in §23.4.)

The upshot, then, is that our *total theory* Θ describing the world both at Level 1 and at Level 2 will be employing primitive terms from both the lower-level vocabulary V_1 and the higher-level vocabulary V_2, not only to describe each level separately ('in its own terms', so to speak), but also to describe various interconnections *between* the two levels. Let this now be tacitly understood when we use the notation $\Theta(V_1, V_2)$ for our total theory.

Assume – very idealistically, and downright unrealistically – that the goal of total science has been reached. That is, we have arrived at a 'total theory' $\Theta(V_1, V_2)$ that is satisfyingly complete, that covers all the available evidence, and that continues to withstand all attempts to falsify it by further experiment and observation. Time now to look inside it, and in particular at the Level 1–Level 2 relationship that it establishes.

According to the supervenience theorist, that 1–2 relationship is one of *determination*, by the Level-1 facts, of the Level-2 facts. This can be beautifully explicated by the mathematical logician as follows.

Take any domain D in which we are to interpret the combined language based on V_1 and V_2. That interpretation consists in assigning *extensions* within the domain D to each primitive expression of the vocabulary. (For example, given any one-place predicate, we need to specify *of which individuals* in the domain it holds; and so on.) We seek in this way to specify a model M based on domain D that will make the total theory $\Theta(V_1, V_2)$ true. Success in this endeavor is possible (says the supervenience theorist) only in accordance with the following *determination constraint*:

> Suppose one has fixed extensions in D for each of the primitive expressions in V_1. Then for each primitive expression in V_2, there is *at most one way* to fix its extension so as to produce a model M that makes the total theory $\Theta(V_1, V_2)$ true.

The mathematical logician summarizes the foregoing by saying that <u>each term in V_2 is *implicitly defined* by $\Theta(V_1, V_2)$ with respect to V_1</u>. And this is the *antecedent* of Beth's Theorem:

> **Beth's Definability Theorem**
>
> If each term in V_2 is *implicitly defined* by $\Theta(V_1, V_2)$ with respect to V_1, then each term in V_2 can be *explicitly* defined relative to $\Theta(V_1, V_2)$ using only terms in V_1.

This leaves thus far unanswered only the following question: what is it to define a term in V_2 *explicitly* relative to $\Theta(V_1, V_2)$ using only terms in V_1? The answer is straightforward. Take, say, a two-place predicate $R(x,y)$ from V_2. It would be explicitly defined by any formula $\varphi(x,y)$ (whose free variables, as indicated, are just x and y) in the language of V_1 such that the *co-extensiveness claim*

$$\forall x \forall y (R(x,y) \leftrightarrow \varphi(x,y))$$

is provable in the theory $\Theta(V_1, V_2)$. And the same would hold for any n-place predicate P in V_2. It would be explicitly defined by any formula $\varphi(x_1, \dots, x_n)$ in the language of V_1 such that

$$\Theta(V_1, V_2) \vdash \forall x_1 \dots \forall x_n (P(x_1, \dots, x_n) \leftrightarrow \varphi(x_1, \dots, x_n)).$$

(Recall that $\Delta \vdash \theta$ means that there is a proof of the conclusion θ from premises drawn from the set Δ.) Of course, any two competing such formulae would themselves have to be coextensive, since each would be coextensive with P.

Note that we are talking here about *intra-theoretic*, or *nomological* coextensiveness of each higher-level predicate P with some lower-level 'reducing' formula φ. It is *according to the total theory* Θ that that P is coextensive with φ. It is not a matter of *analytical connections* or of Humean *relations among ideas*. It is just that our overall best account of the world, as expressed in the theory $\Theta(V_1, V_2)$ dealing with the two levels of reality in question, forces each higher-level predicate to be coextensive with some *lower-level expressible relation*. The world can, as it were, be apprehended, and truly described, *solely in V_1-terms*.

This is a deep, surprising, and perplexing implication of Beth's Definability Theorem. It says, in effect, that

> *supervenience guarantees reducibility-in-principle.*

This view was first articulated in Hellman and Thompson (1975), but with the intention of raising a technical objection to the applicability of Beth's Theorem. (The first source to provide a detailed argument for reductionism on the basis of Beth's Theorem was Bealer (1978). The ensuing debate was assessed in Tennant (1985).)

The anti-reductionist confronted by these considerations has some wiggle room to explore. There are four objections that she can raise.

First, she can challenge the background assumption that the language of total science will be a first-order language, or at least one of those well-behaved languages for which Beth's Definability Theorem holds. In the absence of Beth's Theorem – either because it can be shown *not* to hold for one's chosen langue, or because we do not yet have a proof of it for that language – the reductionist's case for reducibility-in-principle does not even get off the ground.

Secondly, the anti-reductionist can point out that the total theory Θ that effects the assumed *implicit* definitions of the higher-level concepts in terms of the lower-level ones needs to be very powerful indeed in order to accomplish this. The theory Θ is a highly idealized construct. It is most unlikely ever to be attained at any foreseeable stage of our ever-evolving scientific enterprise. The historical record shows that our scientific theories always turn out either to be empirically falsified, or to be cripplingly incomplete, in not being able to so much as offer a positive or a negative answer to certain questions that we wish to pose. So, even if Θ is formulated in a language for which Beth's Theorem holds, we may still be unable honestly to invoke the theorem on behalf of the reductionist. This would be for the simple reason that the antecedent of the theorem is not in fact fulfilled. The theory Θ at hand is not powerful or comprehensive enough to effect the implicit definitions required (of the higher-level notions in terms of the lower-level ones).

Thirdly, the anti-reductionist can point out that Beth's Theorem itself does not impose any constraints on how *long and complicated* the 'reducing' formulae φ might be, whose existence is guaranteed for the higher-level concepts once they are indeed implicitly defined. One can fairly expect many, if not all, of these reducing formulae to be unmanageably complex. They are hardly likely to afford any guiding insights as to how things are at the higher level, even when the supervenience basis of lower-level facts has been pinned down by the preferred story that Θ provides in the lower-level language. It's all very well that her neurons are firing in such-and-such a pattern, and that the concentrations of testosterone, oestrogen, adrenaline, dopamine, serotonin, oxytocin and vasopressin are changing thus-and-so in various parts of her brain … but does she *really* love you?

Fourthly, there is the technical objection in Hellman and Thompson (1975), which was noted earlier but not explained. A word of explanation is now in order. Hellman and Thompson point out that the definition of implicit definability requires generalization over *all possible first-order models* of the scientific discourse in question. Among those myriad models will be ones in which there are *non-standard natural numbers*, in the part of the model that interprets the language of arithmetic. But, they urge, it would be reasonable to restrict the definition of how it is that lower-level facts determine higher-level facts so that it falls short of being tantamount to the antecedent of Beth's Theorem. They wish to restrict attention to just those models for the total theory in which *only standard natural numbers* occur (as the natural numbers of the model in question). This is a technical 'out' that evades the application of Beth's Theorem.

Those who are moved by the foregoing considerations in opposition to the application of Beth's Theorem are left holding an attractive position: *supervenience-without-reductionism*. It is a metaphysical and methodological position that does justice to the overriding and underlying importance of physical reality, while at the same time preserving a useful theoretical niche for the higher-level disciplines such as psychology, biology, sociology, and economics.

Note that supervenience is not being disputed by the 'ecological' theorists of mental content. These are the theorists, such as Hilary Putnam and Tyler Burge (b. 1946), who maintain that the content of an agent's belief depends at least in part on the identity and nature of the external objects or stuffs which the belief concerns. Thus, my belief that water can boil when heated depends for its identity on what, precisely, the stuff called 'water' on this planet essentially is. Imagine Twin Earth, a planet like Earth in every respect except that the stuff called 'water' in Twin-Earth English is actually XYZ rather than H_2O. According to the ecological theorist, the word 'water' on Twin Earth means something different from the word 'water' on Earth. When my *Doppelgänger* on Twin Earth says that water can boil when heated, he is thereby expressing a different belief from the one that we express using the same words. Even if one agrees with this so-called 'wide' or *externalist* theory of content, it nevertheless remains the case that facts about belief supervene on physical facts. Only now the supervenience basis is wider than it is usually thought to be by the proponents of the opposing 'narrow' theory of content. The supervenience basis is wider because it includes the actual stuff, XYZ or H_2O, as the case may be. The latter is an additional lower-level determinant (in addition, that is, to various neurophysiological facts) of higher-level facts about the beliefs held by speakers mouthing the word 'water'.

14.3 Emergentism and epiphenomenalism

Emergentism and epiphenomenalism go hand-in-hand. Emergentism is the view that as various systems of constituents become more complex, they may acquire properties or features that emerge from that complexity. These features could in no way be predicted beforehand, even with the fullest possible knowledge of how all the constituents would behave outside the context of the new system. This is the stuff of Engels's dictum that differences of quantity eventually lead to difference of quality. It is also behind the slogan that the whole is more than the sum of its parts. (This slogan is adopted also by those who believe in the possibility of so-called 'downward' causation, whereby the whole can causally affect or constrain the behavior of its parts. See Campbell (1974).)

The thesis that there are emergent properties may be arresting until we reflect more closely on what it means. Then we begin to acknowledge emergent properties all around us – or so it seems. Physical properties of chemical compounds, for example, appear to be emergent properties. Why is water wet? Could one have predicted that it would be, from a knowledge of the properties of hydrogen and of oxygen in isolation? It would appear not. Why does salt taste salty? Could one have predicted that it would, from a knowledge of the properties of sodium and of chlorine in isolation? It would appear not. Why does the light from lush grass cause the sensation of greenness in the consciousness of the perceiving subject, rather than the sensation of redness? Could the exact nature of the color sensation have been predicted from a knowledge of the wavelength(s) of the electromagnetic radiation, and from knowledge of the neurological workings of the perceiver's brain? It would appear not.

There is a response to such claims of emergence, however. It is to ask simply whether we are doing justice to what there is to know about, say, sodium and chlorine 'in isolation'. What exactly is meant by 'in isolation' here? Are we to preclude knowledge of the sodium (resp., the chlorine) in its relation to other things and stuffs? Why should not the properties of common salt (including its characteristic taste to human beings) simply be included among the properties of sodium ('in isolation') and among the properties of chlorine ('in isolation')? Isn't our problem, rather, that we diagnose emergentism too readily? Isn't this because we fail to explore a wide enough basis of properties of things and stuffs? In particular, shouldn't we refrain from saying that we know the properties of sodium (or of chlorine) until we have studied them in all their possible chemical combinations? Aren't we making the mistake of responding to the (naturally too difficult) challenge of predicting some of those properties from limited knowledge of a few central ones?

One can try in this way to fend off the emergentist claim that a thing or stuff has emergent properties only by pointing to the importance of a vast network of relations into which the constituents of the thing or stuff enter. That is, one can fend off emergentism only by adopting a degree of *holism*, maintaining that the full range of properties of an object can be appreciated only by seeing it in its relations to (many, perhaps all?) other objects. In the case where we try thus to fend off emergentism, we do so by being holist about the constituents of the thing or stuff with the allegedly emergent properties. Holism on constituents is thus tantamount to emergentism on wholes.

Emergentism is also evident in the thinking of non-equilibrium thermodynamics, the theory of dissipative structures and of self-organising systems. (See Eigen and Schuster (1979) and Prigogine and Stengers (1984).) Systems of constituents exhibit all of a sudden fresh patterns of self-organization and self-assembly when the flow of energy through those systems is increased. As a final example of emergentism, we have the age-old view that human consciousness is an emergent phenomenon. Its precise nature and peculiarities could never have been predicted from knowledge of, say, all the truths of theoretical physics. The mind is *sui generis*. On this view, it poses its own special demands for explanation and description. These demands cannot be met by recourse only to the physics of hadrons and leptons.

As a special case of this view, the philosopher of language and mind might hold that the notion of meaning is emergent. At some time in the distant past, after the Big Bang and before the evolution of life, there was no such phenomenon as meaning. That is, nothing ever meant anything to anything else. Now, however, there is lots of meaning. Every day we engage in meaningful exchanges. We tell one another things. We exchange casual information and gossip; we convey extraordinary confidences and secrets. We do so using language. Precisely how sentences of our language could have come to acquire the meanings-in-context that they standardly have, is a question that still exercises the philosopher. (The author's own reflections on this topic can be found in Tennant (1984).) On one proposition, however, most philosophers would now agree: there could not be meaning without intentional human actions (the acts of communication: utterances of sentences and the like). Meaning supervenes (so it would appear) on human behavior.

But whether human behavior itself can in turn be explained without reference to meanings raises the uncomfortable prospect that we are caught in a closed circle of explanation. It is what is sometimes called the *hermeneutic circle*. It is often stressed as an insuperable obstacle to a fully naturalized account of human nature and behavior. Epiphenomenalism is like emergentism in holding that the higher-level phenomena (such as consciousness) arise out of the lower-level ones in an essentially unpredicable way. But it is also an important part of the epiphenomenalist view that the epiphenomena themselves are causally inert or idle. That is, the epiphenomena are mere 'spin-off', mere ineffectual 'fog' generated by the real workings below. They do not themselves constitute loci of causal influence.

The denial of this latter view is characteristic of interactionism. The interactionist can still be an emergentist. He or she maintains that the mind does of course influence the body (even if numerically distinct from it). The most famous interactionist is Descartes, with his account of the mind as an individual substance distinct from the body, but interacting with it in a (perforce) rather mysterious fashion, mediated, he thought, by the pineal gland. Karl Popper and John Eccles (see Popper and Eccles (1977)) are modern proponents of this dualist doctrine. It is characteristic of discoveries in empirical science that they can stoke up renewed interest in hoary old philosophical positions. Popper and Eccles make much of the lateralization of mental capacities across the left and right hemispheres of the brain. The self is seen as a distinct entity interacting with the left hemisphere.

In similar vein, chaos theory has been claimed by some writers to rehabilitate the libertarian view that we have genuine free will: the universe, being in chaos, is not determined after all. In this respect chaos theory is a johnny-come-lately after quantum theory (and Hadamard's theorem, which Karl Popper cites as a precursor-insight of chaos theory). Likewise the Big Bang hypothesis in cosmology has stoked renewed interest in creationist doctrines; and the discovery of the delicate inter-calibration of fundamental constants (such as the speed of light; Planck's constant; the gravitational constant; Hubble's constant) has led to speculation that the cosmos must be a put-up job by God to ensure that we intelligent creatures evolve at long last, to appreciate His handiwork. (This is Wheeler's so-called Anthropic Principle. See Wheeler (1983) and Rees (1999).) Finally, contemporary quantum theorists, pondering such problems as the collapse of the wave packet, seem to be edging towards a Janus-like conception of the universe in which consciousness is as primordial as matter-energy, and not simply an idle epiphenomenon, nor even simply supervenient on the workings of matter-energy.

14.4 Towards a tolerant synthesis

While it may sound as though we are making light of some serious-minded concerns in that fraught region between Science on the one side, and Metaphysics and Religion on the other, we would nevertheless be the last to criticize anyone for seeking to integrate and unify their empirical theories (which are, after all, just a collection of hitherto well-tested speculations) with their metaphysical or religious speculations, leanings, or yearnings.

This author's only distaste is for beliefs that are the result of wishful thinking. Given the tentative conclusion above that emergentism about wholes can at best be avoided by adopting holism with respect to their constituents, it seems that we have to take seriously the complaint that a strictly downward- and inward-looking methodology is unlikely to throw light on the full picture. The sensitivity to surround that comes in large part from the recent sciences of ethology and reproductive ecology represents, in this author's humble opinion, a sensible concession to holistic concerns. That degree of holism in turn is compatible with a methodological preference for bottom-up causal stories wherever these are to be had, over their top-down rivals.

14.5 An alternative to the 'web of belief'

With an underlying belief in supervenience-without-reductionism, we would then be led to a conception of scientific discourse that differs somewhat from that of Quine's famous 'web of belief'. (See Quine (1951) and Quine and Ullian (1970).) Quine's model is of a network or web of sentences forming a ball or sphere. On the periphery are observation sentences, tuned most directly to the impinging of sensory experience. At the core lie logical laws, Mathematics and high-level theoretical hypotheses of well-tested empirical theories. In between lie the generalizations of intermediate importance. Quine has often stressed how the web responds to a change in the distribution of peripheral truth-values by re-distributing truth-values inwards. These re-distributions could in principle reach right into the core, forcing one to abandon a well-entrenched hypothesis. No sentence is immune to revision.

This is a nice model, and it has many happy adherents; but it does not seem to us to do full justice to the theoretical 'layering' that is involved in theories that describe and explain things and happenings at different levels of reality. Nor does it do justice to the idea that there are, locally, rather dense meshes of logical connections among sentences of any one scientific discipline. It does not do justice either to the idea that each scientific discipline on occasion seeks explanatory causal mechanisms at the level below and locates interesting problems by looking to the next level above. That is, it does not do justice to the possible 'bridge laws' that might serve to link theorizing at any one level with theorizing at the levels immediately above and below, without yet underwriting the possibility of theoretic reductions.

So in place of Quine's model of the sphere or ball, it is proposed here that we adopt a new one. We shall call it the Havisham Cake model. (Miss Havisham, in Charles Dickens's novel *Great Expectations*, remember, kept her unused wedding cake mouldering next to her, gathering cobwebs.) The picture is of several layers. As with the cake, the biggest layer is at the very bottom, and layers get smaller as one moves up. This reflects the asymmetry of supervenience. The bottom layer is physics; the next layer up, chemistry; then biology; ... and so on up, perhaps with metaphysics and theology being the miniature bridal pair at the very top.

Now remember that the special thing about Miss Havisham's cake was that it gathered cobwebs. Imagine these cobwebs linking each level to the next one below. We liken these linkages to bridge laws: those hypotheses that involve vocabulary from each of two neighboring levels of theory, and that bring the two otherwise logically independent bodies of theory into fruitful contact. As a matter of mathematical-logical fact, the existence of a rich set of bridge laws is compatible with there being no reduction in principle of any higher-level body of theory to that of any lower level. The different layers of the cake are then loosely connected modules, corresponding to the bodies of doctrine in well-established scientific disciplines dealing with the respective levels of reality as discussed earlier.

Each such discipline has its own periphery, and each its own core. At the periphery of each lie the observation sentences couched in the vocabulary appropriate for the disciplines concerned. The connecting strands between layers still make for the possibility of ramifying reverberations resulting from the re-distribution of truth-values at the periphery of any one of the layers.

We guess logic would have to be the steel rod that goes up the middle through all the layers, that makes the whole cake stand up in the first place. We like this concession of the cake model, because we think that logic is analytic and *a priori* and unrevisable (once we have got it right, that is ...). Logic is a precondition for enquiry, rather than just another slice of the intellectual action. The Havisham Cake model also does justice to another aspect of scientific lore. The explanatory spread of the lowest level is the greatest. And the little bits at the top are just a piece of cake.

14.6 Adequacy conditions on any methodological view

Given the variety of opposing views – reductionist v. anti-reductionist; epiphenomenalist v. interactionist; holist v. individualist; top-down v. bottom-up causal theorist – the following questions arise:

> *What would enable us to decide rationally among these competing alternatives?*
> *What conditions would an adequate metaphysical and methodological picture have to meet?*

The best answer, we submit, is this. Take the theories that are discovered and formulated as a result of following any one of these methodologies. In following such a methodology you will have been imbued with the metaphysical outlook that underpins it. That metaphysical outlook guides your formulation of concepts, your choice of descriptive categories, your mathematical models, your organization of evidence, and your framing of hypotheses. Let the metaphysical outlook (and associated methodology) simply stand or fall with the theories in which it results.

And what do we demand of these theories? Why, as already stated in §13.6, simply that they should:

1 account logically for the evidence;
2 make new and testable predictions;
3 unify explanations across a range of disparate phenomena;
4 be succinct and elegant and simple;
5 mesh smoothly with common sense; and
6 be as spartan as possible in what they postulate as existing.

All one's talk about wholes being more than the sum of their parts, about feedback loops, about top-down causation, and about emergent properties has to yield a payoff somewhere. The only currency in which payment can be made is the explanation and prediction of past and future sense experience. Whatever trendy terms a new theory may employ, it has to face the crunch: it has to explain how it was that things in the past appeared they way they did, and say how in the future they will appear to be.

Problems

1 Explain what is meant by *reducing* one theory to another.
2 What considerations are relevant to the question whether supervenience implies reductionism?
3 Choose one of the popular scientific books referred to in this chapter, and summarize how its arguments and theses bear on the question of reductionism in Science.
4 'It is way too demanding to expect a philosopher, expecially one coming from the humanities rather than the sciences, to understand how the technicalities of a deep and difficult result in mathematical logic can shed light on a central philosophical problem.' Discuss.
5 How do scientific theories cope with system-containments?
6 'There is no point in seeking theoretical reductions if they do not preserve the *meanings* of the higher-level terms that are being reduced.' Discuss.

Part III
The Existence of God

15 A *Priori* Arguments for the Existence of God

In Chapter 13 we looked at the different deductive roles of mathematical theorems and scientific hypotheses. We saw that mathematical theorems stand as the conclusions of proofs using axioms as their premises. By contrast, scientific hypotheses stand as assumptions in proofs whose conclusions are predictions or observation statements. No amount of observational evidence will ever make an hypothesis certain; but the hypothesis can at least serve to explain the observational data, and could, in principle, be refuted by it.

Take, now, the prospect of an argument 'for' **the existence of God**. There would appear to be two possible forms for such an argument.

1. The argument is like a mathematical argument. Its premises are self-evident truths about which all parties, hopefully, can agree. Its steps will be inferentially compelling. Its conclusion will be the statement that God exists.

2. The argument is like a scientific explanation. One of its premises will be the 'theistic hypothesis' that God exists. Other premises will be statements on which, hopefully, all parties to the debate can agree. The conclusion of the argument will be some statement that all parties think is true, and badly in need of explanation. Indeed, using the 'theistic hypothesis' over and over again, one might be able to give a large number of such arguments, each with acceptable side-premises and its own importantly true statement (as conclusion) that is badly in need of explanation. Finally – and this is the difficult requirement – the 'theistic hypothesis' would have to be demonstrably better than any rival hypotheses that might be used to furnish simplifying and unifying explanations of all the true statements that stand in need of explanation.

There are two famous arguments for the existence of God that conform to type (1). They are like mathematical arguments in that they try to reach the existence of God as a conclusion, rather than using it as an explanatory hypothesis. These arguments are called **the Ontological Argument** (due to Anselm) and **the Cosmological Argument** (due to Aquinas). And there is one famous argument for the existence of God that conforms to type (2). It is like a scientific explanation, or set of such explanations, in that it employs the statement that God exists as an explanatory hypothesis, rather than trying to reach it as a conclusion. This argument is called **the Argument from Design**. It is due to Newton and, later, William Paley (1743–1805). (A great irony in the history of ideas is that Charles Darwin made a close study of the writings of William Paley, when he was training to become a member of the clergy.)

In this chapter we deal with the arguments of type (1). In Chapter 16 we deal with arguments of type (2).

15.1 The Ontological Argument

> I had gone out to buy a tin of tobacco, and was going back with it along Trinity Lane, when I suddenly threw it up in the air and exclaimed: 'Great God in Boots! – the ontological argument is sound!'
>
> (Russell (1967), p. 84)

Russell was in his fourth undergraduate year at Cambridge at the time (1894). The mature Russell was perhaps the most famous atheist of the twentieth century.

As a non-smoker, this author urges greater circumspection with the young Russell's conclusion. Let us first examine the outcome of a formal analysis of Anselm's argument, before making up our minds about its soundness and/or validity.

We shall reach a formal analysis only after some extended investigations.

15.1.1 The original Latin version of Chapter 2 of Anselm's Proslogion

Here is the original Latin of Anselm's ontological argument (Anselm of Canterbury (1078), Chapter 2). The reader who does not know Latin may skip it, and proceed to the translation in §15.1.2.

2 Quod vere sit Deus
Ergo Domine, qui das fidei intellectum, da mihi, ut, quantum scis expedire, intelligam, quia es sicut credimus, et hoc es quod credimus. Et quidem credimus te esse aliquid quo nihil maius cogitari possit. An ergo non est aliqua talis natura, quia 'dixit insipiens in corde suo: non est Deus' [Ps. 13,1; 52,1]? Sed certe ipse idem insipiens, cum audit hoc ipsum quod dico: 'aliquid quo maius nihil cogitari potest', intelligit quod audit; et quod intelligit, in intellectu eius est, etiam si non intelligat illud esse. Aliud enim est rem esse in intellectu, alium intelligere rem esse. Nam cum pictor praecogitat quae facturus est, habet quidem in intellectu, sed nondum intelligit esse quod nondum fecit. Cum vero iam pinxit, et habet in intellectu et intelligit esse quod iam fecit. Convincitur ergo etiam insipiens esse vel in intellectu aliquid quo nihil maius cogitari potest, quia hoc, cum audit, intelligit, et quidquid intelligitur, in intellectu est. Et certe id quo maius cogitari nequit, non potest esse in solo intellectu. Si enim vel in solo intellectu est, potest cogitari esse et in re; quod maius est. Si ergo id quo maius cogitari non potest, est in solo intellectu: id ipsum quo maius cogitari non potest, est quo maius cogitari potest. Sed certe hoc esse non potest. Existit ergo procul dubio aliquid quo maius cogitari non valet, et in intellectu et in re.

15.1.2 A canonical English translation of Chapter 2 of Anselm's Proslogion

There are of course many translations of Anselm's famous argument into English. A reasonably canonical one is to be found in Hopkins and Richardson (2000), at pp. 93–94:

CHAPTER TWO
God truly [i.e., really] exists.

Therefore, O Lord, You who give understanding to faith, grant me to understand – to the degree You know to be advantageous – that You exist, as we believe, and that You are what we believe [You to be]. Indeed, we believe You to be something than which nothing greater can be thought. Or is there, then, no such nature [as You], for the Fool has said in his heart that God does not exist?[fn] But surely when this very same Fool hears my words 'something [than which nothing greater can be thought', he understands what he hears. And what he understands is in his understanding, even if he does not understand [i.e., judge] it to exist. For that a thing is in the understanding is distinct from understanding that [this] thing exists. For example, when a painter envisions what he is about to paint: he indeed has in his understanding that which he has not yet made, but he does not yet understand that it exists. But after he has painted [it]: he has in his understanding that which he has made, and he understands that it exists. So even the Fool is convinced that something than which nothing greater can be thought is at least in his understanding; for when he hears of this [being], he understands [what he hears], and whatever is understood is in the understanding. But surely that than which a greater cannot be thought cannot be only in the understanding. For if it were only in the understanding, it could be thought to exist also in reality – something which is greater [than existing only in the understanding]. Therefore, if that than which a greater cannot be thought were only in the understanding, then that than which a greater cannot be thought would be that than which a greater can be thought! But surely this [conclusion] is impossible. Hence, without doubt, something than which a greater cannot be thought exists both in the understanding and in reality.

15.1.3 Our own, slightly more rigorous, English version of Anselm's argument

We shall give below a reconstruction, or exegesis, in 'logician's English', of Anselm's Ontological Argument for the existence of God. Our concern here, in presenting the argument in our own prosaic form with tweakings in 'logician's English', is to focus attention on the very important role played by the two argumentative moves that we have rendered as 'Call such a thing E' and 'Call such a thing F'. Each of these moves marks the introduction, into the discourse, of a so-called *existential parameter* (E and F, respectively).

Such moves are governed by strict logical protocols, taking the modern form of restrictions on modes of occurrence of the parameters involved, when employing the so-called rule of 'Existential Elimination'. (The reader may wish at this point to take a quick look ahead to the end of §27.1, for the formal statement of this rule.) *In order to make such moves assume licit form* within our eventual regimentation of Anselm's argument, we have to be very careful to extract suitable existential statements that can serve as the major premises of the required applications of the rule of Existential Elimination. So, to the extent that our prose exegesis below of Anselm's original argument departs in minor ways from extant forms in the literature, the reader needs to be mindful of this consideration: *these departures are driven by a logician's charitable concern to get the argument into a formal shape that enjoys the best possible chance of being formally correct, and valid.*

After regimenting the argument as charitably as we can, we shall examine various criticisms of it.

15.1.4 Exegesis

Before advancing to any such criticisms, however, we need an *exposition* or *exegesis* of the Ontological Argument itself. The following is the best we can do (in the investigative spirit of the foregoing remarks) to render the argument in the most rigorous logical detail that the original text can support (while still setting it out in prose).

The Ontological Argument for God's Existence

We believe [God] to be something than which nothing greater can be conceived. So we understand the expression 'something than which nothing greater can be conceived'.

Thus something than which nothing greater can be conceived exists *in the understanding*. Call such a thing E. So E is a thing than which nothing greater can be conceived, and which exists in the understanding.

Now suppose (for *reductio ad absurdum*) that E does not exist *in reality*.

We can conceive of something than which nothing greater can be conceived existing *both* in the understanding *and* in reality. Call such a thing F.

Because F exists in reality but E does not, F is greater than E.

We have conceived of F; and F is greater than E.

But E is supposed to be a thing than which nothing greater can be conceived! – a contradiction.

Thus our supposition that E does not exist in reality must be wrong.

Hence E *does* exist in reality.

But E is that than which nothing greater can be conceived.

Hence that than which nothing greater can be conceived exists in reality.
That is, God exists in reality.

The argument is purely conceptual; and it is *a priori*. Like a proof of a mathematical theorem, it seeks to establish its conclusion by taking truth-preserving steps of inference from first principles that are presumed to be self-evident. Criticisms of any such argument can be of two forms:

1 at least one of the 'first principles' used as a starting point for the argument is not true; or
2 at least one of the steps of inference taken in the course of the argument is fallacious, i.e., not truth-preserving.

15.1.5 First objection: Anselm tacitly uses a mistaken principle about linguistic understanding

Anselm's argument, as regimented above, begins as follows:

We believe [God] to be something than which nothing greater can be conceived. So we understand the expression 'something than which nothing greater can be conceived'.

Thus something than which nothing greater can be conceived exists *in the understanding*. Call such a thing E. So E is a thing than which nothing greater can be conceived, and which exists in the understanding.

The emphasized word 'thus' – which we call an *inference marker* – indicates a basic or primitive inference being drawn at this point in Anselm's argument. That inference is an instance of the general form

We understand the noun phrase 'N'.
Thus N exists in the understanding.

A different instance of this same pattern would be:

We understand the noun phrase 'Pegasus'.
Thus Pegasus exists in the understanding.

Here is another one:

We understand the noun phrase 'the square root of Jupiter'.
Thus the square root of Jupiter exists in the understanding.

(One needs to *understand* the expression 'the square root of Jupiter' in order to know that there is no such thing.)

Let us concentrate on the instance involving 'Pegasus'. Could it possibly be true to say that *Pegasus itself* – that winged horse of ancient Greek mythology – actually exists in an individual understanding, or in the collective understanding? What would it *be* for a mythical object so to exist? The answer must lie in the fact that each individual understander has his or her own *mental image* of Pegasus. For the sighted, this is probably a visual image of a steaming, shimmering, silver-gray horse with wings. But *that image* (or *those images*) cannot themselves be Pegasus. For if (miraculously) Pegasus really were to exist, he would not *be* the mental image that I have of him, or the mental image that anyone else might have of him. He would merely be the thing *of which* those various images *are images*. If Pegasus really were to exist, he would not be *in our heads*. Our *images* of him might be in our heads, as well as our thoughts about him; but he himself would be outside our heads, prancing or grazing or doing whatever amuses him. The images we might have of him, *qua* mental images or brain states, would be ontologically distinct from him. They would be an interesting subject matter to investigate, in cognitive psychology or linguistic semantics or neurophysiology; but that investigation would concern Pegasus himself only indirectly. It would be an investigation of intentional states having Pegasus as their object, not an investigation of Pegasus himself.

Anselm's insinuation of *the thing itself* (in the example at hand: Pegasus) into the understanding is therefore objectionable. This is so even when we concede that thinkers often do (perhaps unreflectively) think that part of their understanding of certain expressions of their language consists in their having various mental images associated with those expressions. But even if unreflective thinkers think that this is how they understand their language, their mental images are nevertheless accidental, not essential, to that understanding; and they are irrelevant to an account of what such understanding consists in.

For, there could well be thinkers who understood the expressions of their language *without having any associated mental images*. (Call these thinkers, if you will, *semantic zombies*.) These zombies' understanding would be fully manifest in the *publicly observable uses* they made of the expressions of their language. Indeed, one influential view about linguistic meaning and linguistic understanding – due to the later Wittgenstein – is that it consists precisely in the *use* that we make of our expressions. That usage is all that is available as evidence when we acquire a language; and is all that is available as evidence when we judge others' competence in the language. We look at observable *usage*. We do *not* inquire after people's mental images when we judge of their linguistic competence. Perhaps, then, Anselm is too easily generalizing from what happens to be true, introspectibly, from his own case. He 'looks within' himself, and finds that he has associated mental images for expressions that he understands. Then he mistakenly takes this to be an essential ingredient in anyone's linguistic understanding. But, the objector will say, he is mistaken. He has no entitlement to the inference registered by the emphasized word 'thus' in the quoted passage above.

15.1.6 *Second objection: Anselm mistakenly treats existence as a property of things*

Anselm continues his Ontological Argument as follows. The reader should focus on the claim marked with the asterisk:

> Now suppose (for *reductio*) that E does not exist *in reality*.
>
> We can conceive of something than which nothing greater can be conceived existing *both* in the understanding *and* in reality. Call such a thing F.
>
> (*) **Because** F exists in reality but E does not, [it follows that] F is greater than E.
>
> We have conceived of F; and F is greater than E.
>
> But E is supposed to be a thing than which nothing greater can be conceived! – a contradiction.
>
> Thus our supposition that E does not exist in reality must be wrong.
>
> Hence E *does* exist in reality.

Anselm is effectively treating existence as yet another property of things, to be lumped in with all the other properties, consideration of which helps one to judge individuals' relative greatness.

But, the objector will say – as Kant did, most famously – *existence is* **not** *a property of things*. Comparisons of relative greatness can be made only among *things* – that is, among entities that already exist. It is to substantive properties of actually existing things that we attend when judging of relative greatness. Any non-existent 'thing' would be ruled out of such a comparison on logical grounds. Existence is a pre-requisite for entry into the game of comparison. It is not a feature that would earn its 'bearer' any 'Brownie points' in the Greatness Stakes.

Existence is not a property of things. Rather, existence is a (higher-order) *property of properties* of things. To say that something has the (first-order) property F is not to predicate a property of any particular thing. Rather, it is to predicate (at higher order) a property of the property F: namely, that *F has instances*. This central logical insight into the 'logical grammar' of the word 'exists' (and its cognates in other languages) was the central contribution of the founding father of modern logic, Gottlob Frege.

15.1.7 *Third objection: The Ontological Argument keeps bad company. There are other arguments, of the same form, for patently unacceptable conclusions*

Here is an 'Ontological' Argument for the Non-existence of Zero (courtesy of Saint Anselm). It is patently misguided to think that one could *prove* that zero does not exist. Hence there must be something wrong with Anselm's argument as well, since it has the same form as the following one.

> We believe [zero] to be something than which nothing of greater nullity can be conceived. So we understand the expression 'something than which nothing of greater nullity can be conceived'.
>
> Thus something than which nothing of greater nullity can be conceived exists in the understanding. Call such a thing E. So E is a thing than which nothing of greater nullity can be conceived, and which exists in the understanding.
>
> Now suppose (for *reductio*) that E does exist in reality.
>
> We can conceive of something than which nothing of greater nullity can be conceived existing only in the understanding but not in reality. Call such a thing F.
>
> Because F does not exist in reality but E (by supposition) does, F is of greater nullity than E.
>
> We have conceived of F; and F is of greater nullity than E.
>
> But E is supposed to be that than which nothing of greater nullity can be conceived! – a contradiction.
>
> Thus our supposition that E does exist in reality must be wrong.
>
> Hence E does not exist in reality.
>
> But E is zero, i.e., something than which nothing of greater nullity can be conceived.
>
> So zero does not exist in reality.

15.1.8 Fourth objection (raised by the anti-realist): The Ontological Argument uses a strictly classical form of reductio ad absurdum to which the anti-realist would object

Consider once again the block of argumentation that we examined in connection with the second objection above. This time we place an asterisk in a new position, to draw the reader's attention to an aspect of the argument to which **the anti-realist** would take exception:

> Now suppose (for *reductio*) that E **does NOT exist** in reality. We can conceive of something than which nothing greater can be conceived existing *both* in the understanding *and* in reality. Call such a thing F. Because F exists in reality but E does not, it follows that F is greater than E. We have conceived of F; and F is greater than E. But E is supposed to be a thing than which nothing greater can be conceived! – a contradiction. Thus our

supposition that E does not exist in reality must be wrong. (*) Hence E **does exist** in reality.

The anti-realist refuses to assert a positive on the basis only of a *reductio ad absurdum* of the corresponding negative. Only the realist is prepared to do that. That is to say, only the realist will accept the rule of inference called **classical reductio ad absurdum**. For the anti-realist, reducing **not-P** to absurdity provides justification only for the claim **not-(not-P)** – that is to say, that it is not the case that it is absurd to assert P. Where P is the claim that God exists in reality, the anti-realist agnostic could agree that it is not the case that it is absurd to assert P; while yet she refuses actually to assert P. She will justify her refusal by pointing out that it is one thing to show the impossibility of denying the existence of God (in reality); but it is quite another thing to provide a constructive reason *for asserting* the existence of God (in reality). The impossibility of denial amounts merely to *consistency*; whereas what we want, surely, is some *justification* for asserting what we take to be *true*. The anti-realist is prepared to use classical *reductio ad absurdum* only when the proposition P in question is effectively decidable – that is, when we have an effective method for deciding what the truth-value of P is. An effective method for deciding whether P is one that can be applied in a mechanical way, according to a recipe that can be specified in detail in advance. An effective method requires no ingenuity for its application, and requires only a finite amount of time, for a finite number of steps, before it yields a definite answer (here, to the question whether it is the case that P). It is hard to think of a better example of a proposition that is *not* effectively decidable than the proposition that God exists.

Logical *cognoscenti*, please note: if one accepts the force of this fourth objection, one does not thereby undermine the force of the third objection. For, as casual inspection will reveal, in the Anselmian argument for the non-existence of zero the *reductio ad absurdum* is constructive, not classical. It involves assuming, for the sake of argument, that E *does* exist in reality, and deriving a contradiction, from which it then follows that E does *not* exist in reality. This step is an application of the rule of negation-introduction, not an application of the classical rule of *reductio ad absurdum*.

15.1.9 A completely rigorous regimentation of the argument

The foregoing objections can be underscored or highlighted by more rigorously *regimenting* Anselm's argument as a completely formal proof. The aim would be to use only such axioms and primitive rules of inference as are used by Anselm, or at least only such axioms and rules as would have to be put forward on his behalf, in order to make good certain lacunae in his argument. Once one has constructed a faithful formalization of his argument, the subtleties revealed might also give rise to yet further objections.

With the aim of fully regimenting Anselm's argument, we must first investigate how best to provide his sentences with appropriate logical forms. To this task we now turn.

15.1.10 A translation manual for Anselm's primitives, into suitable logical notation

'We'

It is less likely that Anselm was using the 'royal' or 'authorial' 'We', than that he was addressing his considerations to a community of believers whom he took to share with him certain basic beliefs about God. His aim was to provide his fellow believers with apodeictic grounds for their shared belief. So, for the first-person plural pronoun 'We', we shall use the uppercase constant W, and treat it like a name.

'God'

At the very outset, we have to decide whether (in Anselm's argumentation) we are to understand 'God' as a *name* (perhaps a name introduced as an abbreviation of some definite-descriptive term) or as a *one-place predicate*. The Quinean might say that it matters not, since he (Quine) has famously left on the table a general proposal to treat *all* names as disguised definite-descriptive terms involving one-place predicates, a proposal that invokes Russell's theory of descriptions by way of justification. Thus the name 'Caesar', rather than being rendered in logical notation as the name c, would be rendered as $\iota x C(x)$, i.e., 'the unique thing x such that x Caesars'. But this is a device of such recent vintage that it might not be fair to regiment Anselm's discourse about God in this fashion.

A straightforward reading of various English translations of Anselm's text inclines this author to render 'God' in logical notation as a proper name – g, say. We shall proceed on this simple assumption about translation into logical notation until such time as we might discover any insuperable obstacle to doing so. It might turn out, of course, that we have to construe the name g as an abbreviation for a longer definite-descriptive term of the form 'the being x such that ... x ...'. But we shall deal with such a possibility only if and when we encounter it.

'X believes t to be Φ'

We shall regiment 'X believes that p' as

$$\beta(X, p),$$

where the propositional-attitude (doxastic) operator β joins a singular term and a formula to form a formula. The form of expression 'X believes t to be Φ' can sometimes invite the sternly *de re* reading 't is such that X believes of *it* that it Φs', which the doxastic logician renders as

$$\exists x(x=t \wedge \beta(X, \Phi(x))).$$

On this reading, the singular term t (or its sense, or conceptual content) is neither part of the content that X believes (for it is not within the scope of β), nor part of any reason that X may have for believing the content in question.

But this is emphatically not the case when the term t is the name g for God. For surely both the contents of one's theistic beliefs (should one hold any), as well as one's reasons for holding those beliefs, would hinge crucially on conceiving of the being whom the beliefs concern *as God*. Thus, when the form of expression to be regimented is 'X believes g to be Φ', it is surely the *de dicto* reading that would be called for: 'X believes "of God", *as God*, that He/She/It Φs'.

Note the scare double-quotes around the phrase 'of God'. These are needed in order to quash in advance any assumption, on the part of one's listener, that one is reporting X's belief in such a way as to involve oneself (the reporter) in sharing X's own commitment to the existence of God. One needs to be able to report X's beliefs that are purportedly about God, without necessarily being saddled thereby with X's own commitment to God's existence. That is why we *definitely* cannot use any such regimentations as

$$\exists x(x=g \wedge \beta(X, \Phi(x)) \quad \text{or} \quad \exists x(x=g \wedge \beta(X, \Phi(g))$$

with their up-front ('wide-scope') existential quantifiers. The suitably non-committal reading that we are after (non-committal, that is, for the reporter of the belief) would be regimented more simply as

$$\beta(X, \Phi(g)).$$

This *de dicto* form of belief-attribution absolves the reporter of any supposed commitment to the existence of God. The reporter is merely reporting X's belief *about* (hence also: *in*) God, but without necessarily endorsing any part of it. Moreover, brief reflection on the dialectical situation (on Anselm's behalf) convinces one that the *de dicto* form of belief-attribution has to be correct. For, if we had to regiment Anselm's opening line 'We believe [God] to be ...' by means of the *de re*, existentially committal formula, he would already stand accused of blatant circularity, or begging of the existential question – explicitly assuming God's existence at the very outset, rather than deducing it from less obviously commiting assumptions.

'Greater than'

Anselm considers one thing being (judged to be) *greater than* another. This strikes one as a straightforward binary relation. We shall regiment 'x is greater than y' as

$$x > y.$$

The 'greater-than'-ness in question is of course not to be confused with the usual orderings of familiar mathematical objects, such as the natural, rational or real numbers, that are conventionally represented by the relational symbol '>'.

'Conceiving, conceiving of, and conceiving as'

Anselm only ever uses the verb 'conceive' within the scope of an explicit or implicit 'can'. The verb phrase 'can conceive' can govern an accusative or a subordinate clause:

> x can conceive of t

or

> x can conceive [of the possibility] that p.

We shall regiment these as $C(x,t)$ and $C(x,p)$ respectively. Context will make clear whether the second argument is a singular term (t) or a (possibly open) (recall from §7.1: an open sentence is a well-formed formula that contains a free variable) sentence (p). We shall call the former occurrence of C 'objectual C', and the latter one 'propositional C'.

'Exists in the understanding'

To speak of something as existing in the understanding strikes one nowadays as rather quaint and outmoded, carrying with it a problematic commitment to intentional objects existing only in the mind of an understander. But the regimenter has to be faithful to Anselm's text, and provide some way to regiment this important Anselmian notion. So we shall regiment 't exists in the understanding' as

> Ut,

and avoid having to deal with any explicit existential quantifier prefix that may call for an unusually specialized and problematic meaning.

'Exists in reality'

With 't exists in reality' we are closer to Fregean (and indeed Quinean) turf. A Fregean would say that this is just an equivalent variant, in natural language, of 't exists'. Adding 'in reality' is, as it were, to add nothing to what is being said. On this Fregean and Quinean construal of univocal existence, we could regiment 't exists in reality' as

> $\exists x\, x = t$, or $\exists ! t$.

But it may be unfair to Anselm's text to be that ruthless or peremptory in imposing upon his (translated) words these contemporary forms of logical expression. So we shall 'back off' here, and regiment 't exists in reality' less contentiously as

Rt,

thereby maintaining at least a symbolical analogy with our foregoing treatment of 't exists in the understanding'.

15.1.11 *Translating Anselmian chunks into logical notation*

We are now getting close to the Anselmian chunks that stand in need of regimentation. Consider first Anselm's 'nothing greater than t can be conceived'. This is the negation of 'something greater than t can be conceived'. The only reading of the latter that can serve the purposes of Anselm's argument is 'something actual can be conceived of (by some actual thinker) *as being greater than t*'. This is to be regimented as

$\exists y \exists z \mathcal{C}(z, y > t),$

which uses propositional $\mathcal{C}$.

Thus Anselm's form of words 'nothing greater than t can be conceived' has the regimentation

$\neg \exists y \exists z \mathcal{C}(z, y > t).$

Let us use

$\Psi(t)$

as an abbreviation of this regimentation.

We are now in a position to consider how best to regiment the opening Anselmian line

> We believe [God] to be something than which nothing greater can be conceived.

Note that the final step of his argument involves a substitution of identicals: he substitutes 'God' for 'that than which nothing greater can be conceived'. The latter descriptive phrase implies *uniqueness*, not mere existence. So the very first line of Anselm's argument would serve his argumentative purposes much better if it were to read

> We believe God to be (as a matter of definition) that thing than which nothing greater can be conceived.

This is straightforwardly regimentable as

$$\beta(W, g =_{df} \iota y \Psi(y)),$$

and can be taken as an *axiom*, expressing an analytic (and *a priori*) truth about the language used by Anselm and his interlocutors.

Another axiom to which Anselm could help himself is that *we exist*:

$$\exists!W.$$

It features in the formal proof below, supplying the existential presupposition that is needed in order to infer from the premise that *we* can conceive something to be the case to the conclusion that *someone* can do so.

We regiment Anselm's form of words 'we understand the expression "…"' as

$$\text{Und}(W, \text{'}…\text{'}).$$

In the formal proof below, the axiom marked with an asterisk is seldom remarked upon as an actual premise of Anselm's argument. But it really does feature as an undischarged assumption (hence, as a premise) within his argument. It is the claim that *we can conceive of there being a unique thing than which nothing greater can be conceived existing both in the understanding and in reality*. As an axiom, it is presumably vouchsafed by simply reflecting upon an act of alleged conception that is taken to involve the content in question.

With those final clarifications, we now present a completely formalized proof as a regimentation of Anselm's argument. We do so on Anselm's behalf because of the general principle (which we have invoked before) governing demonstrable validity of argumentation. This is that *no argument can be admitted as compellingly valid unless it really can be regimented at the level of detail that is required in order for all its steps to be justified by appeal to primitive rules of inference*. The diligent reader should identify within this formal proof all the *loci* for the objections already raised against the prose form of the argument; and should also inspect each step within the proof, in order to ask whether it really is a valid move of reasoning. For each step, the reader should try to determine what generally valid form of rule, if any, the step instantiates.

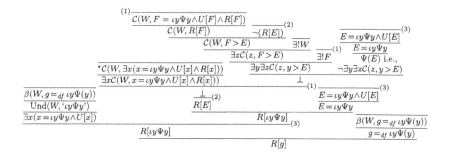

15.1.12 *Further reading on the Ontological Argument*

The interested reader should consult Sobel (2004) and Oppy (2011).

15.2 The Cosmological Argument

The Cosmological Argument is so-called because it involves concepts basic to our understanding of the cosmos: causation and time. The argument was first presented by Aquinas as his 'Second Way' of proving that God exists. Here is the relevant extract from Bratman *et al.* (2009):

> The second way [to prove the Existence of God] derives from the nature of efficient causation. In the world that we sense, we find that efficient causes come in series. We do not, and cannot, find that something is its own efficient cause – for, if something were its own efficient cause, it would be prior to itself, which is impossible. **But the series of efficient causes cannot possibly go back to infinity.** In all such series of causes, a first thing causes one or more intermediaries, and the intermediaries cause the last thing; **when a cause is taken out of this series, so is its effect.** Therefore, if there were no first efficient cause, there would be no last or intermediary efficient causes. If the series of efficient causes went back to infinity, however, there would be no first efficient cause and, hence, no last or intermediary causes. But there obviously are such causes. **We must therefore posit a first efficient cause**, which everyone **understands to be God.**

15.2.1 *Exegesis*

Aquinas is thinking of God as the 'Prime Mover'. He thinks that at the point 'in' time 'at which' the physical universe came into being, there was an act of creation – an event – involving the Deity. God created all things, and ordained the lawful order that has since constrained the behavior, in space and time, of all the physical objects in His creation. From this alleged initial event – the 'prime moving' – flow all causal chains through subsequent time. Take any of these causal chains. According to Aquinas, if we follow it back through time, we shall (in an atemporal sense) eventually arrive at a terminus in the past: the act of creation itself. For Aquinas, there can be no back-tracking infinitely far, without end, into the past, along a causal chain of events. (The causal direction, of course, would be the reverse – it would be the forward-tracking of the same chain.)

15.2.2 *First objection: there can be causal over-determination*

It is somewhat naïve to think that causes and effects come in separable series, each of which can be linearized. If one traces the relation of cause and effect in a large class of events, one can well find structures that look like 'chicken wire' – with both forward-branching and backward-branching (though with all arrows pointing from left to right, as it were). The sheriff offers a large reward for the outlaw, dead or alive. Two bounty-hunters make off to find him. They take different routes to his mountain hide-out. From opposite ends of the valley, they fire at him, simultaneously. Each bullet is deadly accurate (literally as well as metaphorically). But one of them kills the outlaw a split-second before the other hits him. The cause of the outlaw's death was that striking by the first bullet. But even if that event had not obtained, the striking by the second bullet would have killed him. This is a case of causal over-determination. It is not at all clear, in general, that the removal (in counterfactual cases) of any member of a 'series' of causes and effects would prevent the later members from still obtaining. For those 'series' (in the plural, now) are intertwined and intercalated in complicated ways.

Important though this objection is, it is not necessarily fatal to Aquinas's argument. The next objection, however, is.

15.2.3 *Second objection: Aquinas commits the quantifier-switch fallacy*

Aquinas's central inference has the form

> Every event has a (distinct) cause;
> **therefore**, Some event caused all (other) events.

We saw earlier that one way to object to a step of inference is to exhibit another instance of the same form, taking one from an obviously true premise to an obviously false conclusion. (Mere truth and falsity, respectively, would be sufficient; but the objection is even stronger when those truth-values are obvious.) Here now is another inference, of exactly the form displayed by Aquinas's inference:

> Every integer is less than some (distinct) integer;
> **therefore**, Some integer is less than all (other) integers.

Taken as an inference in a discussion of the negative and positive integers, it is clearly fallacious. For the premise is clearly true, while the conclusion is clearly false. There is no 'first' (negative) integer. The series of integers goes backwards (more conventionally: 'to the left') through the negative ones, without end. We might talk of 'minus infinity', but this phrase does not denote any integer. It is just a helpful way of reminding ourselves that the series of integers goes on and on through the negatives, without terminating in any 'least' integer. The series is 'unbounded to the left'.

Aquinas can be squarely criticized for not having said more to secure the conclusion that there is a first cause. He dogmatically rules out the perfectly consistent and imaginable scenario of a class of events extending infinitely far back into the past, without there being any temporally 'first' point. Each event could be caused by a strictly earlier event, while yet no event is initial within the temporal ordering.

15.2.4 Third objection: even in the Big Bang model, there is, strictly speaking, no first cause

Some modern thinkers suggest that Aquinas's Second Way can be redeemed by commitment to the so-called Big Bang model of the universe. The Big Bang itself is supposed to be the 'initial event' that 'caused' all subsequent events. This, however, is mistaken. What cosmologists call the Big Bang is not an event *in time*. It is a singularity sitting as a limit point to, but not in, the spatio-temporal manifold. It is like the way the number 0 sits as a limit point to, but not in, the set of all strictly positive real numbers. In the positive real numbers, one can keep taking ever-smaller 'hops' backwards, *ad infinitum*, without actually reaching 0. So too, in the spatio-temporal manifold, one could take infinitely many hops back in time, from an event E_1 to its cause E_2, thence to the latter's cause E_3, ... and so on, *ad infinitum* into the past – without ever having to reckon the Big Bang itself into the causal chain. For the Big Bang is not in *any* causal series. It 'sits outside' the causal manifold. Indeed, the Big Bang is not even an *event*. An event is a happening *in* space-time; while the Big Bang lies *outside* space-time, as a singularity where no physical laws would be applicable.

In summary, we reject the suggestion that Aquinas's fallacious uniformization (the quantifier-switching move from 'every-some' to 'some-every') can be repaired by borrowing from the most popular current model in scientific (as opposed to philosophical) cosmology.

15.2.5 Fourth objection: why should a first efficient cause, if there is one, be God?

This is not a silly question, from the atheist's point of view. *So what* if some argument about the nature and structure of causation leads one to accept that there *was* indeed some initial event, in which all causal chains have their source? Why should *that* be taken, without further ado, to be God, or even simply to be God's *doing*? Why shouldn't it simply have happened, in a Godless universe?

Problems

1 Is there any reason to believe that anything than which nothing greater can be conceived would have to be the *only* such thing?
2 Might God exist, but only *contingently*?
3 In our formal regimentation of Anselm's Ontological Argument, identify exactly which formal steps are subject to the first, second and third objections raised in §§15.1.5–15.1.7. Do you think that the Ontological Argument could be revised and made compelling, in response to the criticism leveled against it?

4   Are there any more sophisticated versions of cosmological theorizing (such as, say, the theory of inflation, parallel universes, and multiverses) that might lend support to Aquinas's cosmological argument for the existence of God? But even if so, what becomes of the would-be *a priori* status of the argument itself?

5   Anselm's Ontological Argument exploits the notion of conceivability, which needs to be distinguished from the notion of logical or metaphysical possibility. After Anselm, both Descartes and Leibniz (criticizing and seeking to improve upon Descartes) formulated versions of what are commonly called ontological arguments. They did so, however, by using the notion of possibility rather than the notion of conceivability. Read the Fifth Meditation in Descartes (1641b), followed by Leibniz (1969a) and Leibniz (1969b). Regiment as best you can both Descartes's ontological argument, and Leibniz's attempted improvement of it.

6   The greatest logician of the twentieth century, Kurt Gödel, was deeply influenced by Leibniz. Gödel even went so far as to formalize a Leibnizian version of the Ontological Argument. Carefully study Gödel (1995), and try to reach a judgment as to whether it is faithful to the lines of argument to be found in Leibniz (1969a) and Leibniz (1969b).

16 The Argument from Design

We explained earlier how arguments for the existence of God could either seek to derive the existence of God logically from premises acceptable to both parties to the debate; or use the *hypothesis* or *conjecture* that God exists in order to derive from that hypothesis, in combination with acceptable premises, various important statements about the world that call for explanation.

It is the latter kind of argument that we confront in this chapter. The Argument 'from' Design *postulates* the existence of God in order to explain the appearance of design in the natural order, both physical and biological. Thus the claim *that God exists* is functioning, strictly, like a scientific hypothesis, to be tested against the evidence by the predictions that it affords us.

16.1 Main presentations of the Argument from Design

The best statement of the Argument from Design comes, rather remarkably, from Isaac Newton, in the General Scholium that he first put into the second edition of his great work *Principia*. (The source for our quotation is Newton (1726).) Newton was deeply impressed, not by *biological* design (on which he did not remark), but by the design of the *heavens* and the universal laws governing the motions of physical masses quite generally. These were the very laws that he himself had discovered, and they had such mathematical beauty and simplicity that he was moved to see the hand of God at work in the creation of any world in which they held. From what Newton wrote in the Scholium, we quote a representative, if somewhat extended, excerpt from the 1729 translation from Newton's Latin by Andrew Motte.

> This most beautiful System of the Sun, Planets, and Comets, could only proceed from the counsel and dominion of an intelligent and powerful being. And if the fixed Stars are the centers of other like systems, these, being form'd by the like wise counsel, must be all subject to the dominion of One; especially since the light of the fixed Stars is of the same nature with the light of the Sun, and from every system light passes into all the other systems. And lest the systems of the fixed Stars should, by their gravity, fall on each other mutually, he hath placed those Systems at immense distances from one another.

This Being governs all things, not as the soul of the world, but as Lord over all: And on account of his dominion he is wont to be called *Lord God* ... or *Universal Ruler*. ... The supreme God is a Being eternal, infinite, absolutely perfect; ... from his true dominion it follows that the true God is a Living, Intelligent, and Powerful Being; and, from his other perfections, that he is Supreme or most Perfect. He is Eternal and Infinite, Omnipotent and Omniscient; that is, his duration reaches from Eternity to Eternity; his presence from Infinity to Infinity; he governs all things, and knows all things that are or can be done. He is not Eternity and Infinity, but Eternal and Infinite; he is not Duration and Space, but he endures and is present.

It would not be too mischievous to point out that this is from the hand of the same thinker who claimed *Hypotheses non fingo* ('I do not create hypotheses').

The version of the design argument most familiar to philosophers, however, is due to William Paley. (See Paley (1867).) This version stresses the obvious intellectual ease with which we will postulate a designer whenever we encounter a complicated artifact in a stark and barren setting. If one were to come across a chronometer in a lunar landscape, the hypothesis would readily be at hand that some intelligent designer had fashioned the watch, and caused it somehow to be placed there. One would not countenance the possibility that the watch itself might have arisen from the random interplay of natural forces, such as wind erosion, volcanic eruptions, etc. That would be just too implausible. So, thought Paley, when one turned to consider the magnificent design features of the living world, one would be hard-pressed not to attribute it all to the workings of a divine designer. The designer would have to be divine, because to suggest that beautifully designed mortal beings had mortal designers would only drive the problem one step further back. Who or what would have designed those mortal designers? It did not occur to Paley, however, that the answer might postulate natural forces that would slowly bring about the appearance (and reality) of design, without this being the realization of any agent's purposes. An insight of this magnitude was only to come later, with Darwin – see below.

Paley's example of the watch in the desert landscape does not really speak to the Argument from Design concerning biological creatures, except by very weak analogy. Watches do not reproduce; whereas organisms do. This crucial disanalogy gives an important advantage to the opponent of the Argument from Design in the biological realm, as we shall presently see.

The theistic hypothesis (that there is a divine Designer) is really a big conjunction: God exists, and God created the natural order, and God intended the result to have a certain kind of order, beauty, harmony, regularity ... Perhaps even also: God intended part of His creation to bring forth 'intelligent observership', in the form of human beings (and perhaps other rational creatures, elsewhere in this or other galaxies?) who can reason about His creation, ponder its harmony and regularity, stand in awe of its beauty, and investigate its underlying order with all the intellectual tools with which He has furnished them.

16.2 The Anthropic Principle

A contemporary variant of the Argument from Design puts forward the so-called 'Anthropic Principle'. This is the claim, which we encountered in §14.3, that there must have been a divine creator in order for intelligent observership to have been able to evolve in the natural universe. This is supposedly because (it has been discovered that) the numerical values of the various fundamental constants of nature (the speed of light; Planck's constant; Hubble's constant; the gravitational constant; etc.) are amazingly delicately intercalibrated for the 'purposes' of allowing galaxies, stars, and planets to form, and indeed among them a planet, like Earth, with conditions conducive to the origin and evolution of organismic life. If any of the fundamental constants had had a slightly different numerical value, this argument contends, cosmic evolution could not have produced the causal pathway leading to us intelligent observers on the face of the Earth, able to ponder this miraculous arrangement of inter-related numerical values. So the evolution of intelligent observership is *highly improbable* ... so the existence of a divine creator-designer is *all the more probable* ...? For a critique of this kind of probabilistic reasoning, see Mellor (1969).

For all its sophistical sophistication, however, the Anthropic Principle is just another way of postulating the existence of a divine creator, with intelligence and purpose in undertaking the demanding job of creating the whole universe so that we can eventually appreciate what has been achieved. It does not carry any more predictive clout than the conjunctive God-hypothesis set out above.

16.3 The explanatory role of the theistic hypothesis

Given this rather long conjunctive hypothesis, one will be able to derive a rudimentary set of statements that register important features of the world for which we seek explanation. Why are there complicated organs like the eye, the brain, the kidneys, the liver ...? Because God made them so that whole organisms could live and reproduce. Why are there self-replicating molecules? Because it pleased God to make them. Why is there sex? Because God ordained it, and knew it would be enjoyable. Why are there multi-cellular organisms? Because God brought them into existence. Why is there language and mind? Because God made us in His image. In the beginning was the Word (Greek: *logos*), and this means that linguistic consciousness was the primal stuff from which the cosmos derived. So, it's no wonder that we think in language ...

Some may be satisfied by these theistic explanations; others may want something more. But one thing we can agree on: the God-hypothesis is functioning here like a rudimentary scientific hypothesis, indicating the source or origin, and the processes or mechanisms, whereby various things came into existence and now operate and behave the way they do. Just how much more *detail* can be wrung from this theistic hypothesis is of course rather moot.

Is the theistic hypothesis falsifiable? That is, can we imagine consistent circumstances, no matter how far-fetched, that would reveal it to be false? If not, then the theistic hypothesis is not in contention as a scientific hypothesis, and has no standing as an alternative to the scientific hypotheses deserving of consideration in our classrooms. But if it *is* falsifiable, then one must consider seriously any alternative, *naturalistic* theories that would work in place of it. Moreover, one must consider the merits of the theistic hypothesis with the same intellectual demands that one would be prepared to place on any alternative explanatory hypothesis.

So let us suppose that the theistic hypothesis is falsifiable, and consider its further scientific credentials. Can such an hypothesis make detailed, precise predictions about a range of hitherto unobserved phenomena? Can it be tested against accurately measured data? How does the theistic hypothesis fit in with our naturalistic theories about stellar and planetary evolution, about plate tectonics, about population genetics, etc.? Is it *intended* by its proponents that the theistic hypothesis meet such demands? If not, then just how is that hypothesis to be understood as functioning?

16.4 Theory choice

This raises a pressing methodological question, which is of crucial relevance to the status of the Argument from Design:

> *Which theory will a scientist believe or accept?*

Answer: the *best available* one. This would be the theory that is doing best from among all the available alternatives. Science is not monolithic and cumulative. The real activity of science is the rational proliferation of explanatory alternatives, all subject, ultimately, to the test of experience. The prevailing 'paradigm' in, say, physics, might be dominant for the time being; but it will have competitors at various stages of development, waiting to be considered if the dominant paradigm ever falters.

So: how *is* one to choose among competing scientific theories?

In situations where theories compete to explain roughly the same range of data thus far, and where we cannot devise crucial experiments to rule out all but one contender, we appeal to *pragmatic criteria of theory-choice*. These include:

1   simplicity
2   mathematical elegance
3   ontological parsimony
4   wide explanatory scope.

These notions are difficult to analyze or explicate. But they have considerable intuitive appeal, and definitely influence scientists' preferences for one theory over another.

16.4.1 Simplicity

An example of an intuition about simplicity is this: all other things being equal, one would prefer a theory postulating *linear relationships* to one postulating non-linear relationships.

Another way that simplicity is made manifest is in the *curve-fitting problem*: we prefer a curve through a set of data-points that fits the data as closely as possible (so that deviations from the curve can be explained by appeal to perturbating influences on measurement). A well-known method for choosing between two candidate curves $y = f(x)$ and $y = g(x)$ is called the *method of least squares*. For each data-point $\langle x,y \rangle$, the f-curve will 'miss it' by the y-amount $f(x) - y$ (the x-deviation of f from y); likewise, the g-curve will 'miss it' by the y-amount $g(x) - y$ (the x-deviation of g from y). To find out whether f 'misses' the data points, overall, worse than g does, see whether the *sum of squares of the deviations of f* is less than the *sum of squares of the deviations of g*. The lower the sum of such squares, the closer the fit of the curve to the data. In general, the simpler the curve one tries to draw (i.e., the fewer the algebraic parameters that need to be specified in the equation for the curve), the harder it is for the curve to pass through each data-point exactly. So there is an immediate tension between *exactitude* and *simplicity*. Usually, simplicity wins; for the scientist assumes that all measurements are subject to error and perturbation, in either direction (up or down from their 'true values'). Thus, a smoother curve is preferred, especially to the piecewise-linear zig-zag 'curve' that could be drawn by 'connecting the data-points' by straight lines. The smoother curve (whatever it is, algebraically) will be *simpler* than the zig-zag curve, even though the zig-zag curve is 'spot on' the data-points.

A final example of simplicity is Einstein's choice of *non-Euclidean geometries* to describe the structure of space-time. He *could* have stuck to Euclidean geometry instead, had he been willing to put up with an enormous complication in the statement of his dynamical laws. But by opting rather for the unconventional geometry, he achieved a much simpler form for his dynamical laws. And all other scientists now follow him in this choice. This does not show that Euclidean geometry is false. Rather, Euclidean geometry remains true of *Euclidean* spaces; it's just that physical space is now regarded as not Euclidean. This is on the basis of overall theoretical considerations, the most important of them being the preference for simplicity.

16.4.2 Ontological parsimony

The famous dictum 'Do not multiply entities beyond necessity' is called *Occam's Razor*, and is what the requirement of ontological parsimony amounts to. Strictly speaking, it counsels against postulating the existence of too many *kinds* of entity. It does not matter so much if any given kind of entity has a great many exemplars. There are huge numbers of photons in the universe, for example. Occam's Razor counsels only that we avoid postulating new kinds of fundamental particle unless there is a real theoretical payoff to be had from doing so.

16.4.3 Wide explanatory scope

The requirement of wide explanatory scope answers to the intuitive need to 'get to the bottom of things'. A fundamental scientific theory should carry implications for a great variety of different domains within which we observe and measure characteristic phenomena. Think of how Newtonian mechanics unifies into one simple and powerful explanatory scheme such diverse phenomena as planetary orbits, trajectories of projectiles, tides, pendula, spinning tops, gyroscopes, vibrating strings, sound waves, ripples in water, etc. Think of how the modern synthesis in evolutionary and molecular biology reveals the underlying unity in the myriad forms of life on earth. Think of how atomic theory enables one to explain such diverse phenomena as erosion by wind and water; combustion; chemical compounds; acidity and alkalinity; solubility; etc.

16.5 Revolutionary theory-change: a biological analogy

The famous historian of science Thomas Kuhn (1922–96) took the view that periods of scientific development were of two kinds: normal science, and revolutionary science. (See Kuhn (1970).) In a period of normal science, theorists extend the explanatory and predictive reach of their hypotheses, working largely on problems that can be solved. They enjoy a degree of success, working 'within' the paradigm. But when the failings of their theory become apparent – as so-called 'anomalies' crop up, which cannot be accommodated in that theoretical framework – dissident creative minds will seek radically different conceptual and theoretical frameworks in which to formulate a competitor theory.

This begins a period of revolutionary science. Once the competitor theory reaches a certain stage of development, its successful application to resolve the growing numbers of anomalies for the old theory suddenly tips the balance in favor of the new theory. The revolution is completed when a new generation of adherents, trained in the new tradition, replace the old theorists who could not change their intellectual ways.

The picture is very much like that of biological evolution, where a species that has remained unchanged in physical form and forms of behavior, coping with a relatively constant environmental niche, suddenly finds itself confronted with a set of important environmental changes. Mutant variants within the species will suddenly find themselves at a selective advantage, because they have some physical feature or behavioral capacity that enables them to cope better with the new selective pressures. They leave disproportionately more descendants in the next generation. These descendants inherit these features from their parents. Indeed, all that is needed in the way of such 'inheritance' is that there be a weakly positive correlation between parents and offspring in the newly important regards. After sufficiently many generations – and often, surprisingly few – the new features will have become almost universal within the survivors of that species. Or perhaps, by now: this new species.

The analogy between scientific change (evolution of theories) and biological change (evolution of species, and micro-evolution within them) serves two purposes here. The *first purpose* is to emphasize the sequence

- random variation;
- hitherto unencountered problem for survival;
- sudden increase in fitness of mutant strains;
- eventual displacement of the now badly adapted by the now better adapted.

The *second purpose* is to introduce some basic evolutionary ideas and ways of thinking about the world of living organisms. This enables one to appreciate, later, the force of a certain historic challenge to the Argument from Design, whose consequences all theists are wrestling with today. The challenge in question comes from Darwin's alternative, *naturalistic* way of explaining the appearance of design in the living world. As we shall see, Darwin makes no appeal to a divine creator or designer. He appeals only to known physical and chemical forces and quantities in order to explain how, over long enough periods of time, biological design can emerge from completely naturalistic processes and interactions. More of that in due course.

The sequence above can be interpreted easily on each side of the analogy between the biological world and the realm of scientific theories. What is being varied and has to survive, but might become 'unfit' in the face of new problems and be displaced by a mutant competitor, could be either a *kind of organism* or a *set of scientific hypotheses making up a theory*.

Indeed, corresponding to Kuhn's model of normal science (stasis) and revolutionary science (sudden discontinuity and displacement) is the theory of 'punctuated equilibrium', due to Gould and Eldredge, in evolutionary biology. (See Eldredge and Gould (1972).) They stress the long periods of stasis during which evolutionary changes are minimized, punctuated by relatively short periods of rapid speciation (involving changed bodily design and changes in forms of behavior). These short periods of rapid change are probably made possible by such events as heightened solar flares, when the increased radiation reaching earth gives rise to more mutations at the genetic level, in the organisms' DNA. When all species suddenly start changing, there is a non-linear explosion in the way that environments vary, since any one species' environment is made up, largely, by the various predator- and prey-species that are important to it. When the relative stasis is disturbed by a burst of mutations, the effects reverberate and get amplified through the whole ecosystem.

16.6 Evolution of ideas, concepts, theories and methods

And so it is, too, for the world of ideas, concepts, theories and methods.

When a new mathematical technique is invented, whole new areas of scientific investigation can be opened up. Think of co-ordinate geometry; the differential and integral calculus; non-Euclidean geometry; Hilbert-space theory and group-theory; catastrophe theory; chaos theory and non-linear dynamics.

When a new kind of instrument for observation is invented, we gain access to new kinds of data, which provokes new kinds of theorizing. Think of the telescope; the microscope; the electron microscope; X-rays; CAT-scans; PET-scans; the linear accelerator; supercolliders; the Hubble telescope.

When a new kind of instrument for *thinking* about (i.e., processing) the data is invented, all manner of new patterns in the existing information can be discerned, and can pose new demands for explanation. Think here of just one thing: the computer.

New concepts are always born in the context of a new set of axioms or postulates or hypotheses that endow new theoretical terms with content. (Some might say: those contents *are* the new concepts in question.) Novel concepts and theories come hand in hand. *These* are the novelties that represent the greatest breakthroughs. Think here of the following concepts (and theories involving them): gravitation; heat-energy; electromagnetism; quantized physical magnitudes; chemical valencies; natural selection; the gene; double-helical DNA; inertial-frame-relative measurements of space and time. (Note that we are not observing the actual historical order in the development of these concepts and theories.)

16.7 The relation between theory and evidence

Scientists – by training, intellectual inclination, moral conviction, professional aspiration, and communal discipline – submit themselves and the theories that they champion to the test of experience. This instils in them a certain intellectual *humility*. (Or at least: it *ought* to.) The humility consists in being prepared to admit, in the light of rival and better explanations of the data, that their theory is either wrong, or not the best available theory after all.

It is a hard pill to swallow, if things work out badly for one's favorite theory. But one is, after all, engaged in the dispassionate search for the truth about the natural world. Or at least: for an as-yet-unfalsified, elegantly formulated, simply conceived, nicely unifying, broadly explanatory *theory* of the natural world. One has to have a theory meeting this description in order to have any prospect at all of getting at 'the truth'. Indeed, when one reflects on the logical structure of scientific hypotheses, scientific reasoning, and the hypothetico-deductive method, one realizes that one cannot and will never do any *better* than that. That is, one will never have anything more than an as-yet-unfalsified, elegantly formulated, simply conceived, nicely unifying, broadly explanatory *theory* of the natural world. No matter that you might be sitting on 'the true theory'; you will never be able to *know* that you are. At best, if you are that fortunate, you will find that you never have to give up your theory in the face of countervailing evidence. But no amount of confirming evidence is ever going to *prove* your scientific theory with that degree of certainty attained exclusively in Mathematics, or in introspection about one's own states of sensory awareness and intellectual concentration. Scientific theories are never conclusively proved; and they are inherently fallible. But the only source of that fallibility is the rigor of logical and mathematical deduction, combined with acknowledgement of the primacy of observational evidence.

We seem to have ventured some way from our original topic: the Argument from Design for God's existence. But in fact we have not really strayed beyond what is both essential and relevant in building up to confront that argument.

16.8 The Darwinian theory

The range of 'design phenomena' that the theistic hypothesis 'explains' is what Darwinian theory also sets out to explain. The difference, however, as stressed earlier, is that Darwinian theory does not postulate God's existence. The theory is very accessible in its conceptual fundamentals; it does not involve any sophisticated mathematics. (For a detailed case for this claim, see Tennant (2014b).)

The main problem is to account for adaptive change in the design of organisms: changes in their bodies and in their ways of behaving. These changes make them 'fit better' within the niche in which they struggle to survive and reproduce. How is this 'fit' attained?

Darwin's answer was very simple. It involved three observations and an imaginative but logical leap to a startling conclusion.

The *first observation* is that (in any given species) there is *variation* among individuals. They vary in many ways, both in bodily characteristics and their behavioral repertoire. These bodily and behavioral features are what the evolutionary biologist calls the individuals' *phenotypic traits*. Some examples of variable traits are: stature; weight; coloration; immunities to infections; libido; trustworthiness; intelligence; fleetness of foot; balance and co-ordination; acuity of vision; keenness of hearing; appetite for food; need for sleep; etc. It matters not that these traits can be strongly affected by environmental influences during maturation. What matters only is whether there is a non-random correlation between such features on the part of parents and such features on the part of their offspring. Note that all that we have said so far would apply just as much to non-human animals as it would to human beings. (*And*: it applies to human beings.)

The brings us to the *second observation*: there *is* a non-random correlation of the kind just mentioned. Offspring take after their parents; they tend to resemble them more than they resemble other, arbitrarily chosen members of the population. In a word, we have *heritability* of phenotypic traits.

The *third observation* is that individuals vary in the number of offspring they leave behind. Some do not breed at all; some leave very many offspring (comparatively speaking). And, in sexually reproducing species such as our own, there is the further twist that *variation in reproductive success* is greater among males than it is among females. This is the result of the asymmetry between the sexes. Conception involves the male. But, while conception also involves the female, gestation is the female's preserve exclusively (biologically speaking). Moreover, the female knows that her offspring is her own, whereas the male can never attain the same level of certainty. But we digress ...

In summary, we observe:

1 *inter-individual variation;*
2 *heritability; and*
3 *differential reproduction.*

What can we predict, from this? The answer comes from the further consideration that some of the inter-individual variations are responsible for the differential reproduction that takes place. Individuals vary in reproductive success largely because of the traits they have. (Example: the successful male fruit-fly dances more effectively than his competitors. So, in all likelihood, will his sons.) And those traits that make for reproductive success will be handed on to the relatively more numerous offspring that the successful reproducer will leave behind. And so it will go on, generation after generation.

The leap of imagination – which, we stressed earlier, is really only a logical leap – is involved when we consider what will be the result of the repetition, over a great many generations, of this stage-by-stage process of 'natural selection'. The process is called *natural* because it is the 'blind forces of Nature' against which the individuals are struggling for survival, and with which they have to contend in order successfully to reproduce. Natural selection is here contrasted with *artificial* selection, which is the process whereby human beings selectively encourage certain members of other species (such as homing pigeons, hunting-dogs, or racehorses) to breed, with the aim of producing individuals exhibiting certain traits that the *human being* would like them to have. Of course, artificial selection is, ultimately, a form of natural selection, but both the original contrast betwen natural and artifical selection, and the eventual dissolution of that contrast, should be clear to the reader.

The logic of Darwin's explanatory argument is compelling. Given sufficient variation, both existing or arising through further mutations, natural selection alone can, over many generations, effect qualitatively huge changes in the make-up of any species. Indeed, it can explain how a given species can speciate into two distinct species. We need only a mechanism whereby the 'storehouse of variation' can be stocked, as it were, and re-supplied from time to time. If this is how species evolved (or 'descended', through eons), then we can expect traces of their ancestry to exist in the fossil record. Here, evolutionary biology meets paleontology, and the structure of the so-called 'phylogenetic tree' gets revealed in a piecemeal, always incomplete, but very systematic fashion. Darwin gets combined with the geologist Charles Lyell (1797–1875), the zoologist Georges Cuvier (1769–1832), the paleoanthropologist Richard Leakey (b. 1944), and others. This is where interest in dinosaurs, mammoths, Neanderthal man, and ancient pre-hominid species in the eastern African savannah fit in.

The storehouse of variation, which is the engine of evolutionary change, is the complement of *genes* on the *chromosomes* in the *cells* of conspecific individuals. Genes are postulated as particulate bearers of reproductive information, enabling offspring to grow in a way that makes them resemble their parents. They grow that way because they get their complement of genes from their parents, in the form of a sperm cell and an egg cell (both of these being called *gametes*). Each gamete contributes a parental chromosome towards each pair of chromosomes that the new individual needs. Much is known, for various species, about the relative *dominance* or *recessiveness* of the two *alleles* at a great many of the *genetic loci* on a chromosome. Here, organismic biology meets cellular biology, embryology and population genetics. Darwin gets combined with philosopher-biologist Ernst Haeckel (1834–1919) and plant geneticist Gregor Mendel (1822–84). Just over a decade ago, with more detailed knowledge of the underlying molecular genetics, the complete genome of the fruit-fly *Drosofila melanogaster* had at last been mapped. Something on the order of a thousand chromosomal loci were involved. Since then big science has busied itself to completion on the human genome itself – with 100,000 chromosomal loci.

When we inquire further after the mechanism of gene-transmission from parent to offspring, we find that the biochemical basis (or molecular-genetic basis) of the gene is the double-helical strand of DNA, in which sequences of *codons* correspond to genes. The genes' information-theoretic content is determined by how they code for the production of primary proteins, in ways that modern science is still unravelling. Here, Darwin and Mendel get combined with Francis Crick (1916–2004) and James Watson (b. 1928), the co-discoverers of DNA.

16.9 The New Synthesis

The result of combining all these observationally driven, predictively and explanatorily powerful, and *testable* theories, is called the *New Synthesis*. The New Synthesis is a magnificent intellectual product, of broad explanatory reach. Moreover, it is completely *naturalistic* in all its various postulations of mechanisms, processes, constituents, stuffs, forces, etc. Philosophers of science really do mean what they say when they describe such a theory as the result of making an *inference to the best explanation*. 'Best' is judged both with regard to the conceptual and ontological economy of the theory, and with regard to the totality of observational data that needs to be fitted into the overall picture, with adequate logical and explanatory structure superimposed.

There are some propositions that have been uncovered only courtesy of the New Synthesis, and which present a challenge to any previously entrenched, or newly formulated, rival explanatory theory. An example of such a proposition is: *In all known terrestrial species, the genetic code is universal.* Another one is: *Information flows from the genotype to the phenotype, and never in the other direction.* The New Synthesis has ready explanations for these generalizations; its theistic rival would be at some loss to explain them.

To be sure, there are still some hard and exciting explanatory problems facing the New Synthesis. But that is precisely what one would want for any flourishing scientific theory: problems whose eventual solution will drive the theory forward, making it extend its reach, making it uncover new forces or processes or mechanisms or *natural* kinds of thing. (Note the stress on 'natural'.) Examples of such explananda are:

- What might have been the 'ur-species' (the original kind of self-replicating entities)?
- How did cells arise?
- How did sexual reproduction arise?
- How did multi-cellular organisms arise?
- How did sociality arise?
- How did altruism arise?
- How did consciousness arise?
- How did language and logic arise?
- Why are humans nevertheless so beastly?

A thriving scientific tradition is not to be downgraded just because it may not yet have attained a satisfactory theoretical consensus in reply to questions such as these.

16.10 On choosing between the theistic and naturalistic theories

These questions, and the present lack of consensual answers to them, do not represent problems that can *now* be asserted to be *insoluble* within the New Synthesis or any possible future extension thereof. The opponent who says to supporters of a theory T

> No reasonable extension of T, conforming to your broadly naturalistic methodological constraints, will ever succeed in supplying an answer to naturalistic question Q

is actually guilty either of appalling ignorance or of appalling intellectual hubris. The opponent would be guilty of appalling ignorance if the answer to question Q were already well known to the practitioners of theory T. Unfortunately, this is often the case with creationists' objections to the New Synthesis. Frequently they just do not know enough about the Science they are undertaking to criticize.

But even in the case of a question that the practitioners of theory T agree does not (yet) have a satisfactory answer, the objector who baldly asserts that no such answer will ever be forthcoming is guilty of appalling intellectual hubris. For one has to be a logically omniscient scientific genius in order to be able to grasp a theory in its essential *limitations*. Who is to say that there will not be a broadly naturalistic *extension* of theory T, based on some as-yet-unthought-of naturalistic insight, which *will* provide a satisfying answer to question Q?

To make this point vivid: consider the proponents of 'élan vital', or (irreducible) 'living force', who denied that there would ever be a naturalistic explanation of Life itself. They were just plain wrong. (As was Emil du Bois-Reymond, who had the Origin of Life on his list of seven insoluble 'cosmic riddles' – see the discussion in §23.1.) They could not anticipate the discovery of DNA, and our eventual understanding of the mechanism whereby genetic information is transmitted from parents to their offspring. The theorists of 'élan vital' proved to be simply hubristic. What made them think themselves so smart that they could circumscribe in thought all the possibilities concerning what we might one day discover and conjecture, and which would make the naturalistic answer to the question clear? To tell someone else – indeed, the whole scientific community, present and future – that they are just *not smart enough* to figure out a naturalistic explanation is a form of overweening intellectual arrogance.

All this said, we return to confront the Argument from Design with the Darwinian alternative. Why postulate God when more modest postulations of entirely natural things will do? Why continue to be dazzled by the complexity and harmony of nature when there are intellectually satisfying explanations of it? Why not embrace the world in a natural-scientific frame of mind, rather than be hell-bent (if one might use the phrase) on maintaining a theistic one *for the purposes of explaining exactly what natural science sets out to explain, and explains so well*?

These are the challenges facing the person who accepts the Argument from Design. He or she has to show the scientific objector that, *qua scientific hypothesis*, the postulation of God is intellectually more satisfying than the postulation of self-copying organic molecules with coding properties, and the blind, impersonal force of natural selection. And the scientific objectors, for their part, might have to find other grounds or reasons for belief in God – if that is what they want to believe.

Problems

1 What exactly is the fundamental schema of Darwinian evolutionary explanation? Why is it naturalistic?
2 Explain the analogy between theoretical revolutions followed by periods of normal science, and rapid evolutionary change followed by periods of stasis.

244 The Existence of God

3 What are the various branches of Science that contribute to the so-called New Synthesis in evolutionary biology?
4 How did Newton's Argument from Design differ from Paley's?
5 What is the Anthropic Principle?
6 What are the marks of simplicity on the part of scientific theories? (For your answer, do not rely on this chapter's material alone. Take a look at both Quine (1963) and Sober (1975).)

17 The Argument from Contemporary Creationism

17.1 Naturalism v. Creationism

Philip Johnson (b. 1940) is a born-again Christian and founder of the 'Intelligent Design' movement, which attempts to set out an intellectually respectable defense of Creationism. Consider the following argument, to be found in Johnson (1995):

> Scientific theories are based on naturalism.
> Scientific theories have undermined our morals, etc.
> That is a bad thing.
> *ergo*, Naturalism is false.

It was David Hume, the great common-sense philosopher of the Scottish Enlightenment, who first alerted us to the fallaciousness of arguments whose premises stated matters of fact but whose conclusions stated moral norms. Such arguments commit the *naturalistic fallacy*. They try (mistakenly) to infer values from facts. It is not being implied, however, that Johnson's style of argument here commits the naturalistic fallacy. Rather, it does something *even worse*. One of its *premises* is a moral evaluation – indeed, a *meta*-moral evaluation – to the effect that *it is a bad thing* that a particular, traditional moral code of precepts and principles is on the wane. But the argument's *conclusion* is about a great (and purported) metaphysical fact of the matter: *Naturalism is false*.

Johnson is committing what might better be called the *Ostrich Fallacy*. Here we trade on a common (mis)understanding. An ethological myth has it that the ostrich sticks its head in the sand in order to 'pretend to be a bush', so as to fool predators. Hence the metaphor, in English, of 'putting one's head in the sand' – that is, refusing to take a proper comprehending look at a potentially dangerous situation. The author was told by a zoologist, however, that the best explanation for the ostrich's habit is that it is listening for vibrations, below ground level, from the footfalls of potential predators – hence, ironically, very much trying to comprehend what danger it may be in. By way of possibly great injustice to the poor ostrich, however, we shall persevere with the new label.

The Ostrich Fallacy is exemplified by the following argument-forms:

Virus V exists.
Virus V causes sickness S.
Sickness S is horrible.
ergo, We should not believe that virus V exists.

The Second Amendment literally says XYZ.
Citizens of the USA interpret XYZ as protecting their right to carry guns.
Exercising the right to carry guns results in many shooting deaths.
This is horrible.
ergo, We should not believe that the Second Amendment literally says XYZ.

More generally, the pattern of an Ostrich fallacy is:

It is a fact that P.
Its being the case that P tends to bring about condition C.
C is bad.
ergo, We should not believe that P.

The central form of argument in Johnson's *Reason in the Balance*, which was quoted above, commits the Ostrich fallacy. So too does a second, more elaborate form of argument to be found in Johnson's text:

Suppose that God indeed exists.
God is a moral Being with a concern for our moral welfare, and with intentions as to how we ought to live our earthly lives.
So, it behooves us to live according to His moral law.
But naturalism, and/or the scientific theorizing based on it, induces us to cease observing His moral law.
That is a bad thing.
ergo, We should not believe Naturalism.

Having a naturalistic outlook may, as a matter of empirical fact, change one's moral code. *So what?* Even *if* that change in one's moral code is, objectively, for the worse, *so what?* Having adopted a deficient moral code, why should that reflect any discredit on the *truth* of one's scientific theories and/or – if one can speak of truth and falsity here – of one's naturalistic metaphysical outlook? In ignoring the history of the fact/value distinction, Johnson has succeeded only in commiting what the Oxford philosopher Peter Strawson (1919–2006) once called a 'non-sequitur of numbing grossness'. (Strawson was criticizing Kant with this remark, so perhaps Johnson can claim to be in good company.)

The conclusion of Johnson's ostrich-fallacious argument, note, is that naturalism is *false*, not just that naturalism is – *tsk, tsk* – a *morally* bad or unfortunate metaphysical outlook. One wants to ask: why shouldn't a theist accept that naturalism is the correct metaphysical outlook to adopt for the understanding of nature, but that one should not thereby allow oneself to lose one's basic *moral* norms? Why can't we have the new recipe for our metaphysical cake and still eat its old-fashioned moral frosting? *Nothing in the logic of human thought and experience prevents us from having both.* Whatever our current (indeed: perennial) moral failings, they do *not* show that naturalism is false.

There is another major flaw in Johnson's way of seeing things. He expresses himself repeatedly in a way that shows that he thinks that naturalism (as a metaphysical view) *gives rise to*, or *entails* our scientific theories. But it does not. The metaphysical outlook of naturalism is, rather, one that arises, upon intelligent reflection, from the explanatory and predictive successes of the various natural sciences. Naturalism starts as a *methodology* for the discovery of good scientific theories.

This methodology enjoins us to look for efficient causes of the regularities that we detect in observed phenomena. We should try, when framing our explanations of these regularities, to eschew any appeal to spirits, or God's will, or predestination, or the work of the Devil. Instead, we should seek out those laws of cause and effect, those patterns of statistical distribution and correlation, that the phenomena might disclose. Then we should try to put forward logically unifying conjectural theories that explain those regularities. These theories will explain those regularities by appeal to mediating mechanisms and internal constitutions, microscopic or macroscopic, which constitute in some sense the ultimate nature of physical reality. When our theories are spectacularly successful – much more successful than prayer or imprecation, than divination or animal sacrifice, than reading tea leaves or Tarot cards, than burning incense or twirling rosary beads – we get comforting support for a naturalist metaphysical outlook. When our theories give us tremendous technological and therapeutic benefits, we know that we are onto something deep and important concerning how the natural world works. It is the success of theories obtained on a naturalistic *methodology* that gives rise to naturalism as a *metaphysical* outlook; not the other way round. The reason why Johnson, like many a theist, finds it so hard to live with the success of modern science is this: if adequate *theories* render God superfluous for our scientific understanding of the world and of our place in it, what rational reason remains for belief in God? *That* is why Johnson has to sally forth into the fields of Big Bang cosmology, macroevolution and the fossil record, and neurobiology, to lodge his shaky criticisms.

Instead of carving Nature at the joints, Johnson seeks to fill alleged gaps in our scientific understanding. There are important singularities for, and 'thresholds' in, the history of the cosmos, from the self-interested point of view of our own species:

- the origin of universe (caveat: this is a singularity, *not* an 'event');
- the formation of galaxies, stars, planets;
- the origin of the genetic code (i.e., of the first self-replicating molecules);
- the origin of first unicellular organisms;

- the origin of first eukaryotes;
- the origin of multicellular organisms;
- the origin of sexual reproduction;
- the origin of organs of sense;
- the emergence of mammals;
- the emergence of open behavioral programs;
- the emergence of sociality;
- the emergence of consciousness;
- the emergence of intelligence;
- the emergence of *Homo sapiens*;
- the emergence of tool use;
- the emergence of religious practices;
- the emergence of language;
- the emergence of theories.

Of course, from this list it is the Big Bang, the origin of life, and the emergence of *Homo sapiens* that the creationists most frequently cite as requiring the hypothesis of divine intervention for their explanation. But such an hypothesis is actually *devoid* of explanatory and predictive value. It is the last resort of scientifically impoverished imaginations. To guard against this dogmatic intellectual defeatism, one should adopt

THE NATURALIST'S RULE OF THUMB
Interpret

> God has intervened in the natural order to make it the case that P

as saying no more than

> Given our ignorance or misunderstanding of extant naturalistic theories, and/or our inability to apply them and work out their logical consequences, we (the theists) believe that there could not possibly be any naturalistic explanation of its being the case that P.

The hypothesis of divine intervention at any or all of the junctures listed above tells us nothing testable about the mechanisms at work in the divinely effected event of creation or emergence; and it leaves us utterly in the dark as to what one might expect *next* in the way of further supernatural hocus-pocus. The creationists resorting to this hypothesis invariably ignore other, naturalistic accounts that address the question of mechanisms (as in the case of the theory of the genetic code) or treat judiciously of the singularities (as in the case of cosmological models of the Big Bang). (For a detailed argument as to why Big Bang cosmology lends no succour whatsoever to the creationist, see Grünbaum (1995).) These naturalistic theories, moreover, fail to be predictive only because they deal with highly non-linear phenomena; but still manage to give a satisfactory account, retrodictively, of the complexities of emergence.

Most important among the naturalistic theories that, on a proper understanding, would be unsettling to a theist would be those on the following list. But creationists are ignorant of them, or misunderstand them, or fail to appreciate their explanatory reach:

1 general relativity, quantum gravity, and Big Bang cosmology (Einstein (1915), Einstein (1916), and Einstein (1917); Penrose (2004); Hawking (2001));

2 the molecular biological theory of the origins of the genetic code and of unicellular life forms (Eigen and Schuster (1979));

3 the theory of the evolution of species by natural selection (Darwin (1859)) by virtue of particulate inheritance (Mendel (1866 and 1870); Schrödinger (1946)) whose biochemical mechanism is DNA (Watson and Crick (1953)) with the focus of selective forces ultimately being the gene or allele (Williams (1966); Dawkins (1976)), and with sporadic patterns of dramatic phase transitions followed by periods of relative stasis (Prigogine and Stengers (1984), for a theory of systems far from thermodynamic equilibrium; Eldredge and Gould (1972), for a macro-evolutionary theory of punctuated equilibria);

4 the theory of the evolution of the hominid brain: emergence of perceptual categories, causal thinking, tool use, language, sociality, self-consciousness (Darwin (1871); Lorenz (1941); Piaget (1971); Riedl (1980); Premack (1976));

5 the theory of the evolution of forms of social, co-operative behavior (Axelrod and Hamilton (1981); Axelrod (1984)) and the moral codes that re-inforce it (Campbell (1975));

6 the theory of the evolution of consciousness and rationality (Dennett (1981); Jaynes (1976); Sober (1981));

7 the theory of the evolution of scientific concepts and theories themselves (Toulmin (1972); Popper (1972); Tennant (1988); Plotkin (1994));

8 the theory of cultural evolution (Boyd and Richerson (1985); Cavalli-Sforza and Feldman (1981));

9 the theory of complexity at the edge between order and chaos, of dissipative structures and phase transitions (Kauffman (1993)).

Johnson omits even cursory coverage of any of the above theories, despite the fact that they were all published well before he wrote *Reason in the Balance*. Yet they are theories that can claim to fill the important lacunae which, he alleges, demonstrate the impossibility of a naturalistic account of our earthly life in this universe. These theories render toothless Johnson's main criticisms of naturalistic science with regard to its *explanatoriness*.

Note that even if there are some explanatory gaps in the naturalistic theories so far available, the best response to this would be 'more of the same'. That is, one should seek *naturalistic* extensions of those theories, so as to plug those gaps. If, instead, we throw up our hands in craven intellectual defeat and invoke the words or works of God, we do not thereby obtain *any* predictive power or *any* genuine improvement in our state of understanding. Indeed, such an intellectually defeatist theistic attitude makes for very bad science. It makes one give up too soon in one's efforts to apply the scientific method. Science is *hard work*. We should not provide too many excuses in advance for intellectual malingering. If creationists were honest, they would concede that if God moves, then He perforce moves *only* in mysterious ways. Absent the mysteries, and we have naturalistic explanations. It would follow, then, that we should be more willing to tolerate a temporary explanatory gap than to fall back on useless stop-gaps.

But still, the over-ready diagnosis that there are indeed yawning explanatory gaps is entered without any honest attempt, on the creationist's part, to come to terms with the many and varied facts about the biological realm that are so satisfyingly brought within our comprehending grasp by neo-Darwinian evolutionary theory. It is tedious in the extreme to read Creationist arguments that proceed in ignorance of some or all of the basic features of contemporary evolutionary theorizing.

Johnson attacks certain scientific theories, claiming that they are vitiated by available evidence, or explanatorily deficient. His attacks are ill-informed and spurious. He misunderstands the theories he attacks, and wholly ignores whole theories that would plug his alleged gaps. He is itching to get his God in, not just as a God of the Gaps, but really as a God of the Last Gasp, and to find enough gaps in the picture provided by science to be able to join the dots and form a figure in the shape of his Judaeo–Christian God. This figure will emerge, rooted in the interstices of our alleged theoretical failings, as the Be-all and End-all, the force that sustains the universe, who brought it into existence and even now keeps it in existence. The last thinker in the Western tradition who thought that God intervened pretty much continuously in this way to keep everything going was Nicolas Malebranche (1638–1715). One is tempted, today, to decompose this name into its component syllables, and regard the view as out on a limb, and badly wrong.

From his odd perch Johnson crows over or cavils at what he thinks is

1   relativistic cosmology's admission of a singularity in space-time (the so-called Big Bang) that can be thought of as the event of creation, and that can be construed only as the work of God;
2   modern science's inability to account for the *origin* of life;
3   evolutionary theory's inability to account for macroevolution: the emergence of new phyla and species, with new body plans and with too little in the fossil record to fill in all the transitional stages that one would expect on a gradualist Darwinian account; and
4   reductionist neuroscience's inability to account, within the scheme of its own categories and principles, for rationality, consciousness, intentionality, and other aspects of our mental life.

Johnson's allegations (above) of theoretical Achilles heels or shortcomings blithely disregard the resources of certain of the theories that are listed above. His complaints can be countered, respectively, as follows:

1 The Big Bang cannot be regarded as having been *caused* by any agency, not even a supernatural one. For it is not an event *in time*. Rather, it is a singularity that *bounds* space-time. It marks the beginning of time without being at an instant *of* time. Thus it violates no conservation laws of physics: for these laws speak only of certain magnitudes being constant *at all instants of time*. There was (or, timelessly if one wishes: is) no moment of creation, hence no event of creation, hence no act of creation. Therefore God could not have *caused* the universe to come into existence. (Here we are endebted to Grünbaum [1995].)

2 Johnson neglects to mention or to examine the molecular theory of the hypercycle. This theory accounts in great detail for the pre-biotic origin of RNA and DNA. It is due to the Nobel Laureate Manfred Eigen.

3 In the modern synthesis of evolutionary biology, there is an abundance of plausible suggestions as to the genetic and environmental factors that would turn microevolution into macroevolution. Catastrophic events such as flaring sun-spots, impacts of comets and meteorites, melting of polar ice-caps, and volcanic eruptions can both increase the rates of mutation in different gene pools and give rise to tremendous forces of directed selection. Mutations at single loci (of so-called 'control' genes) can result in catastrophic changes in body plans, such as the production of whole new pairs of arms or legs. The first phyla were established in a planet-wide phase transition for life forms known as the Cambrian era – beginning roughly 500 million years ago. We know enough about epigenetic phenomena already to appreciate that there are myriads of potentialities for body-plan innovation within a reasonably large genome. We can acknowledge also that, once various phyla's broad body plans had been established, those phyla would have enjoyed a competitive edge that severely impeded the emergence of yet more radically distinct phyla. Moreover, the relative proportions of lethal and benign mutations are absolutely beside the point: the whole point about natural selection is that it does indeed winnow genotypes ferociously. Hence the survivors are highly adapted; that is, they *appear* to have been designed for the niches that they occupy. Johnson also commits the fundamental error of thinking that adaptation by natural selection can occur only by dint of highly improbable sequences of benign point mutations. He neglects altogether the theory of genetic variability and of heritability in the population geneticist's sense. He does not see variability within a gene pool as always providing an as yet untapped source of potential responsiveness to future environmental challenges, which could thereby induce rapid evolutionary change, including speciation and the emergence of new body plans.

4 On the topic of reductionism, Johnson pays scant attention to the fact that many a naturalistically minded philosopher of science has already made

intellectual room for the determination of higher-level phenomena (such as mental phenomena) by lower-level physical processes, while yet retaining descriptive and explanatory autonomy for the 'higher-level' theories such as psychology (see the conclusions reached in this regard in §14.2). In fact, it would be fair to say that the orthodox view among philosophers of science is that at all neighboring levels one has 'supervenience without reductionism'. This includes the pairs physics–chemistry, molecular biology–organismic biology, neuroscience–psychology, and individual psychology–sociology. Emergent properties of complex wholes are as much a part of nature as are the properties of their constituents. But the latter need not provide us with any explanatory or descriptive purchase on the former. The fact of 'emergence', nevertheless, does not speak for divine or creative intervention.

We do not need God to get the universe going. The universe just *is*. We do not need God to get life going. Life simply arose from large molecules. We do not need God to get life to diversify. Life simply diversified through evolution by natural selection. We do not need God to get creatures to feel and think. They became feeling and thinking creatures because suitably complicated brains and nervous systems enhanced their inclusive genetic fitness. Nor do we need God to get them caring about one another. Perfectly good explanations of sociality and prevalent forms of altruism are to be had from sociobiological theories based on the genetic theory of kin-selection.

Problems

1   What epistemological weight should be accorded to ancient scriptures that put forward creation stories at odds with modern scientific theorizing?
2   Does morality need a foundation in revealed religion? Can we both frame a moral code and abide by it, with an intellectual commitment to a completely secular account of cosmic and biological evolution?
3   Read any one of the scientific works cited in this chapter and assess whether the claims made on its behalf are reasonable.
4   Do any of the internal theoretical disputes within the broadly Darwinian camp (such as, say, the dispute between gene-selectionism and group-selectionism) undermine the credibility of the neo-Darwinian synthesis as a comprehensive naturalistic account of how living things came to be the way they are?
5   Has any creationist thinker ever made an important and original contribution to the advancement of science?

18 Pascal's Wager

Having looked at 'theoretical' arguments for the existence of God, we turn now to an argument of a different kind: Pascal's Wager (see Pascal (1910)). In order both to describe it and then to criticize it, we need to digress into the general topic of rational action and deliberation, especially under conditions of uncertainty.

18.1 Background: the theory of rational decision-making

18.1.1 *Rational decision-making without uncertainty*

First, to keep matters simple, we look at *decision-making without uncertainty*. By this we mean decision-making in situations where one believes that there is only one possible relevant outcome S of whatever action A one is considering. This belief on the part of the rational agent X can be expressed as follows:

X believes that by performing action A, X will bring about situation S.

Examples:

- I believe that by turning the ignition key, I will get the engine started.
- You believe that by reading this, you will learn about Pascal's Wager.
- He believes that by having a good breakfast he will have more energy late in the morning.
- She believes that by betting $100 on such-and-such a horse, she will win a large sum of money (because she believes the race has been rigged so that this particular horse will definitely win).

What would make the agent decide to perform action A? Obviously, the *desire* that the situation S should obtain, and the further *belief* that both the situation S and all foreseeable consequences of the action A are morally and legally permissible. (The rational agent will consider foreseeable consequences in order to avoid possible lawsuits for culpable negligence, and to avoid any future pangs of conscience, and to avoid harming anyone.) In the case of most actions within the course of normal daily events, we don't think explicitly in these terms. I don't find myself saying to myself:

> I would like a coffee.
> I believe that by going into my favorite local coffeehouse and offering $3 I shall get a coffee.
> There is nothing morally wrong about doing this, and there is no legal prohibition against it, and I don't think that there are any foreseeable, untoward consequences of doing this.
> So, I shall go into the coffeehouse and offer them $3 for a coffee.

If I *did* deliberate explicitly in this way, I would be in bad shape, and would either need that coffee or discover that I had been having way too much coffee of late.

In the normal course of events, the features

- desire that S obtain
- belief that by A-ing, one will make S the case
- belief that both A and S are permissible
- decision (formation of intention) to A
- intentionally A-ing

hardly penetrate to the surface of consciousness. One dimly craves, and one acts accordingly. Well-established habits are more reflexive and unthinking. The grooves of daily conduct are morally and legally smooth, free of obstruction. One simply goes with the flow, of life, like-minded people, and coffee.

But in other cases of rational deliberation, these features can be very explicitly foregrounded – indeed, ought to be. This happens at the more critical junctures of one's intellectual and emotional life. Think of major decisions, such as:

- choice of diet, i.e., what to eat on a regular daily basis
- choice of college
- choice of major in college degree
- choice of romantic partner
- choice of graduate education
- choice of more permanent significant other
- choice of first permanent, full-time job
- decision to have children
- decisions about investment of retirement assets
- decisions about how to cast one's vote in presidential elections.

As we shall shortly see, rational deliberation over these things is fraught with uncertainty; and we are supposed, at this stage, to be considering only decision-making in the absence of such uncertainty. Still, these examples serve a useful purpose at this stage. A lot of people, sadly, do not deliberate much about these things. They just fall into certain *de facto* options, without really taking control of their lives, for themselves, at these critical junctures. They might give in to parental pressure, or the unreasonable demands of a casual sexual partner, or the blandishments of a recruiting officer, or to a romantic mood on vacation, or to some fast-talking con-man from a big brokerage house, or to some narrow-minded ideological bandwagon roaring through their tightly-knit neighborhood.

One good reason to become self-conscious and reflective about rational deliberation is to break the hold that these insidious influences can have on the unwary, so as to equip yourself with the wherewithal to think things through for yourself, with an independent and critical mind.

Let us go back, however, to the schematization

- X desires that situation S obtain.
- X believes that by A-ing, X will bring it about that S.
- X believes that both A-ing and S are morally and legally permissible.
- So, X (intentionally) As.

We have here the essential components of a *rational explanation of an intentional action* by a rational agent, in situations unaffected by uncertainty: a certain desire; a certain means-end belief; and a subsidiary belief that these means and this end are permissible. A given action is made intelligible by attributing an appropriate belief-desire pair to the agent. We rationalize the agent's action *locally*. But we should also have an eye to rendering the agent *globally* rational, by re-using our attributions of those same beliefs and those same desires, but in different combinations, to explain yet other actions on the agent's part. In all projects of so-called *rational interpretation* of people from a radically different culture, who speak a radically different language, we think of them as possessed of the same basic sorts of beliefs and desires as we have, and we try to work out from there what various words might mean in their mouths. But we also have to allow for the possibility that they have some very strange (to us, irrational) beliefs, as well as some very strange desires. These will only be identifiable over the course of time, as we try to make increasing sense of all that they do – both with their words, and to one another, ourselves included.

18.1.2 *Rational decision-making under conditions of uncertainty*

Now we turn to the topic of decision-making in *conditions of uncertainty*.

Typically in such situations we are confroned with a range of alternative (and, let us suppose, mutually exclusive) actions $A_1, \ldots, A_n$. By performing any one of them we *might* make a partial causal contribution to how things subsequently will work out. But exactly how they do work out is not entirely in our hands, or under our control. We have to leave a lot (indeed, in some cases, everything) to fortune, destiny, fate, Nature, or (less portentously) to circumstances beyond our control. Typically, for each action A_k, there will be various ways $W_1, \ldots, W_m$ in which things could work out (perhaps as a result, partially, of our performing action

A_k – but then again, perhaps not). At best we will be able to assign probabilities (numbers lying between 0 and 1) to these possibilities $W_1, \ldots, W_m$. These m probabilities will sum to unity.

To simplify matters, let us take $m = k = 2$. So we shall be considering two alternative actions A_1 and A_2, and two different ways W_1 and W_2 that the world might be, perhaps as a partial result of those actions, perhaps independently of them.

This gives us four possibilities:

1   action A_1 is undertaken; W_1 turns out to be the case;
2   action A_1 is undertaken; W_2 turns out to be the case;
3   action A_2 is undertaken; W_1 turns out to be the case;
4   action A_2 is undertaken; W_2 turns out to be the case.

Example: in a two-horse race between Horse$_1$ and Horse$_2$:

1   bet that Horse$_1$ will win; Horse$_1$ wins;
2   bet that Horse$_1$ will win; Horse$_2$ wins;
3   bet that Horse$_2$ will win; Horse$_1$ wins;
4   bet that Horse$_2$ will win; Horse$_2$ wins.

Here is a case where the action (the placing of a particular bet) has no bearing on the future outcome of the race. But in other decision-theoretic situations, the particular action undertaken might foreclose existing, or create new, possibilities, while still leaving several possibilities open, and with probabilities that are themselves affected by whichever action has been undertaken.

The problem facing the agent is always: *which of the available actions should I perform?* Let us assume that this problem is to be solved in an entirely self-interested way. That is, the agent cares only about his or her own welfare, and cares about the welfare of others only to the extent involved in avoiding doing any legally or morally impermissible harm to anyone.

The rationally self-interested agent (also sometimes called a *prudential* agent) has to ask:

- What is the cost or benefit to me, in each of the combinations $[A, W]$ consisting of my action A, and of the way W that things turn out to be? (In the simplified case under discussion, there are four such combinations: $[A_1, W_1]$; $[A_1, W_2]$; $[A_2, W_1]$; $[A_2, W_2]$.)
- What are the respective probabilities of those ways the world might be, conditionally on the action I might perform? That is,

  –   What is the probability of W_1, conditional on my performing A_1?
  –   What is the probability of W_2, conditional on my performing A_1?
  –   What is the probability of W_1, conditional on my performing A_2?
  –   What is the probability of W_2, conditional on my performing A_2?

The payoff, or *Utility*, of way W when action A has been performed, is denoted $U(W,A)$. This quantity $U(W,A)$ will be the result of adding together all the various *benefits* of having performed A when W turns out to be the case, and then subtracting all the various *costs* associated with A.

The *probability of W conditional on A* is denoted prob$(W|A)$. By prob(W) we shall mean the *absolute probability* of W, independent of any condition such as A. If A has no influence one way or the other on W, then prob$(W|A)$ = prob(W).

The *expected Utility* of any action A (in our simplified case, where W_1 and W_2 are the only ways things can turn out) is

$$\text{prob}(W_1|A).U(W_1,A) + \text{prob}(W_2|A).U(W_2,A).$$

The *downside* of action A (in our simplified case) is the minimum value of $U(W,A)$ as W ranges over the various ways things might turn out to be. Note that in the definition of downside there is no mention of probabilities. The downside is simply the worst possible outcome, no matter how improbable. When the downside is bad enough (e.g., death) the rationally 'risk-averse' hesitate to 'weight' it with probabilities.

The Utility, or net cost or benefit of each outcome (consequent to the action performed) and the various conditional probabilities all contribute importantly to the rationality of the final choice of action. Once the agent has answered the earlier questions posed, there are *two questions that usually guide decision-making under uncertainty*:

1   Which action will *maximize my expected gain*, – i.e., for which action A will

$$\text{prob}(W_1|A).U(W_1,A) + \text{prob}(W_2|A).U(W_2,A)$$

be maximized?

2   Which action will *minimize any possible loss*, i.e., for which action A will the downside of A be minimized?

An ideal solution to a decision-making problem will be an action A serving as the answer to both these questions. When there is no ideal solution, then one has to examine more closely one's levels of risk-tolerance for the worst-case scenarios.

Note that all the actions we have talked about have been doings or undertakings – making a payment for services, laying a bet on a horse, making an investment decision, etc.

What makes Pascal's Wager rather singular is that the 'action' considered is that of forming, or not forming, a certain belief – in this case, the belief that God exists. The only way that Pascal's Wager could convince one that one ought to believe that God exists, is for one to be convinced that forming a belief (or refraining from forming it) is something that we can do on *prudential* grounds. Normally, rational agents avoid *wishful thinking* – that is, forming beliefs on the basis of what one would like to have be the case. Instead, rational beliefs ought to be formed only on the basis of relevant evidence and proper logical (or probabilistic) argumentation. Beliefs should *force themselves upon* the rational intellect, once it is apprised of the appropriate theoretical grounds for them. Beliefs should not be adopted simply because of prudential self-interest. Many a novelist has decried the inauthenticity or self-deception involved when a character adopts (or makes out that he or she has) particular beliefs, when the apparent holding of such beliefs is really only designed to promote the self-interest of that character, regardless of where the truth itself might lie.

18.2 Exposition of Pascal's Wager

That having been said by way of preparatory prophylactic, here is the *structure of Pascal's Wager*.

A_1: Form the belief that God exists; and then live accordingly, by giving up certain pleasures of the flesh, making certain financial sacrifices, putting up with minor inconveniences (such as worship), etc.

A_2: Do not form the belief that God exists; and then live accordingly, by enjoying those pleasures of the flesh, not making those financial sacrifices, and not having the inconveniences of worship, etc.

W_1: God exists, and is just how the religious tradition describes Him: wrathful and judgmental, ready to send both non-believers and the non-repentant to Hell for eternity.

W_2: God does not exist.

$\text{prob}(W_1|A_1) = \text{prob}(W_1|A_2) = \text{prob}(W_1) > 0.$
$\text{prob}(W_2|A_1) = \text{prob}(W_2|A_2) = \text{prob}(W_2) = 1 - \text{prob}(W_1).$
$U(W_1,A_1) \gg 0$ (possibly even positively infinite).
$U(W_2,A_1) < 0.$
$U(W_1,A_2) \ll 0$ (possibly even negatively infinite)
$U(W_2,A_2) > 0.$

By dint of the foregoing, we have the following.

Expected Utility of A_1
$= \text{prob}(W_1|A_1).U(W_1,A_1) + \text{prob}(W_2|A_1).U(W_2,A_1)$
$\gg 0.$

Expected Utility of A_2
$= \text{prob}(W_1|A_2).U(W_1,A_2) + \text{prob}(W_2|A_2).U(W_2,A_2)$
$\ll 0.$

On these grounds alone, it should be prudent to opt for A_1 (belief in God, and correspondingly becoming conduct). Here we are appealing to only the first principle, which tells one to maximize expected utility. Now, could the second principle, which tells one to minimize the downside, counsel us the other way? As it happens, no; the downside of A_2 is $U(W_1,A_2) \ll 0$; whereas the downside of A_1 is $U(W_2,A_1) < 0$. Thus for the rationally risk-averse, A_1 would be by far the safer bet than A_2. So the two principles point to the same choice of A_1 over A_2.

Pascal's Wager, then, counsels belief in God, and conducting oneself in a God-fearing manner, as the best course of 'action' for the rationally self-interested agent.

Now we have to ask: is this a rationally compelling argument for the existence of God?

There are two main criticisms to be made of Pascal's Wager.

18.3 The first criticism of Pascal's Wager

Pascal's Wager makes the fundamental error of treating *forming a belief* as a kind of *action* to which the theory of rational decision-making would be applicable. The view that belief-formation is a kind of action, which can be *freely chosen* after *prudential* deliberation, is mistaken on both italicized scores.

First, the rational agent *does not freely choose* when forming any belief. Rather, the rational agent is *compelled*, by the weight of evidence, and logical or probabilistic argumentation, to form the belief in question. And, when the rational agent does *not* form the belief in question, this is because the evidence and argumentation fall below whatever threshold is required for rational conviction. We are prepared to exculpate a wrongdoer who is in the grip of an addiction, and who is thereby *compelled* (by forces *currently* 'beyond the agent's control') to commit their wrongdoing. We do not regard the addict as capable of the kind of free decision-making for which the addict could reasonably be required to bear responsibility. So too, ironically, should it be in the case of belief-formation. The rational agent finds him/herself rationally compelled (by the evidence and the argumentation) to believe a certain proposition. The resulting belief-state, when rational, is not a state of mind for which the agent could ever be praised or reproached. The agent cannot take any credit for it. The rational agent cannot be reproached for it. The rational agent is simply *compelled* by the force of reason to adopt the belief in question.

Of course, the rational agent who forms a particular belief might be criticized on *other* grounds, such as: there was not enough evidence available to justify that belief; or there was a fallacy in the reasoning that lead to that belief; or ... Here, the grounds for criticism are reasons for reproaching the rational agent *qua* rational agent. They concern the manner in which the agent responded to what was available, as putative grounds, for forming the belief. But when the response is right – when all rational agents would agree that the available evidence and argumentation really do establish a given conclusion – *one's forming the belief that the conclusion in question is true* is not the kind of 'action' for which one bears any kind of responsibility at all.

Rational compulsion closes off all avenues to praise or blame. The rational agent is beyond all reproach; but not in the same way that the morally saintly person is beyond all reproach. The moral saint is beyond reproach (in doing good things) because *what the moral saint freely does* is morally good. The moral saint really does choose. The rational agent is beyond reproach (in forming rational beliefs) because *what the rational agent is compelled to believe* is rationally dictated by the evidence and argumentation. The rational agent really has no choice. Indeed, having no choice in the matter is what makes one a rational agent. By contrast, the moral saint does have a choice. Indeed, having a choice in the matter (and always making the right choice) is what makes one a moral saint.

Secondly, forming a belief on *prudential* grounds is the worst thing one can do, as a rational agent. One's own self-interest should be irrelevant when considering matters of fact – which is what one's beliefs aim to represent. It is a strong criticism to accuse someone of *wishful thinking*. One is a wishful thinker if one naïvely and over-optimistically believes that something is the case simply because one *wishes* it to be the case. The wishful thinker makes the fundamental mistake of not attending to the available evidence; or not actively seeking it out and only then reasoning with it, so as to form the *correct* belief about the matter. Likewise, the prudential belief-former is letting self-interest cloud the issue of fact. Instead of asking 'What is it right to believe, on the basis of evidence and argumentation?', the prudential belief-former is asking 'What is it in my best interest to believe, regardless of evidence and argumentation *based on it*?' To be sure, Pascal's Wager presents a kind of argumentation; but it does not present any evidence, with the ensuing argumentation *based on it*. Instead, Pascal's Wager seeks to derive the conclusion that *it would be in one's best interests to believe that God exists*. But this is very different from an argument whose conclusion is *that God exists*. Yet it is an argument of the latter kind that the rational agent really needs in order to be rationally compelled to believe that God exists.

18.4 The second criticism of Pascal's Wager

Even on its own terms, the prudential conclusion is arrived at too hastily. When one makes decisions under conditions of uncertainty, the uncertainty concerns *which of a given range of ways the world might be* (consequently upon, or independently of, the decision made) is the way the world actually turns out to be. The uncertainty is registered by assigning probability-values, lying strictly between 0 and 1, to the various alternatives explicitly entertained. The probabilities should sum to unity.

Clearly, the rational decision-maker deserves criticism if any important, salient, relevant alternative is left out of consideration. That is, the range of ways the world might be should be suitably exhaustive, given the background constraints on the decision-making situation. There is no point in agonizing over which horse to back in a race (the action here being: laying a bet on a particular horse) if, in all one's deliberations, one thinks only about *some but not all* of the horses concerned.

The second criticism of Pascal's Wager can be made metaphorically as follows: Pascal was mistakenly backing one of what he took to be the only two horses in the race. His horses were: *Believe that God exists* and *Do not believe that God exists*. To be sure, to the unsuspecting mind this might seem exhaustive. For, surely, these two alternatives divide up logical space. One of these two horses must win.

But now consider the alternatives: *Horse₁ will win* or *Horse₂ will win*. In the context of a mishap-free two-horse race, these two choices are exclusive. They divide up logical space. Another way of putting the alternatives in a two-horse race would be: *Horse₁ will win* or *It is not the case that Horse₁ will win*. But what if it's not a two-horse race? What if Horse₃ takes part?

Similarly, in Pascal's Wager, we can ask: What if there is some other God to think about, quite apart from the Judeo-Christian God that so occupied Pascal's thoughts? *What about God*?*

For those who do not know any theo*logy, let me tell you a little about the super*natural, divine* Being* that is God*. God* created the Universe, with the Big Bang, and so arranged the fundamental physical constants that everything that happens in the Universe happens according to natural laws. God* is so knowing and powerful that He* does not ever *need* to make any divine* interventions in the natural course of things. He* saw to it that intelligent observership would evolve, just the way it has, by putting all His* design-thought into the choice of fundamental *naturalistic* laws at the outset. On the moral side, however, God* is rather different from God. God* intends to send to Hell anyone foolish enough to postulate His* existence, or foolish enough to be persuaded by fallacious arguments like the Ontological Argument or the Cosmological Argument, or the Argument from Design, for His* existence. God* intends to reward with a blissful, eternal afterlife only the atheistic, naturalistically minded thinkers who seek to use their God*-given intellects to work out the basic laws of God*'s creation.

The challenge to one who thinks that the divine creator must be God, rather than God*, is to produce a cogent argument for their conception of the creator's *moral* make-up. None of the arguments for God's existence that we have examined thus far contain the seeds of such a conception. The *moral* aspects of a divine creator appear to be logically independent of the metaphysical aspects with which those attempted proofs of existence are concerned. Just as no geometer can establish Euclid's axiom of parallels from the remaining axioms of Euclidean geometry, so too no *metaphysical* considerations about a divine creator secure any conclusions about the *moral* make-up of that creator. And just as Science came to grips with the idea that relativistic space-time geometry is actually non-Euclidean, so too the theologian should consider the possibility that the moral make-up of a divine creator is that of God* rather than that usually ascribed to the Judeo-Christian God.

Enough said about God*. God* complicates Pascal's Wager in a way that completely undermines its prudential recommendation. For, with God* to consider *as a relevant possibility*, belief in God no longer maximizes expected gain. Indeed, belief in God brings with it a terrible downside, namely an eternity in Hell. For those who like trinities, we have to realize that there is now a third horse in the race. The three alternative ways the world might be are:

1 God exists (but God* does not).
2 God* exists (but God does not).
3 Neither God nor God* exists.

This is a genuine, tripartite division of logical space. It cannot be ignored or wished away by the Pascalian posing his Wager. Faced with these three alternatives, rather than his previous two, Pascal can no longer recommend his original Wager 'Believe that God exists, and act accordingly'. For the new possibilities generated by consideration of God* overturn (or at least undermine) the recommendation based on the previous calculations of expected utilities and downsides.

The reader can easily check that there is no more 'prudential reason' (of the kind that Pascal urges, and which we have already criticized on independent grounds as suspect, anyway) for believing in God than there is for believing in God*. Pascal's Wager contains the seeds of its own discrediting, as it were. There do not appear to be any conceptual reasons (as opposed to habits of theological tradition) for thinking that it is only Pascal's *bipartite* range of possibilities that the Wager must address, rather than the *tripartite* one just suggested.

Problems

1 Explain the basics of decision-making under conditions of uncertainty.
2 *Is* it always wrong or irrational to form a belief solely because one wishes it to be true? (See Williams (1973a) for further food for thought in this connection.)
3 Examine carefully how the payoff matrix (with reference to the then conventional conception of the Judeo-Christian God) is set out in Pascal's Wager. Do you have any disagreements with any of the entries?
4 Do you think that Pascal's Wager is just a fancy formal exercise, masquerading as some sort of intellectual argument, when its author should rather be simply confessing to an *overwhelming need to take certain things on faith*?
5 Assess whether, even if the voluntarist can make a successful case for being entitled to form certain beliefs on purely prudential grounds, Pascal's Wager will nevertheless succumb to a different objection.

19 The Problem of Evil

19.1 Exposition of the Problem of Evil

Thus far we have considered only arguments *for* the existence of God. The criticisms leveled at these arguments have at best left us in the position of the agnostic. That is, if the criticisms are sustained, then we have no good argument so far *for* the existence of God.

Now we consider an argument *against* the existence of God. It takes the form of a *reductio ad absurdum*. The claim being reduced to absurdity is the claim that

> G. God exists.

Of course, there are other 'side assumptions' on which the argument relies. First, there are four *conditional* statements about God, whose consequents a theist would regard as 'obviously true'. The conditionals themselves might even be acceptable to certain kinds of agnostic:

1 If God exists, then God created the Universe, including all sentient creatures.
2 If God exists, then God is omniscient.
3 If God exists, then God is omnibenevolent.
4 If God exists, then God is omnipotent.

Secondly, there is the main premise that gives this argument its name:

5 There is evil in the world, and much misery and pain and suffering as a result, on the part of sentient creatures.

Thirdly, there is a premise to the effect that

6 If God exists, then God is morally perfect: He does everything that He ought to do.

Here now is the **Argument from the Problem of Evil**:

Suppose (for *reductio ad absurdum*) that

>   G. God exists.

By (G) and (1), God is responsible for the existence of all sentient creatures.

By (5), many of these are in misery, pain and suffering.

By (G) and (2), God knows this, and indeed would have known this when He created the Universe.

By (G) and (3), God would have intended otherwise for His sentient creatures; He would have wished them *not* to have to suffer in this way.

By (G) and (4), God could have acted otherwise: He could have created a Universe without that suffering.

By a universally accepted principle of morality, God therefore *should* have acted otherwise. He *should* have created a Universe free of that suffering; yet He did not.

But that, with (G), contradicts (6).

So we have a contradiction from (1)–(6) in conjunction with the assumption (G) that God exists.

Holding on to (1)–(6), we conclude that

>   God does not exist.

19.2 Responses to the Argument from the Problem of Evil

Having set out the Argument from the Problem of Evil (for the atheist's conclusion that God does *not* exist), we now consider various critical responses to that argument. We shall here manage only one more dialectical layer, by offering the atheist's rebuttal to each objection raised.

19.2.1 The 'Polarity' response

This response takes the following form.

>   Good could not exist without there being at least some evil with which it could be contrasted. Thus the existence of evil is, as it were, a necessary evil, if there are to be moral beings capable of pursuing the good.

Rebuttal by the atheist: Not so. An ordinary moral sensibility could be nurtured, or acquired, without exposure to any instances of evil. Extrapolating from minor instances of accidentally self-inflicted pain could give the imaginative moral agent a conception of *what it would be intentionally to inflict pain and misery on an innocent, sentient being.* This was reportedly the young Buddha's experience. He was several years old when, for the first time in his life, he witnessed the suffering of a sentient creature: a bird overhead pierced by an archer's arrow. He was able to understand immediately the moral enormity of intentionally inflicting suffering on an innocent, sentient being. One does not need actual exemplars of a property F in order to be able to conceive what it would be to have property F. Our counterfactual imaginations are vivid enough.

19.2.2 The Leibnizian response

This response takes the following form.

> Unknown to the limited intellects who are moved by the Argument from the Problem of Evil, this world, even with all the evil within it, happens to be *the best of all possible worlds that God could have created.* Our intellects are simply too limited to grasp the deeper wisdom behind God's having created the world the way it is.

Rebuttal by the atheist: Read Voltaire's novel *Candide*.

19.2.3 The 'Cosmic Justice' response

This response takes the following form.

> Sure, there is intentionally inflicted pain, misery, and suffering in this world. But that doesn't make it a case of incomprehensible or reprehensible evil on a cosmic level. Rather, the individuals' suffering is meet and right: for they are being punished for their own past wrongdoings, in a cosmos in which justice is always done.

Rebuttal by the atheist: So those innocent babies, pitchforked by SS thugs in the concentration camps, were paying for 'their' own past sins? This is repulsively counterintuitive. There is, however, a further problem with the 'cosmic justice' suggestion. If current sufferers are being punished for their supposed previous evildoing, what about the victims of those evildoings? Were they in turn being punished, at long last, for *their* own, yet earlier, evildoings? In order to sustain this response consistently, one is driven to postulate that the chain of evildoings whose victims are being punished stretches back infinitely far into the past. Otherwise, there will be some original, undeserved evildoing (from the point of view of its hapless victim), and the Argument from Evil would once again gain purchase. This enforced picture, however, is at odds with that urged by Aquinas's Cosmological Argument. Not that that matters much, since the Cosmological Argument is invalid anyway – but at least we see that this theistic defense against the Argument from the Problem of Evil knocks out one of the positive possibilities of argumentation *for* God's existence.

19.2.4 The Libertarian response

This response takes the following form.

> God's greatest gift to humankind is the granting of free will. He had to 'let go' of His control over our actions in order to bestow genuine free will upon us. He cannot be held responsible for the evil which *we* do. The moral deficit in this universe is to be laid at *our* door. We have no ground to reproach God for having created a universe in which His creatures freely choose to do evil.

Rebuttal by the atheist: This presupposes that we do have genuine free will; and this is another deep metaphysical debate to be joined. But let us grant free will for the sake of argument. God could still have given us free will, but simply restricted the range of abominable possibilities open to us. He could, for example, have ensured that we never developed the technologies of mass torture and extermination used in Hitler's concentration camps. God could have ensured that, free though we were, we were always inclined to *use* our free will so as to do the right thing. Is a moral saint any the less free for never doing wrong? If not, then why couldn't we all have been created moral saints? Tempted at times, to be sure, but in the end always capable of resisting temptation to do evil.

19.2.5 The 'Reconceptualization' response

This response takes the following form.

> Having derived a contradiction from certain assumptions about God's nature (should He exist), why not simply give up some of those assumptions, rather than conclude that He does not, after all, exist? Perhaps God is *not* omnibenevolent, after all. Or perhaps He could *not* have foreseen the abominable things that His creatures would do, once granted their freedom of will. Or perhaps he is/was powerless to improve on His creation.

Rebuttal by the atheist: This is dramatic concession. It certainly detracts from our usual idea of God as a being worth worshipping, and as the source of our morality. It would also sabotage Anselm's Ontological Argument, which involved a conception of God as a being greater than which nothing could be conceived. But Anselm's argument was defective on other scores, so perhaps that is not too disastrous for the theist. Now, pray tell, what kind of positive argument can the theist provide for the existence of this somewhat diminished Deity?

19.2.6 The 'Incommensurability' response

This response takes the following form.

> You (the atheist) are employing a notion of moral *commensurability* of alternative possibilities of creation. You think you are able to contemplate this universe, with the evil in it, and compare it with yet another (non-actual) universe with no (or less) evil in it, and then pronounce that the latter universe is better – hence morally preferable – to the former. You then conclude that God ought to have avoided creating the former, and ought to have preferred, instead, to create the latter.
>
> But isn't this idea of commensurability broken-backed? One cannot compare one whole universe with another whole universe when making moral judgments. At best you can compare one act with another act *within one and the same universe*, in order to determine which one is morally preferable.

Rebuttal by the atheist: Whence, then, our moral intuition that we can effect moral improvements in our lives and our societies? Idealistic reformers are motivated by their conception of a better life, whether or not it is ever realized. They can imagine possible futures for this world of ours, in which things seem clearly better than they actually are (or probably turn out to be, despite the reformers' best efforts). There does not seem to be anything counterintuitive here if we describe the idealistic reformer's intuition as based on a comparison of two whole worlds or universes: one of these is the actual universe, past, present and future; the other is a universe that has the same history as the first one up to a certain point, after which it 'diverges morally' at the societal level, with greatly reduced evil from that point on. It seems pretty clear that this moral comparison can be made, and holds good, for the two worlds in question.

19.2.7 The 'Deep Constraint' response

This is a variation of the Leibnizian response, and is suggested here only because of its novel flavor. It takes the following form.

> It is generally agreed that God is constrained by the limits of what is logically and mathematically possible or necessary. For example, God could not have made a universe in which $2 + 3 = 7$. Nor could God have made a universe in which a square had three sides. Nor could God have made a universe in which 0 was the number of things identical to 0 ..., etc. Now, it has recently been argued that the emergence of life (self-replicating systems of organic molecules) is actually a *'combinatorial' necessity*, once given enough basic chemicals and a certain density of interactions among them. Far from being a highly improbable 'cosmic accident', the emergence of Life, on this view, is virtually guaranteed by the conditions found on Earth shortly after its formation. Perhaps there are similar deep constraints, deriving from

the mathematics of combinations, on the kind of *behavior* that God could Himself constrain, on the part of complex organisms. Their evolutionary origin and behavior is to be governed by the laws of nature, which God is putting in place. But perhaps *any* laws of nature in accordance with which life is at all possible are laws that must permit (and indeed make inevitable, at least on occasion) those behaviors that we regard as evil. Perhaps God could not even prevent creatures *without* free will from *intentionally, on occasion, doing things that inflict pain and misery on other sentient beings.*

Rebuttal by the atheist: In all probability, this is the right picture. But, surely, God can be removed from it? For what we have here, after all, is a description of the world as the atheistic naturalist sees it, once it is stripped of the God-talk.

Problems

1 Regiment the Argument from Evil *against* the existence of God, so that it is laid out as a formal proof (like the one that we proposed as a regimentation of Anselm's Ontological Argument *for* the existence of God).
2 Consider any one of the seven responses to the Argument from the Problems of Evil, and develop it in as much detail as you can, by exploring the extensive literature. You could begin with Mackie (1955); Plantinga (1977); and Adams and Adams (1990).

Part IV

Mind, Body and External World

20 The Pivotal Figure of Descartes: Dualism and Skepticism

Three important ideas or schools of thought are named after the great rationalist philosopher, scientist and mathematician René Descartes: Cartesian coordinates, Cartesian dualism, and Cartesian skepticism.

20.1 Cartesian coordinates

To keep matters simple, consider a space of two dimensions – a *plane*. Every high-school student is familiar with the way we can represent points in a plane by means of an *x-coordinate* and a *y-coordinate*.

We choose two perpendicular *axes* in the plane ('perpendicular' here meaning 'intersecting at a right angle'). (Interestingly, Descartes, in *La Géométrie*, did not require that the axes be perpendicular to each other. He managed with coordinates for points with respect to axes not meeting that condition.) We label one of these axes the *x*-axis, and the other the *y*-axis. They each extend to positive infinity in one direction, and to negative infinity in the other. So each axis is a 'copy' of the real numbers. The axes' point of intersection is called the *origin*, and is described by the ordered pair $\langle 0,0 \rangle$.

Given any point P in the plane, we find its *ordered pair* $\langle x_P, y_P \rangle$ as follows. Draw a line-segment from P to the *x*-axis, parallel to the *y*-axis. This line intersects the *x*-axis at x_P. Draw another line segment from P to the *y*-axis, parallel to the *x*-axis. This line intersects the *y*-axis at y_P. These two numbers x_P and y_P are called the *x*-coordinate and the *y*-coordinate of P respectively.

In this way a *geometric point P* in a plane can be represented by, or identified with, an *ordered pair of real numbers* $\langle x_P, y_P \rangle$. (If the point were in a three-dimensional space, we would use instead an ordered *triple* of real numbers, $\langle x_P, y_P, z_P \rangle$, availing ourselves of a third axis, the *z*-axis. Here we shall make do with the two-dimensional case.)

Likewise, *lines* and *curves* in general (lying in the plane) can be described as *sets of geometric points*. Many of them will be definable by means of *algebraic relationships among the coordinates* x and y of their constitutive points. Thus for example a *circle* with *radius r* and *center* $\langle a,b \rangle$ is the set of points $\langle x,y \rangle$ obeying the algebraic relationship

$$r.r = [(x-a).(x-a)] + [(y-b).(y-b)].$$

Another example: the *straight line* that passes through the y-axis at *b* and through the x-axis at *a* is the set of all points $\langle x, y \rangle$ such that

$$a.b = (b.x) + (a.y).$$

Cartesian coordinates provide a fruitful way of re-conceiving spatial figures as algebraic interrelationships among numbers (that is, among the coordinates of the points involved). This is called the *algebraicization of geometry*, and it was a major breakthrough in mathematical thinking. What is essentially involved are *two different systems of representation*: two different ways of thinking about the same things. Given the system of Cartesian coordinatization, one can regard spatial forms (one can 'construe' them, as philosophers sometimes say) as 'no more than' sets of pairs (or triples) of numbers; and one can regard geometrical properties as amounting to 'no more than' the algebraic relationships among numerical coordinates.

The great irony is that Descartes conspicuously failed to do, or avoided doing, the same thing with the phenomenon of mind. That is, he did not construe mental phenomena as no more than physical states of the physical organism, and mental processes as no more than physical relationships among the physical realizations of mental states.

Instead, he left an intellectual legacy at the other extreme, quite at odds with his pioneering insight about space and numbers.

20.2 Cartesian dualism

Cartesian dualism is the view that the mind is a *radically different kind of entity* from the physical body to which it 'belongs'. This is a *dualism of substance*, not just a dualism of attributes. Descartes does not simply maintain that mental attributes are special, and cannot be reduced to physical attributes; while, nevertheless, both kinds of attributes are enjoyed by just one kind of thing, namely bodies. Rather, he goes even further, by maintaining that minds are *things* quite different from bodies (whence of course it will follow also that their attributes are not physical attributes). Minds, said Descartes, exist in time but *not in space*: they are not 'extended'. They could also survive the destruction of the physical bodies to which they seem to belong.

This extreme kind of dualism gives rise to the *problem of mind–body interaction*. If minds are not in space, and are not themselves physical things, how then do they interact with bodies? Conscious experience of the things we perceive must involve some sort of causal process beginning in those things and ending in our minds. Conversely, there are intentional actions that result in the movement of physical bodies (our own bodies, and the things outside us that we move around and manipulate). Surely this involves some sort of causal process – desiring or deciding – that begins in our minds and ends in the world of physical objects? If so, what sort of causation is this? Could there be a science of this causation? Or would parts (or all) of it be inaccessible to the methods of science? What is the mechanism (or 'mentalism'?) of mind–body interaction?

20.3 Cartesian skepticism

We shall expound Descartes's skepticism by quoting quite a few important passages from the text of his *Meditations on First Philosophy*, and interpolating both expository and critical comments as we proceed. The material we have to deal with here is better suited to this form of engagement than to our earlier procedure of setting a view out, and only thereafter raising criticisms.

In the order of presentation in *Meditations*, Descartes's skepticism actually preceded his dualism. His dualism was invoked by way of some sort of solution to the prior skepticism that he had raised. We have chosen a different order of exposition here in order to make the ironic contrast between Descartes's 'reductive' numerical coordinatization of space (about which he says nothing in his *Meditations*), and his extremely *anti-reductive* dualism about mind and body.

There are many varieties of skepticism. We touched on them briefly in Chapter 6. Cartesian skepticism concerns our *empirical knowledge of the external world*. The common-sense view is that the external world consists of various physical things 'outside of' ourselves (the perceiving subjects); and that we come to know facts about these things by means of sensory perception (sight, hearing, touch and proprioception, smell, and taste).

It is this common-sense view that Descartes directly challenges. Noting that we are occasionally subjected to dreams and hallucinations, he generalizes the worry that awareness of dreams and hallucinations induces. We know that sometimes we are dreaming, and that the world is not at all the way it is represented as being in the dream. But how can we be sure that we are not *dreaming all the time*? Our senses sometimes deceive us: or at least, one sensory channel does, and we have to correct it by recourse to other sensory channels. (Think of how the senses of touch and proprioception reassure us that the stick in the water is really straight, although it may *look* bent.) How can we be sure that it is not the case that *all our senses deceive us all the time*?

Cartesian skepticism concerns our *knowledge of the external world*. The Cartesian skeptic pursues the method of *radical doubt* about all our alleged knowledge of the external world.

Why, one might ask, would anyone wish to pursue such skepticism? The charitable answer would run as follows. The Cartesian skeptic earnestly wishes to secure the foundations of empirical knowledge, or of natural science, against the possibility of serious error. In order to do so, he invents the strongest challenge he can think of. In defending empirical knowledge against such a challenge, we would uncover our real reasons and justifications for holding the beliefs we do. And that is the only way to confirm these beliefs as genuine knowledge, not just fanciful opinion, or prejudice, or over-credulous speculation.

The uncharitable answer would run differently. Some have alleged that Descartes was a naturalistically inclined scientist who had developed his natural scientific method, and pursued it, for a long time before he wrote the *Meditations*. Nowhere in his earlier writings had there been any hint of radical doubt, or skepticism. So why did these ideas suddenly appear later in the *Meditations*? The answer is that Descartes had been chilled by the Inquisition's treatment of Galileo, who himself was following the naturalistic method of experimental inquiry, and putting forward the Copernican view that the Sun, not the Earth, was the center of the (then known) universe. So Descartes set about providing a *metaphysics* that would be acceptable to the Church authorities, and cleverly fashioning within this metaphysics a permissible space for the pursuit of empirical and experimental inquiry. (In order to explore this interpretative possibility more carefully, the interested reader can begin with Clarke (1982); Gaukroger (1995); and Davies (2001).)

Whatever the correct explanation of Descartes's motives, he has given Western philosophy one of its most celebrated thought-experimental figures: that of the *evil demon*. Descartes asks his reader to imagine that there is an all-powerful evil demon who is constantly deceiving us, by making it *seem* to us as though there is an external world of material objects.

This thought-experiment calls into question both the existence of physical objects (including our own bodies), and our supposed knowledge of their various properties and relations – color, shape, size, category or kind, internal constitution, motion, etc. Descartes asks us to consider seriously the possibility that *all* our supposed knowledge of these things is illusory, or false. Thus he casts doubt on common-sense reports of observation. Examples: 'The dog is barking'; 'The cat is on the mat', etc. Also, naturally, he casts doubt on higher-level generalizations and hypotheses that are logically connected with such observation reports. Examples: 'All metal bars, when heated, expand'; 'Bread nourishes'; 'Bodies attract each other with gravitational forces'; 'All men are mortal', etc.

If all such beliefs of ours are false, then we must at least be able to *entertain the thoughts* involved. That is,

Point 1:
We must still have a conceptual apparatus, and logical operations, for the framing of our thoughts – even if the ones we choose to believe turn out to be false.

Moreover, Cartesian skepticism is capitalizing on the appearance/reality distinction. The master thought is that appearances can and (perhaps always) do deceive us (or, if we prefer to put it this way, it is through those appearances that the evil demon succeeds in deceiving us). We are deceived as to the very existence of the external world, or as to the true nature of the external world, should it exist. But if appearances can thus deceive us, then: *how the world seems to us* (how things appear to us) would *not* be *how things really are*. The appearances, or seemings, would misrepresent how things are. And in order for us to be deceived in this way,

Point 2:
There is a fact of the matter as to how things *appear* to be (even if it is the evil demon who is subjecting us to these appearances).

These two simple points yield certain significant classes of thoughts or propositions that would remain *unaffected* by Cartesian doubt.

1 *Phenomenological truths about current experience.* If I sincerely claim *There is a red patch in my visual field now*, this is not the sort of claim that can be made subject to Cartesian doubt. The evil demon's malevolent ministrations depend on the prior truth of claims of this kind.
2 *Truths about the structure of phenomenological possibilities.* I can still confidently claim that anything red is colored; and that nothing (not even an *appearance*) could (seem to) be solidly red all over and solidly green all over at the same time.
3 *Logical truths.* Whatever the evil demon does, he cannot make the logical Law of Non-contradiction, *not-(P and not-P)*, fail. He is supposed to be deceiving us about, say, *P* by having us believe *not-P*, or vice versa. The evil demon's whole point is to make us adopt a consistent set of beliefs that are false. So in fact the evil demon would want us to carry on believing all the laws of Logic, since these help to structure the very thoughts that are going to be factually mistaken.
4 *Mathematical truths.* Likewise for mathematical truths. If the evil demon makes me think, falsely, that there are two pink elephants and three green ones in the lecture theater, then he will happily allow me to believe that there are five (pink-or-green) elephants in the lecture theater. The evil demon has no interest in making me cease to believe that $2 + 3 = 5$.
5 *Conceptual truths.* The evil demon will not interfere with my belief that, say, all bachelors are unmarried men. This I know by virtue of the meanings of the words alone; my (deluded) sense perception plays no role in justifying this belief. Hence this belief, and others relevantly like it, are immune to Cartesian skepticism.
6 *Introspective truths.* I have a stomach ache. I know I do. I know I feel this way, even if the evil demon caused me to so to feel. This is an example of an introspective truth to which I have authoritative, privileged, infallible access. You ask me, in a world in which the evil demon may be at work, 'Do you have a stomach ache?' I do not have to lay to rest doubts about empirical knowledge, or convince myself that there is no evil demon, in order to be able to answer you truthfully and with certitude.

Although these kinds of 'invulnerable' knowledge do not tell us much about the external world, they provide at least a starting point for a line of defensive argument against the possibility that we are constantly being deceived by an evil demon. In the next chapter we shall examine Descartes's complete response to his own problem: a response that begins with his famous introspective dictum

'Cogito ergo sum' ('I think, therefore I am'). For the rest of this chapter, we focus on some of the more important claims in the first two *Meditations*, leading up to the famous *Cogito*.

20.4 The structure of the reasoning in the first two *Meditations*

All quotations are taken from Bratman *et al.* (2009).

20.4.1 Meditation I: On what can be called into doubt

Descartes intends to call *all* his previous beliefs into doubt. This is what earns his method the title 'method of *radical* doubt'. But we shall have to ask ourselves whether it isn't philosophically unsettling enough to confine the doubt to beliefs about *the external world*, while leaving intact all our beliefs of a purely logical, conceptual, or mathematical nature.

> I would need to tear down *everything* and begin anew from the foundations if I wanted to establish any firm and lasting knowledge. ... I can justify the rejection of *all* my beliefs if I can find some ground for doubt in each.

Is Descartes really justified in doubting the conclusions of mathematical proofs that he has carefully worked through? What about mathematical *axioms* that he formerly took, upon reflection, to be self-evident? And does it follow from the fact that each belief, taken one at a time, is dubitable, that one can doubt *all of one's beliefs* simultaneously?

> I have occasionally caught the senses deceiving me, and it would be prudent for me never completely to trust those who have cheated me even once.

Note the moral analogy. Would the point be as persuasive if it read, instead, as 'I have occasionally discovered that my senses have malfunctioned, and it would be prudent for me never to rely wholly on senses that have malfunctioned even once'? Probably not – because when one sense is malfunctioning, we can always have recourse to other senses in order to make the necessary correction. Consider, for example, how one would resort to the sense of touch in order to determine that a stick is straight, even though it looks as if it is bent when put into water.

> [T]here are no reliable signs by which I can distinguish sleeping from waking.

Is this really so? Might there not be some requirement of overall systematicity and coherence of beliefs arrived at in a waking state, which is not met in the case of 'dream-beliefs' that the dreamer 'forms' when dreaming?

> [M]ightn't I be deceived when I add two and three?

You might be deceived, say, by your sense of vision when looking at the page in the course of trying to follow a written proof of the claim that $2 + 3 = 5$. But what about the purely intellectual process of running through the proof in one's mind, unaided by symbols or diagrams written or drawn on paper?

> Nothing I used to believe is beyond legitimate doubt ... because I have valid and well-considered grounds for doubt. I must therefore withhold my assent from my former beliefs as carefully as from obvious falsehoods, if I want to arrive at something certain.

Nothing? What about conceptual, logical and mathematical truths that you have already proved to your satisfaction?

> [I]t will be good ... to allow [that I am] deceived, and to suppose that *all* my previous beliefs are false and imaginary.

Once again, it may be that we can save conceptual, logical, and mathematical truths from this skeptical doubt, while allowing the skepticism to apply only to all beliefs (based on perception) about *the external world*.

> I will suppose, then, ... that there is an evil demon, supremely powerful and cunning, who works as hard as he can to deceive me.

Bear in mind that this is a *supposition*. Descartes is not claiming that such a demon really exists. He is only saying that, *for all we currently know* (after calling various beliefs into doubt), it is *prima facie* consistent to suppose that such an evil demon exists. The task will be to discover considerations and reasoning that would reduce this supposition to absurdity.

20.4.2 Meditation II: On the nature of the human mind, which is better known than the body

We should bear in mind a distinction made later in philosophy, between 'knowledge by acquaintance' and 'knowledge by description'. Perhaps Descartes can claim only that we are better *acquainted* with our minds than we are with our bodies. For mental introspection gives indubitable knowledge-by-acquaintance; whereas we have knowledge (by acquaintance) of our bodies only through the mind's exercise of the senses.

> I can hope for great things if I can even find one small thing that is certain and unshakable.

This is a display of typical rationalist optimism. One needs only to find some overarching principle from which one can generate an enormous stock of knowledge.

> Let [the evil demon] deceive me all he can, he will never make it the case that I am nothing while I think that I am something. ... I must finally conclude that the statement 'I am, I exist' must be true whenever I state or mentally consider it.

Note that the stating or mental considering here is what is covered by the Latin verb 'cogito'. 'I am, I exist' abbreviates, in Latin, to 'sum'. And Descartes is inferring the truth of the latter from the truth of the former (whenever it holds). Hence the usual Latin formulation 'cogito, ergo sum'. Note the reflective robustness of this insight. No matter how little one has in the way of justified beliefs, the mere awareness of one's own intellectual *questionings* or *doubtings* or *wonderings whether* suffices to make the claim 'cogito' (= 'I am thinking/cogitating') true. For these intellectual attitudes are a species of cogitation. One does not have to be thinking some proposition in a confident, assertive frame of mind in order to be able to describe oneself as cogitating. It is enough, for example, to be wondering whether one will ever arrive at a justified belief. As soon as one is aware of that mental activity, one knows that one exists. And the evil demon cannot take this away.

> [I]t comes down to this: There is thinking, and thought alone cannot be taken away from me. I am, I exist. That much is certain. ... I know that I am a real, existing thing, but what kind of thing? As I have said, a thing that thinks. ... I know that I exist, and I ask what the 'I' is that I know to exist. It is obvious that the conception of myself that I arrive at in *this* way does not depend on anything that I do not yet know to exist and, consequently, that it does not depend on anything of which I can shape a mental image.

Descartes is clearly embracing the possibility here that he might exist only as a disembodied mind.

> [Even if dreaming] it is still certain that I *seem* to see, to hear, and to feel.

Again, even the victim of the evil demon can cogitate; and, in doing so, be certain of his/her/its own existence.

What point have we now reached? Descartes has, by the end of Meditation II, responded to the specter of the evil demon with the single certitude 'I think, therefore I am'. It is still possible that he exists only as a mind, without any physical body; and that what *seems* to him as perceptual experience 'of' external objects is no more than a train of hallucination visited upon him by the evil demon. The problem still facing him is: How can he move from the *cogito* to a newly justified and fully recovered system of belief about the external world?

20.5 Descartes's resort to the existence of God

Having adopted the method of radical doubt, and having invoked the possibility that he is being deceived systematically by an evil demon, Descartes has attained, in response thus far, only the reflective insight that he exists in so far as he thinks. Moreover, he exists as a *thinking thing*, i.e., a mind. He does not yet have any secure knowledge of his own body, or of any other external things. How is such knowledge to be recovered?

The short answer is that he aims to prove that God exists – a God, moreover, who would not deceive him, especially about matters that Descartes takes himself to perceive *clearly and distinctly*.

In Meditation III, Descartes gives an argument for God's existence that has a form similar to that of Aquinas's Cosmological Argument. Recall that Aquinas considered the cause–effect relation among things and events, and maintained that chains of causation could not stretch infinitely far back into the past. Aquinas concluded that there must be some 'prime mover', which was God. Descartes likewise considers instead the chain of events terminating in his having the idea of God with all His perfections. He argues that this chain, extending back in time, must terminate in God himself; for from none other than God, with His supreme perfections, could his (Descartes's) idea of God have derived.

> I seem to be able to establish the general rule that whatever I clearly and distinctly grasp is true.

Descartes makes this claim *before* proving that God exists. Moreover, he proceeds to use this claim as a premise when proving that God exists. Later, however, he appeals to the existence of God in order justify this claim (or, at least, one that is plausibly equivalent to it). This is known as the *Cartesian circle*. (There is an extensive literature on the Cartesian circle. See the anthology Doney (1987).) Any interpretation that would save Descartes from the embarrassment of having engaged in such circular argumentation is well worth considering.

> [I]f [God] wants, He can make it the case that I err even about what I take my mind's eye to see most clearly. ... I ought to ask as soon as possible whether there is a God and, if so, whether He can be a deceiver. For it seems that, until I know these two things, I can never be completely certain of anything else.

This is known as the 'notorious' fourth paragraph of Meditation III. Many a commentator cannot understand why and how God could deceive the 'mind's eye' about purely conceptual and/or mathematical matters having nothing to do with sense-perception.

> [T]he central question is about the ideas that I view as derived from objects existing outside me. What reason is there for thinking that these ideas resemble the objects? I seem to have been taught this by nature. ... When I say that nature teaches me something, I mean just that I have a spontaneous impulse to believe it – not that the light of nature reveals the thing's truth to me. There is an important difference. When the light of nature reveals something to me (such as that my thinking implies my existing) that thing is completely beyond doubt, since there is nothing as reliable as the light of nature by means of which I could learn that the thing is not true.

The phrase 'light of nature' is being used here as an important philosophical *metaphor*. Descartes does not literally mean that the physical phenomenon that we now understand as a stream of photons is illuminating whatever it is that he understands to be true. Instead, he is alluding to some sort of perfectly unimpeded intellectual perspective, from which the truth of a proposition is crystal clear, fully illuminated for the understanding. Still speaking metaphorically: one would grasp all the boundaries, all the appropriate contrasts, all the textures and hues. All salient features would shine with self-evidence; nothing relevant to the determination of the truth of the proposition would be left shrouded in any darkness or shadow or obscurity. It would yield the same kind of certainty of recognitional judgment that one achieves when one sees a dear friend's face fully revealed by light flooding from the appropriate angle. Descartes, however, offers no clarifying taxonomy of the sorts of propositions whose truth can be determined thus definitively by the light of nature. Do they include mathematical propositions? observation statements, under ideal conditions of observation? introspective reports of the contents of one's own consciousness? fundamental propositions about the nature of space, time, and causation? propositions about the metaphysics of self? ... There is a great variety of candidates for illumination by the light of nature. One would like to have a general account of our epistemic access to them, and what the 'throwing of light' in each case would consist in. Instead, Descartes tends simply to help himself, wherever needed, to the claim that such-and-such proposition is revealed (as true) by the light of nature.

> [T]he light of nature has revealed that there is at least as much in the complete efficient cause as in its effect. ... It follows ... that what is more perfect – or, in other words, has more reality in it – cannot come from what is less perfect and has less reality.

Perhaps Descartes is more sensitive to the light of nature than lesser mortals.

> [E]ach idea contains one particular presentational reality which it must get from a cause having at least as much formal reality as the idea has presentational reality. ... Although one idea may arise from another, this can't go back to infinity; it must eventually arrive at a primary idea whose cause is an 'archetype' containing formally all that the idea contains presentationally. Hence, the light of nature makes it clear to me that the ideas in me are like images which may well fall short of the things from which they derive, but which cannot contain anything greater or more perfect. ... [I]f the presentational reality of one of my ideas is so great that I can be confident that the same degree of reality is not in me either formally or eminently, I can conclude that I cannot be the cause of that idea, that another thing must necessarily exist as its cause, and consequently that I am not alone in the world.

Here is the foreshadowing of a form of Cosmological Argument for the existence of God ...

> [A]s to my ideas of physical objects, it seems that nothing in them is so great that it couldn't have come from me. ... All that is left to consider is whether there may be something in my idea of God that couldn't have come from me. By 'God' I mean infinite substance, independent, supremely intelligent, and supremely powerful – the thing from which I and everything else that may exist get our existence. The more I consider these attributes, the less it seems that they could have come from me alone. And I must therefore conclude that God necessarily exists.

... And here is its conclusion.

> [I]t's clear to me that there is more reality in an infinite than in a finite substance, and, *hence*, that my grasp of the infinite must somehow be prior to my grasp of the finite – my understanding of God prior to my understanding of myself. For, how could I understand that I doubt and desire, that I am deficient and imperfect, if I don't have the idea of something more perfect to use as a standard of comparison? (Emphasis added)

The present author, for one, is not convinced by the 'hence' here.

> It suffices for me to understand that, being finite, I cannot fully comprehend the infinite and to judge that, if I grasp something clearly and distinctly and know it to have some perfection, it is either formally or eminently present in God.

What would be the argument that finite minds cannot comprehend the infinite?

> I ought to ask myself ... whether *I* have the power to ensure that I, who now am, will exist a little while from now. Since I am nothing but a thinking thing ... I would surely be aware of this power if it were in me. But I find no such power. And this very clearly shows that there is an entity distinct from me, on whom I depend.

Note that Descartes is simply assuming here, without argument, that he would be introspectively aware (as a mind) of every power of his mind. But *can* any one mind be so fully aware of itself?

> [S]ince I am a thinking thing with the idea of God in me, my cause – whatever it is – must be a thinking thing having in it the idea of every perfection that I attribute to God. And I can go on to ask whether this thing gets its existence from itself or from something else. But ... if my cause gets its existence from itself, it must *be* God: having the power to exist in itself, it must also have the power actually to to give itself every perfection of which it has an idea – including every perfection that I conceive of in God. On the other hand, if my cause gets its existence from some other thing, I can go on to ask whether this other thing gets its existence from itself or from something else. Eventually, I will come to the ultimate cause: God.

This is a restatement of the Cosmological Argument foreshadowed earlier.

> ... [My parents] do not preserve me. Insofar as I am a thinking thing, they did not even take part in creating me. They simply formed the matter in which I used to think that I resided. (By 'I' I mean my mind, which is all that I now grasp of myself.) ... The fact that I exist and have an idea of God as a perfect entity conclusively entails that God does in fact exist.

The purpose of Meditation III is now achieved. Descartes began this Meditation with only himself in the picture. Now he has God as well.

> The idea [of God] must ... be innate in me, like my idea of myself. ... [I]t's not at all surprising that in creating me God put this idea into me, impressing it like a craftsman's mark on His work.

Descartes is neglecting the possibility that the human mind has a wonderful (but often misleading) capacity for over-generalization, over-extension and over-extrapolation. Why can't we simply say that we attain a conception of God by thinking of certain extremes along certain dimensions of comparison – but that our doing so affords us no guarantee that anything really answers to the aggregate extremal conception thus formed?

I know that I could not exist with my present nature (that is, that I could not exist with the idea of God in me) unless there really were a God – the very God of whom I have an idea, the thing having all the perfections that I can't fully comprehend but can somehow reach with thought, the thing that clearly cannot be defective. From this, it is obvious that He can't deceive, for the natural light reveals that fraud and deception arise from defect.

Descartes has finally made the epistemological application that he sought at the outset, of the conclusion that God exists. Because God is perfect, He would not deceive us. (The natural light reveals this.) Hence, what we clearly and distinctly *perceive* to be the case must *be* the case.

Later, in Meditation V, Descartes writes:

[I]f I were ignorant of God, I might come to *doubt* [the] truth [of a mathematical theorem that I have proved] as soon as my attention wandered from its demonstration, even if I recall having mastered the demonstration in the past: I could convince myself that I have been so constructed *by nature* that I sometimes err about what I *believe* myself to grasp most plainly ... But now I understand that God exists, ... and that He's not a deceiver. From this I infer that *everything I clearly and distinctly grasp must be true*. ... *I can't err about what I clearly and distinctly understand*. ... Thus ... the certainty of all my knowledge derives from my knowledge of the true God.

Note that the emphasized principle is derived *from* the existence of God. If, for Descartes, the following two principles are equivalent:

- I clearly and distinctly grasp that *p*
- the light of nature reveals to me that *p*

then we have a *circular argument* from Descartes. For recall the earlier point we made about how Descartes relies on revelations of the light of nature in order to prove that God exists.

Problems

1 Regiment clearly the pattern of logical dependencies among important claims that critics regard as constituting the Cartesian circle.
2 How severe can skepticism about one's erstwhile beliefs be, without incurring a charge of logical or conceptual irrationality?
3 Why was Descartes concerned to establish the existence of God *a priori*, before allaying his radical doubts?
4 Put yourself imaginatively into Descartes's predicament of being beset with radical doubt about at least all of your erstwhile empirical beliefs. Suppose, for

the sake of argument, that not only do you not believe that God exists, but that you are, moreover, convinced that you will never be persuaded to believe that God exists. In what way might you alleviate, mitigate, or overcome your radical doubt about your erstwhile empirical beliefs?

5   Is it metaphysically possible for a disembodied Cartesian soul to so much as *form* any purportedly empirical beliefs, even if only ones that are false?

6   Could a disembodied Cartesian soul entertain any *geometrical* thoughts about the structure of two- or higher-dimensional *space*?

21 Problems about Mind

What must any solution to the mind–body problem account for?

The mental realm is generally agreed to consist of the goings-on inside a person's head: mainly, the brain and important parts of the central nervous system. These goings-on are variously called *events, states, processes, phenomena, occurrences*. There are also more enduring systemic conditions called *dispositions*. These are tendencies to behave in certain ways when certain triggering conditions are met.

We have purposely avoided using the word 'mental' in the previous paragraph, except as its second word. Please re-read that paragraph now. Then consider this: these goings-on could be *physical* goings-on; or they could be *mental* goings-on. Indeed, the main thesis of *philosophical materialism* is that *the same goings-on are both mental and physical*. Thus every mental event, state, process, phenomenon, or occurrence is a physical event, state, process, phenomenon, or occurrence. (This is the 'is' of identity, or of what is – sometimes a little misleadingly – called 'numerical identity'.)

But the converse generalization need not hold. That is, it need not be the case that every physical event, state, process, phenomenon, or occurrence is a mental event, state, process, phenomenon, or occurrence. Indeed, it is rather obviously not the case. Not even every physical event, state, process, phenomenon, or occurrence *within a human body* is a mental event, state, process, phenomenon, or occurrence. Think of perspiration, or excretion, or osteoporosis.

Moreover, the mental aspects of a physical system are *fixed by* its physical aspects: there can be no change in one's mental states without some underlying change in one's physical states. Philosophers call this the *supervenience of the mental on the physical*. We discussed it in §14.2. Supervenience does not mean that determinism is true (i.e., that the future is determined by the past and the present). Rather, it means that, at any given time, mental reality is determined by how things are, physically, *at that time*.

Obviously there are going to be many physical goings-on *even in one's head* that would not count as mental goings-on. Accumulation of phlegm in one's sinuses is just one example of a physical going-on in one's head that is highly unlikely to be a mental going-on. (Although sometimes, given the sluggish nature of some people's thoughts, one wonders …)

The philosophical materialist invites one to view the mental not as a thing, namely a mind, interacting with the body (or brain); but rather as a system, or functioning assemblage, of mental goings-on. These take place in the brain, and indeed *are* physical goings-on. These physical goings-on, however, also enjoy a *mental aspect*. Bodies, when animated, remain completely physical. Thus the philosophical materialist replaces Descartes's entity dualism with an *entity monism* in combination with a *dualism about aspects* (or features, or qualities, or properties, or attributes) of physical things.

When discussing the phenomenon of mind, we can start with our own case – the human condition. Alternatively, we can try to think in much more general terms. We can conceive of the possibility that features of human mentality might be present (in varying forms) in other terrestrial species, even if not all of them are co-present.

For example, a rodent might have visual impressions even if it has no reflective self-awareness. A snake might be able to experience something like fear, even if it could never be guilty of premeditated deceit. A beetle might have a 'sense of balance' (a proprioceptive sense), even if it never thinks about the three-dimensionality of space. The ethologist Konrad Lorenz famously claimed that the water-shrew has a somewhat deficient conception of physical space. He found that a water-shrew would never catch on to the fact that if it could get from A to B and then from B to C, then there might be a shorter and more direct way from A to C than going via B. Nevertheless, the water-shrew makes do with whatever impoverished spatial conceptual scheme its little brain affords.

The suggestion is that we can 'decompose' mentality into separate components. We can conceive of the possibility that different species might have just some of them; or perhaps all of them, but to lesser degrees. They may even have some of them to a much higher degree than we do – think of a dog's sense of smell, compared with ours, or the visual acuity of an eagle.

There is also the distinct possibility that other species have modes of awareness that would be quite alien to us. As already noted in §4.3, the philosopher Thomas Nagel advanced the thesis that there are objective facts about radically different subjective modes of being. He invites us to consider the curious sense of bat-sonar. This sensory modality of the bat is somewhat like seeing; but also somewhat like hearing. The bat's method of echo-location enables it to map out the arrangement of solid objects (rocks, walls of the cave, tree stumps, other bats, flying insects . . .) in its immediate environment. So it is like human vision in giving that intellectual awareness of things being 'out there' in three-dimensional space. But the bat does this with soundwaves bouncing back to its very sensitive ears from those distant objects. So presumably it 'hears' their presence out there. It is difficult for us to form an imaginative conception of what it might like to *be* a bat. What would it be like to enjoy sensory impressions of the echo-locating kind? But, Nagel suggests, we must countenance the possibility that, for all its inherent inaccessibility (to us human beings, who are differently constituted), there is a *metaphysical fact of the matter* as to *what it is like to be a bat*.

This is what the French Existentialist philosophers call *être-pour-soi* – being-for-itself. Conscious existence can be a matter of mere primitive sentience, with very little intellectual processing; or it can be highly self-reflective, like a Cartesian mind engaged in the thought 'Cogito, ergo sum'. The tiny paramecium, waving its flagella in swampy water in search of shoals with just the right alkalinity, might be possessed of felt states with the sensory content 'Too acidic here!', 'Too alkaline here!', and 'Just right here!'. Of course, the paramecium will not have any chemical concept of acidity and alkalinity. Instead, it will have, we are suggesting, something like a burning or a soothing sensation, that will induce it to paddle along to get relief, or to stay put to enjoy being soothed. Of course, we are the ones who deploy the scientific concepts in order to explain why they behave the way they do, and what features of the water they are sensitive to.

No matter how primitive or advanced – no matter how low or high in the phylogenetic tree of biological being – mental states will no doubt come paired in two complementary kinds. There will be belief-like states; and there will be desire-like states. Desires provide the motivation for action; beliefs guide one's action. To stop desiring something (which is often, itself, highly desirable) one needs to be able to form the belief that the state of affairs obtains that would satisfy that desire. As the philosopher John Searle puts it, belief involves a *mind-to-world* fit, and depends, crucially, on sensory perception; while desire involves a *world-to-mind* fit, prompting actions intended to change the world so that it will better fit the mind's conception of how it would like the world to be.

Every species with a behavioral repertoire complicated enough to invite mentalistic description will have some kind of *sensory apparatus*, coupled with some kind of *percept-* or *belief-forming mechanism*. Likewise, it will have some kind of *appetitive structure*. Desire for food, desire for sex, desire for social status, etc., motivate individual creatures to 'keep on the go'. The resulting behavior will tend to improve each individual's chances of reproductive success.

The sensory apparatus will give rise to perceptual representations of the way the outside world is, in ways salient to the species' concerns. The most important things it needs to 'register', perceptually, are potential prey, potential mates, kin, potential foes, potential predators, and inanimate environmental resources or conditions important to its survival. One could expect early evolutionary pressures for development of both perceptual and cognitive mechanisms. Those creatures would flourish who were best able to translate sensory stimuli (in the various modalities the species possesses) into effective representations of the salient objects, events, and causal processes in the creatures' environment.

Likewise, as any species' habitat becomes more complicated, one would expect the motivational states to become more differentiated. One would expect the capacity for different kinds of *emotions* to evolve. The different emotions like fear, jealousy, rage, resentment, lust, affection, love, hate, sympathy, and pity all have their place in a well-functioning, inner mental ecology. ('Well-functioning' is used here from the evolutionary point of view. This stresses the constant struggle to leave behind as many successful offspring as possible. Obviously this is not the point of view of the Christian or Buddhist monk or nun who has taken a vow of celibacy, and who seeks to purify his or her soul of all the 'negative' emotions just listed.)

The fundamental constrast between belief and desire is marked, terminologically, in various other ways: cognitive/affective; representational/motivational etc. There must be an evolutionary story to tell about each side of the divide in question. Mind is Life's evolved answer to the two questions 'How do we find the world to be?' and 'How would we like the world to be?'. Even the most cranial geek has to take a break to eat now and again; and even the most lustful gourmand has to have an eye for the dish of the day. One cannot have beliefs without having desires; and one cannot have desires without having beliefs. Call this the *Principle of Analytic Equilibrium* for belief and desire.

In the dim theater of incipient perceptual awareness, our earliest ancestors started to keep track of their surroundings. Primitive sensory channels became more sophisticated as a result of aeons of natural selection. Evolutionists tell of sixteen different lines of descent of a complex, functioning eye from a single light-sensitive cell. When 'parallel' evolution happens like this, we know that tremendous selective advantage must be conferred by the developing organ in question. Perceptual representations become, under the pressure of natural selection, richer, finer-grained and more informative.

We human beings (and no doubt other species) have in this way come to enjoy *qualia*. Philosophers also call these *sense-data*. Think of a quale as a relatively atomic piece of sensory information about a small region of some sensory field. Examples: red-patch-here-now; tone-of-middle-C-now; pin-prick-on-tip-of-right-index-finger-now. Somehow the mind/brain integrates such qualia, holistically, into informative and life-preserving representations of what things are doing what, and how, all around us.

Within social groups of creatures, brains have developed highly task-specific capacities such as individual face-recognition, and memory for biographical details. (Someone who has cheated you in the past is likely to cheat you again; so, best to remember his face and what he did to you, so as not to be duped again in the future.) It is in the context of social living that some of our most complicated cerebral functioning in all likelihood arose. Examples:

- the capacity to detect deception from observable behavior;
- the ability to attribute states of belief and desire to conspecifics (so as to be able to predict their future behavior);
- the ability to bear lasting grudges, as well as lasting debts of gratitude.

Both cognitive and emotional differentiation and fine-tuning would have received an enormous boost from the exigencies of social life. Acute observers find evidence for this claim even in the behavior of rats and chimpanzees.

So we have, in some sort of ascending evolutionary order:

- modality-specific sentience, both endogenous (e.g., nausea) and exogenous (e.g., burning sensation all over);

- more localized qualia (e.g., bright-red-patch-here-now; sickening-pong-just-below-my-nose-right-now; stabbing-pain-in-my-right-hoof);
- modality-integrating percepts, involving categorization of objects (offspring-of-mine-at-my-knee-now; hairy-predator-in-tree-over-there-now);
- singular causal beliefs about interactions of objects (lion-ate-mom; bee-stung-hand; eating-caterpillar-made-me-feel-yuck);
- low-level generalized beliefs about causal powers (beware-of-lions; stinky-water-bad-to-drink; get-sex-more-easily-if-offer-fresh-kill);
- high-level hypotheses (all bodies attract one another with a force proportional to the product of their masses and inversely proportional to the square of the distance between them).

We see this last stage as involving quite a jump. In terms of evolutionary development, however, it is but the tiniest step. (One small step for the primates, one huge step for mankind?) Much more groundwork had to be laid at the neurogenetic level in order to get any species to even the second-to-last stage listed above.

Most importantly, thought had to acquire its mysterious property of 'aboutness'. Singular terms (like proper names, for example) have to *refer* to their bearers. How does the mind direct its attention-in-thought to an object by means of a symbol standing for it? This is known as the *problem of intentionality*. All the stages except the last one involved examples of hyphenated representations. The tacit suggestion was that these would be 'internal tokenings' on the creature's part, in some inner *'language of thought'*, along lines suggested by the philosopher Jerry Fodor (b. 1935). (See Fodor (1975).) The problem of intentionality arises already for the language of thought. How do tokenings-in-the-brain of symbols in the language of thought manage to refer to things outside the head? Even if we could supply a satisfactory answer to this question, there would still be some way to go in order to handle the phenomenon of natural language. We would still need to give an account of how an *external code of public communication* could have evolved. How did human beings come to acquire their incredibly complicated spoken languages, complete with recursive grammars that provide for infinitely many well-formed utterances that we have never heard before, but understand with ease?

There are many naturalistic suggestions as to how this might have come to pass, but to enter into any of them would be too much of a digression here. The main point is: public languages presumably somehow 'piggy-backed' off some already pretty sophisticated cognitive apparatus. This apparatus would already be in place for representing, in private thought, how things were in the world, and especially how one's fellow creatures were geared to behave towards one. A strong case can be made that public language could have entered the evolutionary arena only in the hands or mouths of creatures able to discern one another's *intentions* from their observable behavior. To be able to do that, they would already need a sophisticated perceptual and conceptual apparatus.

All the aforementioned stages involve only the cognitive side. We must not lose sight of the fact (according to our Principle of Analytic Equilibrium) that the affective side would be developing as well. We have been assuming the evolution of increasingly complex and (presumably) accurate representations of the way the objective world happens to be. Each species will be in the grip of its own enforced modes of subjectivity, arising from the peculiar means they have of *sensing* their environment. Ecologically-minded theorists talk of the 'affordances' enjoyed by creatures of a given kind, as they sense the world after their own peculiar fashion – ordinary vision, infra-red vision, ultraviolet-vision, echo-location, water-borne electromagnetic emanations, or what have you. (See Gibson (1977).) But all individual organisms, of every species, are striving, as it were, to track accurately what is actually going on around them: the main players, and the main plays, on their little bit of turf in the evolutionary arena.

Here, we want to say, the facts are objective and in principle knowable. They do not depend on the 'inner subjectivity' of any species' modes of sensing.

This is where the ability to *categorize* comes in. When categorizing objects, an intelligent system will be integrating the sensory information it receives from its various sensory channels, and forming a unified *representation* of whatever is the current focus of its attention. In this way, the mind tries to break free from, or transcend, its own modality-imposed subjectivity. This is the great Kantian problem of how we move from the deliverances of our *sensibility* to *objective knowledge of an external world*. Kant's own suggestion was that we do so by applying *categories*, or *concepts of the understanding* (specifically: the concepts of *substance* and of *causation*) to the *manifold of apperception* – this being the (English translation of) his fancy German term for something like 'field of spatio-temporally organized sensations'.

What we have been sketching above is a sort of 'naturalized' version of Kant's account. (Kant of course was not himself a naturalist in the current philosophical sense.) The main challenge to the naturalizer, however, is to explain why any of these cognitive states – ranging from detection of acidity, say, through to beliefs in causal regularities – need involve *conscious awareness* of any kind. Why couldn't the evolving systems simply be devoid of consciousness? Does consciousness itself – hence, whatever physical substrates might give rise to it – have any selective advantage for the creature possessed of it? What is the *function*, if any, of consciousness? How and why do the 'mentalistic aspects' of our brains' inner workings intrude themselves upon the merely physical aspects? Why (or to what end, if there is one) do we have consciousness at all? Is consciousness just an inevitable metaphysical spin-off of a certain level of self-organizing complexity within a neural network? Or does it contribute something to the functioning of the system over and above the physical happenings that give rise to consciousness? To those skeptics who think that consciousness cannot add anything to the physical story, and that it must be 'mere epiphenomenal fog', one can pose two pointed questions: Why is pain awful? Why is orgasm fantastic? And the follow-up question: Would zombies be as good at self-preservation and self-propagation as those who can experience both pain and orgasm?

We sense the world in various ways. And there is *something that it is like* to be a locus of consciousness capable of this sensing. We integrate our various kinds of sensory information, to form stable, objective *representations* of things in the world. These representations involve the use of *concepts*, both to classify things and to track their causal interactions; and the use of *referential devices* that latch thoughts onto the objects they are about. The more we can learn about reliable regularities in the behavior of different kinds of things, the better off we are.

An important class of things whose workings we need to track and understand are our fellow human beings. We can 'read off' from their external behavior a great deal as to what their mental states might be. But we also have a wonderful instrument for fine-tuning our *attributions of mental states*: we have *language*. We can ask one another how we think and feel about things. Language can be used to express belief, to manifest emotion, and to avow intentions: to inform or to lie, to woo or to warn, to promise or to threaten. Language can also be used to reason, to theorize, to hypothesize, to run 'what if ...?' thought-experiments. Its sentences come equipped with a *logic* that tells one how one is *permitted* to infer conclusions from premises, and what one *ought* to acknowledge as a consequence of what one says. These notions of (logical) permission and obligation are *normative*. And it is a great challenge for any naturalistic account to explain how norms can arise from the workings of material things (such as the neurons in our brains).

Beliefs and desires are called *propositional attitudes*. If I see wet ground, I form the belief (i.e., the attitude of belief involving the present-tensed proposition) *it is raining*. If I see cracked, parched earth, I form the desire (i.e., the attitude of desire involving the future-tensed proposition) *that it rain*. Of course, I can't do much to bring it about that it rains. Long ago, I might have sacrificed a virgin, but we have now come to accept that doing so doesn't seem to have the desired effect on barometric pressure. So let us try a different example.

I see the bare inside of my refrigerator, and I form the belief that I have no food. I feel my stomach rumbling, I feel that light-headedness that comes from a blood-sugar drop, and I form the desire that I have some food. (I am weird; I don't feel hunger-pangs. I just have my own ways of forming the desire that I have food.) So I intentionally go out to get food. This new intention-state in turn engages other beliefs and desires. I believe there is a supermarket around the corner, open for business, and that I have my wallet with me. I guess I also have the desire not to be incarcerated for simply making off with the food without paying; so I tender cash at the register. Note also that other beliefs and desires might well have been involved (however implicitly, habitually and subconsciously) in my not stopping, on the way to the supermarket, to decapitate and cannibalize the first passer-by.

The point of all this is that we are guided, or driven, or led along, in our daily routines by all manner of tacit beliefs and desires, with contents ranging from the sensory through the perceptual to the conceptual and the ethical. We are immensely complicated *intentional systems*. An intentional system is one basically capable of beliefs and desires, in consequence of various pairings of which there arise intentional actions. When we interpret someone's actions, seeking to make their behavior intelligible, we try to work out what beliefs and desires can reasonably be imputed to them, on the basis of what we might know about their own sources of perceptual evidence, testimony of others, etc., and their own needs, addictions, deprivations, idiosyncratic preferences, etc. We try to map out both their cognitive and their appetitive structures, in an effort to explain, understand and predict their behavior as intentional systems. Dennett (1989) describes this as taking *the intentional stance*. Earlier, Wittgenstein had called it *eine Einstellung zur Seele* (roughly: the attitude appropriate for dealing with a soul). Davidson (1973) called it *radical interpretation*.

Human beings are not the only creatures deserving to be treated as intentional systems. Many others have been so, with marked success: rats, chimpanzees, baboons, dolphins, elephants, crows, to name but a few. The naturalist has no reason to be stingy with intentional attributions. (See Routley (1981).) But at the same time we need to apply Occam's Razor, and not *over-hypothesize* mental states when the behavior of the creatures concerned does not really call for it. We must also think carefully before adopting the intentional stance towards thermostats; heat-seeking missiles; and ants. But what about robots? And what about extra-terrestrial life forms? (But let us not get too excited about the possibility of communicating with these: see Tennant (1993).)

The tremendous efficacy of intentional explanation, even if only of *human* behavior, provokes the pressing question: What is the relationship between *intentional explanations of behavior* and the *non-intentional explanations* that one would be able to give within some *completed physical science*? It does not matter that current physical science is not up to the task. We can still imagine future developments of present science which might be. These future developments would involve only explanations in terms of efficient causation, and would reveal the complex details of the internal mechanisms giving rise to the overall behavior in question. If we but had such a neurophysiological explanation, say, of a given stretch of human behavior, what would its relation be to the usual intentional explanations of the same behavior?

There are various options in response to this question. Some, like Paul and Patricia Churchland, say we should *eliminate* intentional explanations, and make do just with scientific theorizing about the brain. (See Churchland (1981).) Others, like Donald Davidson, say that intentional explanation is *irreducible* to physical explanation, and hence *sui generis* and indispensable. And yet others say that even if intentional explanation were ultimately reducible to physical explanation, the reduction would be hopelessly complex, and so intentional explanation is *practically indispensable*. (See Tennant (1985).)

Problems

1 Why *consciousness?* How did it emerge? Does it *supervene on* some physical substrate? If so, could there be a science that investigates how it does so?
2 Explain the cognitive/affective distinction; and the analytic equilibrium of belief and desire.
3 Language is a means to communicate both about the external world and about one's own mental states. How might language have evolved?
4 Norms of reasoning have a problematic status in a material world. How and why, do you think, have they arisen?
5 How does intentional explanation relate to physical explanation? Is intentional explanation *reducible* to physical explanation? Is it *indispensable?*

22 Cartesian Dualism v. Logical Behaviorism

22.1 Cartesian dualism

Descartes's dualism is a dualism about *entities*: *minds* and *bodies* are distinct kinds of entities. They form radically different, indeed disjoint, *categories*. This metaphysical conclusion Descartes bases on an epistemological consideration, in Meditation VI: 'On the existence of material objects and the real distinction of mind from body':

> I have a clear and distinct idea of myself insofar as I am just a thinking and unextended thing ... I have a distinct idea of my body insofar as it is just an extended and unthinking thing. It's certain, then, that I am really distinct from my body and can exist without it.

In Meditation IV: 'On truth and falsity', he had written:

> The mind is just a thinking thing which isn't extended in length, breadth or depth and which doesn't have anything in common with physical objects.

With mind and body thus radically separate, it is no surprise that the Cartesian tradition offers up the prospects of two types of extreme (by way of philosophical thought-experiment). First, there is the possibility of *zombies*: creatures (even humanoid, if you like) that behave *as though* they have minds, but do not really have minds. Zombies are supposed to be devoid of consciousness or awareness; they have no qualitative experience. They might *seem* (to us human observers, if we were to encounter them) to perceive things in their environment, and act accordingly; but they will have no 'internal phenomenology', no conscious mental states, no visual images, or auditory images, or tactile images, or after-tastes, or what have you. No afterglow; no rock-butt from sitting for an hour on a hard bench in a lecture theater. (Maybe this is one good thing about being a zombie.)

At the other thought-experimental extreme is the *disembodied Cartesian mind (or soul)*. This is supposedly a locus of pure consciousness, endowed with reason, but with no sensory access to the external world (if there is one) and with no way of effecting changes in such a world. All it can do is meditate, cogitate, draw inferences; do mental arithmetic; play mental tic-tac-toe; think about what it might be like to have a body. Like the zombie, the disembodied Cartesian mind cannot see, hear, smell, taste, or feel; it has no qualitative sensory experiences. Unlike the zombie, however, the disembodied Cartesian mind would be able to *think what it might be like to have such experiences.*

These two extremes – zombies and disembodied Cartesian souls – invite consideration as soon as one draws as radical a distinction as Descartes does between minds and bodies.

Yet even Descartes the dualist conceded

> I am very tightly bound to my body, and so 'mixed up' with it that we form a single thing. … a certain physical object, which I view as belonging to me in a special way, is related to me more closely than any other. I can't be separated from it as I can from other physical objects.

Nevertheless, by way of reinforcing the distinct natures of minds and bodies, the dualist (call him/her X) claims to know of X's own *mental* life by introspection; whereas X knows of X's *body* by (i) internal sensation, (ii) observation and (iii) conscious control of the course of 'internal' sensation and observation.

By way of contrast with this, consider X's knowledge about any *other* person Y. X knows of Y's body only by observation; and X knows of Y's mental life via the *Argument by Analogy.*

What is the Argument by Analogy? Basically, it is a way of justifying claims about the mental life of others besides oneself, offered as an answer to the *Problem of Other Minds.* It has the overall form of an inference to the best explanation. Here is how it proceeds.

X can do no better than make problematic inferences from the observed behavior of Y's body to Y's supposed states of mind. These are the states of mind which, by analogy with X's own conduct, are supposed to be revealed, or made manifest, by Y's behavior. Those mental states will be the causal source of Y's behavior. In the 'first-person' case, X knows of X's own states of mind very intimately – by introspection – as the cause of X's behavior. X also knows some of X's states of mind to be caused by external stimuli. But in the 'third-person' case, where we are talking of X's knowledge of the states of mind of some *other* person Y, there is not the same 'first-person privileged access' to the linkage between mental states and bodily behavior. X can observe only Y's (outward) *behavior.* X has no direct knowledge, first hand, of Y's *mental states.* Nor has X (in normal circumstances) any kind of perceptual access to micro-events in Y's brain and central nervous system. All that X can rely on (as evidence for Y's states of mind) is Y's publicly observable bodily behavior: gestures, movements, spoken words, etc. The Arguer by Analogy claims that this behavioral evidence is enough; from it, X can reasonably and reliably infer to knowledge of Y's states of mind.

The Arguer by Analogy agrees that there is no such thing as telepathy. There is no direct connection between what happens in one mind and what happens in another. There is no 'reading of minds', unmediated by bodily interaction. There is no way for one person genuinely to experience another person's pain, say – despite assurances by an American ex-President to the contrary. When lovers gaze into each other's eyes, and think their souls are mingling, they are simply deluded. The phenomenology of ecstatic embrace is falsidical. The lovers in mystical spiritual union are still, on this view, actually arguing by analogy – albeit with the analogy on the brink of homology and the argument no lover's quarrel.

What about *mind–body interaction*? According to the Cartesian, these interactions cannot be introspected. Nor can they be studied in the laboratory. Why? First, when the mind introspects, it has access only to mental states; it cannot penetrate beyond the boundary of putative mind–body interaction so as to yield any knowledge of what is on the bodily side of that interface. At all performances in the inner theater, the exit doors are closed. Secondly, when the laboratory experimenter studies a physical system, all that is directly observable are the *physical* events, states and processes. Although the Arguer by Analogy might infer *from* some of these *to* the existence of mental states that explain them, no experiment is going to reveal anything about the nature of mind–body interaction. At best it can reveal something about the extent of the physical-evidential basis from which the argument by analogy might proceed.

For the Cartesian, physical existents are in space and time; whereas mental existents are in time but not in space. What has physical existence is composed of matter, or is a function of matter; whereas what has mental existence consists of consciousness or else is a function of consciousness. For the Cartesian, everything in the mind is accessible to the introspecting gaze. The mind is *self-transparent*. It cannot hide anything about itself from itself. It is utterly, and veridically, reflexive.

This assumption or article of faith has been challenged by the school of Freudian psychoanalysis. Freudians believe that the mind is compartmentalized, with conscious access limited to a certain zone, while another zone – the 'subconscious', or 'unconscious' – is inaccessible to introspection. Freudian theory holds that traumatic memories, or deviant desires that have been punished, can be 'repressed' into the unconscious. They will become unknown to the conscious, introspecting part of the mind; for it harbors them in the unconscious, beyond the reach of introspection. These memories and desires will affect the person's behavior in perhaps pathological ways. The person might become a neurotic or a psychotic, propelled by repressed mental states of which (s)he has no knowledge, and over which (s)he has no control. The purpose of psychoanalysis is to enable the patient, through autobiographical monologue, to unearth the causes of such repression in the distant past; and to bring the repressed mental states to consciousness, where they can be dealt with at long last. There may be catharsis, there may be cure; there is great controversy over the efficacy of psychoanalysis. (See Grünbaum (1984).) But at the very least, the Freudians have mounted a strong challenge to the Cartesian dogma that the mind is a full-length mirror unto itself.

By the time of the Second World War, advances in science generally, and especially in psychology and medicine, along with wider cultural acceptance of Freudian vocabulary, had induced critical strain on the Cartesian concept of mind. It was being eroded on all sides by discoveries about the material basis of mental processes. Ryle's great achievement, in his book *The Concept of Mind* (Ryle (1949)), was to offer a re-conceptualization of mind itself. First, he launched a scathing critique of Descartes's dualism, which he called the Official View. Secondly, he articulated an alternative view, which has come to be known as *Logical (or Analytical) Behaviorism*. In §22.2 we look at Ryle's critique of Descartes. In §22.3 we look at Ryle's Logical Behaviorism.

22.2 Ryle's critique of Cartesian dualism

We began the last section with the claim

> Descartes's dualism is a dualism about *entities*: *minds* and *bodies* are distinct kinds of entities. They form radically different *categories*.

While that is true, these radically different categories are nevertheless sub-categories of a yet wider category: that of *entity with causal powers*. In *The Concept of Mind*, Ryle claims that this is Descartes's crucial error. He calls it a *category mistake*. According to Ryle, Descartes fundamentally misapprehends the nature of mind by treating minds as entities that causally interact with bodies. But, says Ryle, minds do not belong to the category of 'causal agent', or 'entity with causal powers'. Indeed, minds are not entities at all. We have to *reconstrue* or *reconceptualize* the mental, so that we can arrive at a better understanding of mental phenomena, mental states, mental events, mental processes, mental faculties, etc.; and, hopefully, arrive at a theory about mind that is closer to the truth than Cartesian dualism.

Before we can say what minds *are*, then, for Ryle, we need to explain his notion of a *category mistake*.

22.2.1 Category mistakes

The best way to do this is to list Ryle's own examples of such mistakes. In the following table, each row represents a different category mistake. The mistake consists in assimilating the item in the second column to those in the first column. The mistake lies in not appreciating how the items in the second column are *constituted by* the items in the first column, or are abstract constructions out of them, or arise out of their organization or co-functioning.

Christ Church, Bodleian Library, Ashmolean Museum …	The University of Oxford
Battalions, batteries, squadrons	The Division
Bowlers, batsmen, fielders, umpires, scorers	Team spirit
Home Office, Church of England, Ministry of Defence …	The British Constitution
John Doe, Richard Roe …	The Average Taxpayer
A left-hand glove, a right-hand glove	The pair of gloves

Armed now with the notion of a category mistake, we can understand Ryle's criticism of Descartes more fully: the Official Doctrine, says Ryle, is a philosopher's myth, the dogma of the Ghost in the Machine. It is generated by 'a family of radical category mistakes'.

Here is what Ryle says:

- Descartes had mistaken the logic of his problem. Instead of asking *by what criteria* intelligent [i.e., mind-driven] behavior is actually distinguished from non-intelligent [mindless] behavior, he asked 'Given that the principle of mechanical causation does not tell us the difference, what other *causal principle* will tell it us?'
- The belief that there is a polar opposition between Mind and Matter is the belief that they are terms of the same logical type. [By which one can understand Ryle to mean something like 'terms for entities that can causally interact' – NT.]
- Both Idealism and Materialism are answers to an improper question. The 'reduction' of the material world to mental states and processes, as well as the 'reduction' of mental states and processes to physical states and processes, presuppose the legitimacy of the disjunction 'Either there exist minds or there exist bodies (but not both)'.
- It is perfectly proper to say, in one logical tone of voice, that there exist minds and to say, in another logical tone of voice, that there exist bodies.

The origin of the category mistake in Descartes's thinking is to be found in two conflicting motives: to explain the *workings* of the mind; but to do so without making the mental a variety of the mechanical. Ryle wrote:

> The differences between the physical and the mental were … represented as differences inside the common framework of the categories of 'thing', 'stuff', 'attribute', 'stage', 'process', 'change', 'cause' and 'effect'.… [T]he repudiators of mechanism represented minds as extra centers of causal processes, rather like machines but also considerably different from them. Their theory was a paramechanical hypothesis. Minds are not bits of clockwork, they are just bits of not-clockwork.

According to Ryle, there are three ensuing difficulties for this view:

1 how to account for Freedom of the Will;
2 how to recognize the differences between rational and irrational utterances, and between automatic and purposive behavior;
3 how to correlate overt behavior with mental powers and processes.

None of these difficulties can be overcome by Cartesian dualism; so, as Ryle was one of the first to argue, we need to fashion a different *concept* of mind.

22.2.2 Invoking supervenience

We have seen that Philosophical Materialism asserts the thesis of supervenience: that the mental facts are fixed by the physical facts. As it happens, the thesis of supervenience was originally formulated in the context of moral philosophy, finding its first clear formulation in Moore (1922), at p. 261 (but without *using* the word 'supervenience') and Hare (1952), at pp. 80–81 (using the word 'supervenient', which was in the air in Oxford at the time).

In his re-fashioning of the concept of mind, Ryle did not go so far as to formulate supervenience explicitly as an underlying metaphysical principle. It is reasonable to suppose, though, that *if* Ryle had been presented with the thesis of supervenience for consideration, he would have assented to it.

In the twentieth century, two of the most influential forms of Philosophical Materialism were Ryle's Logical Behaviorism, and Putnam's Functionalism. We close this chapter with an explanation of how Logical Behaviorism sought to construe the nature of mental states and processes; and with some criticisms of Ryle's own position. Chapter 24 is devoted to Functionalism.

22.3 Ryle's Logical Behaviorism

22.3.1 Dispositional properties

A *disposition* is a tendency to behave in a certain way in specified circumstances. For example, solubility (in water) is a dispositional property of sugar. Given any piece of sugar X, one can say:

If X were to be placed in water, then (all other things being equal) X would dissolve.

This kind of statement is called a *subjunctive conditional*. This is because it is of conditional form, namely of the form 'if P then Q'; and its antecedent P is supposed to be unfulfilled at the time the statement is made.

The rider '(all other things being equal)' is called a *ceteris paribus* clause (because that is what the Latin words mean). The clause is put in to cover oneself against the possibility of an interfering condition that may thwart one's expectation. For example, the lump of sugar should not have been covered with a coat of varnish. Philosophers are good at thinking up all manner of thwarting conditions, which are impossible to rule out explicitly when framing the subjunctive conditional.

We could go even further, and strengthen the subjunctive conditional to a *counterfactual conditional*, by saying:

If X *had been* placed in water (which it has not), then (once again, *ceteris paribus*) X would have dissolved.

The solubility of X makes this counterfactual conditional true. The solubility of X also makes the following explanatory exchange satisfactory:

Q: Why did X dissolve when I placed it in the water?
A: Because X was a lump of sugar, and sugar is soluble in water (that is, dissolving in water is the characteristic behavior of sugar). And there were no thwarting conditions to prevent the expected manifestation, in these conditions, of the sugar's solubility.

It is of course usually taken for granted that a further story needs to be told about the micro-constitution of sugar, and how and why sugar molecules are made to separate from one another by molecules of water. This is called finding the *categorical basis* for the disposition in question. When in a given 'higher-level special science' like organic chemistry one specifies a dispositional property of something, one almost always has recourse to a 'lower-level science' like physics for the specification of the categorical basis of that dispositional property.

Science is full of dispositional talk. Having mass, being magnetic, having a certain modulus of elasticity, being a good conductor of heat or of electricity – these are all dispositional properties. So are: having 20/20 vision; having high blood pressure; being autistic; being a miser. As an exercise, you should think up what the respective test conditions would be for each of these, and what the ensuing 'manifesting behavior' of the substance or individual in question would be.

So: a dispositional property of an object X is a property of X in virtue of which under certain conditions C, the object X will behave in manner B. We call C the *test conditions*, and we call B the *manifesting behavior*.

22.3.2 Dispositional analyses of mental states

How does this bear on the mind–body problem? In a nutshell: because the logical behaviorist offers a *dispositional analysis* of what it is for a particular person (say X) to be in a particular mental state (say M). The general template for such an analysis is:

X is in state of mind M
if and only if
in the various circumstances $C_1, C_2, \ldots, C_n, \ldots,$
X tends to behave
in the respective ways $B_1, B_2, \ldots, B_n, \ldots.$

The idea is that attributing mental states to people is a matter of trying to say, in some shorthand way, that they are disposed to behave in such-and-such ways when placed in such-and-such circumstances.

All this makes being in a mental state look suspiciously like having the property of solubility. You specify certain conditions, you specify the manifesting behavior to be expected in those conditions, and the job is done.

22.4 Criticisms of Logical Behaviorism

But it's not as simple as that; and, even though more complex, it makes an extraordinarily simplifying claim about the metaphysical nature of mind.

First, on the matter of the dispositions in question not being simple: notice that we have provided, in the case of a single mental state M, for a potentially infinite spectrum $C_1, C_2, \ldots, C_n, \ldots$ of different kinds of test conditions, and for a correspondingly potentially infinite spectrum $B_1, B_2, \ldots, B_n, \ldots$ of behavioral manifestations. Why do we do this? Because a moment's reflection convinces us that a given mental state M can be 'infinitely various' in the ways it can disclose itself in human behavior. Being in a state of belief-that-P – for example, believing that it is raining – is not a straightforward matter. There is no single dispositive test of whether a person believes that P, the way there is for finding out whether a lump of white stuff is soluble in water. In the latter case, we would simply immerse the lump in water and wait a while to see whether it dissolved. If it did, we'd say it was soluble; if not, we'd say it wasn't soluble. And that would be dispositive.

But being in a mental state – even one as simple as believing that it is raining – is not that straightforward. This is because so much depends on what *other* mental states one is in at the time. John believes that it is raining. John is quite a predictable fellow. If he goes outside (C_1), he will take his umbrella (B_1). If he is asked 'John, is it raining?' (C_2), he will answer 'Yes' (B_2).

But now consider Jake, who is not quite a psychopath, but who has problems. Jake too believes that it is raining. But he thinks, for whatever reason, that it will seem ultra-cool to the girl on whom he has a crush if he ventures out without his umbrella, and arrives bedraggled at his next class. He is also full of disdain for naïve questioners, so, when asked 'Jake, is it raining?' he lies, and says 'No, it's sunny outside'.

Now consider Jech, a recently arrived immigrant who is struggling with English, and is too poor to afford an umbrella, and too proud to acknowledge that getting wet discomfits him. Jech too believes it is raining. And Jech has to go outside. So he simply walks, just as he would were it sunny instead. And, if asked whether it is raining, he smiles politely and offers the only English sentence he knows, with the use of which he was trained by a malicious immigration official on arrival: 'I am sorry, I do not have enough information at my disposal; but I assure you that I take your question seriously.' This utterance comes out in a slightly labored, halting way, but is complicated enough to convince listeners that he is reasonably fluent in English, and it leaves them completely befuddled.

So much for the ease with which we thought we could specify test conditions and manifesting behavior, even in the case of a belief as simple as *that it is raining*.

Given the potentially infinite variety of test-conditions $C_1, C_2, \ldots, C_n, \ldots$, and the corresponding variety $B_1, B_2, \ldots, B_n, \ldots$ of manifesting behaviors, the dispositional theorist of mental states could follow the time-honored strategy, in the special sciences, of plumping for the relatively few conditions that account for most of the variance. That is what we did above, in focusing on the pairs (C_1, B_1) and (C_2, B_2) with the normal fellow John. We naïvely think that having beliefs amounts, roughly, to being disposed to behave in some *canonically criterial, non-linguistic* way in some *canonically criterial, non-linguistic* condition, and to being disposed also to behave in some *canonically criterial, linguistic* way to some *canonically criterial, linguistic* condition. Respectively: taking one's umbrella when going outside; and answering affirmatively when asked whether it is raining.

Our examples of John, Jake and Jech should, however, succeed in showing that this is a pipe dream. There is no way to 'nail down', in an explicit 'if and only if' form, everything that flows from one's being in a given state of belief. We have seen that the manifesting behavior depends too crucially on what *other* beliefs one has, on what *desires* one has, and on *what meanings one associates with what strings of sounds*.

This is known as the *Problem of Holism*, and it is fatal for any form of dispositional analysis of the kind proposed by Ryle.

But it is worth reflecting for a moment on the metaphysical possibilities that Ryle's proposal opened up, which are still being pursued by contemporary philosophers of mind.

1   'The mind' is not a thing. Having a mind, or being possessed-of-a-mind, is a matter of being in many different kinds of mental state, each to be construed as a complicated dispositional property.
2   If the dispositional analysis were to succeed, we would have, in principle, a way of *reducing* talk of the *mental* to talk of the *physical-behavioral*.
3   Consciousness would be analyzed mainly in terms of dispositions to say appropriate things and otherwise react in appropriate ways to various stimuli. The importance of an intensely first-person, phenomenological understanding of consciousness would give way to a *more third-person construal* of the public criteria by means of which we warrant our assertions that a given person or creature is conscious.

4 The 'evolution of mind' becomes a chapter of *evolutionary ethology*: acquiring a mind is a matter, across evolutionary time, of coming to be able to behave in increasingly fine-tuned ways in response to challenging circumstances.

So we see that there is some progress toward answering some of the important questions posed at the end of Chapter 21. Even if Logical Behaviorism does not answer all of those questions satisfactorily, it at least gets one out of the Cartesian 'mind-set', and into a new way of conceptualizing mind itself. And that is no mean achievement.

Problems

1 Explain the holism of the mental, and why it poses a problem for Logical Behaviorism.
2 Mass in physics is defined in terms of a body's tendency to accelerate at a certain rate when a force of a particular magnitude is applied to it. So *mass* is a dispositional notion. Might *every* basic property postulated in Science be dispositional? What, if so, makes a dispositional theory of *mind* at all distinctive?
3 Might there be scientific strides to be made by abandoning a first-person perspective on the mind, which is based on introspection, and adopting instead a third-person perspective that can investigate structures, states, processes, and mechanisms that are inaccessible to the person whose mind is being studied?
4 How did Freud's theory of mind clash with Descartes's theory?
5 How do emotions differ from thoughts? Could there be minds without emotions?
6 How does Logical Behaviorism improve (if at all) upon ordinary 'folk-psychology', in offering useful predictons about human behavior?

23 Materialism and Supervenience

23.1 The gradual emergence of Materialism about mind

The main divide among various philosophical attempts to solve the mind–body problem is the one that has finally emerged between dualists and *materialists*. Dualism was the default position for almost all thinkers in an age of widespread religious convictions, well into the nineteenth century (which was why Ryle was able to refer to it as the Official View). They were inclined to believe that minds (or souls) were somehow *supernatural*, somehow beyond the reach of natural science. Human beings were thought to be somehow *special*, and set apart from the rest of the animal kingdom. That all changed with the publication of Darwin (1859), as explained in §2.1. For the first time a credible alternative and *naturalist* account was on offer, as to how we human beings could be understood to be part of the natural order. Darwinism made it possible for us to view our own kind as just one more social-living species within the animal kingdom, even if, admittedly, we are singularly and exceptionally well endowed in certain respects (innate mastery of recursively structured languages not the least of these).

Still, it took some time for the full *philosophical* implications of Darwin's theory of evolution to sink in. Educated lay persons did not become gung-ho materialists overnight. Even in the 1870s, when the famous *Ignorabimusstreit* broke out in continental Europe and across the Channel in England, some of the most influential philosophically minded *physiologists* involved, such as Emil du Bois-Reymond (1818–96) and Thomas Huxley (1825–95), were pessimistic about the prospects of science revealing how consciousness might emerge from the workings of mere matter. This was one of du Bois-Reymond's famous (or notorious) allegedly insoluble *Welträthsel* (cosmic riddles). His list of seven riddles, and his Latin slogan *Ignorabimus* (We shall not know), set the agenda for the late nineteenth-century debate about possible limits, in principle, to science itself. (See du Bois-Reymond (1898).) The sea-change against dualism began a little later, as we have already seen, with Ryle's Logical Behaviorism. After Ryle, the critical turning point for analytical philosophers of mind was the pair of now-classic papers Place (1956) and Smart (1959), by the Australian materialists Ullin Place (1924–2000) and Jack Smart (1920–2012).

A materialist holds that every mental event, state or process is to be *identified* (metaphysically) with some physical (or 'material') event, state or process in the brain and/or central nervous system. So there *is* nothing more to having a mind, and a mental life, than having a brain and central nervous system that operate in a suitably complex way. For the materialist, a particular state of the brain and/or central nervous system that is being identified with a given mental state has two different *aspects* – a physical one, and a mental one. The physical aspects fall under the purview of the appropriate branch of natural science – in this case, neuroscience.

The mental aspects, too, may be studied scientifically, as happens with cognitive and social psychology; but they also fall under the purview of our common-sense 'folk theory of mind', which views human beings as *intentional* (and *rational*) *agents*. An agent is a being who is capable of *perceiving* things and events in its environment; who forms *beliefs* about the external world on the basis of those perceptions; who has various *desires* to fulfill (many or most of them related to the project of survival and reproduction); and who accordingly makes *choices* and *decisions* and performs *intentional actions* on the basis of particular beliefs and desires. When we commonsensically describe people as doing certain things for certain *reasons*, we are taking the 'folk psychological' view of them as intentional agents.

23.2 Supervenience as central to Materialism

Supervenience, which we have already broached in §14.2, is the central notion for an understanding of materialist philosophies of mind. Materialist philosophers of mind are *entity monists*. Unlike the Cartesian dualist, they deny that minds are separate entities from bodies. But they are at least also committed to a *dualism about attributes*. Certain events, states and processes have both mental attributes and physical attributes. As already emphasized, however, materialists insist that all *mental* events, states or processes are *physical* events, states or processes respectively. All that there *is*, is *physical*; but *some* of it is also mental, in the sense that it has mental attributes. (The 'some' here will be mainly hidebound, and largely within heads of a certain complexity.)

The priority of the physical is stressed by the materialist's *supervenience thesis*:

The mental supervenes on the physical.

That is, the physical facts (about all the individuals and stuffs in the universe) *fix* or *determine* whatever mental facts there may be, involving (some of) the individuals in question. Put another way: there could be no change in the mental state(s) of any individual without some corresponding change in its physical state(s) (or in its physical environs).

We repeat the word of caution sounded in Chapter 21: do not confuse the supervenience thesis with any thesis of determinism, to the effect that the future states of the world are fixed or determined by its present state. Determinism has to do with causality 'all at the physical level', as it were. The present and future states mentioned in the determinist's claim can be thought of as exclusively physical states. Moreover, deterministic causation involves the lapse of time: the *present* state causes each *later* state to be what it is.

By contrast, the supervenience theorist's 'fixing' or 'determining' of the mental by the physical is a *simultaneous* fixing or determining. It has to do with synchronic relations between two levels of reality; causation is not involved. What the supervenience theorist is getting at with her talk of the physical facts fixing or determining the mental ones, is the *synchronous metaphysical pinning down* of one level of factuality by another. This is compatible with saying that some mental events can cause physical effects (murderous intentions can cause fingers to pull triggers), and that some physical events can cause mental effects (photons striking your retinas can cause you to form perceptual beliefs). Those sorts of claims would still be true, involving, as they do, the lapse of time. They are, however, compatible with the supervenience theorist's insistence that *all causation occurs at the physical level only*.

Why is this so? *Can* causation really be ultimately confined to just the physical level? Another way of putting the question is this: *Do we really have causal closure of the physical?* In order to pose the question more vividly, and appreciate the form of the supervenience theorist's answer, let us consider the following diagram, displaying a snippet of the mental life of some individual. Time is understood to lapse from left to right. At the 'mental level' of description or theorizing, we are inclined to say that mental event m_1 caused mental event m_2 (as indicated by the top arrow):

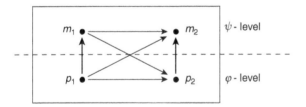

The arrows pointing straight up represent the synchronous 'fixing' of the mental by the physical, as claimed by the supervenience theorist. *There are no arrows pointing straight down.* The supervenience theorist is a materialist because of this order of determination chosen: it is the physical that fixes or determines the mental. (Had it been the other way round, we would have been dealing with an idealist rather than a materialist. For the idealist metaphysician claims that the fundamental level of reality is that of ideas, and that material objects are at best constructions out of these. That is to say, for the idealist it is the mental that would fix or determine the physical.)

Arrows in the diagram that traverse any horizontal distance (and always from left to right) represent possible relations (or instances) of causation. The top arrow represents mental event m_1 causing mental event m_2. An example might be Macbeth's being appeared to daggerishly causing his belief that there was a dagger before him. (It matters not that in this instance the event m_1 would be hallucinatory, and the belief whose formation is event m_2 would accordingly be false.) The hallucinatory event m_1 would supervene on some brain-state p_1 of Macbeth; which, as represented by the bottom arrow, causes some further brain-state p_2 which, according to the supervenience theorist, *is* the formation of the belief that there was a dagger before him.

There does not seem to be any need to make room for a mental event causing a physical event (the downward-sloping arrow in the diagram), or for a physical event causing a mental event (the upward-sloping arrow). If someone were to suggest that we ought to allow for mental event m_1 to cause physical event p_2 (the downward-sloping arrow), the supervenience theorist can reply that mental event m_1 supervenes on physical event p_1, and it is the latter which *really* causes p_2. Likewise, if someone were to suggest that we ought to allow for physical event p_1 to cause mental event m_2 (the upward-sloping arrow), the supervenience theorist can reply that mental m_2 event supervenes on physical event p_2, and it is the latter which is *really* caused by p_1. The whole causal story can then, as it were, be confined to the physical level.

This is compatible with conceding that causal stories almost always reflect our human interests. We regard only certain things as salient, and when we interpret human behavior we almost always prefer to tell a *mental* or *intentional* story, invoking causal relations among *mental* events. Causal closure of the physical is nevertheless compatible also with conceding to the 'mentalist' that we even rely on such mental narratives to *identify*, theoretically, exactly what the physical events p_1 and p_2 *are* (or conjecturally *might be*), upon which the mental events m_1 and m_2 respectively supervene.

Philosophical materialism insists on an asymmetry between the mental and the physical. This asymmetry is underscored in three ways:

1 Every mental event is a physical event. But the converse does not hold; some physical events are not mental events.
2 The physical facts determine the mental facts (the supervenience thesis).
3 Evolutionarily, the physical preceded the mental. Once upon a time, there were no minds; there was only matter. Now, there are minds; and their behavior is determined by the matter of which they are made. Mentality somehow *evolved* and arose *out of* the functioning of certain bits of matter (i.e., brains and nervous systems).

23.3 The main Materialist accounts of mind

23.3.1 *Logical Behaviorism*

The physical aspects of our selves that are important for the 'fixing' or 'determining' of our mental lives are our brains and central nervous systems, along with the patterns of behavior in which we engage. The Logical Behaviorist (such as Ryle) stresses only the behavioral patterns (or dispositions), and does not inquire after neurological structure or functioning. The Logical Behaviorist is content to treat the mind/brain as a 'black box' mediating between sensory stimuli and overt behavior. The structure and micro-functioning of the 'wiring' inside the black box is seen as irrelevant for our possession of mental states. Or, if not irrelevant, then: inconsequential. For it possesses relevance only in so far as it creates and sustains the behavioral dispositions which themselves are definitive or constitutive of our occupying whatever mental states we do.

23.3.2 Biological Essentialism

Once we move away from Logical Behaviorism, however, while remaining philosophical materialists, that internal structure and micro-functioning of the brain and central nervous system can assume new importance. For it can be incorporated into the *supervenience basis* of those physical facts that serve to fix or determine what the mental facts happen to be. The possibility now arises that mental states are enjoyed only by beings with a particular kind of 'meatware' (brains); and that, no matter how similar in behavioral dispositions a differently constituted being (such as an android, or an alien silicon-based life form) might be, it cannot, metaphysically, have mental states, because it is simply not made of the right kind of *meat*. This view might be called *Biological Essentialism*: it is essential, for mental life, to have a brain that is biologically broadly like ours. As John Searle puts it, it is only the brain that can secrete consciousness. No artificial gland could secrete the same. His case for biological essentialism can be found in Searle (1992).

23.3.3 Functionalism

In between the Logical Behaviorist, who does not care at all about the structure of the brain, and the Biological Essentialist, who might, arguably, care too much about it, is a third position: that of the *Functionalist*. Functionalism is such a widely held and thoroughly discussed position that we shall be devoting the rest of our discussion of the mind–body problem in Part IV to its clarification, and to the criticisms that it faces.

The Functionalist cares about the structure of the brain only insofar as it needs to be able to harbor the various *states* in the *program* that, as far as the Functionalist is concerned, constitutes the mind. The *mind-as-program* 'runs on' the *brain-as-hardware*. Different hardwares can run the same program. Running a program is a matter of being able to make various transitions among '*logical states*' within the program. These transitions will be triggered by *sensory inputs*, and will produce *behavioral outputs*. Thus the Functionalist is moved to say of mind that *it's not the meat, but the logical motions that matter*. (I owe this saying to Kim Sterelny.) The Functionalist, unlike the Biological Essentialist, will think of a human being having the same kinds of mental states as an android or silicon-based alien, provided only that they all 'function' the same way in producing like behavior in response to like sensory stimuli. If their programs are the same in each case, then so are their minds: for, according to the Functionalist, the mind simply *is* the program.

23.4 Identity theories

Despite their differences on matters of detail, the Logical Behaviorist, the Functionalist and the Biological Essentialist are all agreed on the more central materialist claim: that the mental supervenes on the physical. Their disagreements arise over exactly *how* such supervenience obtains. Are token mental events, states and processes associated with the underlying token physical ones only in a non-rule-governed, chaotic way? Not surprisingly, those answering affirmatively to this question are known as '*token-token' identity theorists*. Or are there interesting *regularities* to be discovered, linking certain *types* of mental events, states and processes with underlying physical types of the same? Not surprisingly, those answering affirmatively to *this* question are known as '*type-type' identity theorists*. The most extreme form of the latter would be the full-blown *reductionist*: the theorist who maintains that *every* mental event, state or process is an *explicitly definable physical* event, state or process. It would then follow that our 'mental theorizing' at the 'higher level' could, in principle, be *replaced by* purely physical theorizing, and that the latter form of theorizing would be every bit as adequate (in predicting and explaining human behavior) as theorizing at the mental level.

The type-type identity theorist, then, sees a plethora of potentially dscoverable *bridge laws* linking mental phenomena with happenings at the 'lower', physical, level. For reductionism to be possible, there would have to be a very replete set of such bridge laws. It is perfectly possible (and conceivable), however, for the mental level and the physical level to be linked only by the occasional bridge law, with the total set of such laws falling far short of what would be needed for a thorough reduction of mental theorizing to physical theorizing.

We shall not dwell here on these early forms of materialism, except in so far as these general points need to be made at this stage of our exposition of materialist theories. The early materialists were overridingly concerned only with making a case for the *prima facie* plausibility of a materialist account of mind *of some kind or other*. They did not present anything like detailed accounts of the nature of the possible connections between the mental and the physical. By the late 1950s, as would be evident to any reader of Feigl (1958), the battle lines had at least been shifted far enough for it to be plausible (prescinding from any of the empirical details) that there might be a considerable range of what Feigl called 'φ-ψ correlations' – systematic and discoverable links between kinds of physical events, and kinds of mental events (between φ-events and ψ-events).

Before we embark on a detailed discussion of Functionalism, we need to mention, in closing, that Functionalism is not the *only* materialist philosophy of mind to have been put forward since the 1960s. It is worth mentioning here at least two others – Davidson's *Anomalous Monism*, and the Churchlands'

Eliminative Materialism – which help to round out a fuller picture of materialist positions. They make one realize just how replete is the spectrum of possible materialist positions.

23.4.1 Anomalous Monism

Anomalous Monism is a materialist position put forward by Davidson (1970). Its distinguishing feature is its denial that there are *any bridge laws at all* linking the mental to the physical. The anomalous monist is committed to the Supervenience Thesis, and is therefore *at least* a token-token identity theorist. Davidson's main intent, however, was to secure *complete autonomy* for the mental level of description and theoretical explanation of human action. Even though he postulated the causal closure of the physical, he insisted that the mental level of theorizing is absolutely indispensable, and the one that we naturally inhabit when understanding both individual persons and social forces. The mental level of description and explanation will never be, and *could* never be, replaced by or reduced to a purely physical level of description and explanation. If we were (*per impossibile*, according to Davidson) able somehow to make such a transition, we would lose all grasp of what it means to be human; of what the wellsprings of human action really are; and of what is involved in treating each other as persons.

Davidson's anomalous monist respects the age-old divide between the *Geisteswissenschaften* and the *Naturwissenschaften*, with a principled view as to why the former could never be abandoned, replaced, usurped, or reduced to the latter. Yet anomalous monism also embodies the fundamental metaphysical concession that Materialism about mind is nevertheless true: the mental facts supervene on the physical facts. The anomalous monist is a physicalist about *entities only*; but is also an *attribute dualist* with a vengeance.

23.4.2 Eliminative Materialism

The Churchlandish eliminative materialist (whose most prominent statement is Churchland (1981)) agrees on two important scores with the Davidsonian anomalous monist: *there are no bridge laws*; and *all causation is physical causation*.

The eliminative materialist is, however, diametrically opposed to the anomalous monist on one important matter. In fact, the eliminative materialist is so far out on the left end (or would it be the right end?) of the spectrum of materialist positions that one ought perhaps hesitate to say that she subscribes to the supervenience thesis at all. This is because the supervenience thesis seems at least to presuppose that the mental level of description is meaningful, useful, and/or by-and-large true when it comes to describing the behavior of perceiving and thinking beings like ourselves. For the eliminative materialist, however, this is emphatically not the case. Rather, the mental level of description is claimed to be fundamentally confused; at best, meaningful but radically false; at worst, meaningless and useless in gaining true insight into, and understanding of, what makes us tick. The eliminative materialist likens talk about beliefs and desires to earlier, misguided talk about phlogiston (in the early theory of combustion), and about the ether (in the transition from Newtonian theory to the theory of relativity); and to earlier misguided talk about witches. There is no phlogiston; there is no ether; there are no (and never have been any) witches.

There is therefore nothing much to be gained, according to the eliminative materialist, by talking about the physical facts fixing the mental facts – *because there really aren't any mental facts at all.* An uncompromising search for the truth about how we function would confine itself to the findings of *neuroscience*, and avail itself of such branches of mathematics as the computational theory of neural networks (of the kind, say, in Rumelhart *et al.* (1986)). The supposedly more accurate and predictively successful science that would emerge from this might not even warrant the label 'reductive', since its categories and revealed causal pathways might not correspond at all with what the pre-scientific mentalistic theorizing incorrectly postulated. Why look for 'reductions' of false or meaningless levels of theorizing? Why not learn, instead, to inhabit a new, and better, level of scientific description, and simply *outgrow* the felt need to describe human behavior mentalistically?

For the eliminative materialist, respect for the theoretical autonomy of the *Geisteswissenschaften*, so precious to the anomalous monist, can be extended as mere good-humored indulgence. The eliminative materialist would regard any *Geist*-imbued account with the same diffident (even if undisclosed) intellectual attitude as one would bring to the observation of rain dances performed by some pathetically drought-stricken tribe. The theorizing, like the dance, will be impotent. It will only distract one from pursuing real causes by the scientific method, and discovering the deeper truths that we need to grasp in order to put things right, both in the physical world and *among ourselves*.

Problems

1 Read up on du Bois-Reymond's list of seven cosmic riddles. Assess whether, on the basis of scientific developments since the time he drew up his list, we would be justified in keeping on that list the riddle of how consciousness emerges from the workings of mere matter.

2 Construct a classification scheme for all the different positions that we have mentioned or discussed thus far on the nature of the mind–body relationship. Use as few *differentiae* as you can in order to 'pigeonhole' each position uniquely within your scheme.

3 Can you think of an evolutionary argument for the implausibility of Eliminative Materialism?

4 What is meant by 'causal closure of the physical'? Can it be denied by any anti-dualist?

5 Is it the case that every reductionist account of the mental would have to take the form of a type-type identity theory?

6 'Anomalous Monism is case of trying to have your cake and eat it.' Discuss.

24 Functionalism

Functionalism is perhaps the most dominant species of materialist philosophy of mind today. It is due in its original variety, known as 'machine functionalism', largely to the influential work of Hilary Putnam. The classic papers are Putnam (1960) and Putnam (1967). (Putnam, however, has since disavowed his machine functionalism. See Putnam (1988).) A metaphysically and logically sophisticated variety of functionalism due to David Lewis is called 'causal functionalism'. The classic source for causal functionalism is Lewis (1972). We shall examine these two forms of functionalism in turn. Then we shall cover various criticisms of functionalism as a philosophy of mind.

24.1 Machine Functionalism

Chapter 10 explained the concept of a Turing machine. This chapter seeks to explain its application in the Functionalist philosophy of mind. Our earlier discussion accounted for how the concept of a computable function was explicated in different but provably co-extensive ways. Here we expand on that discussion, to provide the material necessary for a proper appreciation of Functionalism in the philosophy of mind.

It is important to realize that a particular Turing machine computes *exactly one* numerical function – that is, *exactly one* many-one mapping from natural numbers to natural numbers. Thus any given Turing machine constitutes *both* the hardware *and* the software for the computations of which it is capable. It is, however, the *program* or *software* sense of 'Turing machine' that the Functionalist philosopher of mind wishes to exploit. The nuts-and-bolts engineering aspects of actual Turing-machine *physical devices* are completely irrelevant to the Functionalist's concerns.

Turing's abstract model of computation is a far cry from mentation. How does the process of computing a function by means of a finite-state machine connect with human thinking, to the extent that the former can provide a theoretical model of the latter?

The brief answer to be developed in this chapter is that it is possible, in principle, to 'encode' the simultaneous stimulations of sensory nerve-endings at any given time as a term (a finite string of symbols) composed out of symbols in a very large but still *finite* 'alphabet'; and likewise to 'encode' the simultaneous efferent signals to the body's motor system. Thus the brain can be thought of, abstractly, as a computational device effecting the transitions between sensory inputs and motor outputs. And on this conception, a *state of mind* would be identified as one of the states involved in the specification of the Turing-machine program that 'is' that mind. Such a state of mind would be like a temporal cross-section of everything that is going on in one's mind: it would be made up of raw feels, beliefs, desires, hopes, fears, regrets, repressed memories, introspective convictions, etc. – in short, every kind of 'mental state' in the ordinary sense, that one is occupying as of the given moment.

It all sounds beautifully simple and compelling. Now we must inquire after the strengths and weaknesses of Functionalism as an account of our mental lives.

As a materialist, the Functionalist is committed to the *supervenience thesis* (see Chapter 23). But the Functionalist's intention is to be uncommitted to any thesis of reducibility – indeed, to deny it. The Functionalist regards both ordinary and theoretical talk about the mental as irreducible to talk about the physical. The mentalistic level of description and explanation of human behavior is *sui generis* and indispensable.

Functionalism can be understood as a natural development of Logical Behaviorism, aimed at remedying the latter theory's shortcomings. (See the relevant discussion of the Problem of Holism towards the end of our account of Ryle's Logical Behaviorism.) To anticipate: for the Functionalist, to be in a mental state is to occupy a certain 'logical state' in the execution of the 'program', or 'software' that is running on the brain as 'hardware'. The Functionalist does not follow the Logical Behaviorist's strategy of trying to describe, locally as it were, the behavioral dispositions in which occupancy of such a state consists. Instead, Functionalists content themselves with specifying the complicated interconnections among such states, allowing them to interact in multifarious ways in mediating between sensory input and motor output.

This raises another difference between Logical Behaviorism and Functionalism. Logical Behaviorists are content to see the mind/brain as a *black box*, whose internal structure – either physical or functional – is irrelevant to their conception of what the occupancy of a mental state consists in. For the Logical Behaviorist, it does not matter how the dispositions to behavior might arise – only that they be in place. By contrast, the Functionalist needs to break into the functional structure or organization of the mind/brain, in order to attain a deeper characterization of mental states. Our ultimate understanding of that functional structure or organization might well involve understanding exactly how our gray matter works. That is, we might need to learn everything we can about neurons, axons, dendrites, synaptic thresholds, neurochemicals, etc. But we shall be doing this only with an eye to abstracting the crucial functional structure and organization.

The Functionalist's emphasis on abstraction here marks an important difference from the Biological Essentialist. For the Biological Essentialist, the human brain 'secretes consciousness' because of its essential biological make-up. *These* neurological structures, *these* neurochemical concentrations, *these* foldings and fissures of the cortex, etc., are, on this essentialist view, what give rise to consciousness. The Biological Essentialist maintains that an artificial behavioral duplicate of a human being – an android, say, like Sean Young's character in the movie *Blade Runner*, or like Arnold Schwarzenegger's *Terminator*, or like Nanette Newman's character in *The Stepford Wives*, or like the Yul Brunner character in *Westworld* – would lack consciousness, for want of the right kind of brain matter.

This is where the Functionalist begs to differ. As the label suggests, all that should count is the *function* of the physical state one is in; not the physical nature of that state. Thus the Functionalist would ascribe a mental make-up (even: *consciousness*) to any behavioral duplicate of a human being, be it an artifact with a 'brain' of silicon chips, or an extraterrestrial creature with a radically different biology. The technical term used in this connection is *multiple realizability*. Just as the same software can run on radically different kinds of hardware (think of Word for the Mac v. Word for an IBM-clone PC), so too the same 'mentality' can be realized on radically different kinds of meatware *or* hardware.

Nor should too much emphasis be placed on exact *duplication*. There is no reason, on the Functionalist's view, to refrain from saying that chimpanzees are conscious, or that extraterrestrials with radically different sensory modalities and behavioral repertoires are conscious. Presumably these cases would transcend some minimal 'threshold' of complication in internal organization to count as conscious (or as having beliefs and desires, if we wish to stress the psychological rather than the phenomenological).

The Functionalist conceives of one's mind as a *program*. A program specifies how the system is to make transitions among different (logical) *states*, in response to current monitored *inputs*; and also specifies how it is to create *outputs*. In the simplest case, these transitions will be *deterministic*, in that everything about one's immediate next state, in response to current input, will be exactly specified by the program. In the more general case, the transitions will be *probabilistic*, allowing for a range of possible successor states, each with a different probability of being the state actually entered into. Unless the Functionalist opts for the probabilistic model of 'mind-as-program', she will face difficulties with the problem of free will.

Before we examine the next variety of Functionalism, it is necessary to clarify the implications of one authoritative statement about Functionalism's commitment to (some version of) Materialism. We have in mind here the apparently bold assertion to the contrary in Levin (2013):

> [S]ince descriptions that make explicit reference only to a state's causal relations with stimulations, behavior, and one another are what have come to be known as 'topic-neutral' (Smart (1959)) – that is, as imposing no logical restrictions on the nature of the items that satisfy the descriptions – then it's also logically possible for *non-physical states* to play the relevant roles, and thus realize mental states, in some systems as well. So functionalism is compatible with the sort of dualism that takes mental states to cause, and be caused by, physical states. (Emphasis added)

It should be emphasized, however, that taking 'mental states to cause, and be caused by, physical states' can be construed as 'taking certain physical states that admit of description *as* mental states to cause, and be caused by, (other) physical states'. But Levin seems to imply that genuinely 'non-physical states' can play the role that Functionalism assigns to what it *calls* mental states (but which Functionalism wishes to identify, metaphysically, with certain physical states).

The crucial question to ask is 'What are the *bearers* or *occupiers* of these "non-physical" states?' It is difficult to understand how Functionalism can have its point if the bearers are postulated to be (possibly) non-physical entities (such as Cartesian souls). Indeed, the main point about multiple realizability, which is the hallmark of the functionalist's position, is that the realizers are always *physical* entities or structures. So the physical facts will fix the emerging functional facts of the realization in question. Supervenience of the mental on the physical holds, according to the functionalist. Only *physical* entities and structures are eligible to be bearers of mental states. Functionalism crafts an understanding of how these physical entities or structures can nonetheless be regarded as occupying 'non-physical, i.e., mental' states while yet *also* admitting of yet other descriptions in purely physical terms. That is, Functionalism can entertain *attribute dualism*, but is rather obviously committed to rejecting *entity dualism*.

24.2 Causal Functionalism

Lewis's Causal Functionalism arises from what he takes to be the best logical account of how theoretical terms (such as psychological ones) are embedded within a total theory based on certain kinds of evidence (observational and behavioral). His aim is to allow for – indeed, to secure – the possibility that one can make theoretical *identifications* of mental with, say, neural states. As Lewis put it (see Lewis (1972), at p. 249):

> [T]heoretical identifications *in general* are implied by the theories that make them possible – not posited independently. This follows from a general hypothesis about the meanings of theoretical terms: that they are definable **functionally**, by reference to **causal** roles. (Boldface added)

Hence the name for his position: causal functionalism. As the ensuing account will make clear, this is a 'functionalism' rather different in kind from that of the Machine Functionalist. Different notions of function are involved in these respective forms of Functionalism about mind. But, in the serendipitous circumstance that a Lewisian theory had its theoretical terms playing the same role as the terms denoting logical states of a Turing machine, the two kinds of Functionalism would coincide in spirit, even if not in detailed predictions of observable behavior.

Lewis dichotomizes scientific vocabulary into T-terms and O-terms, for 'theoretical' and 'observational' respectively. The observational predicates could include color- and shape-predicates ('x is tawny', 'x is round'), as well as predicates describing episodes of observable behavior ('x is chasing y', 'x is snarling at y'). He writes (1972, p. 253):

> Suppose we have a new theory, T, introducing the new terms $T_1, \ldots T_n$. These are our T-terms. ... Every other term in our vocabulary, therefore, is an O-term. The theory T is presented in a sentence called the *postulate* of T. ... It says of the entities – states, magnitudes, species, or whatever – named by the T-terms that they occupy certain *causal roles*; that they stand in specified causal (and other) relations to entities named by O-terms, and to one another.

(We depart slightly from Lewis's original text, by using upper-case letters suggestive of predicate terms. Lewis used lower-case letters, confining himself to theoretical terms that were names. This was an unnecessary restriction. Our exposition is intended to clarify and make more accessible Lewis's own rather terse presentation.)

The postulate of the theory therefore takes the form of a single sentence (no doubt in the form of an immensely long conjunction):

$$\theta(T_1, \ldots, T_n, O_1, \ldots, O_m).$$

Then, in a move borrowed from Ramsey, Lewis invites us to consider the sentence resulting by existentially quantifying into the places occupied by the theoretical terms:

$$\exists X_1 \ldots \exists X_n \; \theta(X_1, \ldots, X_n, O_1, \ldots, O_m).$$

The latter sentence is called the *Ramsey sentence* of the theory based on the postulate θ. It is easy to see, as a matter second-order logic, that for any sentence φ containing only observational terms,

$$\exists X_1 \ldots \exists X_n \; \theta(X_1, \ldots, X_n, O_1, \ldots, O_m) \vdash \varphi$$

$$\Leftrightarrow$$

$$\theta(T_1, \ldots, T_n, O_1, \ldots, O_m) \vdash \varphi.$$

That is, the Ramsey sentence of the theory based on the postulate θ has the same 'observational content' as the postulate θ itself.

Lewis proceeds to assert more, concerning what the theorist is committing herself to when postulating θ. According to Lewis (1972, p. 254),

> [I]n presenting the postulate as if the T-terms ha[ve] been well-defined thereby, the theorist has implicitly asserted that [θ] is *uniquely* realized. (Emphasis added)

So, as far as Lewis is concerned, we are entitled, when regimenting the theorist's own theoretical convictions, to use the *modified Ramsey sentence* that contains a string of initial existence-*and-uniqueness* quantifiers:

$$\exists_1 X_1 \ldots \exists_1 X_n \, \theta(X_1, \ldots, X_n, O_1, \ldots, O_m).$$

Lewis then suggests that the theory axiomatized by θ should really be understood as consisting of the following set of conditionals. First, there would be the claim that, if θ *does have* unique realizers, then these realizers are (denoted by) the respective erstwhile theoretical terms $T_1, \ldots, T_n$:

$$\exists_1 X_1 \ldots \exists_1 X_n \, \theta(X_1, \ldots, X_n, O_1, \ldots, O_m) \;\rightarrow\; \theta(T_1, \ldots, T_n, O_1, \ldots, O_m).$$

Secondly, there would be the further claims, for each i from 1 to n, that the theoretical entity or state or property T_i *does not exist* if unique realizability fails:

$$\neg \exists_1 X_1 \ldots \exists_1 X_n \, \theta(X_1, \ldots, X_n, O_1, \ldots, O_m) \;\rightarrow\; \neg \exists X \, X = T_i.$$

Upon adopting these conditionals, Lewis claims:

> The T-terms have been defined as the occupants of the causal roles specified by the theory [θ]; as *the* entities, whatever those may be, that bear certain causal relations to one another and to the referents of the O-terms.

He goes on to claim (without explaining how this would be so) that if this account of the content of a theory is correct, then T-terms are *eliminable*. The elimination he regards as available (given the logical preconditions laid out above) takes the form of a definite-description identifier of the form

> $T_i = the$ entity X_i of the appropriate kind (object, state, property, relation or whatever) such that $\theta(\ldots X_i \ldots)$.

Since, in this last occurrence of θ, bound (second-order) variables are introduced in place of the theoretical terms $T_1, \ldots, T_n$, only observatonal vocabulary is left therein; whence, Lewis thinks, each theoretical term T_i is eliminable in favor of a complicated definite description within which only observational vocabulary appears.

   To this logician's eye, this is the murkiest spot in Lewis's account; for it is not made at all clear how, in forming the definite descriptive phrase for any *particular* theoretical term T_i, all the *other* theoretical terms somehow disappear. One can only conjecture that something like the following happens. Let us focus on the term T_1. The definite description that is to do duty for T_1 is perhaps the following (with ι regimenting the definite article 'the'):

$$\iota X_1 \exists X_2 \ldots \exists X_n \theta(X_1, X_2, \ldots, X_n, O_1, \ldots, O_m).$$

It is not difficult to see how this suggestion would generalize to the cases $i = 2,\ldots,n$. Thus for each theoretical term T_i, its purely observatonal *definiens* would involve quantification over *all the other* 'theoretical roles' to be occupied by *their own* definientia. This is not to say that the treatment is viciously circular; but it *is* to cast some light on the disconcerting fact that the causal functionalist one can never quite get away from the overall mesh of (theoretical) causal roles respectively filled by the terms he is seeking to *eliminate* in favor of the purely observational.

Lewis, as already noted, did not cite any dispositive metalogical reason for assuring his reader that his account of Causal Functionalism would afford eliminations (in principle) of all theoretical terms. One is put in mind here of the rather more agreeable account of explicit definability afforded by Beth's Definability Theorem, discussed in §14.2. Lewis appears to have shaped his account of a causal-functional theory of mental and bodily behavior in such a way that it would meet the requirement that the mental terms T_i be *implicitly defined* in terms of the O-terms (in the model-theorist's sense of implicit definability explained in §14.2.1). So this reader of Lewis, for one, would be happier simply to invoke Beth's Theorem in support of the contention that the causal-functional theorist is entitled to regard his theoretical terms as eliminable. It is because, courtesy of Beth's Theorem, they are all definable using only the O-terms. What is more, the definitions in question will all be at *first order* (in 'Grade A idiom'). They will not need any of the second-order variable-binding that Lewis's own definientia involve.

24.3 Criticisms of Functionalism

As with any philosophical account of mind, Functionalism has its critics (including its own originator).

24.3.1 The Disentanglement Problem

Their first critical focus is Functionalism's alleged analogy between mental states of feeling, perceiving, thinking and acting subjects, on the one hand, and, on the other hand, the logical states of a Turing-mechanical program that would effect the same transitions between sensory inputs and motor outputs. Normally we think of mental states as 'compartmentalized', despite their holistic interdependencies. We distinguish beliefs from desires, and hopes from fears; and each of these has its own specific propositional *content*. We distinguish sensory awareness from idealistic imaginings. We can run through trains of factual reasoning without any intrusion of felt desires. Likewise, we can fantasize about indulging our wildest desires without any intrusions from beliefs concerning the feasibility, local satisfiability, or morality of those desires. We occupy different 'mental modes' at different times.

The challenge to the Functionalist would be: how do the postulated 'logical states' in your program-description 'of' the functional structure of my mind answer to these separable modes? Can you disentangle the belief-states from the desire-states? When I explain an action, I attribute (at the very least) a particular belief and a particular desire. These are understood to be two relatively enduring states of the mind responsible for the action in question. Yet in the running of your 'program' representing the structure of that mind, how could such states co-determine the action in question? Isn't it the case, by your own admission on the Turing model of computation, that the running of the program (corresponding to the unfolding of my mental life) proceeds serially, thereby not affording us the means for discerning which state might be a belief-state, and which state might be a desire-state?

Let us call this the *Disentanglement Problem* for the Functionalist's logical states, in so far as they are supposed to correspond to genuine mental states. It is not offered as an insuperable problem for Functionalism. Rather, it serves to put the Functionalist on notice that there are certain strong intuitions about mental make-up and the temporal flow of mental states. These intuitions act as constraints on the formulation of any would-be Turing-mechanical simulation of a genuine mind at work.

24.3.2 The Problem of Sensory Qualia

The second focus for criticism is Functionalism's alleged inability to account for sensory *qualia*. Qualia are the 'atoms' of subjective experience: small, subjectively homogeneous regions of quality space. Typical examples of qualia are 'red patch here now', 'middle C on clarinet for a brief moment, ending now'. The idea is that all our subjective *sensory* experience is a *manifold* that can, as it were, be pixellated into a mosaic of such qualia.

The critic of Functionalism will lodge a complaint along the following lines (due to Chalmers (1996)):

> All that the Functionalist manages to do is give an account, from a *third-person point of view*, of the connection between sensory stimuli and bodily behavior. But such an account could hold true of a functional (hence behavioral–dispositional) duplicate of me, who happens to be a zombie, with no inner awareness, and no subjective experience. Yet *I* have inner awareness and subjective experience! How come Functionalism pays no attention to this central fact about my mental life?

(Of course, the critic herself could be a zombie, lodging this complaint; we shall just have to take her at her word.)

This does indeed seem to reveal a gaping topical hole in the Functionalist account of mind. Nor will it be enough for the Functionalist to retort as follows:

> Sorry, zombies are metaphysically impossible. By some means that we could never be in a position to explain, any system that instantiates a functional program of the kind I envisage will have a mind, and will enjoy all the

usual conscious aspects of mental life. *It just happens that way* – you can't have these complicated co-functioning logical states realized on a system's hardware without the system thereby becoming conscious.

This retort by the Functionalist will not do, because of a famous problem of some vintage: the *Problem of the Inverted Spectrum*. Let us allow for the sake of argument that zombies are a metaphysical impossibility. Let us grant that any instantiation of one's own 'mental program' is going to have an inner, subjective, conscious course of experience. Let us agree, then, that such systems will always 'get a [mental] life'. Now take yourself and any other system (call it S) instantiating 'your' functional program. Consider the following suggestion:

> It is possible that what you see as 'your' red, S sees as 'your' green, and vice versa. This spectral inversion will not be detectable no matter how minutely we examine your respective nerve-stimulations and resulting behavior, including linguistic behavior. For, when you learned language, you learned to associate the word 'red' with what looked red to you; whereas the system S learned to associate the word 'red' with what looked [your] *green* to S. So you both call London buses, say, *red*, thinking you agree on their color; while those buses nevertheless look [your] red to you but look [your] green to system S.

Being undetectable by any considerations involving nerve-stimulations and causal-functional roles of subsequent information-processing, these postulated subjective differences between you and S cannot be accommodated by the Functionalist. Indeed, it is questionable whether the Functionalist (if genuinely committed to Functionalism) could even *make sense* of the suggested possibility of spectral inversion.

24.3.3 *The Knowledge Argument*

There is another variation on this theme by the self-styled 'qualia freak' Frank Jackson. The case he presents in Jackson (1982) has come to be known as the *knowledge argument*. Consider, says Jackson, a brain-scientist called Mary, who knows absolutely everything that neuroscience can tell us about the brain and its functioning. Mary is not a zombie; she has an inner subjective life. She just happens to be radically color-blind. She sees everything in black, white, and various shades of gray. This color-blindness, it turns out, has a simple cure. An operation can be performed, which will restore to the patient a normal range of color-vision. Mary undergoes the operation. When she regains consciousness, she is dazzled by the new colors she can see. At long last, she knows what red really looks like. Before the operation, she knew, as a compleat brain-scientist, exactly how other people's brains would work in yielding them the visual sensation of redness. But she didn't know what that visual sensation would be like. The post-operative Mary, however, does know. But she hasn't learned any more brain science. She has simply undergone a change in her optical and neural functioning that allows her to know, in the only way possible – *what it is like to be able to see red.* She has learned something that science couldn't teach her. A *fortiori*, she has learned something that escapes expression by a Functionalist theory of mind.

These three objections – the possibility of zombies; the problem of the inverted spectrum; and what Mary didn't know – all stress the ineffability of phenomenal experience, of inner awareness, of *what it feels like* to be a conscious, perceiving subject. All three objections stress the *first-person phenomenology of sensory experience.* This is the Achilles heel of Functionalism.

In suffering from these 'phenomenalist' objections, however, Functionalism is not alone. These objections affect *all* materialist theories of mind. The one possible exception here might be biological essentialism, which claims that inner subjectivity will arise as a metaphysical inevitability from the complex functioning of a biological brain and nervous system. But the biological essentialist will still only be able to characterize inner subjectivity by relying on the first-person perspective of interlocutors. Subjectivity, like jazz, is something that cannot be explained to anyone who has never experienced it.

24.3.4 The Problem of Semantic Qualia

So far we have covered the 'phenomenalist' objections to Functionalism. They all alleged that Functionalism cannot be the whole story about subjective sensory experience. We also mentioned the Disentanglement Problem.

An *even more radical line of objection* to Functionalism would maintain that it actually fails where it is thought to be at its strongest and best. Usually, critics focus on the phenomenal, agreeing (concessively) that Functionalism might still be a workable model of what can be known about the mind from a third-person, psychological point of view. But what if we refuse to make even this concession?

One intriguing line of possible objection would be that there are not only sensory qualia; there are *semantic qualia* as well. Genuine communication, in language, is accompanied by a kind of subjective experience that can loosely be described as *really knowing that you understand the words and grammar involved.* (This was remarked on by Moore (1953). More recent contributions sympathetic to this idea are Strawson (1986), Strawson (1994), Siewert (1998) and Tennant (2009).) When one hears or makes an assertion, there is a 'subjectivity' to the experience; there is something that it is like to be trying to *represent the world as being this way rather than that.* When you make an assertion, you know what it is you are trying to do; and you can also imagine what it would be like to be at the receiving end, and acquire (for the first time) the information that you are seeking to convey. This sort of subjective experience is very different indeed from exerience made up of sensory qualia; but it is genuinely subjective, for all that.

This semantic subjectivity would, however, arguably be absent from a mere 'information-processing' device like a computer, even if it instantiated the program that the Functionalist says underlies our linguistic competence. The suggestion here is that 'semantic zombies' might be easier to imagine than 'sensory zombies'. And zombies of any kind are bad news for the Functionalist.

24.3.5 The Chinese-Room Argument

A related, though different, line of objection to Functionalism comes from Searle (1980), and is called the *Chinese-Room Argument*. Searle attacks the Functionalist's claim even to have characterized linguistic understanding of a 'non-qualitative' kind, devoid of any 'semantic qualia'.

> *The Chinese Room*
> Take a person who has absolutely no knowledge of, say, Chinese. Put him in a room with an in-window and an out-window. Through the in-window, feed him input in the form of stories written in Chinese ideography, followed by questions (again, in Chinese) intended to test his understanding of the stories. Let him be equipped with the functional program of the fully competent speaker/reader/writer *of Chinese*. This takes the form of a manual of instruction, *written in English*, for the manipulation of sequences of Chinese ideograms into other sequences of Chinese ideograms. Require him to deliver his answers to your questions through the out-window.

The Functionalist, note, insists that all there is to linguistic understanding is this functionally describable ability to manipulate symbols (either sounds or written marks). *If the Functionalist's claim is true*, then Searle's monoglot English-speaker inside the 'Chinese Room' will be instantiating such a program, but – and this is Searle's main point – *with absolutely no understanding of Chinese*, qualitative or otherwise. Yet his output, in the form of answers written in Chinese in response to questions put to him in Chinese about the story told in Chinese, would convince any Chinese-speaker that he understood Chinese. (He would, of course, have to work very fast when implementing the instructions from the manual he is given; but let us suppose he is somehow motivated to do that, and succeeds at it.)

The conclusion, says Searle, is that linguistic understanding cannot be captured by any Functionalist account. Whatever program is put forward as embodying one's competence in Chinese, it could be given to the monoglot English-speaker in the room as a manual written in English, for the manipulation of Chinese characters. And he could successfully manipulate these characters in accordance with the program's instructions, all the while being blissfully unaware that his output was even interpretable as a response in any kind of language at all.

The Functionalist's reply to Searle's Chinese-Room argument is known as the '*Systems Response*'. In my imagined version, it runs as follows.

> You, Searle, are focusing on the wrong 'locus of understanding' in your set-up of the Chinese room. To be sure, the man inside the room knows no Chinese. You get to legislate on that point – it is, after all, your

story. But you have misunderstood where we Functionalists would locate the alleged linguistic understanding that is involved when Chinese-speakers outside the room are impressed by the apparent fluency in Chinese of the 'system' as a whole. Imagine that the room were inside the head of some artificial android, and that the inputs were not only the written Chinese characters of your story, but also perhaps other characters encoding sensory information from sensory transducers with which the system is equipped. And suppose further that the outputs were not only the written Chinese responses to questions, but also motor-system commands being issued by the Room (the system's Brain) to its locomotive apparatus. Call the big system Godzilla. Godzilla uses sensory information and written Chinese input to determine his course of actions, which include not only the emission of Chinese outputs but also locomotion, grasping of objects, consumption of fuels, etc. Suppose, moreover, that the streams of input and output could interlace, so that Godzilla could receive, say, a written instruction in Chinese to raise his arm, and he would do so. Or he could receive an invitation to a dinner party at the local gas station pump, and he would arrive there, tank-cap unscrewed and fuel-bladders panting. *Godzilla as a whole* really would understand (written) Chinese. You ask about the man inside Godzilla's head? He's just a sub-personal cog inside Godzilla's hardware, running a bit of his own sub-personal software in his own head. We call such bits of sub-routing software *modules* in computer science, and we call such partial bits of system-hardware *homunculi*. No one ever requires a homunculus to possess any properties that could only be emergent properties of the system as a whole. So, the ignorance of Chinese on the part of the homunculus (the man-in-the-room) within Godzilla's head is irrelevant; it's Godzilla whom we are claiming to understand Chinese, not the homunculus.

24.3.6 The Out-Gödelizing Argument

Functionalism is a form of *mechanism about mind*. It denies that the mind is a creative spirit that transcends the capacities of any machine. Each particular mind can be captured, in principle, by the action of a Turing machine. That is what the Machine Functionalist believes.

This means, in turn, that the intellectual wherewithal of an individual mind can be captured, in principle, by (or as) a Turing machine. In particular, the ability of the individual in question to come to know, or to 'see the truth' of, propositions about the natural numbers can be captured by a Turing machine. The Machine Functionalist holds that each of us embodies *some* 'axiomatization' of number theory. Any person X is capable of seeing the truth of arithmetical propositions only to the extent that those propositions are provable from the axioms that are implicit in, and limited to, that part of the Machine M's operational capacity – where M is the Turing machine that 'exhaustively captures the mind' of X.

Of course, the Machine Functionalist is *not* going so far, or making so bold, as to claim that any of us would be able to work out for ourselves just which machine M captures our own cognitive abilities. The Machine Functionalist is maintaining only that each of us *is* no more than such a machine (as far as our cognitive abilities are concerned), even if we might never, even in principle, be able to find out *which* machine that is. But that does not imply that *others* would be incapable of working out which machine *I* 'am'; or that others and I would be incapable of working out which machine *you* 'are'.

Now we face the problem that was raised by John Lucas (see §13.3): for any sufficiently strong consistent system $\mathcal{A}$ of axioms for arithmetic (number theory), there are true statements about numbers that cannot be decided by those axioms. Among these statements is the 'Gödel-sentence' for the system $\mathcal{A}$, which says (something equivalent to) 'I am not provable in the system $\mathcal{A}$'. Lucas points out that we, Gödel's interlocutors, have a way of seeing that this Gödel-sentence is *true*. Indeed, we can *prove* that it is true, admittedly by going 'outside' the system $\mathcal{A}$ – but in a way that is intuitively compelling and rather obvious, namely by adopting the further explicit assumption that the system $\mathcal{A}$ is consistent. So, says Lucas, *we* can 'out-Gödelize' the Turing machine whose arithmetical capacity is equated with the system $\mathcal{A}$ of axioms. *Minds transcend machines*, he concludes.

Lucas's critics respond here with a 'Not so fast!'. They point out that we can out-Gödelize a machine's arithmetical system only when we can *identify* exactly which set $\mathcal{A}$ of axioms it involves. For the independent Gödel-sentence is constructible only on the basis of detailed information about the axioms available. Thus we could all form a population of closet Turing machines, each of us unable to descry the axioms at work within any other. Yet each of us would be able to work through Gödel's famous proof of the incompleteness of first-order arithmetic, by virtue of being machines powerful enough to do at least *that* much. (Gödel himself, despite his genius, would still have been a machine, by these lights.)

Lucas's opponent could actually afford to sail even closer to the wind here, and make more concessions without conceding the main argument to Lucas. One could concede that we form a *hierarchical* population of Turing machines, some with the ability to work out the Turing-Mechanical basis of *others'* particular arithmetical abilities, but not necessarily capable of working out the similar basis for *their own*. Almost all of us might be able to out-Gödelize certain others, but not necessarily ourselves. (Also, in order to avoid inconsistency, one would have to stipulate that no 'loops' are allowed in the relation 'individual X can out-Gödelize individual Y'.) In response to Lucas one can therefore say that each human mind, *qua* machine, can be transcended by some other mind – but there is no guarantee that the latter mind is not, itself, a machine. There is no mind that can transcend all machines (on the assumption that every mind *is* a machine), because no mind can transcend itself. Thus Mechanism about Mind would appear to be intact.

We end this discussion by drawing attention to what *would* be a strange irony, *if* the Lucasian argument for transcendence of mind over mechanism in general were to prevail. We explained in Chapter 10 how Turing's and Gödel's explications of the notion of computable function were provably coextensive. Each of them had captured exactly the right class of functions, namely the computable ones. Turing did so with his account of functions calculable by Turing machines; and Gödel did so by means of a mathematician's elegant inductive definition of *recursive functions*, in terms of certain basic recursive functions, and certain computability-preserving operations for creating yet more recursive functions.

We point out, first, that Putnam's Machine Functionalism was inspired, clearly, by the proposed analogy between our mental states and the logical states in the execution of a Turing machine's program. The resulting Philosophy of Mind is a form of Mechanism. We point out, second, that the incompleteness phenomena in arithmetic were discovered only by dint of Gödel's method of encoding finite syntactic objects such as sentences and proofs as natural numbers, by means of recursive functions. This afforded an entering wedge for a form of 'diagonal argument' by means of which the incompleteness of arithmetic could be established.

It would be bizarre if these two complementary and coextensive explications of the notion of computable function could have given rise, by these two ensuing routes, to a warrantedly assertable Thesis of Mechanism and a warrantedly assertible Thesis of Anti-mechanism, respectively. One's trust in the overarching harmony of conceptual explication with metamathematical reasoning must surely put a question mark over the Thesis of Anti-Mechanism, and Lucas's arguments for it. Otherwise one will be faced with a very deep incoherence indeed, in the very foundations of Exact Philosophy.

Problems

1 What were Putnam's own reasons for eventually abandoning the Machine Functionalism that he originated?
2 What is the Disentanglement Problem?
3 Explain what the functionalist means by 'multiple realizability'.
4 Suppose you agree with Nagel that there is something it is like to be a bat. Does it follow that there is something it is like to be an android equipped with a very sophisticated computer program running on the silicon chips in its 'brain'?
5 Suppose zombies are metaphysically possible, but not actual. Does it follow that there could be no scientific explanation, in such worlds, of why organisms that *do* feel pain when their bodies are injured, do so?
6 What, in your considered view, is the most serious problem facing Functionalism about mind? Is it not among those covered here? Or is it just insufficiently developed above?

25 Free Will v. Determinism

As we have already stressed, there is a principle shared by all materialist philosophies of mind: the supervenience thesis. Mental facts are said to supervene on the physical facts. It follows that any kind of mind–brain (or brain–mind) interaction is really a matter of one *brain*-state causing another *brain*-state to arise. In other words, supervenience commits us to the *causal closure of the physical* – even though some of the physical can be construed as being also mental.

When we try to explain any sort of happening, we try to identify earlier conditions that are causally responsible for making it happen. The 'making' is supposed to be in accordance with hypothesized universal laws, be these laws of physics or chemistry or biology. The happenings in question could range from my dropping a pen to the floor, through the speciation of dinosaurs, to Tolstoy's composition of *Anna Karenina*.

What?! one might ask. How can you categorize something like Tolstoy's extended act of literary creation alongside the physical and biological examples you gave? Were not all sorts of free and creative decisions involved in his putting pen (repeatedly) to paper so as to produce that imaginative masterpiece? How could this have been determined only by physical laws? How could this possibly have been so determined, even by the totality of physical conditions obtaining at the time, say, of the union of the sperm and egg cells that gave rise to Tolstoy?

Good question. Reply: so are you withdrawing your allegiance to the supervenience thesis? For, if not, then – though you may find this surprising or even appalling – you are committed to the following:

> Let the totality of physical laws be L. Let the totality of physical facts at the moment of Tolstoy's biological conception be P. Let the writing of *Anna Karenina* be A. Then: even if L and P together do not guarantee that A would happen when it did, nevertheless there is *nothing else* besides L and P that could have contributed to the bringing about of A.

The point is: any element of *randomness* in the sequence of events leading from P to A or any measure of *underdetermination* of A by $(L + P)$ is just that: randomness or underdetermination. It is emphatically *not* the basis of, or source for, the *causally efficacious intrusion* of free will.

Somewhat ironically perhaps, some accounts, by fiction-writers themselves, of the phenomenon of literary inspiration *play down* the phenomenon of 'feeling as though one is doing something by exercising one's free will'. Here is Virginia Woolf describing her composition of *Orlando*:

> Yesterday morning I was in despair ... I couldn't screw a word from me; and at last dropped my head in my hands: dipped my pen in the ink, and wrote these words, as if automatically, on a clean sheet: Orlando: A Biography. No sooner had I done this than my body was flooded with rapture and my brain with ideas. I wrote rapidly till 12 ... How extraordinarily unwilled by me but potent in its own right ... Orlando was! as if it had shoved everything aside to come into existence.

Is this not more like the phenomenology one would expect if the act of literary creation resulted simply from the boiling-over of a mental cauldron of bubbling ideas, with the writer herself merely acting as a selective filter for the resulting linear stream?

Yet the countervailing phenomenological evidence for the exercise of free will is compelling from other quarters. We have all had the experience of deliberating hard and long over a difficult decision in complex circumstances. It could be anything from a choice of appetizer, to a long-term investment, or the choice of a life-partner. We mull over the pros and cons, weighing this consideration against that one. We try to recognize in ourselves sources of irrational feelings or compulsions, so as to minimize their influence. We reflect on our desires, and ask ourselves which of these we desire to have satisfied. (First-order desires can be in conflict: for example, the desire for an ice cream and the desire to look slim. And first-order desires can be overridden by higher-order desires: for example, the first-order desire for sexual gratification and the higher-order desire not to be governed by passions of the flesh.) We try to get the 'big picture' in full view, without losing any of the details that we have thought through. We look ahead to likely consequences, and ask ourselves how our decision might affect other people. Eventually (if we are lucky) we 'make up our minds'. We make a *decision*, and form an *intention*. We choose how to act. In doing so, we are often aware of *making a moral effort* (or of failing to make one). (The making of moral effort is emphasized by Campbell (1957), an excellent discussion of free will and determinism.)

If we stick to our decision, we act accordingly. If we falter, without reflectively altering any of the considerations leading us to our earlier decision, then we suffer from *akrasia*, or weakness of will.

It is this first-person phenomenology of the exercise of free will that seems so intuitively convincing to the *libertarian*, as the philosophical advocate of free will is called. (Not to be confused with 'libertarian' in the political sense, namely someone with the conviction that intrusion by government into the lives of individual citizens should be kept to an absolute minimum.) The philosophical libertarian claims we have free will; the *determinist* claims we do not.

The determinist, however, has a reply. What is being described here is simply *what it feels like* for a conscious mind to be undergoing certain (admittedly very complex) trains of mental events, i.e., brain events. But those brain events are structured in a physico-causal sequence, for all that. And even if some of them are not fully determined by their immediate antecedents, nevertheless there is not any further force (a ghostly free will) helping to determine them either. This is just what it is like to be a subject undergoing a process of deliberation. It is just a more extended process than, say, an outraged reflex in instantaneous revenge for a grievous harm inflicted upon one. More of the neo-cortex is involved when we deliberate. And our introspective convictions about our own imagined exercise of free will are just an illusory epiphenomenal concomitant of all that complex neural processing.

Deprived of the 'introspective phenomenology argument' for free will, the libertarian can try another tack. Our possession of free will, she claims, seems to be an indispensable premise on which our moral and legal institutions of blame, conviction and punishment are based. The very fabric of social life is based on the express acknowledgement of free will. From the Nuremberg Tribunal down to the parking warden, transgressions are treated as though *committed* by free agents *who could have done otherwise*.

Now, why is it important that we say that the freely acting agent could have done otherwise? Why, that is, do we subscribe to the principle

X acted freely in A-ing → X could have refrained from A-ing?

Just as no one would punish a grandfather clock for chiming every hour (since that is how it is determined to behave, by its very structure and the laws of physics governing its motions), so too no one would think it right to *punish* a creature for behavior beyond its deliberative control. If the creature couldn't help doing what it did, it is not to blame. (This was the argument advanced by the Australian eco-feminist Valerie Plumwood when she criticized the agents of government who hunted down and killed the crocodile that had seriously mauled her.)

And is this not the intuition that inclines us to regard as mitigating or exculpating such circumstances, on the part of a criminal defendant, as their alcoholism or drug-addiction, or obsessive-compulsive disorders, or paranoid schizophrenia, or any of a host of other conditions that render them *less able to have done otherwise*? The thought seems to be that the normal person who is free of such *inner coercions* and who is therefore genuinely able to do otherwise, is fully responsible for the acts they perform, for these acts are *free*.

Again, the determinist has a reply. In the case of inner coercion, the causal sequences are all too painfully obvious. The addict craves his fix, steals the TV and sells it, and makes off to the pusher. In the grip of his addiction, his behavior is out of his control. He is not responsible. He is not free. *However*: the same is true, in principle, of the healthy subject supposedly free of all inner coercions. It's just that the way the deterministic course of events unfolds within her healthy, educated, drug-free mind/brain is not as painfully obvious as it is in the case of the addict. She has just arrived at an informed consumer choice of the very TV that the addict stole, but she has done so after reading consumer reports, studying their wiring diagrams, imagining their aesthetic appeal in the corner of her boudoir, looking at their prices and studying her most recent bank statement in combination with her current unpaid utility bills. And after all this, and because of all this, she freely chose *that* TV. *Wrong!* says the determinist. After all this, and because of all this, she chose the TV. That much is agreed. But what was free about her doing so? That she could have done otherwise? How so? How do you really *know* that she could have done otherwise? Perhaps, for all you know, she was *pre-determined to undergo exactly that course* of pre-purchase deliberations.

Is the intuitive conviction that we really do have free will able to withstand the onslaught of considerations from a thoroughgoing philosophical materialism? How might the determinist accommodate the *concept* of free will, and explain our *apparent possession* of free will (from the first-person perspective), while yet maintaining that libertarianism is deeply, metaphysically, *false*? Can experimental findings in neuroscience (such as the famous experiment reported in Libet (1985)) be brought to bear profitably on the question whether our phenomenological conviction that we possess free will is illusory?

Alternatively, how might the libertarian accommodate the causal closure of the physical, and the supervenience of the mental upon the physical, and explain away our *apparent lack* of free will (from the third-person perspective), while yet maintaining that it is *determinism* that is deeply, metaphysically false?

Can the conflict between determinism and libertarianism be resolved, and thereby be shown to be merely apparent? Is there a position that can do justice to the strength of both the pre-theoretical, first-personal intuitions which seem to favor libertarianism, and the high-level, third-personal theoretical principles which seem to favor determinism? Such a view would be called *compatibilism*.

25.1 A form of compatibilism that is more deterministic than libertarian

We intend here to give an argument for our own view in the contentious free-will debate.

> *Thesis:* We do not have free will. We just think we do. And there are good evolutionary reasons for maintaining this metaphysical illusion, and living as though it were true.

Call this position, if you like, *compatibilism with attitude*. Here is how it goes, in more detail.

The mental supervenes on the physical. The physical is causally closed. Whatever can be explained can, under suitable physicalistic description, be explained in physical terms. Whatever cannot be explained physically cannot be explained at all, not even in mentalistic terms.

Note that this 'deterministic' view is *not* as extreme as that of Pierre Simon Laplace (1749–1827), after whom *Laplacean determinism* is named.

> We ought ... to regard the present state of the universe as the effect of its anterior state and as the cause of the one which is to follow. Given for one instant an intelligence which could comprehend all the forces by which nature is animated and the respective situation of the beings who compose it – an intelligence sufficiently vast to submit these data to analysis – it would embrace in the same formula the movements of the greatest bodies of the universe and those of the lightest atom; for it, nothing would be uncertain and the future, as the past, would be present to its eyes. (Laplace (1820), p. 4)

Writing at a time when the successful application of Newton's laws of motion, and theory of gravitation, could inspire such intellectual optimism, Laplace's statement of determinism conflates the *determining* with the possibility of some intelligence *being able to track that determining*. This it would do by making accurate *predictions* about the position of every particle in the universe at any instant of time in the future. It would, of course, need similar universe-wide information regarding some past instant of time; but that assumption is granted for the sake of argument (or for hyperbolic statement), so to speak.

In this regard, Laplacean determinism overstepped the mark. There is no principled reason to believe that a universe whose evolution in the future *is* actually (fully) determined by its present state would allow one to track this by means of theory. The reality of determinism could, as it were, evade theoretical capture. In order to capture it, we would need some *statement $\mathcal{L}$ of laws*, in an appropriate scientific language, that would allow one to derive, by means of deductive logic, from the correct description D_1 of the state of the universe at time t_1, the correct description D_2 of its state at any later time t_2. We would need, that is, for any such instants t_1, t_2,

$$\mathcal{L}, D_1 \vdash D_2.$$

And there is no reason to think that this could be guaranteed, in general, even for a fully deterministic universe. (For an extremely rigorous treatment of theories that do succeed in expressing determinism in the world, see Montague (1974).)

To make matters worse: our *contemporary* scientific picture of the microcosm is that it is (*pace* Laplace) *in*deterministic. There are random events in the small: uncaused happenings, like decays of radioactive particles. Only 'in the large' do reasonably reliable statistical laws emerge – as, for example, when we say that the half-life of radium is so-and-so. Still, whenever we are dealing with *caused* happenings, we want to say: *that* much is *physically* deterministic. This falls far short of what Laplace confidently asserted; but it is enough to thwart the libertarian.

The unpredictability of human behavior furnishes no warrant for asserting freedom of the will. This is because not even strict, classical, Laplacean or Newtonian determinism implies the predictability of all events. There is a non-trivial bound on how accurately any measurement of a real-valued magnitude can be carried out. Hence we can never feed exact real numbers into the 'initial- and boundary-condition' statements of Newtonian predictions. In highly non-linear systems, these inaccuracies of initial values will 'blow up' super-exponentially, so that at any reasonably later time the predicted values of the magnitudes we are interested in will be way off their actual values. The world, we have learned, is (only roughly ordered) *chaos*. A lot of what happens is entirely unpredictable: radio-active decay, genetic mutations, speciations, conceptions, religious conversions, onset of schizophrenia, the lottery, the stock market, the human condition one thousand years from now, and whether she will say 'Yes' if the ring is CZ.

But it is *physical* chaos. It is not chaotic because of free will. And it is not hospitable to free will just because it is chaotic. Free will does not get a look-in. The best one can do is look for certain kinds of order-in-chaos, and ask why and how we came to think in terms of free will, and why and how that helps us in a chaotic world that doesn't really allow free will a foothold.

We human beings are bits of order in this chaos. Our bodies, and the psyches that operate within them, have to negotiate many other bodies, the most important of these being human bodies. Our psyches, in order to cope with these challenges, needed to have a workable model of what is reasonably reliable in human behavior 'wired in'. Evolution by natural selection has seen to that. (That is a long story, and one into which we do not venture here.)

Whatever dispositional-behavioral properties individual human beings have, these are of intense interest to other human beings who have to have dealings with them. These properties are called character traits. One needs to be able both to predict the behavior of one's fellow human beings, and also influence it in various ways, in order to make one's own way in the world. Keeping track of character traits maximizes one's chances of doing so.

So it is that we are equipped with an innate grasp of folk-psychology, and are ready to exercise it with varying degrees of discernment and maturity as we grow older. We learn to detect good intentions, bad intentions, and indifference. We learn to anticipate nastiness and avoid it. We learn to enjoy the pleasures of civilized human company and to cultivate the benefits of reciprocity. We take stock and keep tabs. Why? Because the character traits that we detect represent valuable information about likely future behavior of these probabilistic automata called persons.

Being prepared to display justified or warranted anger or indignation, or to issue a reasoned reproach or rebuke, can have deterrent effect on other people's otherwise untoward conduct. The con-artist is less likely to exploit the wary. The slanderer is less likely to carry on defaming the angry and indignant victim. The adulterer is less likely to go near the spouse of the enraged cuckold.

So we have developed a whole repertoire of emotions, tailored as responses to various kinds of social behavior. The appropriate exhibiting of these emotions affects the probabilities of subsequent episodes of behavior on the part of others that, generally, would adversely affect one's own reproductive fitness.

The concomitant phenomenological states have to be highly motivating as well. If revenge is 'objectively' needed in order to maximize one's chances of survival and reproduction, then it would be more effective if the vengeful behavior were driven by a *desire for retribution* rather than by *an intellectual conviction that inflicting revenge in this way will in all likelihood lower the probability of future actions on their part that might adversely affect one's own chances of survival and reproduction; i.e., will have a deterrent effect.*

Now, who should be the best targets for retribution? Why, those who have *wilfully done us harm.* What was wilful about it? Well, they used their complex cranial circuitry to work out how to harm us. And if they've done it once, they'll do it again, unless we put an end to it. ... And so the cycle begins.

Note, ironically, how the fear for one's future is premised on the likelihood of repetition, which in turn lends support to the view that there is a quasi-deterministic regularity here. Those guys over the hill, because of the way they are wired, are probably going to do this to us again ... It's like a deterministic premise for the conclusion that we must now act (freely!) in our own self-defense. But that is not how we represent matters to ourselves. We work ourselves to a fever-pitch of retributive anger precisely by representing them (perhaps falsely?) as having made a free choice to act against us. We *blame* them, and hold them responsible, in order to feel justification for what we are about to do to them in return.

By treating them as free, we accord them the status of deviant deliberators, a real challenge to contend with. That both keeps us on our toes, and stokes the burning resentments within.

Another irony: when submitting to patriotic fervor and a supposed moral imperative to take revenge, one feels that it would be unthinkable to do otherwise. Yet at that point one is at one's most free. The moral law can coerce one onto a single course of action. But first one has to submit oneself to the moral law; and in doing so one is free.

Of course, from an evolutionary standpoint all this talk about the moral law is a matter of yet more cranial machinery being bent to the service of a particular pattern of reaction to other people's behaviors perceived and experienced in a certain morally loaded way. The underlying contention remains: the point of our having a concept of free will is to make us (hopefully) better able to suffer less harm and to act so as to enjoy better prospects of survival and reproduction. Genes (i.e., alleles) that code for thinking of oneself (and others) as possessed of free will should spread at the expense of those alleles (for the genetic loci concerned) that do not.

That takes care of the phenomenology and psychology of free will. What about free will as a premise for our institutions of punishment?

Again, an evolutionary argument is powerful. Those societies flourish that have effective systems of criminal deterrence and imprisonment. We have claimed already that a desire for retribution is a better motivator than any intellectual conviction about the deterrent effect of what one intends to do. Yet it is the deterrent effect that is contributing to the evolutionary emergence, stability and selective value of institutions of punishment and imprisonment. The value of imprisonment is another irony here: it is best explained or justified in terms of the likelihood of recidivism, should the convicted offender not be imprisoned. And this once again invokes a quasi-deterministic premise about the criminal's dispositions to anti-social behavior.

It seems to be no accident that the two most influential theories of punishment are the retributive and deterrence theories. The desire for retribution is a highly effective epiphenomenon of a system whose behavior is really being selected because of the effects of deterrence (or because of the *lack of opportunity to commit crime*, on the part of those criminals who have been incarcerated).

Because of the way we have been shaped by natural selection, we need to think of ourselves and others as free. If we stopped thinking of ourselves as free, and really followed through on that intellectual conviction, our behavior would become socially maladaptive. So we have to continue with the illusion that we are free. But, deep down, we are not. Deep down, it is just a matter of matter moving in accordance with the laws of nature, where applicable. The rest is randomness, leaving no room for genuine free will. But in the emerging evolutionary order out of that chaos, self-organizing systems emerge that have to think of themselves as free, in order to maintain that level of organization.

The illusion is a happy one, and its discovery should set us free.

Problems

1   Compare and contrast the compatibilism put forward in this chapter with *quasi-realism in metaethics*, of the kind advocated by Blackburn (1993).

2   What do you think is the *point* of trying to decide between the doctrines of libertarianism and determinism? Is it *just* an exploration in metaphysics? Why would any settled answer be important to an individual thinker, or to society at large?

3   How does the phenomenon of *randomness* in the physical world bear on the debate over whether we have free will?

4   How does the *impossibility of attaining absolute precision in our measurements of magnitudes* in the physical world bear on the debate over whether we have free will?

5   Is the debate between determinism and free will an entirely *a priori* one, that should, in principle, be able to be resolved *without* regard for any empirical findings and theories in the natural sciences?

6   Does determinism imply predictability? Does predictability imply determinism?

Part V

Representation, Inference and the Elusive Infinite

26 Representation and Evaluation

It is an orthodox view that sentences acquire their representational powers (their *contents*) by having *truth-conditions* somehow associated with them; and that those truth-conditions in turn determine what logical relations obtain among the various sentences of one's language. The slogan would be: *truth-conditions first; inferential relations second*.

I am of the converse persuasion. I am an inferentialist, not a representationalist. I believe matters should be explained the other way round: *inferential relations first; truth-conditions second*. (Perhaps the best known recent version of inferentialism is the 'pragmatist' version to be found in Brandom (1985), Brandom (1994), and Brandom (2000). For an account of how the author's own brand of inferentialism differs from Brandom's, see Tennant (2014d).) Everything one does with language is tacitly governed by rules of inference – *even* something as simple as hearing a sentence, looking at a situation, and 'telling' whether the sentence is true, or false, in that situation. Let us develop some illustrative details, to convey the deeper gist of this view.

Imagine that you are observing a simple scene or situation. It consists of a few individuals with salient properties and standing in salient relations to one another. You might, for example, be observing a roomful of people. There might be some chairs and tables. Some of the people might be seated, others standing. Some might be talking to others. They might vary in height (making it appropriate to use the relation 'x is taller than y'). They might vary in girth (making it appropriate to use the relation 'x is fatter than y').

Using the vocabulary appropriate for describing features of the situation, you can consider various sentences, constructed in accordance with the rules of grammar. By 'appropriate vocabulary' we mean:

- the *names* that one might have at one's disposal for referring to some of the individuals involved (names such as 'John' and 'Mary'); and
- the *primitive predicates* that pick out salient features of the situation (such as 'x is standing'; 'x is sitting'; 'x is next to y'; 'x is taller than y'; 'x is a person'; 'x is a chair'; 'x is a table').

Here are four examples of sentences in such a vocabulary:

1   John is fatter than Mary.
2   Mary is standing.
3   Someone is standing and talking to someone who is seated at a table.
4   Everyone who is standing is taller than someone who is sitting.

You can determine a *truth-value* (**True** or **False**) for each such sentence, in the situation under consideration.

Before considering how we do this, note that there is an interesting difference between the sentences (1) and (2), on the one hand, and the sentences (3) and (4), on the other. Sentences (1) and (2) are called *atomic* sentences, because such internal complexity as they enjoy arises from their being put together out of *names* and *primitive predicates*. They do not contain any *logical* vocabulary – words like 'not', 'and', 'or', 'only if', 'some' and 'all'.

Sentences (3) and (4), by contrast, *do* contain items of logical vocabulary. This is what makes them *logically complex*, rather than atomic.

Now consider how one determines the truth-value of a sentence against the background of a given situation. We may presume that the situation is presented 'at one remove', so to speak, as a diagram. It will contain dots for the individuals, labeled by their names, with Venn-Euler regions representing extensions of one-place predicates, and with sundry arrows representing two-place relations, etc. If the sentence in question is atomic, one simply 'looks at the diagram' for the presence or absence of the appropriate 'simple fact of the matter'. Does John love Mary? – here is how one decides: one locates the individual John; locates the individual Mary; then one 'looks to see' whether he loves her (as represented by, say, an arrow in the diagram). If the 'arrow of loving' is there, the sentence receives the value **True**; otherwise, it receives the value **False**. We might say that the truth-value of an atomic sentence can simply be 'read off the diagram'.

Here is how it works, in an utterly basic case. We shall consider a situation so restricted that it contains only the two (distinct) individuals John and Mary. Call the situation M. (The letter M is suggestive of *model*, the formal semanticist's standard term for an interpretation of this kind for a language with names, predicates, quantifying phrases and identity predicate =)

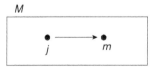

As the saying goes, a picture is worth a thousand words. Here is how (some of) the information 'in' the diagram for M can be rendered inferentially. On the left are the inferential renderings; on the right are English sentences providing the same information:

$$\frac{j=m}{\bot}{}_{\mathrm{M}} \qquad\qquad \text{John is distinct from Mary}$$

$$\frac{Ljj}{\bot}{}_{\mathrm{M}} \qquad\qquad \text{John does not love himself}$$

$$\frac{\quad\quad}{Ljm}{}_{\mathrm{M}} \qquad\qquad \text{John loves Mary}$$

$$\frac{Lmj}{\bot}{}_{\mathrm{M}} \qquad\qquad \text{Mary does not love John}$$

$$\frac{Lmm}{\bot}{}_{\mathrm{M}} \qquad\qquad \text{Mary does not love herself.}$$

Note how the distinctness of the two individuals is registered by the 'M-relative' rule of inference that tells us that from the sentence $j = m$ one may infer absurdity ($\bot$). One could also reckon to the stock of inferences expressing the 'basic information' about M the rule

$$\frac{m=j}{\bot}{}_{\mathrm{M}}$$

in which the names occur in the reverse order. But that would be to make the stock of such inferences unnecessarily redundant. The identity predicate '=' is subject to two important logical rules that fix its logical meaning; and by using them we can *derive* this last rule from the one that expresses the distinctness of John and Mary, in that order. The two logical rules governing identity are *Reflexivity* and *Substitutivity*.

Reflexivity.   For any term t that denotes an individual: $\dfrac{\quad\quad}{t=t}$.

That is, one may infer $t=t$ from 'nothing', i.e., from the *empty set* of premises.

Substitutivity.   For singular terms t and u: $\dfrac{\varphi \quad t=u}{\psi}$,

where the result of replacing every occurrence of t in φ with an occurrence of u is the same as the result of replacing every occurrence of t in ψ with an occurrence of u. That is, one may replace any occurrence(s) of t in φ (not necessarily all of them) by occurrences of u, and *vice versa*, in order to obtain ψ.

Now we are in a position to derive the rule

$$\frac{m=j}{\bot}{}_{M}$$

from the rule

$$\frac{j=m}{\bot}{}_{M}.$$

The derivation, using both Reflexivity and Substitutivity of identity, is

$$\frac{\overline{j=j} \quad m=j}{\frac{j=m}{\bot}{}_{M'}}$$

Let us move now from the relation of identity to that of loving. The atomic fact that John loves Mary is registered by the 'zero-premise' inference rule that tells us that from 'no assumptions at all' one may directly infer the conclusion $L(j,m)$. (In our diagram, a two-place relation like loving will be represented by arrows – a different style of arrow for each of the relations in question. In M, we have only one two-place relation, so the arrows are of just one kind.)

Importantly, though, the inferential method of 'saying how things are' requires *separate specification* of the 'negative' facts. In the diagram, an absence of loving is registered by *having no arrow* in the appropriate place. John loves Mary, but his love is unrequited. The diagram *explicitly* reveals that John loves Mary, by means of the 'arrow for loving' going from John to Mary. That Mary does not reciprocate is *tacitly* revealed by the *absence* of any arrow in the converse direction. By contrast, the inferentialist registers this unhappily asymmetric situation by means of two separate M-relative rules. The 'positive fact' of John's loving Mary is registered by the zero-premise rule

$$\frac{}{Ljm}{}_{M}.$$

The 'negative fact' that Mary does *not* reciprocate John's love is registered by *another* rule, a rule that allows one to *infer absurdity* from the *assumption* that Mary *does* love John:

$$\frac{Lmj}{\bot}{}_{M}.$$

We see, then, that the inferentialist can handle atomic sentences directly, by consulting the list of atomic inferential rules for a verdict. This list is also called the *atomic diagram* of the model or situation in question. It is subject to the *coherence condition* that for no atomic sentence A does one have *both* the rule $\dfrac{}{A}\text{M}$ *and the rule* $\dfrac{A}{\bot}\text{M}$.

The non-identities like the one just displayed do not serve to 'fix' exactly which individuals feature in the situation M. That John is not Mary does not entail that John and Mary are *all* the individuals in M. The only way we can express the latter fact inferentially is to allow two important further M-relative rule-schemata.

The first of these rules tells us that in order to *verify* a universal sentence $\forall x\varphi x$ it suffices, since John and Mary are *all the individuals there are*, to *verify* just the two instances φj and φm:

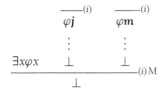

Note that verifying a sentence is a matter of producing it as the *conclusion* of an arrangement of subsentences, which arrangement we shall call a *verification* of that sentence (relative to M).

The second rule tells us that in order to *falsify* an existential sentence $\exists x\varphi x$ it likewise suffices to *falsify* just the two instances φj and φm:

$$
\begin{array}{ccc}
& \overline{}^{(i)} & \overline{}^{(i)} \\
& \varphi j & \varphi m \\
& \vdots & \vdots \\
\exists x\varphi x & \bot & \bot \\
\hline
& \bot &
\end{array}\; {}^{(i)}\text{M}
$$

Note that falsifying a sentence is a matter of deriving $\bot$ as the conclusion of the final step of what we shall call a *falsification* of that sentence (relative to M). The sentence in question is the major premise of the final step of the falsification. In the rule just stated, the overlinings of assumptions (marked with a numeral *i*) indicates that the bottommost absurdity ($\bot$) no longer depends on them. They are *discharged* by the application of the rule, likewise labeled with the same numeral *i*.

With a logically complex sentence, one has to accomplish two kinds of task in order to determine its truth-value. First, one has to have an eye to all the 'basic facts' in the diagram – or at least, to all those that might be relevant to the determination of truth-value. Secondly (and very importantly) one has to be able to marshall those facts in the right kind of way in order to work out whether the complex sentence should receive the value **True** (i.e., be derived as the conclusion of an M-relative verification) or should instead receive the value **False** (i.e., be the major premise of the final step of an M-relative falsification). In this process, it is particularly important, when dealing with the contribution of quantifying phrases like 'everyone' and 'someone', to know who all the people are. In general, the quantifiers are read as 'everything' and 'something', and the domain is said to consist of *individuals* or *objects*. They make up the so-called 'range' of these quantifiers. The two new rules we have just discussed – the M-relative rules of Universal Verification and of Existential Falsification – succeed in specifying exactly which individuals comprise the domain of M. The individuals in question are the ones that the two rules say must be taken into consideration when verifying universals or falsifying existentials, relative to M.

Let us illustrate these ideas with a very simple example. Consider once more a situation consisting of just the two distinct individuals, John and Mary. Suppose further that the following 'atomic facts' obtain:

John loves Mary;
Mary loves John;

and that *that is all the loving taking place*. In the situation as described (call it M′), there are the following further basic facts about the *domain of individuals*:

John is distinct from (i.e., not identical to) Mary;
Everyone is either identical to John or identical to Mary.

The diagram of the situation M′ that has just been described is as follows:

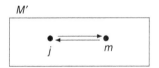

26.1 Verifying a sentence in a situation

Consider now the logically complex sentence

Everyone loves someone else,

interpreted against the background of the situation M′. You may think that you can 'see in a flash' that this sentence is true. But in so thinking, you are probably unaware of the several *steps of logical inference* that you must be performing subconsciously in order to arrive at that determination. I want to suggest that the process really does consist of several steps, and that they are as follows.

First, the sentence is built up in grammatical stages, as revealed by the following constructional pedigree. It begins, at the top, with **simplest possible expressions**, and successively introduces *layers of logical complexity* as one proceeds downwards to the sentence being formed.

	x **is identical to** y	
x **loves** y	not(x is identical to y)	(prefixing with 'not')
[x loves y and not(x is identical to y)]		(joining with 'and')
someone y[x loves y and not(x is identical to y)]		(prefixing with 'someone')
i.e., x loves someone else		(abbreviating by using 'else', and suppressing bindings of variables)
everyone x(x loves someone else)		(prefixing with 'everyone')
i.e., everyone loves someone else		(suppressing bindings of variables).

It is this constructional pedigree that makes for what we call the underlying *logical form* of the sentence. The underlying logical form here is

Everyone x[someone y(x loves y and not(x is identical to y))].

We can re-do the foregoing construction tree more succinctly by using formal logical symbolism as follows:

	$x = y$	
Lxy	$\neg x = y$	(prefixing with '¬')
$[Lxy \wedge \neg x = y)]$		(joining with '∧')
$\exists y Lxy \wedge \neg x = y$		(prefixing with '∃y')
$\forall x \exists y Lxy \wedge \neg x = y$		(prefixing with '∀x')

i.e., everyone loves someone else.

English grammar (like the grammar of any natural language) has ways of 'smoothing out' all the logical wrinkles displayed above so that one's speech flows more easily. But 'beneath' that smooth flow of words in 'Everyone loves someone else' there is the foregoing underlying logical form that can be brought out by being very pernickity about simplest constituents, their order of composition, prefixings and compoundings, bracketings, and variable bindings. Arguably, this more detailed structure is available to be processed in the mind/brain, the smooth phonological contours of the English sentence notwithstanding.

Once we have the underlying logical form of the sentence, we can proceed to work out its truth-value in the situation described above. Here is how that determination would go.

John loves Mary (given).
John is distinct from Mary (given).
So, John loves Mary **and** John is distinct from Mary.
So, **John** loves **someone else**.
Mary loves John (given).
Again, John is distinct from Mary (given).
So, Mary loves John **and** John is distinct from Mary.

So, **Mary** loves **someone else**.
But **everyone** is either identical to **John** or identical to **Mary** (given).
So, **everyone** loves someone else.

What we have here is an informal 'M'-relative' *proof* of the conclusion 'Everyone loves someone else' from basic ('axiomatic') information about the situation M'. That is what makes the sentence **True** in M' – it can be M'-*relatively deduced* from the basic information about M'.

The following formal M'-relative verification, using the logical forms introduced above, 'regiments' the foregoing reasoning by means of which we determined that the sentence is True in M'. In this verification, we see that the sentence is M'-relatively deduced as a conclusion, using as premises the basic information about M', expressed inferentially. M'-relativity is evident also in the use of the M'-relative rule of '∀-Verification' at the final step.

$$\cfrac{\cfrac{M'\cfrac{}{Ljm} \quad \cfrac{\cfrac{}{j=m}^{(1)}{}_{M'}}{\cfrac{\perp}{\neg j=m}^{(1)}}}{\cfrac{Ljm \wedge \neg j = m}{\exists y(Ljy \wedge \neg j = y)}} \quad \cfrac{M'\cfrac{}{Lmj} \quad \cfrac{\cfrac{\cfrac{}{j=j} \quad \cfrac{}{m=j}^{(2)}}{j=m}{}_{M'}}{\cfrac{\perp}{\neg m=j}^{(2)}}}{\cfrac{Lmj \wedge \neg m = j}{\exists y(Lmy \wedge \neg m = y)}}}{\forall x \exists y(Lxy \wedge \neg x = y)}{}_{M'}$$

Definition 6. *We write*

$$M \Vdash \varphi$$

to say that there exists an M-relative verification of a sentence φ. One can read this as 'M makes φ true'.

26.2 Falsifying a sentence in a situation

Similarly, but by way of interesting contrast, a sentence that has the truth-value **False** can be **refuted** by appeal to the basic information that we have about the situation in question. Consider now, for example, the sentence

Someone loves everyone.

Here is how we determine that it is false (in the same situation M'):

Suppose, for the sake of *reductio ad absurdum*, that someone loves everyone.
Now, everyone is identical to John or identical to Mary (given).
So, either John loves everyone or Mary loves everyone.

Suppose, then, that the first case holds: that John loves everyone.
It would follow that John loves John.
But John does *not* love John (given). *Contradiction* (in the first case)
Suppose, then, that the second case holds: that Mary loves everyone.
It would follow that Mary loves Mary.
But Mary does *not* love Mary (given).
Contradiction (in the second case)
We have considered both possible cases; so, *Contradiction!* overall.
We have now reduced to absurdity the assumption that everyone loves someone.

What we have here is an informal 'M′-relative' *disproof* of the assumption 'Everyone loves someone' *modulo* basic ('axiomatic') information about the situation M′. That is what makes the sentence **False** in M′ – it can be M′-*relatively refuted modulo* the basic information about M′.

The following formal M′-relative falsification, using the logical forms introduced above, 'regiments' the foregoing reasoning by means of which we determined that the sentence is **False** in M′. In this falsification, we see that the sentence is M′-relatively refuted as an assumption, using for other premises the basic information about M′, expressed inferentially. M′-relativity is evident also in the uses of the M′-relative rule of '∃-Falsification'.

Definition 7. *We write*

$$M, \varphi \Vdash \perp$$

to say that there exists an M-relative falsification of a sentence φ. *One can read this as* '*M makes* φ *false*'.

26.3 An example to motivate rules for the conditional connective

Logicians standardly regiment sentences of the form 'All As are Bs' by means of the formal sentence $\forall x(Ax \rightarrow Bx)$. They are thereby treating

All As are Bs

as having the same content as

Everything is such that **if** it is an A, **then** it is a B.

Here, the two-place connective → is the *material conditional*. Consider now another little situation, M*:

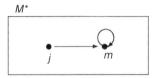

and consider the English sentence 'Anyone who loves themselves is loved by someone else'. Intuitively, we can tell that this sentence is **True** in M*. It generalizes about people who loves themselves. The only such person is Mary. And she is indeed loved by someone else, namely John.

How would this reasoning be regimented, though, when using the universal quantifier in combination with the conditional connective to formalize the English sentence in question? The formal sentence to be evaluated is

$$\forall x(Lxx \to \exists y(\neg y = x \land Lyx)).$$

For this universal sentence to be evaluated as **True** in M*, both its 'John-instance' and its 'Mary-instance' need to be evaluated as **True** in M*:

$$\frac{Ljj \to \exists y(\neg y = j \land Lyj) \quad Lmm \to \exists y(\neg y = m \land Lym)}{\forall x(Lxx \to \exists y(\neg y = x \land Lyx))}\text{-M*} \cdot$$

The 'John-instance' is **True** by default, as it were – because its *antecedent* Ljj is **False**. Intuitively, when evaluating the English sentence we simply ignored the 'John-instance' for this very reason, and focused solely on the 'Mary-instance'. But logical formalization keeps us honest; we are obliged to explain why we count the 'John-instance' of this universal claim as **True**. The reason, to repeat, is that it is a conditional whose antecedent is **False**.

Now consider the 'Mary-instance'. Here, we have a conditional that is **True** simply because its *consequent* is **True**.

We are now in a position to complete the sought verification of the formal sentence

$$\forall x(Lxx \to \exists y(\neg y = x \land Lyx))$$

in the situation M*:

$$\cfrac{\cfrac{}{\boldsymbol{j=m}}_{M^*}^{(2)}}{} $$

$$\cfrac{\cfrac{\cfrac{}{Ljj}_{M^*}^{(1)}}{\bot}}{Ljj \rightarrow \exists y(\neg y = j \wedge Lyj)}^{(1)} \qquad \cfrac{\cfrac{\cfrac{\cfrac{\cfrac{}{\boldsymbol{j=m}}_{M^*}^{(2)}}{\neg j = m}^{(2)} \quad \cfrac{}{Ljm}^{M^*}}{\neg j = m \wedge Ljm}}{\exists y(\neg y = m \wedge Lym)}}{Lmm \rightarrow \exists y(\neg y = m \wedge Lym)}_{M^*}$$
$$\cfrac{}{\forall x(Lxx \rightarrow \exists y(\neg y = x \wedge Lyx))}$$

26.4 What is the role of inference in understanding the representational content of a sentence?

I am not suggesting that there is a Little Logician in one's head constructing tedious formal proofs and disproofs like this when one evaluates sentences as true or false. For that would involve a regress – what about further Little Logicians in *her* head? What I am suggesting rather is this. Just as the visual cortex of a person's mind/brain effortlessly and subconsciously processes an enormous amount of structured information about their visual field, so too does their 'logico-linguistic module', when working out the truth-values of not-too-complex sentences about not-too-complicated situations, process effortlessly and subconsciously computational objects that can be regimented by shortish proofs and refutations such as these.

It is easy to convince oneself that the correct execution of the procedures involved becomes much more complex very rapidly, as the size and complexity of the situation increases, and as the logical complexity of the sentence being evaluated increases. It is in the more difficult cases that one really comes to rely on the above theoretical insights as to how to conduct the determination of truth-value from the basic facts given.

I advance the following thesis.

> The logical moves that are involved in the **determination of truth-values** of complex sentences on the basis of *atomic* information are subsequently employed also, in suitably generalized forms, for the **deductive transitions** that we make from *complex premises* to complex conclusions, even when we do not have enough information to tell whether the premises are true.

Inferential logical moves are involved in recognizing what is true and what is false, even in relatively simple situations and with sentences that are not simple, but are not overly complex either.

So the possibility (indeed, necessity) of logical inference is involved at the very beginnings of language. It is essential for logically complex propositional *representation* itself. In looking at the world, and then reporting on it by means of complex sentences, we have to be able to make logical inferences, from basic information to those complex reports. In hearing someone else's complex reports about the world, and in trying, ourselves, to construct a mental picture of how things must stand if those reports are true, we also have to be able to make logical inferences, so as to be able to adjust the mental picture to fit the reports received.

Logic governs language from the very start. Even the most ordinary kind of thinking – propositional representation of an observed scene – is impossible without it.

26.4.1 *Isomorphisms among models*

Let us re-visit the first simple model that we introduced above:

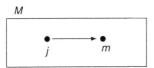

Consider another model, $M^\dagger$, say, containing different individuals in its domain (as indicated by using triangular dots in the following picture, instead of round ones), and structured as follows:

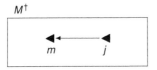

Note that there is no essential difference between M and $M^\dagger$, *qua* models or structures. They are said to be *isomorphic*. This is because they can be put into a structure-preserving, one-one correspondence. If we map the domain of $M^\dagger$ to that of M as follows, indicated by the dashed arrows:

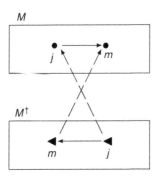

we see that the following holds:

1   the mapping is one-one from the domain of $M^\dagger$ onto the domain of M;
2   the individual named j in $M^\dagger$ is mapped to the individual named j in M;
3   the individual named m in $M^\dagger$ is mapped to the individual named m in M;
4   the extension of L in $M^\dagger$, consisting of just the ordered pair

   $\langle$denotation of j, denotation of $m\rangle$,

   is mapped to the corresponding extension of L in M.

The mapping represented by the dashed arrows is therefore said to be an *isomorphism* from $M^\dagger$ to M; and obviously its converse is an isomorphism from M to $M^\dagger$. The two models M and $M^\dagger$ are said to be *isomorphic*; and in symbols we write $M \cong M^\dagger$.

It is straightforward to generalize the definition of isomorphism that we have just illustrated with our two-element models M and $M^\dagger$. A one-one mapping from the domain of any model M_1 onto that of any model M_2 (for the same extralogical vocabulary) is an isomorphism just in case it 'lifts' the M_1-extension of each extralogical expression onto its M_2-extension. And isomorphism, thus defined, is obviously an equivalence relation. For, first, every model is isomorphic to itself, under the identity mapping; secondly, if $M_1 \cong M_2$, then $M_2 \cong M_1$ (by the converse mapping, as just remarked); and thirdly, if $M_1 \cong M_2$ and $M_2 \cong M_3$, then $M_1 \cong M_3$ (by composition of the two isomorphisms involved).

When we say that we have succeeded in describing a situation M 'up to isomorphism' we mean that (i) M satisfies our description, and (ii) any situation or model M' that satisfies our description is isomorphic to M. (The description in question will be a particular set of sentences using the extralogical vocabulary appropriate for M.) In such circumstances we also say that we have given a *categorical description* of the model M.

What we are concerned to emphasize here is a deep fact that makes *finite* situations (abstract or concrete) very special indeed:

   any finite model can be described up to isomorphism;

or, equivalently,

   any finite model can be categorically described.

Indeed, the categorical description is effected by a *single sentence*:

> For every *finite* model M, there is, in the first-order language apt for describing M, a sentence φ_M such that:
>
> 1 M $\Vdash \varphi_M$; and
> 2 for every model M', if M' $\Vdash \varphi_M$, then M' $\cong$ M.
>
> Moreover:
>
> 3. for every sentence θ in the language of M:
>   if M $\Vdash \theta$, then $\varphi_M \vdash \theta$; and
>   if M $\nVdash \theta$, then $\varphi_M, \theta \vdash \perp$.

One ought also to add here that the deducibility relation $\vdash$ used in the statement of (3) is that of *Core Logic*, which will be described in §27.1.

The following paragraph to end this section is a little more technical, but will repay careful study. It also serves to foreshadow the major theme of Chapter 29.

By contrast with finite models, no infinite model can be described up to isomorphism using a first-order language. At best (and none too frequently) one can describe an infinite model M precisely enough to ensure that M is the only model *of its size*, up to isomorphism, satisfying one's description. But in that case one's description Δ of M is also satisfied by models larger than M.

One might wonder how success on the part of a theory Δ in describing a model up to isomorphism *for a particular infinite size (or 'power')* relates to potential such success for other infinite sizes. A very deep result in model theory, due to Michael Morley (b. 1930), is that the following three possibilities for 'categoricity in power' are exhaustive:

1 Δ succeeds in this regard for all infinite powers.
2 Δ succeeds in this regard for exactly the uncountable powers.
3 Δ succeeds in this regard for exactly the countable powers.

Most infinite structures in which mathematicians are interested, however, fail to be describable up to isomorphism even in just their own power. There are other models of their size that are not isomorphic to them, but which satisfy their complete descriptions.

26.5 The rules of verification and falsification

Now let us get back to basics. The rules for verifying and falsifying sentences in models, as we have already seen from the examples dealt with above, are 'intercalated': more complex verifications can be constructed out of simpler falsifications, and more complex falsifications can be constructed out of simpler verifications. A *verification* of φ has φ as its *conclusion*, and its last step will be an application of a rule of verification. A *falsification* of φ has $\bot$ as its conclusion, and has φ as the major premise of its final step, which is an application of a rule of falsification. In a verification, the only assumptions used are (positively or negatively) 'atomic'. Logicians call atoms and negations of atoms *literals*, and we shall borrow this terminology here. So we can say that in a verification, the only assumptions used are literals. Likewise, in a falsification, the only assumptions used, apart from the main sentence for *reductio* (the major premise of the final step), are literals. The reader should re-visit the earlier worked examples to confirm the correctness of this general characterization.

26.5.1 Rules of verification

In our examples above of verifications and falsifications, we used certain rules without pausing to explain them – mainly because it is pretty obvious, on inspection, why the rules are in order. But in this section we shall pull together all the basic 'evaluative' considerations, in order to give a definitive list of the rules that are permitted, and are put to work, when either verifying or falsifying a sentence in a given situation.

The following rules of verification, apart from the rule for verifying universals, do not depend on the model in which the sentence is being evaluated.

The rule for verifying negations is

$$(\neg\mathcal{V}) \qquad \begin{array}{c} \dfrac{\quad}{\varphi}{}^{(i)} \\ \vdots \\ \dfrac{\bot}{\neg\varphi}{}^{(i)} \end{array}$$

The vertical dots indicate the presence of some falsification of φ. Note that upon applying this rule, the assumption φ in the subordinate falsification is discharged.

The rule for verifying conjunctions is

$$(\wedge\mathcal{V}) \qquad \begin{array}{cc} \vdots & \vdots \\ \varphi & \psi \\ \hline \multicolumn{2}{c}{\varphi \wedge \psi} \end{array}$$

The vertical dots indicate the presence of verifications of φ and of ψ.

The rule for verifying disjunctions comes in two halves:

$$(\vee\mathcal{V}) \qquad \begin{array}{cc} \vdots & \vdots \\ \dfrac{\varphi}{\varphi \vee \psi} & \dfrac{\psi}{\varphi \vee \psi} \end{array}$$

The vertical dots indicate the presence of some verification of φ or of ψ, respectively.

The rule for verifying conditionals likewise comes in two halves:

$$(\to\mathcal{V})\qquad \begin{array}{c} \dfrac{}{\varphi}{}^{(i)} \\ \vdots \\ \dfrac{\bot}{\varphi\to\psi}{}^{(i)} \end{array} \qquad\qquad \begin{array}{c} \vdots \\ \dfrac{\psi}{\varphi\to\psi} \end{array}$$

In the left half of the rule, the vertical dots indicate the presence of some falsification of φ. Note that upon applying this half of the rule, the assumption φ in the subordinate falsification is discharged. In the right half of the rule the vertical dots indicate the presence of some verification of ψ.

The rule for verifying existentials is

$$(\exists\mathcal{V})\qquad \begin{array}{c} \vdots \\ \dfrac{\psi(\alpha)}{\exists x\psi(x)} \end{array} \qquad \text{where } \alpha \text{ is an individual in the domain.}$$

Let N be a finite model, and suppose its domain consists of exactly the n individuals $\alpha_1,\dots,\alpha_n$. Then the N-relative rule for the verification of universals is

$$(\forall\mathcal{V})\qquad \dfrac{\psi(\alpha_1)\ \dots\ \psi(\alpha_n)}{\forall x\psi(x)}\,N$$

The restriction here to finite models is for ease of exposition only. The formal theory of truthmakers and falsitymakers (verifications and falsifications) deals also with infinite domains. In such cases, the steps of 'universal verification' and of 'existential falsification' involved give rise to infinitary sideways-branching of the trees in questions. But the trees are still of finite *depth*. It is straightforward to show that for any sentence φ and model M interpreting its expressions (regardless of the size of its domain), there is an M-relative verification of φ just in case φ is true-in-M in the sense of Tarski; and, likewise, that there is an M-relative falsification of φ just in case φ is false-in-M in the sense of Tarski. See Tennant (2014e) for further details.

So much for verifications. It remains to specify the rules for *falsifying* sentences.

26.5.2 Rules of falsification

The following rules of falsification, apart from the rule for falsifying existentials, do not depend on the model in which the sentence is being evaluated.

The rule for falsifying negations is

$$(\neg\mathcal{F})\qquad \dfrac{\neg\varphi \quad \overset{\vdots}{\varphi}}{\bot}$$

The vertical dots indicate the presence of some verification of φ.
    The rule for falsifying conjunctions comes in two halves:

$$(\wedge\mathcal{F})\qquad \dfrac{\varphi\wedge\psi \quad \overset{\overset{\underline{\quad}(i)}{\varphi}}{\underset{\vdots}{}}\;\bot}{\bot}{}^{(i)}\qquad\qquad \dfrac{\varphi\wedge\psi \quad \overset{\overset{\underline{\quad}(i)}{\psi}}{\underset{\vdots}{}}\;\bot}{\bot}{}^{(i)}$$

The vertical dots indicate the presence of a falsification of φ, or of ψ, respectively.
    The rule for falsifying disjunctions is

$$(\vee\mathcal{F})\qquad \dfrac{\varphi\vee\psi \quad \overset{\overset{\underline{\quad}(i)}{\varphi}}{\underset{\vdots}{}}\;\bot \quad \overset{\overset{\underline{\quad}(i)}{\psi}}{\underset{\vdots}{}}\;\bot}{\bot}{}^{(i)}$$

The vertical dots indicate the presence of falsifications of φ and of ψ.
    The rule for falsifying conditionals is

$$(\rightarrow\mathcal{F})\qquad \dfrac{\varphi\rightarrow\psi \quad \overset{\vdots}{\varphi} \quad \overset{\overset{\underline{\quad}(i)}{\psi}}{\underset{\vdots}{}}\;\bot}{\bot}{}^{(i)}$$

Note that a falsification of a conditional $\varphi\rightarrow\psi$ consists in a *verification* of the antecedent φ and a *falsification* of the consequent ψ.
    The rule for falsifying universals is

$$(\forall\mathcal{F})\qquad \dfrac{\forall x\psi(x) \quad \overset{\overset{\underline{\qquad}(i)}{\psi(\alpha)}}{\underset{\vdots}{}}\;\bot}{\bot}{}^{(i)}$$

The vertical dots indicate the presence of some falsification of some instance $\psi(\alpha)$.

With N as before, the N-relative rule for falsifying existentials is

$$
(\exists\mathcal{F}) \quad
\begin{array}{cc}
\dfrac{}{\psi(\alpha_1)}^{(i)} & \dfrac{}{\psi(\alpha_n)}^{(i)} \\[2ex]
\vdots & \vdots \\
\end{array}
$$

$$
\cfrac{\exists x\psi(x) \quad \perp \qquad \cdots \qquad \perp}{\perp}{}^{(i)\,N}
$$

It is easy to establish that for every situation M and every sentence φ it is impossible for φ to enjoy both a verification and a falsification relative to M.

26.5.3 The semantic upshot of the rules of verification and falsification

Let us confine our attention to the connectives $\neg$, $\wedge$, $\vee$ and $\rightarrow$. Consider the table below, representing the four possibilities for determinate evaluation of φ and of ψ, as either **True** or **False**.

φ	ψ	$\neg\varphi$	$\varphi \wedge \psi$	$\varphi \vee \psi$	$\varphi \rightarrow \psi$
T	T				
T	F				
F	T				
F	F				

Our task is to fill in the empty cells.

It suffices, for each connective @, to consult the rules ($@\mathcal{V}$) and ($@\mathcal{F}$). For each of the four rows in the table just given we have, respectively, the following information about the constituents φ and ψ:

1 There is a verification of φ and there is a verification of ψ.
2 There is a verification of φ and there is a falsification of ψ.
3 There is a falsification of φ and there is a verification of ψ.
4 There is a falsification of φ and there is a falsification of ψ.

The $\mathcal{V}$- and $\mathcal{F}$-rules are then able to generate, for each row, a verification or falsification, as appropriate, for any sentence formed from these constituents by applying the connective in question. The reader will easily confirm that the resulting table of truth-values is the orthodox one, as follows.

φ	ψ	$\neg\varphi$	$\varphi \wedge \psi$	$\varphi \vee \psi$	$\varphi \rightarrow \psi$
T	T	F	T	T	T
T	F	F	F	T	F
F	T	T	F	T	T
F	F	T	F	F	T

Thus our inferentialist account generates the standard truth-tabular semantics for the connectives.

Problems

1 For each of the models whose diagrams appear above, work out for yourself a first-order sentence using the names j and m, and the two-place predicate L, that describes the model in question up to isomorphism.

2 For each of the models whose diagrams appear above, provide a formal verification or falsification of each of the following sentences:

$\forall x \forall y (Lxy \rightarrow Lyx)$

$\forall x \exists y (Lxy \wedge Lyx)$

$\forall x \exists y (Lxy \wedge \neg Lyx)$

$\exists x (\neg Lxx \wedge \forall y Lyx)$

$\exists x (\neg Lxx \wedge \forall y Lxy)$

$\exists x \forall y (Lxy \vee Lyx).$

3 Describe an important contrast, apart from size, between finite and infinite models of first-order languages.

4 Explain how the rules of verification and of falsification for a connective express its truth table.

5 Explore how, even with small models, verifications or falsifications of multiply quantified sentences can be of considerable complexity.

6 'The informal notion of the truth of a sentence φ in a situation M is satisfactorily explicated in terms of the existence of an M-verification of φ; and likewise for falsity and the existence of a falsification.' Discuss.

27 From Evaluation to Deduction

27.1 From evaluation to deduction

We saw in Chapter 26 how there are two rules for each logical operator – a $\mathcal{V}$-rule and an $\mathcal{F}$-rule – enabling one to evaluate as **True** or **False** any sentence φ containing occurrences of those operators, in any situation providing extensions for the primitive, non-logical expressions occurring in φ. We have stressed how the assumptions relative to which verifications and falsifications are constructed take the form of *literals* – atomic sentences in the positive case, negations of atomic sentences in the negative case. Or, as the inferentialist would put it: the atomic axiom $\dfrac{}{A}\,M$ in the positive case, and the atomic rule $\dfrac{A}{\bot}\,M$ in the negative case. Mindful of this restriction on verifications and falsifications, we shall adopt the notational convention of using the uppercase Greek letter Λ (Lambda) for (coherent) sets of such 'literals'. We shall also use V to stand for verifications, and F to stand for falsifications. (These letters Λ, V, and F may occur with or without subscripts.)

The $\mathcal{V}$-rules and $\mathcal{F}$-rules that were stated in Chapter 26 can now be written as follows. (Note that we are now also allowing for the model M to have an infinite domain.)

$$
\dfrac{\Lambda \ , \ \overset{\rule{1.2em}{0.4pt}(i)}{\varphi}}{\underset{\underset{\neg\varphi}{\rule{0pt}{1.2em}\dfrac{\bot}{}\,(i)}}{F}}
\qquad\qquad
\dfrac{\dfrac{\Lambda}{V}}{\dfrac{\neg\varphi \qquad \varphi}{\bot}}
$$

$$
\begin{array}{cc}
\Lambda_1 & \Lambda_2 \\
V_1 & V_2 \\
\varphi & \psi \\
\hline
\multicolumn{2}{c}{\varphi \wedge \psi}
\end{array}
\qquad\qquad
\cfrac{\overbrace{\Lambda \;,\; \varphi}^{(i)} \quad F \quad \cfrac{\varphi\wedge\psi \quad \bot}{}\;{}^{(i)}}{\bot}
\qquad
\cfrac{\overbrace{\Lambda \;,\; \psi}^{(i)} \quad F \quad \cfrac{\varphi\wedge\psi \quad \bot}{}\;{}^{(i)}}{\bot}
$$

$$
\begin{array}{c}
\Lambda \\
V \\
\varphi \\
\hline
\varphi \vee \varphi
\end{array}
\qquad
\begin{array}{c}
\Lambda \\
V \\
\psi \\
\hline
\varphi \vee \psi
\end{array}
\qquad\qquad
\cfrac{
\varphi\vee\psi \quad
\overbrace{\Lambda_1 \;,\; \varphi}^{(i)} \;\; F_1 \;\; \bot
\quad
\overbrace{\Lambda_2 \;,\; \psi}^{(i)} \;\; F_2 \;\; \bot
}{\bot}\;{}^{(i)}
$$

$$
\begin{array}{c}
\Lambda \\
V \\
\psi \\
\hline
\varphi \rightarrow \psi
\end{array}
\qquad
\cfrac{\overbrace{\Lambda \;,\; \varphi}^{(i)} \;\; F \;\; \bot}{\varphi \rightarrow \psi}\;{}^{(i)}
\qquad
\cfrac{\varphi \rightarrow \psi \quad
\begin{array}{c}\Lambda_1\\ T\\ \varphi\end{array}
\quad
\overbrace{\Lambda_2 \;,\; \psi}^{(i)} \;\; F \;\; \bot}{\bot}\;{}^{(i)}
$$

$$
\cfrac{
\begin{array}{ccc}
\Lambda_1 & & \Lambda_n \\
V_1 & \cdots & V_n \quad \cdots \\
\psi(\alpha_1) & & \psi(\alpha_n)
\end{array}
}{\forall x \psi(x)}\;{}_{M}
\qquad\qquad
\cfrac{\forall x \psi(x) \quad \overbrace{\Lambda \;,\; \psi(\alpha)}^{(i)} \;\; F \;\; \bot}{\bot}\;{}^{(i)}
$$

where $\alpha_1,\ldots,\alpha_n \ldots$ are all
the individuals in the domain

$$
\begin{array}{c}
\Lambda \\
V \\
\psi(\alpha) \\
\hline
\exists x \psi(x)
\end{array}
\qquad\qquad
\cfrac{\exists x \psi(x) \quad
\overbrace{\Lambda_1 \;,\; \psi(\alpha_1)}^{(i)} \;\; F_1 \;\; \bot \quad \cdots \quad
\overbrace{\Lambda_n \;,\; \psi(\alpha_n)}^{(i)} \;\; F_n \;\; \bot \quad \cdots}{\bot}\;{}^{(i)\,M}
$$

where $\alpha_1,\ldots,\alpha_n \ldots$ are all
the individuals in the domain

So: verifications have possibly complex conclusions φ; while falsifications have conclusions $\bot$. Moreover, both kinds of construction use only *literals*. They are used as the assumptions for a verification of φ, and as the assumptions (other than φ) for a falsification of φ.

But what happens when one does not have full enough access to the basic (atomic) facts about a situation? One cannot always be in a position to work out for oneself the truth value of a given sentence in any situation in which one finds oneself. Often one has the benefit of some sincere assertions from fellow speakers, in a situation of which one is not fully apprised. One needs, under such circumstances, to be able to work out at least some of the major *consequences* of what one has been told. That is, one needs to be able to *deduce* (possibly complex) conclusions from *complex* premises in general, and not only from *literals* (i.e., atomic sentences and negations of atomic sentences). How might that be done?

We offer for consideration the following methodological suggestion. Let our $\mathcal{F}$-rules be formulated with general (possibly complex) conclusions θ in place of $\bot$. ($\bot$ will of course still be allowed as a *special case* of such θ.) And let the sets Λ of *literals*, in both our $\mathcal{V}$-rules and our $\mathcal{F}$-rules, be replaced by sets Δ of possibly complex premises in general. (Sets of literals will of course still be allowed as special cases of such Δ.)

We are retaining the overall *form* of our $\mathcal{V}$- and $\mathcal{F}$-rules, but allowing particular symbols therein to admit of a more general interpretation. Under the suggested modification, the foregoing $\mathcal{V}$-rules morph into what are known as *Introduction rules*, and the $\mathcal{F}$-rules morph into *Elimination rules*. An Introduction rule tells one under what circumstances one can infer a conclusion of a particular form. The corresponding Elimination rule tells one what can be *inferred from* such a sentence, when it is used as the so-called *major premise*.

Here, then, are the Introduction and Elimination rules that respectively result from making the changes just suggested to the foregoing $\mathcal{V}$- and $\mathcal{F}$-rules. Both verifications and falsification now become *proofs*, for which we shall use the symbol Π (with or without subscripts). Note the following points.

1   In the rules for negation ($\neg$), there is no reason to substitute θ for $\bot$.
2   In the case of disjunction ($\vee$) there are three distinct patterns in which it would be permissible to replace $\bot$ by θ. We retain all three of them.
3   The second half of ($\rightarrow \mathcal{V}$) keeps its conclusion $\bot$ in its subordinate proof, since it is only in erstwhile $\mathcal{F}$-rules that we are substituting θ for $\bot$.

$(\neg\text{-I})$

$$\underbrace{\Delta \; , \; \overset{\rule{1.2em}{0.4pt}{\scriptstyle(i)}}{\varphi}}$$
$$\Pi$$
$$\frac{\bot}{\neg\varphi}{\scriptstyle(i)}$$

$(\neg\text{-E})$

$$\Delta$$
$$\Pi$$
$$\frac{\neg\varphi \qquad \varphi}{\bot}$$

$(\wedge\text{-I})$

$$\begin{array}{cc} \Delta_1 & \Delta_2 \\ \Pi_1 & \Pi_2 \\ \varphi & \psi \end{array}$$
$$\frac{}{\varphi \wedge \psi}$$

$(\wedge\text{-E})$

$$\underbrace{\Delta \; , \; \overset{\rule{1.2em}{0.4pt}{\scriptstyle(i)}}{\varphi}}$$
$$\Pi$$
$$\frac{\varphi \wedge \psi \qquad \theta}{\theta}{\scriptstyle(i)}$$

$$\underbrace{\Delta \; , \; \overset{\rule{1.2em}{0.4pt}{\scriptstyle(i)}}{\psi}}$$
$$\Pi$$
$$\frac{\varphi \wedge \psi \qquad \theta}{\theta}{\scriptstyle(i)}$$

$(\vee\text{-I})$

$$\begin{array}{c} \Delta \\ \Pi \\ \varphi \end{array}$$
$$\frac{}{\varphi \vee \varphi}$$

$$\begin{array}{c} \Delta \\ \Pi \\ \psi \end{array}$$
$$\frac{}{\varphi \vee \psi}$$

$(\vee\text{-E})$

$$\underbrace{\Delta_1 \; , \; \overset{\rule{1.2em}{0.4pt}{\scriptstyle(i)}}{\varphi}} \qquad \underbrace{\Delta_2 \; , \; \overset{\rule{1.2em}{0.4pt}{\scriptstyle(i)}}{\psi}}$$
$$\Pi_1 \qquad\qquad \Pi_2$$
$$\varphi \vee \psi \qquad \theta \qquad\qquad \bot$$
$$\frac{}{\theta}{\scriptstyle(i)}$$

$(\vee\text{-E})$

$$\underbrace{\Delta_1 \; , \; \overset{\rule{1.2em}{0.4pt}{\scriptstyle(i)}}{\varphi}} \qquad \underbrace{\Delta_2 \; , \; \overset{\rule{1.2em}{0.4pt}{\scriptstyle(i)}}{\psi}}$$
$$\Pi_1 \qquad\qquad \Pi_2$$
$$\varphi \vee \psi \qquad \bot \qquad\qquad \theta$$
$$\frac{}{\theta}{\scriptstyle(i)}$$

$(\vee\text{-E})$

$$\underbrace{\Delta_1 \; , \; \overset{\rule{1.2em}{0.4pt}{\scriptstyle(i)}}{\varphi}} \qquad \underbrace{\Delta_2 \; , \; \overset{\rule{1.2em}{0.4pt}{\scriptstyle(i)}}{\psi}}$$
$$\Pi_1 \qquad\qquad \Pi_2$$
$$\varphi \vee \psi \qquad \theta \qquad\qquad \theta$$
$$\frac{}{\theta}{\scriptstyle(i)}$$

$$(\rightarrow\text{-I}) \quad \begin{array}{c} \Delta \\ \Pi \\ \psi \\ \hline \varphi \rightarrow \psi \end{array} \qquad \begin{array}{c} \overline{\Delta \;,\; \varphi}^{\,(i)} \\ \Pi \\ \psi \\ \hline \varphi \rightarrow \psi \end{array} \qquad \begin{array}{c} \overline{\Delta \;,\; \varphi}^{\,(i)} \\ \Pi \\ \dfrac{\bot}{\varphi \rightarrow \psi}{}^{(i)} \end{array}$$

$$(\rightarrow\text{-E}) \quad \begin{array}{ccc} & \Delta_1 & \overline{\Delta_2 \;,\; \psi}^{\,(i)} \\ & T & \Pi \\ \varphi \rightarrow \psi & \varphi & \theta \\ \hline & \theta & {}^{(i)} \end{array}$$

There is a subtle and important story to be told, about how the Introduction rule for $\rightarrow$ achieves the tripartite form just given – in particular, its second part. (The first and third parts are already covered by our methodological suggestion above.) The reader is asked to accept the assurance that this story, too long to be included here, is fully in keeping with the spirit of the intended generalization from evaluation to deduction-in-general.

All the Introduction and Elimination rules, where they indicate discharge of assumptions (by means of overlining with discharge strokes, labeled with a numeral *i*), involve the presupposed requirement that assumptions of the indicated form really have been used, and are accordingly available for discharge. Moreover, all the Elimination rules are stated on the presupposed requirement that their major premises *stand proud*, with no proof-work above them. These features are inherited directly from the evaluation rules that we called the $\mathcal{V}$- and $\mathcal{F}$-rules. They are crucial in ensuring that the resulting deductive logic guarantees that in any proof the premises (i.e., undischarged assumptions) are *relevant* to its conclusion.

The foregoing rules constitute (propositional) *Core Logic*. The same method succeeds in generalizing the quantifier rules from the evaluation setting to the deductive setting. There is, however, a slight complication in the case of the quantifiers, which we did not have to deal with in the case of the connectives.

Two of the quantifier rules make the transition smoothly from the case of evaluation to the more general case of deduction. The rule $(\exists\mathcal{V})$ becomes the rule of $\exists$-Introduction:

$$(\exists\text{-I}) \quad \begin{array}{c} \Delta \\ \Pi \\ \psi(\alpha) \\ \hline \exists x \psi(x) \end{array}$$

And the rule ($\forall \mathcal{F}$) becomes the rule of $\forall$-Elimination:

$$
(\forall\text{-E}) \quad
\frac{\forall x \psi(x) \quad \begin{array}{c} \overline{\Delta \ , \ \psi(\alpha)}^{\,(i)} \\ \Pi \\ \theta \end{array}}{\theta}{}^{(i)}
$$

In the transition from evaluation rules to rules of deduction-in-general, however, further changes have to be made in the case of our two 'M-relative' quantifier rules. When evaluating sentences in a model M, we required instance-by-instance verifications, or falsifications, depending on whether the rule being applied was ($\forall \mathcal{V}$) or ($\exists \mathcal{F}$) respectively. But deductive reasoning does not concern any situation M in particular; rather, it is concerned with preserving truth-in-M, whatever the model M may be. We therefore replace all those 'instance' proofs (and disproofs) for α_1, ..., α_n ... with a single *proof-template*, involving a *parameter* a in place of the various α_i. Thus the M-relative rule ($\forall \mathcal{V}$) –

$$
\frac{\begin{array}{ccc} \Lambda_1 & & \Lambda_n \\ V_1 & \cdots & V_n \quad \cdots \\ \psi(\alpha_1) & & \psi(\alpha_n) \end{array}}{\forall x \psi(x)}\text{-M}
$$

where $\alpha_1,\ldots,\alpha_n$ ... are all the
individuals in the domain of M –

becomes the rule of $\forall$-Introduction:

$$
(\forall\text{-I}) \quad \frac{\begin{array}{c} \Delta \\ \Pi \\ \psi(a) \end{array}}{\forall x \psi(x)}
$$

where a does not occur in any sentence in Δ or in $\forall x \psi(x)$.

The subproof Π is the proof-template just mentioned; it takes over from all the various V_i of the verification rule.

Likewise, the rule $(\exists \mathcal{F})$ –

$$
\begin{array}{ccc}
\underbrace{\Lambda_1 \quad, \quad \overline{\quad \psi(\alpha_1) \quad}^{(i)}}_{F_1} & \quad \cdots \quad & \underbrace{\Lambda_n \quad, \quad \overline{\quad \psi(\alpha_n) \quad}^{(i)}}_{F_n} \\
\exists x \psi(x) \qquad \bot & & \bot \\
\end{array}
$$
$$
\overline{\qquad\qquad\qquad\qquad\qquad\qquad\qquad\qquad\qquad\qquad}^{(i)} \\
\bot
$$

where $\alpha_1, \ldots, \alpha_n \ldots$ are all
the individuals in the domain –

becomes the rule of $\exists$-Elimination:

$$
(\exists\text{-E}) \qquad
\begin{array}{c}
\underbrace{\Delta \quad, \quad \overline{\quad \psi(a) \quad}^{(i)}}_{\Pi} \\
\exists x \psi(x) \qquad \theta \\
\overline{\qquad\qquad\qquad\qquad}^{(i)} \\
\theta
\end{array}
$$

where a does not occur in any sentence in Δ or in $\exists x \psi(x)$ or in θ.

Once again, the proof-template Π, with its parameter a, takes over from the various falsifications F_i of the falsification rule.

We now have in place all the rules of *first-order* Core Logic – for which, see Tennant (2012a) and Tennant (2014c).

27.2 An evolutionary perspective: how could language have acquired its logic?

It is useful to consider thought and language in an evolutionary perspective. It is reasonable to assume that our evolutionary ancestors could see and hear and 'grasp mentally' some of the rudimentary things and events around them. Moreover, they could probably do this well *before* they ever acquired as complicated a language as we speak now. 'The ape who could not see the branch of the tree to grasp it was very quickly a dead ape' (Huxley).

The visual cortex and auditory cortex, as well as the other parts of the brain for smell, touch and taste would have been well developed in pre-linguistic hominids. They would have been able to perceive what they would correctly take to be stable and enduring objects, from fleeting impressions, both visual and auditory. They would have been able to categorize them in rudimentary but survival-relevant ways. Various predator- and prey-species would be obvious candidates for prompt *recognition* and *memory*. So too would different types of food, and useful natural implements, such as reeds, sticks and stones; and different kinds of shelter, such as shade trees and caves.

Assuming that there are regularities in the natural environment, it is to one's advantage to be able to grasp them. This one does by means of appropriate categorizing concepts, and by understanding which kinds of events involving various objects cause what other kinds of events. Our most basic recognitional concepts are designed to 'track the stable order' of things. From enough cat-glimpses and overheard meows, one posits an enduring *cat*, which one can then expect to be a continuing source of such sensory stimulations, from different angles and distances. For 'cat' here one can substitute any of a great number of predator- and prey-concepts; the point holds quite generally.

Let us assume, then, that our hominid ancestors would have had reasonably well-developed conceptual schemes by means of which they could form *mental representations* of situations around them. Individual observers and thinkers who, because they perceive well, and remember important perceived facts, and recall those memories later when they are salient, tend to make better decisions affecting their chances of survival and reproduction than do observers and thinkers who cannot perceive well, or who do not learn from experience, or who cannot apply what they have learned on later occasions. So, well before the advent of language (whether gestural or spoken), one can expect natural selection to have honed our hominid ancestors' ability to register, remember and recall. They would have been able to form and hold 'proto-beliefs' about the external world. These would then have informed their decision-making and the actions they would undertake in order to satisfy their desires.

> *The solitary case.* In a well-functioning observer and thinker, the causal chain would be:
>
> Past or present situation → perception → *mental representation (in observer/ thinker)* → memory → recall → *same mental representation (in observer/thinker)* → suitable decisions and actions in future situations.

27.3 Communication

In any social-living species, the ability to *communicate survival-relevant information* would have been favored by strong selective forces. Genes that made brains that could support linguistic behavior would have been favored by natural selection. The most basic *speech act* would have been *assertion*: the transmission of the information in a 'proto-belief', often acquired from the *speaker*'s own hard-won experience, and which would have been to the great benefit of the *listeners* present. The benefit would derive from being apprised of what they were being told, *without* having to take the risks, themselves, of learning the hard way. Think how valuable it would be to be able to learn, simply by being told, that there is a leopard in that cave, without having to go peering into the cave oneself. Likewise with being told where to find clean water; where to find various sources of food; and so on.

We know that vervet monkeys have distinctive screeches to warn other members of the troop about the presence of (particular kinds of) eagle, leopard and snake. The *listeners'* reactions are tailored to the specific kind of threat posed. One gets out from under trees or rocky outcrops whenever one hears the leopard-warning, looking up to see the danger; one gets away from long grass whenever one hears the snake-warning, looking down at the ground to see the danger; and one ducks under cover when one hears the eagle-warning, looking up at the sky to see the danger.

The different kinds of warning screeches could well be 'hard-wired' into the vervet monkeys' brains by now, both for production and for processing. As soon as the would-be warner's brain forms a mental representation, from perceptual impressions, of an impending threat, a warning cry would be emitted. As soon as a *listener* receives such a cry, a cascade of appropriate reactions would be triggered.

When urgent action is called for, it may well be that the brain of the *listener* short-circuits the formation of a mental representation of the danger at hand, and simply sets the avoidance behavior in train. But sometimes survival-relevant information of great value is obtained at high cost to the *speaker*, and shared in low-cost fashion with *listeners* in situations in which no urgent action is called for. The *listener* can store away the information at leisure, and have recourse to it only later, as and when needed. With communicative interactions such as these, it would be reasonable to suppose that the result, in the *listener*, is a mental representation serving roughly (or exactly) the same functions as does the mental representation already borne by the *speaker*. The mental representation in question functions like any (proto-) *belief*: it can couple with various *desires* to produce various *intentional actions*. The more (correct) beliefs one has, the better one is equipped to choose the best actions in order to satisfy one's desires.

Learning by testimony is a wonderful proxy for learning the hard way. The foregoing account is roughly that of the British empiricist John Locke, laced with some modernizing ideas from neo-Darwinian evolutionary theory. With the advent of communication by means of language, there is a new kind of causal chain in nature:

> *The communicative case.* Past or present situation → perception → *mental representation (in observer/speaker)* → *asserting* → *hearing* → *mental representation (in listener)* → suitable decisions and actions in future situations.

Note how the causal chain originates with one organism's perception of the environment, and terminates with other organisms' actions within it. In the communicative case, the genes shared by speaker and listeners are bound to spread more effectively than in the solitary case.

27.4 Harmony and truth-telling

As soon as a channel of communication evolves in a social-living species, some will try to exploit it to their selfish advantage by lying, or misrepresenting. In response, there will be selection for any increased ability on the part of others to detect such lying and misrepresentation. The quality of information will be as jealously guarded as the quality of mates and other resources. The forces of selection will ensure a balance between (i) the justification that a listener can expect a speaker to have for a sincere assertion, and (ii) the implications that the listener can draw from the assertion. Do not, as a speaker, make frivolous or unwarranted assertions on matters of great importance for survival; and do not, as a listener, jump to unwarranted conclusions on the basis of what the speaker has asserted. The listener should be able to extract from an assertion only what must have been able to go into it. The speaker should put into an assertion (by way of evidence-checking, etc.) as much as a listener can be expected to feel entitled to extract from it.

This fundamental principle of harmony between the speaker's obligations and listeners' entitlements is what underlies all our moral norms concerning truth-telling. The philosopher who gave us this notion of harmony and underscored its importance for the primitive rules governing logical operators was Michael Dummett (1925–2011). See, for example, Dummett (1973). (We are venturing to supply the evolutionary suggestions in connection with harmony, having first put them forward in von Schilcher and Tennant (1984) and Tennant (1984).)

Speakers, as we have seen, are responsible for the conclusions they assert, because their listeners are entitled to infer certain things from those assertions. Now, conclusions are typically drawn by means of *introduction rules*, if the speaker wishes to be justified in asserting them. And listeners can use those assertions as the major premises of the corresponding *elimination rules*. A quick example will make this clear.

Suppose the speaker asserts $A \wedge B$ sincerely and with justification. Then she must have established that A is the case, and established that B is the case, before applying $\wedge$-Introduction to infer $A \wedge B$:

$$\frac{\begin{array}{cc} \vdots & \vdots \\ A & B \end{array}}{A \wedge B}(\wedge\text{-I})$$

Note that the conjunction $A \wedge B$ features here *below* the inference stroke, as the *conclusion* of the elimination.

The speaker is *obliged* to have furnished for herself a justification for asserting A (as indicated by the vertical dots above A), and a similar justification for asserting B, if she is then to make so bold as to assert (sincerely), to a trusting audience, the conjunction $A \wedge B$. Her listener is *entitled*, upon hearing such a conjunctive assertion, to assume that the speaker has discharged those obligations. So he can infer, from the conjunction, that A is the case; and he can also infer that B is the case. That is, he may apply either or both of the following two *elimination* rules:

$$(\wedge\text{-E}) \qquad \frac{A \wedge B}{A} \qquad \frac{A \wedge B}{B}.$$

Note that the conjunction $A \wedge B$ features here *above* the inference stroke, as the *major premise* of the elimination rule(s).

It is clear that the introduction rule for $\wedge$ is in harmony with its elimination rule. The listener is able to wring from the asserted conclusion as much, but no more, than the speaker had to put into it in order to be justified in asserting it. If the two rules were not balanced in this way – if they were *disharmonious* – then one or other of two bad things would happen. First, speakers might get away with needing to establish *too little*, while yet their listeners feel themselves entitled to infer *too much*, from what the speakers assert. That could result in overly rash actions on the listeners' parts, on the basis of beliefs that they have inferred from what they have been told, but without any genuine justification. Secondly, at the other extreme so to speak, listeners might be chronically under-equipped to enjoy the full benefit of the information conveyed to them in a complex assertion, because the elimination rule they are using is unable to extract from the speaker's assertion *all* that the speaker had to put into it. There could then be much wasted altruistic breath on the speaker's part, as she offers her audience more than they take themselves to be entitled to rely upon. (Florian Steinberger handily labels these two kinds of situation respectively as cases of *E-strong* and *E-weak* disharmony. See Steinberger (2011).)

Either way, disharmony (or disequilibrium) between introduction and elimination rules makes them ill-suited for sustainable exchanges within dangerous environments where information is at a premium. People who use mismatched introduction and elimination rules for a would-be logical operator are going to write themselves out of the evolutionary competition. And, as they go, so too goes their language, defective rules for logical operators and all.

27.5 Inference and truth-preservation

We venture now the following hypothesis. It lies, somewhat unusually, somewhere *between* science and philosophy.

> Introduction and elimination rules for any logico-linguistic operator need to be in harmony in order to be *selected for* as the language evolves.

Put another, more impressive-sounding way: harmony between introduction and elimination rules for a logico-linguistic operator is a *necessary precondition for the very possibility of continued communication*. It has a Kantian ring. It is meant to. It is almost *a priori* in its obviousness; and it strikes one as the closest thing the naturalist can get to an explanation of the 'hardness of the logical *must*'. The reciprocal patterns of obligation and entitlement that bind parties to a discourse have a moral quality to them. Communicating really does involve a *social contract* – a 'meeting of minds' as to what we shall take our words to mean. *That* is why we can 'police' one another's use of logical words, and 'keep people honest' when they stray from the inferential norms that are in place. If those norms were *not* in place, then our logical words would not – *could* not – mean what they do. Even the most self-interested persons, if they are to be able to exploit social conventions – including language – to their greatest advantage, must at least *abide by the meanings of words*. And an absolutely central feature of so abiding is to respect the meanings of the logical words in use. Perhaps it is for this reason that Otto Weininger (1880–1903) once wrote the following passage (Weininger (1903), p. 207) by which Wittgenstein was much impressed:

> [L]ogic and ethics are at bottom the same, they are no more than duty to oneself ... all ethics is possible only in accordance with the laws of logic, all logic is at the same time ethical law.
>
> *Logik und Ethik aber since im Grunde nur eines und dasselbe – Pflicht gegen sich selbst ... Alle Ethik ist nur nach den Gesetzen der Logik möglich, alle Logik ist zugleich ethisches Gesetz.*

As language becomes more complex, so the trains of *reasoning*, or *inference*, that it can support become longer. Thus our concern for truth-telling broadens so as to include also *truth-preservation* from the starting points of one's reasoning (the premises) to its end-point (the conclusion). If one has learned, or has been sincerely told, $Premise_1$, ..., $Premise_n$, one may be able to *infer* a certain *Conclusion*. One will do this, in general, by taking several *steps of inference*. These steps are of forms that enable one to extract various aspects of the information encoded in $Premise_1$, ..., $Premise_n$, and to re-arrange them so as to form the sought *Conclusion*.

Naturally, the selective forces governing the utility of language will tend to ensure that the characteristic steps of inference that we are wont to make will be of forms that ensure that they are *truth-preserving*. In the worst case, these steps of inference ought to be *reliably* truth-preserving within the domains that are the subject matter of the premises and the conclusion (usually, matters of survival-relevance in the external world). In the best case, these steps of inference will be *absolutely guaranteed* to preserve truth. Put another way: in the worst case, the steps of inference that we make should be *inductively valid*; in the best case, they will be *deductively valid*.

One might object to the foregoing hypothesis that only harmonious pairs of introduction and elimination rules can be favored by natural selection. The objector's thought would be: is it not both rather strange and almost certainly false that a language would have acquired its logical operators in this fashion? For, with any trait – even that of being inclined to reason classically – it would appear that one could devise (thought experimentally, at least) some environment that would select for that trait. (The author is grateful to a referee for raising this possible objection, occasioning the rejoinder that follows.)

The rejoinder to such an objection is as follows. Such thought-experimentally devised environments would be statistically rare. The actual environment of evolutionary adaptation would have favored only those behavioral strategies that prove to be *evolutionarily stable* in the long run, across reliably recurring situations.

A similar point holds for the rule of conduct, among social-living creatures, known as Tit-for-Tat. Famously, it beats any other strategy in computational game-theoretic modeling of evolutionary trends generated by interactions which are in accordance with these strategies, and from which the interacting organisms gain or lose in a fitness-affecting way.

Problems

1   Investigate the notion of harmony between introduction and elimination rules for the logical operators, by conducting your own research using sources beyond those cited in this chapter.

2   Use the rules of Core Logic to prove the following arguments:

$$\frac{\neg(A \lor B)}{\neg A \land \neg B} \qquad \frac{A \land \neg B}{\neg(A \to B)}$$

$$\frac{\forall x(Fx \land Gx)}{\forall x Fx \land \forall y Gy} \qquad \frac{\exists x \forall y Rxy}{\forall y \exists x Rxy}$$

$$\frac{\forall x(Ax \to Bx) \quad \forall x(Ax \to Bx)}{\forall x(Ax \to Cx)} \quad \frac{\forall x(Ax \to Bx)}{\neg \exists x(Bx \land Cx)}$$
$$\frac{\forall x(Bx \to Cx)}{\forall x(Ax \to Cx)} \quad \frac{\neg \exists x(Bx \land Cx)}{\neg \exists x(Ax \land Cx)}$$

28 Paradoxes

A paradox is something 'above and beyond belief': more precisely, an apparent contradiction generated by deep, important principles that we believe to be true. That belief turns out to be insufficiently reflective: for with a paradox we are confronted with an argument that brings out that there is a contradiction, or incoherence, or confusion implicit in the concepts or principles to which we were committed.

Paradoxes are worth studying for a number of reasons. First, they are deeply puzzling, and often inspire young thinkers to pursue Philosophy more seriously. Secondly, they provide a fount of wisdom about how *not* to proceed in formulating the basic principles of very ambitious or fundamental theories. Thirdly, paradoxes make us aware of the dangers of what might be called *conceptual overreach*. They reveal the strains that will arise as one pushes one's concepts to the very limits of their ranges of applicability. The present author was drawn into Philosophy upon encountering various paradoxes among those covered briefly here; so it is appropriate, for my beginner reader, to make this almost valedictory chapter an echo of inspiration past.

There are different kinds of paradox, and some examples of these different kinds will follow.

28.1 Inductive paradoxes

28.1.1 Hempel's Paradox

All the paradoxes in later sections involve deductive reasoning. There are, however, some paradoxes peculiar to inductive reasoning. We consider first the *Paradox of the Ravens*, due to Hempel (1945). Here are some reasonable assumptions:

1 Any generalization of the form 'All As are Bs' is confirmed by finding A-type things that are also B.
2 If evidence E supports an hypothesis H, then E supports (to the same degree) any statement H' (deductively) logically equivalent to H.

Now consider: the hypothesis

(H) All ravens are black

is (deductively) logically equivalent to the statement that

(H') All non-black things are non-ravens.

Hence any evidence supporting (H') must support (H) to the same degree. But the observation of a white tennis-shoe supports (H'). Hence it supports (H) to the same degree. But what has a white tennis-shoe got to do with *ravens* being *black?*

28.1.2 Goodman's Paradox; or, the 'New Riddle' of Induction

The strange predicate 'grue'

In the list of examples in §8.4 of logically unjustifiable inductions, we mentioned a strange expectation: that the next emerald we examine will turn out to be *grue*. It is time now to explain this concept.

As one might expect, it is an amalgam of *green* and of *blue*. We are going to describe how to make this amalgam with respect to what is known as a *cut-off predicate* $T(x)$. Let $T(x)$ be a predicate that holds of everything mentioned in the evidence so far. An example might be 'x is examined before the year 2020'; but it is not essential for the notion of examination to play any role. All that matters is that every emerald thus far examined should satisfy $T(x)$. Thus another possibility for $T(x)$ is 'x is located within 10,000 kilometers of the centre of mass of the earth' – assuming, of course, that all emeralds that have ever been examined have never been more than 10,000 kilometers away from the centre of mass of the earth. Another, simple possibility for $T(x)$ is that it be a *statement* T (rather than a predicate) that actually makes no mention of x. An example would be 'it is before the year 2020'. We shall choose this simple alternative for the exposition that follows.

The predicate *grue*(x) is to be thought of as an amalgam (less elliptically, $(green(x), blue(x), T)$) defined as follows:

(T and *green*(x)) or (not-T and *blue*(x)).

Thus x is grue if and only if either it is before 2020 and x is *green* or it is 2020 or later and x is *blue*.

We can define *bleen*(x) similarly:

$bleen(x) \equiv_{df} (blue(x), green(x), T)$
$\qquad\quad\ \equiv_{df} (T$ and *blue*(x)) or (not-T and *green*(x)).

Now it might appear as though the concepts *grue* and *bleen* are curiously complex, having as they do the forms

$(green(x),blue(x),T)$

and

$(blue(x),green(x),T)$

respectively. But they have this appearance of unnatural complexity only because we think that *green* and *blue* themselves are simple and natural concepts.

Try to see it from the point of view of the *gruester* – an imaginary being who actually works with the concepts *grue* and *bleen* as simple and natural. From the gruester's point of view, it is the concepts *green* and *blue* that are unnaturally complex. For they have the forms, respectively,

$(grue(x),bleen(x),T)$

and

$(bleen(x),grue(x),T).$

Where is all this taking us? We want now to make a simple and devastating observation – devastating, that is, for the person who takes the concepts *green* and *blue* for granted and thinks that they can be used in valid inductive inferences about emeralds, saphires and the like.

Making predictions using 'grue'

Consider the past evidence concerning those emeralds $e_1,\ldots,e_n$ that we have so far managed to lay eyes on: $green(e_1)$, ..., $green(e_n)$. All those observations took place while it was before the year 2020. Therefore the evidence could just as well be expressed as $grue(e_1)$, ..., $grue(e_n)$.

Now the normal inductivist makes the inductive leap to

for every emerald e, $green(e)$.

In like fashion the gruester will make the inductive leap to

for every emerald e, $grue(e)$.

For does not the gruester's evidence support her hypothesis just as well as the normal inductivist's evidence supports his hypothesis?

The crucial point to make now is that the gruester and the normal *cannot both be correct*. (Of course, it is logically possible that *neither* is correct. The next emerald we examine may turn out to be *red*.) All we need to grasp here is the simple point that the gruester and the normal *disagree in their predictions*.

To see that this is so, consider the case of an emerald 'for which' *T* fails. An example would be the first hitherto unexamined emerald that is examined after the year 2020. Concerning this emerald *e* we have the following predictions:

> **Gruester:** Emerald *e* is grue.
> **Normal:** No, emerald *e* is *green*.

If the emerald turns out to be green (which you, as a normal, no doubt think likely), the normal is right and the gruester is wrong. If, however, it turns out to be blue (which you, as a normal, no doubt think unlikely) then it is the gruester who will be right, and the normal who will have been proved wrong. Either way, we see that they disagree in their predictions. They cannot both be right.

But who is to say, before the cut-off predicate *T* ceases to hold, just which one will be vindicated by the evidence 'beyond the cut-off point'? Do we have no more than brute intuition and bias to rely on? Or can we give a principled argument for preferring the concept *green* and eschewing the concept *grue*? – and, correlatively, preferring the inductive generalization 'all emeralds are *green*' to the apparently deviant one 'all emeralds are *grue*'?

This is the 'new riddle of induction', posed by Nelson Goodman (1906–98) in Goodman (1955). The literature on this problem is enormous, and the problem survives as a deep and baffling one. No one, in the author's humble estimation, has given a satisfactory solution. Failures to do so can usually be attributed to a basic failure to appreciate how, from the gruester's point of view, all the arguments marshaled against her by the normal apply, *mutatis mutandis*, against the normal.

Possible objections to the use of 'grue'

The discontinuity objection

The first example of this sort of failure is as follows.

Scientists prefer so-called 'no-change' hypotheses to 'change' hypotheses. It is but one example of a preference for simpler theories. (For the various aspects of simplicity, and an interesting attempt to give a unified theoretical account of them, see Sober (1975).) Smoothness is preferable to discontinuity; and constancy is preferable to change. This preference gives rise to the 'discontinuity objection' to the gruester.

Consider the normal's complaint:

> You, the gruester, are putting forward an hypothesis that postulates *change* in emeralds. You are saying that at the cut-off point emeralds *change color* from green to blue. But I, the normal, am putting forward a *no-change* hypothesis. I am saying that emeralds will have the same color, regardless of the cut-off

point. A no-change hypothesis is simpler than a change hypothesis; so my hypothesis is preferable to yours.

To this the gruester simply replies:

You, the normal, are the one who is putting forward an hypothesis that postulates change in emeralds. You are saying that at the cut-off point emeralds *change grulor* from grue to bleen. But I, the gruester, am putting forward a *no-change* hypothesis. I am saying that emeralds will have the *same grulor*, regardless of the cut-off point. A no-change hypothesis is simpler than a change hypothesis; so my hypothesis is preferable to yours.

Stalemate. Neither side, it appears, can win. It all has to do with what we take to be basic, natural, simple or primitive in our conceptual scheme. The normal takes *green* and *blue*. The gruester takes *grue* and *bleen*. The disagreement is irresoluble.

The complexity objection

You, the greenster, may complain that grulors (like grue and bleen) are 'unnatural' or 'complicated' or 'overly complex', because of the way they have been defined above. Alright then, the gruester replies: we shall define your color concepts in a way that shows that *they* are highly unnatural (since of course it's my grulor concepts that are really natural). So here we go. Define '*x* is green' as follows:

x is examined before 2020 and is found to be grue – or *x* is not so examined, and is bleen.

And define '*x* is blue' as follows:

x is examined before 2020 and is found to be bleen – or *x* is not so examined, and is grue.

The integration-with-science objection

We require science to be continuous with common sense. The scientific image must mesh with the manifest image. Science must explain the way the world appears to us. In this regard, says the greenster, he is ahead of the gruester. He explains his theoretical superiority as follows.

Greensters (such as I) have a deep scientific explanation of why it is that emeralds appear to us to be green. It is because, owing to their particular chemical composition and crystalline structure, they emit light of such-and-such wavelength. All objects that emit light of this wavelength appear to us to be green.

Not to be outdone, the gruester replies as follows.

> Gruesters (such as I) have a deep scientific explanation of why it is that emeralds appear to us to be grue. It is because, owing to their particular chemical composition and crystalline structure, they emit light of such-and-such *lavewength*. All objects that emit light of this lavewength appear to us to be grue.

Now, of course, the gruester owes us a definition of 'lavewength', but you are sure to be able to see how it will go.

We see, then, that there is a thoroughgoing symmetry between the greenster (i.e., you) and the gruester (i.e., me). Your complaint against me can be turned into my complaint against you. There is no independent position from which this conceptual dispute can be arbitrated. *That* would appear to be the unsettling lesson of Goodman's Paradox. The riddle is called 'new' because it takes induction itself for granted, and shows how shakily it depends on a *particular choice of concepts* in order to get matters inductively right. The challenge is, in effect, to justify the choice of the concepts that we actually use when we apply the inductive method.

An unsettling consequence of Goodman's Paradox

The following possibility rears its ugly head: *there may be hidden gruesters among us.* The very symmetry of considerations buttressing the normal against the gruester, and vice versa, leads one to ask: might not someone out there be speaking what appears to be normal English, but actually meaning *grue* by the word 'green' and meaning *bleen* by the word 'blue'?

Because we have not yet reached the cut-off point, we are unable to winkle such a person out as the linguistic deviant she must be. Since it is not yet 2020, nothing in the hidden gruester's sensory experience or conversation with other 'English' speakers will alert anyone – normal, or hidden gruester – to the fact that she is indeed a (hidden) gruester. That fact about her will emerge only when (if the normals are right) she suffers 'world shock' on the morning of January 1, 2020. It will only be when this cut-off point is upon us that we might suddenly discover that she no longer agrees that new grass is green (like the old grass before the cut-off point). She might go berserk, rushing around complaining that the grass is 'blue', when it appears green to us (as did grass before). Of course, it is still appearing green to her; it's just that that's what makes it *bleen* for her, which is why (by our assumption that she means *bleen* by 'blue') she now calls it 'blue'.

Goodman's paradox thus cautions us that our concepts, as expressed in our everyday language, might be worryingly indeterminate. The problem with induction is now not only that we cannot get a determinate grip on the future on the basis of the past; it is also that we may not have a determinate grip on any portion of it, *past or* future.

If there *are* any hidden gruesters among us, they (and we) are in for a nasty shock sometime, after chugging along in communal harmony so nicely. But when? 2020? 2030? … Perhaps quietism about induction is the only refuge, if not for the sane, then at least for those who wish to remain so.

28.2 The Sorites Paradox

This one earns a section all to itself; the literature it has generated, especially recently, is enormous. A good place for the interested student to start would be Keefe and Smith (1996).

The Sorites Paradox (also known as the *Paradox of the Heap*) makes one wonder whether the use of vague concepts, or of linguistic predicates that can have 'borderline cases', is at heart inconsistent. It can be laid out as follows (in one of its many variant forms).

> If one has a heap of sand, it will still be a heap after the removal of one grain of sand. So, begin with a heap. Remove one grain. What is left is still a heap. Remove another grain. What is left is still a heap. … Eventually, what is left is not a heap at all. For there are only finitely many grains of sand in any given heap, and by removing them one by one they will, eventually, all be gone. But your governing principle tells you that you will still have a heap. Contradiction.

The same flavor of paradox applies in the case of a sufficiently long chain of (neighboring pair)-wise color-indiscriminable patches, beginning, say, with a patch that is obviously red, and ending, say, with one that is obviously orange. At no point in the chain does the observer notice any color difference between adjacent patches. So, by the transitivity of the relation '*x* is apparently of the same color as *y*', the observer ought not to notice any color-difference between the red and orange patches at each end of the chain. But of course she does. Paradox.

Finally, there is an arithmetical version of this paradox, due to Hao Wang (1921–95). The natural number 0 is small. If the natural number *n* is small, then so is the successor of *n*. Hence, by Mathematical Induction, every natural number is small.

28.3 Logical or semantical paradoxes

Logical or *semantical* paradoxes arise when language is used to describe the relationship between itself and its subject matter. Instead of simply sticking to the 'object-level' subject matter, and expressing straighforward truths about *it*, the language (or its user) ventures now to express thoughts – and therefore truths – about its *own relationship* to the subject matter (which has now been expanded so as to include the language itself).

Two kinds of expressive power generate these paradoxes:

(1) singular terms that refer to linguistic expressions, and
(2) semantic predicates such as '... is true' and '... is false', or '... holds of – ', or '... defines – '.

Languages containing such terms and predicates are called *semantically closed*.

28.3.1 The Liar Paradox

The most famous, and perhaps simplest, of the logico-semantic paradoxes for semantically closed languages is the *Liar Paradox*:

   This sentence is false.

The embedded singular term 'This sentence' refers to the very sentence in which it is embedded. Moreover, the predicate '... is false' is best understood as the negation of the predicate '... is true'. So the Liar could be re-expressed as

   This sentence is not true.

The Liar therefore combines features (1) and (2) with a vengeance. The paradox arises because we cannot stably assign a truth-value to the Liar sentence. For, suppose the Liar is true. Then, since it says that it is false, it must be false. Suppose, then, that it is false. Then, since it says of itself that it is false, it is true. So: if the Liar is true, then it is false; and if it is false, then it is true. It cannot be 'stably true'; and it cannot be 'stably false'. Its truth-value seems to flip-flop.
   Here are the main possible reactions to the Liar:

1 The Liar is meaningless.
2 The Liar is meaningful, but the question of its truth or falsity cannot arise, since it does not 'engage with' any language-independent subject matter in a suitably 'grounded' way.
3 The Liar is meaningful, but is *neither* true *nor* false.
4 The Liar is meaningful, but is *both* true *and* false.
5 We should not use a language in which the Liar can be expressed; for such a language is incoherent.
6 We can and should use a language in which the Liar can be expressed; the alleged incoherence arising from the paradox is neither here nor there, and cannot threaten any serious scientific purposes.

It is left to the reader to ponder which response is the best. Again, the literature is huge. A very good recent guide to all extant attempts to deal with the logico-semantical paradoxes can be found in Scharp (2013).

28.3.2 The Postcard Paradox

Note that paradox can arise without the *self*-reference that is involved in the Liar. Here is the so-called *Postcard Paradox*:

1 Sentence (2) is true.
2 Sentence (1) is false.

Neither sentence contains any term referring to that same sentence. But still the result is paradoxical. For, suppose that (1) is true. Then (2) is true; that is, (1) is false. Now suppose that (1) is false. Then (2) is not true, i.e., (2) is false. So (1) is true. Once again, we have unstable assignments of truth and falsity to either of the two sentences involved. Any assumed definite truth-value for one of them is upset by straightforward reasoning that exploits basic properties of truth and the (apparently clear) meanings of the two sentences.

28.3.3 Grelling's Paradox

Grelling's Paradox is constructed by exploiting the idea that some words or phrases apply to themselves, while others do not. For example, the word 'short' is indeed short; whereas the word 'long' is *not* long. The phrase 'begins with the letter "b"' applies to itself; whereas 'written in German' does not. When an expression E applies to itself, we say that E is *autological*. When E does *not* apply to itself, we say that E is *heterological*. Now we can ask: Is the word 'heterological' heterological? Suppose it is. Then it doesn't apply to itself; i.e., it is not heterological. So now suppose that it is not heterological. So it doesn't apply to itself. Hence it *is* heterological. If it is, then it isn't; and if it isn't, then it is – we have here the same flip-flopping as we had in the case of the Liar.

28.4 Mathematical Paradoxes

Mathematical Paradoxes have long been a stimulus to deeper understanding of the abstract quantities, structures and entities studied by mathematicians. They arise because of our attempt to deal both with infinity and with extreme generality. It was Frank Ramsey who first made a principled distinction between the logico-semantical paradoxes and the mathematical ones. It was very prescient of him to do so; for the mathematical paradoxes have turned out, one and all, to be *resoluble*; whereas great controversy continues to rage over whether, and, if so, how, one can either avoid, or learn to live with, paradoxes of the logico-semantical kind.

Here now are just a few examples of famous mathematical paradoxes.

28.4.1 Zeno's Paradox

Zeno's Paradox is very ancient, and is actually no longer considered paradoxical. It is now regarded as arising from a deficient understanding of the process of summing an infinite series. Zeno 'proves' that an arrow cannot hit its target as follows.

> The distance to be traversed from the bow to the target is D, say, as the arrow flies. Before it reaches the target, the arrow will have to reach the midpoint of the trajectory, which is a finite distance $D/2$ away. So the arrow will take some finite time to reach the mid-point. Once it has reached the mid-point, it will have to reach the mid-point of the remaining part of the trajectory, at point $3D/4$; and this will take some finite amount of time. Iterate these considerations, and you end up with an infinite number of finite times having to be added together. That's how long the arrow will take – and Zeno (mistakenly) thought that this temporal sum would have to be infinite. So, he concluded, the arrow would never reach its target.

We can see today exactly how Zeno's reasoning was mistaken. It is possible for an infinite series of finite numbers (such as $\frac{1}{2}$, $\frac{1}{4}$, $\frac{1}{8}$, ...) to have a finite sum. Zeno did not realize that. Paradox dissolved.

28.4.2 Richard's Paradox

Richard's Paradox exploits the axiomatic principle that if there is a natural number with a given property P, then there is a *least* natural number with property P. Consider the property of being a natural number not nameable in fewer than nineteen syllables. Since there are only finitely many syllables, there are only finitely many strings of fewer than nineteen syllables. The 'namings' would have to be effected by these finitely many strings. So only finitely many numbers get named in this way. Hence there is some number that does *not* get named in this way. Now take the least such number, i.e., the least number not nameable in fewer than nineteen syllables. We have just named it in fewer than nineteen syllables. Contradiction.

Richard's Paradox involves a curious blend of semantical and mathematical features. Naming, and nameability, are semantical notions; while the least-number principle is taken from mathematics. The most straightforward resolution of this paradox would involve prohibiting instantiations of the least-number principle that involve properties in which semantical notions are embedded. Mathematics, after all, aims to deal with mathematical objects (such as the natural numbers) and their *mathematical* properties and relations (such as *being prime*, or *being less than*).

28.4.3 Russell's Paradox

Russell's Paradox is perhaps the most famous and vexing of all mathematical paradoxes. It gave rise to the 'crisis in foundations' in the early twentieth century. It bedevils any attempt to give an absolutely general notion of *class* or *set*. Some logician-philosophers thought that all mathematics could be reduced to, or coded as, talk about sets. For example, the number 0 might be identified with the empty set (the set that has no members); the number 1 with the set of all one-membered sets; the number 2 with the set of all two-membered sets; and so on. This led to a search for deep underlying principles governing set-existence. The principle displayed below, now called *Naïve Abstraction*, was in effect proposed in Frege (1893; reprinted 1962). We say 'in effect', because it is a quick consequence of Frege's Basic Law V, which was the actual principle he proposed. Basic Law V says

$$\{x|Fx\} = \{x|Gx\} \;\leftrightarrow\; \forall x(Fx \leftrightarrow Gx).$$

That is to say, the set of all Fs is identical to the set of all Gs just in case the Fs are exactly the Gs.

Here now is the Principle of Naïve Abstraction:

For every property F there exists the set of all things with property F. In symbols:

$$\forall F \exists! \{x|F(x)\}.$$

The reader is reminded here of the notation '$\exists! t$', for singular terms t, that was introduced and explained in §7.3.3. Note that set-abstracts, namely terms of the form $\{x|F(x)\}$, are singular terms.

Naïve Abstraction is easy to illustrate. There is the set of all people; the set of all hydrogen atoms; the set of all natural numbers; the set of all dinosaurs; and so on. Sets are simply extensions of properties, and are to be treated as things that can have further properties.

Now, properties can be specified by using two-place relations. For example, from the relation 'x hates y' one can obtain the property 'x hates x' (i.e., x is a self-hater) by making x occur in both places. From 'x killed y' one can likewise obtain 'x killed x' (i.e., x committed suicide). One can also append a negation sign: 'not(x loves x)' would mean that x does not love himself. And 'not(x is a member of x)' would mean that x is not self-membered.

Russell's devastatingly clever idea was to consider the property of not being a member of oneself. By Naïve Abstraction, there is a set (let us call it R, for 'the Russell set') of all and only those things that are not self-membered. (In symbols: $\{x|\neg x \in x\}$.) So now we can ask: Is R a member of R? In search for an answer, we reason as follows.

Suppose R is a member of R. Then R must possess the property that defines membership in R – that is, R must *not* be a member of R. So, it must after all be the case that R is not a member of R. But then R possesses the defining property for membership in R; whence R *is* a member of R, after all. Contradiction.

The now orthodox reaction to Russell's Paradox is to recognize that Naïve Abstraction is far too ambitious an abstract existential principle. It postulates 'too many' abstract existents, some of which are *too large* to be sets. This leads to inconsistency. A more measured approach, now codified in so-called Zermelo–Fraenkel set theory, is to postulate the existence of certain unproblematic sets, and then to postulate that various other, more complicated, sets can be built up out of them by iterable operations (such as pairing, union, taking the set of all subsets of a given set, etc.). One still obtains in this way enough sets to 'do' mathematics; but sets are no longer regarded as logical objects answering to a single, powerful abstraction principle. (Indeed, one obtains much more than enough in the way of sets. A relatively small initial segment of the cumulative hierarchy V of sets – namely, the segment $V_{\omega+\omega}$ – contains surrogates for all the objects talked about in all the different branches of classical mathematics. See Friedman (1971).)

The modern set-theorist uses as primitive the notation '$\{x|F(x)\}$' (for 'the set of all and only those x such that $F(x)$'). Russell's Paradox teaches us that one of these 'set-abstraction terms' – namely, $\{x|\neg x \in x\}$ – *fails to denote*. This means that the underlying logic itself needs to be revised, in order to accommodate the presence of *non-denoting singular terms* in the language. But this, fortunately, can be done (as already observed in §7.3.3). Not only have we had to surrender Frege's naïve principle of set-abstraction; we have also had to abandon his ideal of a 'logically perfect language' in which every singular term denotes. The result is a so-called *free logic* – free, that is, of the otherwise crippling assumption that every singular term denotes. (For a detailed account of free logic, see Tennant (1978), Chapter 7.) The tacit adoption of free logic was in fact the quiet revolution in logic that was the real and lasting legacy of Russell's Paradox. It is rather peculiar that philosophers of logic still acquiesce in Frege's description of a 'logically perfect' language as one in which all singular terms denote. The lesson of Russell's Paradox (and of the Burali–Forti Paradox, to be discussed in §28.4.4) is that the assumption that all singular terms denote is a great logical *imperfection*.

Russell's Paradox, in modern set theory developed with free logic, is now a mere *negative existential theorem*: there is no set that has as members all and only those sets that are not members of themselves. This should not really be any great surprise. Pure logic tells us also that there is no barber who shaves all and only those barbers who do not shave themselves. Exactly the same logical considerations apply in each case. Paradox dissolved (though only after a great deal of logical headache, and the administration of some very powerful logical analgesics).

28.4.4 The Burali–Forti Paradox

Georg Cantor (1845–1918) pioneered informal set theory, which was only later fully formalized through the efforts of Ernst Zermelo (1871–1953) and Abraham Fraenkel (1891–1965). One of the most important concepts in set theory is that of a *well-ordering*. We shall investigate here how it gave rise to the Burali–Forti

Paradox of the ordinal of the class of all ordinals (equivalently: the well-order type of the class of all well-order types).

Some words of advice at the outset. Our discussion of this particular paradox will make greater than usual demands on the reader's concentration, and willingness to engage with material at a high level of abstraction. It is, in fact, a difficult paradox to set out properly, without distorting where the emphases are to be placed, and without entering considerations that could strike the reader with a critical eye as potentially fallacious. The reader who is not 'symbolically minded' or who is averse to technical material may therefore be satisfied with skimming the formal treatment, and just reading the prose for the main message about the Burali–Forti Paradox. **End of words of advice.**

It is important to stress, at the outset, that this paradox afflicts our *informal* mathematical thinking about well-orderings and their order types, and does not arise solely within the context of formal set theory. It is to be expected, of course, that if formal set theory too slavishly regiments the deductive development of that informal theorizing, without any reforming of naïve intuitions, then something like the Burali–Forti Paradox lies close at hand.

Background to the Burali–Forti Paradox: the theory of well-orderings, and of their order types

Limitations of space, and the formidable mathematical details involved in establishing the following theorems, force this discussion to confine itself just to the statement of necessary results, and to definitions of the notions involved, that enable one to explain the Burali–Forti Paradox. Readers whose interest is piqued by the following theorems about well-orderings, and in particular about the well-ordering of well-order types, are encouraged to try to devise their own proofs.

Definition 8. [Well-ordering] *A binary relation $<$ is said to be a well-ordering of a non-empty set X if and only if it satisfies the following conditions (where the quantifiers range over X):*

1 **Transitivity:** $\forall x \forall y \forall z((x < y \wedge y < z) \rightarrow x < z)$
2 **Anti-symmetry:** $\forall x \forall y(x < y \rightarrow \neg y < x)$
3 **Totality:** $\forall x \forall y(x < y \vee x = y \vee y < x)$
4 **Least elements:** *Suppose Φ is a property possessed by at least one element. Then there is a unique element x with the following property:*

$$\Phi(x) \text{ and for every element } y, \text{ if } y < x \text{ then } \neg \Phi(y).$$

A helpful picture is as follows, where the ordering of X goes from left to right, and matters are idealized by having a line to represent X, rather than some pattern of discrete dots (which would be more faithful to the notion of a well-ordering, but which cannot be represented, pictorially, with the necessary degree of generality):

We shall call $X_<$ the well-ordering (it is the 'structure', or 'model'); and we shall call X its *domain*.

As with any kind of structures, there can be isomorphisms between distinct well-orderings.

Definition 9. [Isomorphism] *Let* $A_<$ *and* $B_<$ *be well-orderings. A one-one function* ϕ *from A onto B is called an isomorphism of* $A_<$ *to* $B_<$ *if and only if*

$$\text{for all } a, a' \text{ in A}, (a < a' \text{ (in } A_<) \quad \Leftrightarrow \quad \phi(a) < \phi(a') \text{ (in } B_<)).$$

Definition 10. [Initial segment] *An initial segment of a well-ordering* $A_<$ *is a well-ordering of the form* $\{x \in A | x < a\}_<$, *where* $a \in A$.

With considerable ingenuity and careful compilation of auxiliary concepts, one can establish the following result.

Theorem 2. *For any two well-orderings* $A_<$ *and* $B_<$, *either* $A_<$ *is isomorphic to* $B_<$, *or* $A_<$ *is isomorphic to an initial segment of* $B_<$, *or* $B_<$ *is isomorphic to an initial segment of* $A_<$.

Cantor included in his informal set theory an informal theory of *well-order types*, or *ordinals*. (He called them *Zahlen*.) Well-order types were, at the time of their introduction, new *mathematical objects*.

The new entities were governed by the following fundamental (but, as the Burali–Forti Paradox will reveal, somewhat naïve) principle:

Principle 1. *Every well-ordering R of a domain D has a unique well-order type, which is also the well-order type of any well-ordering isomorphic to R.*

We shall assume, as Cantor did, that well-order types, as mathematical objects *sui generis*, exist in abundance, and that we can state and prove various general results about them. To that end, we shall use the sortal variables α, β, γ for well-order types.

We now define a relation $\prec$ on well-order types as follows.

Definition 11. [Ordering of well-order types] $\alpha \prec \beta$ if and only if some well-ordering of well-order type α is isomorphic to an initial segment of some well-ordering of well-order type β.

Theorem 3. $\prec$ is a well-ordering of well-order types.

Proof. One can prove each of the following, where the quantifiers range over well-order types:

1 **Transitivity of** $\prec$: $\forall\alpha\forall\beta\forall\gamma((\alpha \prec \beta \wedge \beta \prec \gamma) \to \alpha \prec \gamma)$
2 **Anti-symmetry of** $\prec$: $\forall\alpha\forall\beta(\alpha \prec \beta \to \neg\beta \prec \alpha)$
3 **Totality of** $\prec$: $\forall\alpha\forall\beta(\alpha \prec \beta \vee \alpha = \beta \vee \beta \prec \alpha)$
4 **Least elements of** $\prec$: Suppose Φ is a property possessed by at least one well-order type. Then there is a unique well-order type α with the following property:

$$\Phi(\alpha) \text{ and for every well-order type } \beta \prec \alpha, \neg\Phi(\beta).$$

The proof of **Totality of** $\prec$ makes crucial use of Theorem 2. □

Theorem 4. *Every well-order type α is the well-order type of the well-ordering by $\prec$ of all the well-order types $\prec \alpha$.*

Now for the Burali–Forti Paradox itself . . .

By Principle 1, the well-ordering by $\prec$ of all order-types has its own unique well-order type. Call this well-order type Ω.

It follows, as a particular instance of Theorem 4, that

Ω is the well-order type of the well-ordering by $\prec$ of all order-types $\prec \Omega$.

Now let $\prec^*$ be the well-ordering that properly extends $\prec$ as follows:

for all $\alpha \prec \Omega$ and $\beta \prec \Omega$, $\alpha \prec^* \beta$ just in case $\alpha \prec \beta$; and
for all $\alpha \prec \Omega$, $\alpha \prec^* \Omega$.

By Principle 1, the well-ordering $\prec^*$ (of all well-order types $\prec \Omega$ along with the well-order type Ω itself) has its own unique well-order type. Call this well-order type Ω^*.

Note that the identity mapping on all well-order types $\prec \Omega$ is an isomorphism onto an initial segment of the well-ordering $\prec^*$ (of well-order types $\prec \Omega$ *and the* well-order type Ω itself). It follows that

$$\Omega \prec \Omega^* \tag{28.1}$$

But since Ω is the well-order type of the well-ordering by $\prec$ of *all* well-order types, and Ω^* is a well-order type, we have

$$\Omega^* \prec \Omega \tag{28.2}$$

(28.1) and (28.2) contradict **Anti-symmetry of** $\prec$.

Resolving the Burali–Forti Paradox

As with Russell's Paradox, the underlying problem giving rise to the Burali–Forti Paradox is the naïve willingness to postulate the existence of an abstract 'object' that is 'too big' to exist as a completed entity. The class of all well-order types is simply too big to be a *domain* for which a well-ordering, however natural, can be expected to 'produce', or have associated with it, *its* very own well-order type. The way to resolve the Burali–Forti Paradox is to restrict the unbridled generality of Principle 1. This is difficult to do in the informal setting within which Cantor originally developed his ideas about well-orderings and their well-order types. But in formal set theory we are much more careful about postulating the existence of certain sets that the by now familiar paradoxes reveal to be 'too large' to exist as completed totalities. The lesson of the Burali–Forti Paradox is that the property of *being an ordinal number* (the set-theoretic surrogate for *being a well-order type*) has too large an extension to admit of set-abstraction. There is no such thing as the set of all ordinal numbers. Zermelo's Axiom of Infinity, to be sure, permits one to assert the existence of the set of all *finite* ordinal numbers. But no consistent extension of Zermelo's axioms can permit one to assert the existence of the set of all ordinal numbers, finite *and infinite*.

28.4.5 Skolem's Paradox

A set y is said to be a *subset* of a set x (in symbols: $y \subseteq x$) just in case every member of y is a member of x (in symbols: $\forall z(z \in y \rightarrow z \in x)$).

We shall now state and prove a result of absolutely stunning simplicity and beauty, which has far-reaching implications for the universe of sets. It is an intellectual object of such fascination that it is included here as much for aesthetic reasons as for theoretical ones.

Theorem 5 (Cantor). *For no set is there a function mapping its members onto all its subsets.*

Proof. Let X be any set. Suppose, for *reductio ad absurdum*, that f is a function mapping the members of X **onto** all the subsets of X.

Consider the 'diagonal set' $\{x \in X | x \notin f(x)\}$. By Separation, this set exists, and it is a subset of X. Since f is onto all subsets of X, there is some $d \in X$ such that

$$f(d) = \{x \in X | x \notin f(x)\}.$$

Suppose for subsidiary *reductio* that $d \in \{x \in X | x \notin f(x)\}$. Then $d \notin f(d)$, i.e., $d \notin \{x \in X | x \notin f(x)\}$. Contradiction. This ends the subsidiary *reductio*. We conclude that

$$d \notin \{x \in X | x \notin f(x)\},$$

i.e., $d \notin f(d)$. But now, since $d \in X$, we have

$$d \in \{x \in X | x \notin f(x)\}.$$

Contradiction. So there is no such function f.   □

Note that the only set-theoretic existence-axiom used in the proof of Cantor's Theorem is an instance of the Axiom Scheme of Separation. This is a very innocuous *conditional existence* principle. It says the following.

Suppose one is *given* a set X. So X's existence is not in question. X exists along with its members. It seems, on this supposition, intuitively compelling to claim that, for any property Φ, one can *cull* from the set X that *subset* (call it X_Φ) of X whose members are all and only those members of X that satisfy Φ. That is, X_Φ exists. (Why not? – it is, as it were, no bigger than X.)

This, then, is the so-called principle of *Separation*. Expressed as a formal rule:

$$\frac{t = X}{\exists! \{x | x \in X \wedge \Phi(x)\}} \ .$$

The picture for Separation is as follows. Within the set X:

$X_\Phi = \{x | x \in X \wedge \Phi(x)\}$

some members (i.e., some bullets in the diagram) may have a certain property Φ. We can separate out the set of all members of X that have property Φ. Obviously, this set X_Φ exists if X does.

The *power set* $\wp(x)$ of a set x is the set of all subsets of x:

$$\wp(x) =_{df} \{y | y \subseteq x\}, \text{ i.e., } \{y | \forall z(z \in y \rightarrow z \in x)\}.$$

Another conditional existence axiom of set theory is the *Power Set Axiom*:

Given any set x, $\wp(x)$ exists.

By contrast with Separation, this is a very powerful principle, allowing one to generate more and more sets of 'higher rank'. But it is also an intuitively compelling principle. It invites one to imagine all the various possible ways that one might cull subsets of a given set X (applying Separation, as it were, over and over again); and then gathering all the results together into a completed set – the power set of X. Interestingly, in the presence of Separation, the existence of *anything* guarantees the existence of a very special set: the *empty set*. This is the set $\{x|\neg x=x\}$, usually abbreviated as $\emptyset$. Given any thing at all – call it a – Separation tells us that we can separate out the set consisting of all and only those members of a *that are not identical to themselves*. But of course there are no such things. So the empty set exists, courtesy of this instance of Separation.

Thus far, we have mentioned only *conditional* set-existence principles; and have not yet encountered what one might call an *outright* set-existence principle. But there is a very important one on which all reasonable set theories agree: *the set of all natural numbers 0, 1, 2, 3, … exists*. This is usually stated in set-theoretic terms as follows.

Consider the *finite ordinals*

$\emptyset$,
$\{\emptyset\}$,
$\{\emptyset,\{\emptyset\}\}$,
$\{\emptyset,\{\emptyset\},\{\emptyset,\{\emptyset\}\}\}$,
$\vdots$

where each one is the set of all those preceding it. *The set of all these finite ordinals exists.* We call it ω.

This is the *Axiom of Infinity* of Zermelo–Fraenkel set theory. Stated as a single sentence in abbreviated form, it would read

$\exists!\{x|x$ is a finite von Neumann ordinal$\}$,

where the predicate 'x is a finite von Neumann ordinal' can be spelled out explicitly in terms of $\emptyset$ and $\in$. (The definitional details need not detain us.)

With its existence secured by outright postulation, ω (the set of all finite von Neumann ordinals), becomes the gold-standard for *countability*. An infinite set is said to be *countably* infinite just in case its members can be put into one-one correspondence with the members of ω.

All modern systems of set theory, such as Zermelo–Fraenkel set theory with Choice (so-called ZFC) – are committed to the existence of ω and to the existence of power sets. Hence, by Cantor's Theorem, they are committed to the existence also of:

the **uncountable** set $\wp(\omega)$;
the **even more uncountable** set $\wp(\wp(\omega))$;
⋮
and so on, *ad infinitum*.

This is what the great mathematician and foundationalist David Hilbert called 'Cantor's paradise'. We precipitate the existence of *infinitely many ever-greater infinities*, as soon as we postulate the existence of the comparatively humble, *countably* infinite set ω.

Aristotle refused ever to acknowledge the existence of any 'completed' infinity, construed as a single totality. Rather, he insisted, infinity is at best *potential infinity*. Modern set theory both vindicates Aristotle and ignores him. It vindicates him in so far as he would be able to point out just how committal it proves to be to postulate even the *very first* completed infinity, namely ω. But set theory scorns his fear of completed infinities in general by incurring commitment to all of these infinities 'in one go', as a consequence of the Power Set Axiom. The set-theoretic universe needs no further stage-by-stage postulation, in order to create each of its infinitely many ever-greater infinities. Rather, they all coexist, as soon as one asserts both the existence of ω and that of power sets.

But modern set theory (ZFC, for the sake of definiteness) is a *first-order* theory, formulated in a countable first-order language. Let us assume that ZFC is consistent. That is, there is no proof of absurdity from any of the axioms of ZFC. Then it follows, by an important result in mathematical logic known as the **Countable Models Theorem** (due to Löwenheim and Skolem – see especially Skolem (1919)), that ZFC has a *countable* model. Such a model consists in a countably infinite domain of individuals, the *sets*, furnished with an extension for the binary relation '∈' (which one may read as '…is a member of …').

This is seemingly paradoxical; it has earned the name 'Skolem's Paradox'. Set theory is, *par excellence*, our way of committing ourselves to the infinite, especially the *uncountably* infinite. It explicates the precise sense in which certain sets might be uncountably infinite. It even *proves* the existence of an *uncountably* infinite set, namely $\wp(\omega)$. Yet, because set theory has a countable model, it appears to be unable to ensure that $\wp(\omega)$ *really is* uncountably infinite.

How can this be?

Resolving Skolem's Paradox

Like the other mathematical paradoxes, Skolem's Paradox can be resolved. We need to draw a distinction between seeing things from 'within' a model, and seeing them from 'outside' it.

Any model of ZFC must have an individual in its domain serving as the supposedly uncountable set $\wp(\omega)$. But in any countable model M this set will be represented as having at most *countably* infinitely many members! From 'inside' the model M, one cannot 'see' that the individual serving as $\wp(\omega)$ is 'really' countable. This is because, in accordance with Cantor's Theorem, there is no element *in the model* M counting as (no pun intended) a one-one mapping from ω onto (the individual which, in M, counts as) $\wp(\omega)$. And this is so even though $\wp(\omega)$ is 'really' countable. That is, it is borne the $\in$-relation by only countably many individuals in the domain of M.

This latter fact can be appreciated only by viewing the model M from 'outside', and supplying in one's mathematical imagination the one-one mapping that is 'missing' from M. This shift of perspective involves semantic ascent from the original theory to a more powerful metatheory. But now that very same metatheory, if consistent, has a countable model; ... and one launches on an infinite regress. As Skolem concluded, the notion of uncountability is *relative*, not absolute. Indeed, one might even say: it is *ineffable* – at least, at first order.

Problems

1   There are many suggested solutions to the Paradox of the Ravens. Explore them and try to decide whether any of them is succesful.
2   Given the definitions in the text of *x is grue* and of *x is bleen*, show that *x is green* and *x is blue* may be defined, respectively, as

    (T and *grue*(x)) or (not-T and *bleen*(x)).

and

    (T and *bleen*(x)) or (not-T and *grue*(x)).

3   Regiment the reasoning behind the Liar Paradox as a proof in Core Logic supplemented with simple inferential principles (which you will have to formulate) governing the predicate '... is true'.
4   Regiment the reasoning behind Russell's Paradox as a proof that there is no such set as the set of all sets that are not members of themselves. Make it a proof in Core Logic supplemented with simple inferential principles (which you will have to formulate) governing the notions of set-abstraction and membership.
5   Explain why set theory cannot just 'stop' with the infinity of natural numbers, and refuse to countenance the existence of any greater infinity.
6   Explore the implications of the Countable Models Theorem for first-order real number theory. Does it mean that there cannot really be uncountably many real numbers?

29 Description v. Deduction: The Clash of Ideals

We saw in Chapter 26 and Chapter 27 how our canons of deductive inference, governing truth-preservation across situations *in general*, can be obtained by smooth generalization from the rules of verification and of falsification that govern the evaluation of sentences as **True** or **False** in *particular* situations.

One might therefore expect a larger-scale 'harmony' to assert itself, between our powers of *representation* or *description*, and our powers to *deduce all logical consequences* of our representations or descriptions.

The purpose of this chapter, however, is to reveal an absolutely ineluctable conflict between those two would-be powers. *They cannot be maximized together.* It is ironic indeed that this irresoluble tension should arise between any attempted maximization of our powers of description and any (simultaneously) attempted maximization of our powers of deduction. For should not the two powers go hand in hand? – the latter feeding off, because rooted in, the former?

29.1 The Noncompossibility Theorem

The profoundly disquieting answer is negative, in the form of the Noncompossibility Theorem below. (This theorem was first proved in this completely general form in Tennant (2000).) The reader is reminded here of the notion of a categorical description of a given model or structure, which was explained in §26.4.1. If you aspire to *describe* certain mathematical structures *categorically*, pinning down precisely how many things are in them, and how those things are related to each other, *then* you had better abandon (because it is *irreconcilable* with that 'expressivist' aspiration) any hope you might entertain of being able to *deduce* from your description everything that *actually follows from it* (in the sense of being *logically implied by it*, regardless whether one can actually *deduce* it by means of finite proof). Likewise, *if* you aspire to be able always to *deduce* from your description of a particular mathematical structure everything that *actually follows from* your description, *then* you had better abandon (because it is *irreconcilable* with that 'deductivist' aspiration) any hope you might entertain of being able to *describe* precisely how many things are in that mathematical structure, and how those things are related to each other.

This result bedevils *all* discourse, no matter what the language. The expressivist or descriptivist aspiration is incompatible with the deductivist aspiration. The problem is rooted in the fact that we *state* and *prove* matters of fact in a perforce *finitary* fashion; whereas some of those matters of fact have to do with *infinite domains*, especially in Mathematics.

The Noncompossibility Theorem requires remarkably little for its proof. There are only two concepts that need to be revivified for the reader at this stage.

First, there is the concept of *soundness of proof*. Proofs are sound (and so is the system of proof that generates them) when the truth of their respective premises guarantees the truth of their respective conclusions. Thus: if Π is a proof of conclusion Q from premises $P_1,\ldots,P_n$, then: *any* interpretation of (or model for) the extralogical vocabulary in the sentences involved that makes $P_1,\ldots,P_n$ true makes Q true also.

Secondly, there is the concept of *isomorphism of models*, which we have already encountered in §26.4.1 and in §28.4.4. Two models dealing with the same extralogical vocabulary (names, functions signs, and predicates) are said to be *isomorphic* to each other just in case there is a one-one correspondence between their domains, under which their respective denotations for names, mappings for function signs, and extensions for predicates correspond exactly. For example, if ϕ maps the domain of M one-one onto the domain of M', and P, say, is an n-place predicate of the language being interpreted by both M and M', then we have

$\forall \alpha_1,\ldots,\alpha_n$ in the domain of M,

$$\langle \alpha_1,\ldots,\alpha_n \rangle \in M(P) \iff \langle \phi(\alpha_1),\ldots,\phi(\alpha_n) \rangle \in M'(P).$$

Likewise, if a is a name being assigned a denotation by both M and M', then we have

$$\phi(M(a)) = M'(a).$$

Finally, if f is an n-place function sign being assigned a mapping as its denotation by both M and M', then we have

$$M(f)(\alpha_1,\ldots,\alpha_n) = \beta \iff M'(f)(\phi(\alpha_1),\ldots,\phi(\alpha_n)) = \phi(\beta).$$

For models, being isomorphic means *having exactly the same structure*.

Isomorphism is, in fact, the logician's and mathematician's criterion for *sameness of structure*. When a mathematician seeks to describe a particular mathematical structure exactly, the most she can hope for is to describe it 'up to isomorphism'. That would involve *saying so much* about 'the' model she has in mind, and saying it so precisely, that *any* model making true what she says is isomorphic to the model she has in mind. Mathematicians freely speak of 'intended' models, and they experience no intellectual discomfort or embarrassment in invoking what might strike the uninitiated listener as surprisingly psychologistic discourse. Moreover, if they wish to avoid the charge of psychologism altogether, they speak instead of 'the *standard*' model, rather than 'the intended' model. But this does not obscure the fact that they have a particular model *in mind* – the standard one. And they are trying to convey a grasp of that model to other minds. This is what happens, for example, when a mathematician tries to get a learner to understand what is meant by *the* structure of natural numbers. They call it $\mathfrak{N}$, or $\mathbb{N}$, or something similarly portentous. Then they emphasize that its domain contains *exactly* the 'standard' natural numbers 0, 1, 2, ... *and no other individuals at all.* That done, the learner's grasp of the (extension of) the successor function, the addition function, and the multiplication function is supposed to fall effortlessly into place. Any model that the learner 'thinks up' in response to this course of instruction is going to be isomorphic to the model that her teachers had in mind.

Definition 12. *Let L be any language with identity. Let a be a name not in L. We define $L_{\neq}^{a}$ to be the set of non-identities*

$$\{\neg a = t \mid t \text{ is a term in } L\}.$$

We define L^{a} to be the set $L_{\neq}^{a} \cup \{\exists! a\}$.

Here is one way in which *complete expressive power* of a language L would have to be able to manifest itself: that there be some model M of particular interest to the user of L, such that

1 *Δ is a set of sentences in L;*
2 *M is an infinite L-model of Δ;*
3 *every element of M is the denotation of some term in L; and*
4 *every L-model of Δ is isomorphic to M.*

When these conditions obtain, the L-theory Δ can be said to *categorically describe* the structure of the model M.

Here is one way in which **complete deductive power** of a language L would have to be able to manifest itself: that it be furnished with

1 **a sound proof-system S for its logical operators, such that**
2 **for any set Γ of L-sentences that has no model, there is an S-proof of $\bot$ from Γ.**

We now carry forward the notational convention just established. The conditions in italics below seek to maximize expressive power. The conditions in boldface seek to maximize deductive power. (Note how (7) here is but a special case of the earlier 'boldface' condition (2) for complete deductive power.)

Theorem 6. [Noncompossibility]
It is impossible that the following hold:

1 L is a language
2 Δ is a set of sentences in L
3 M is an infinite L-model of Δ
4 every element of M is the denotation of some term in L
5 every L-model of Δ is isomorphic to M
6 S **is a sound proof-system for the logical operators in** L
7 **for any name** a **not in** L**, if** $\Delta \cup L^a$ **has no model, then there is an** S**-proof of** $\perp$ **from** $\Delta \cup L^a$**.**

Proof. Suppose (1)–(7) hold. We shall derive a contradiction. We shall do so with diagrams copiously provided for intuitive guidance. The non-technically minded reader is encouraged to persevere, and to let the chain of reasoning unfold step by utterly basic step.

Extend L by adding a new name a. Suppose, for a subsidiary *reductio ad absurdum*, that $\Delta \cup L^a$ has a model. Call this model N. The model N must provide a denotation for the new name a. Call that denotation α:

Let N_L be the restriction of N to the language L:

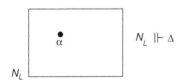

N_L is a model of Δ. Hence by (5), N_L is isomorphic to M. That is, there is a 1-1, structure-preserving mapping from N_L onto M. Call the mapping ϕ:

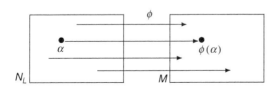

By (4), the individual $\phi(\alpha)$ is denoted in M by some L-term t:

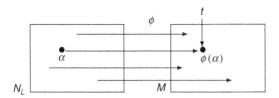

Hence by the isomorphism ϕ between N_L and M, the individual α is denoted in N_L, hence also in N, by that same term t:

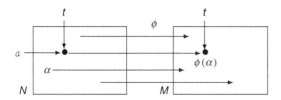

So N makes the identity $a=t$ true. But N is a model of $L^a_{\neq}$. Hence N makes $\neg a=t$ true. Contradiction. It therefore follows that $\Delta \cup L^a$ has no model. (This ends the subsidiary *reductio ad absurdum*.)

It now follows by (7) that there is an S-proof of $\bot$ from $\Delta \cup L^a$. Let Π be the proof of $\bot$ in question. Π has the form

$$\Theta, \Xi$$
$$\Pi$$
$$\bot$$

where the undischarged assumptions of Π form a finite set $\Theta \cup \Xi$, with $\varnothing \subseteq \Theta \subseteq \Delta$ and $\varnothing \neq \Xi \subseteq L^a$.

Ξ is finite and non-empty. Note that $\Delta \cup \{\exists! a\}$ has a model (let the name a denote any individual in M). So by (6) there is no S-proof of $\bot$ from $\Delta \cup \{\exists! a\}$. Hence Ξ contains at least one member of $L^a_{\neq}$. So Ξ has the form $\{\neg a=t_1,\ldots,\neg a=t_k\}$.

Let the respective denotations of the terms $t_1, \ldots, t_k$ in the domain of M be $\alpha_1, \ldots, \alpha_k$:

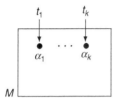

Since M is infinite (by (3)), there is an individual in the domain of M that is not denoted by any of the terms $t_1, \ldots, t_k$. Let β be such an individual:

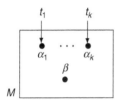

Extend the model M of Δ by making the name a denote β. Call the extended model M_a^β:

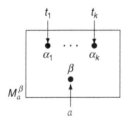

Since $\Theta \subseteq \Delta$, M is a model of Θ. Moreover, M_a^β interprets L exactly the way M does. So M_a^β is a model of Θ:

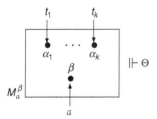

By choice of β, each of the non-identities $\neg a = t_1, \ldots, \neg a = t_k$ is true in M_a^β. So too is $\exists! a$. Hence M_a^β is a model of Ξ as well:

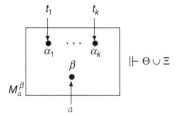

So M_a^β makes true the premises of the proof Π:

$$\Theta, \Xi$$
$$\Pi$$
$$\bot$$

By (6), the proof Π is sound. Hence the conclusion of Π is true in M_a^β. But the conclusion of Π is $\bot$, which is false in every model. Contradiction.

We have reduced (1)–(7) to absurdity.   □

29.2 The foundational consequences of noncompossibility

It is worth stressing that this impossibility result is *utterly general*.

L can be *any language at all*. It could contain higher-order quantifiers, or branching quantifiers; it could enable plural quantification; it could contain unusual first-order quantifiers, such as the plurality quantifiers (*few*, *several*, *many*, *most*, *almost all*, *domain-many*, etc.), or even infinitary quantifiers (*there are infinitely many*, *there are uncountably many*); it could contain modal operators. None of these expressive stengthenings will enable one to elude the impossibility just established. For its proof relies on only the most banal and basic logical properties of the identity predicate, and negation.

The fundamental tension that Theorem 6 exposes between descriptive and deductive aspirations arises (as already intimated above) from the facts that (i) proof has to be finite, whereas (ii) some of the important structures that we wish to characterize 'up to isomorphism' are infinite. What has been uncovered here is a completely general form of the *ineffability of the infinite*.

The important structures that mathematicians wish to describe up to isomorphism include the natural numbers; the (positive and negative) rational numbers; and the hereditarily finite pure sets. The first two kinds of mathematical object will be familiar. But in case the reader needs reminding: the natural numbers are the finite counting numbers 0, 1, 2, ... *ad infinitum*; and the rational numbers take the form $\frac{p}{q}$ or $-\frac{p}{q}$, where p and q are natural numbers within no common factor > 1. The third kind of mathematical object is perhaps less familiar. A hereditarily finite pure set is simply one that can be built up from the empty set ∅ by forming finite sets finitely many times.

The crucial feature that these three structures have in common is that they contain only individuals that are denoted by some term of the language. That is, there are no 'anonymous' individuals in their domains. This makes every individual uniquely identifiable; there are no multiplicities of distinct but mutually indiscernible individuals lurking within the domains in question.

It is rather ironic: for these models M, *even with* (indeed: *because of*) their exhaustive 'guest lists', *if* the language L has a complete proof system, *then* any description Δ of M that one attempts to give in L cannot exclude from the intended model gatecrashers with unauthorized IDs. (This remains true *even if* we could somehow 'get our hands on' the complete theory Th(ℕ) of first-order arithmetic. For Th(ℕ), see Chapter 30, Definition 18. In Chapter 30 we shall learn that we cannot actually 'get our hands on' Th(ℕ). It is unaxiomatizable.)

On the other hand, *if* one manages, by means of some highly expressive language L, to provide a description Δ that excludes the gatecrashers and captures M as intended ... *then* it turns out that L is bereft of a complete proof system. So there will be logical consequences, within L, of one's description Δ that one will *not be able to deduce from* Δ – despite the fact that of course all such consequences are true in M.

Such is our predicament with first- and second-order languages vying to codify arithmetical truth. On the one hand, if we adopt a first-order arithmetical language in order to describe the intended model ℕ of natural numbers, then, no matter what we assert about ℕ, we shall not be able to rule out non-standard models – models that contain ℕ as a submodel, but which *also* contain infinitely many non-standard intruders within their domains. On the other hand, if we adopt a second-order arithmetical language in order to describe ℕ exactly as intended ('categorically'), then we shall succeed – but only at the unavoidable cost of having to live with the *deductive incompleteness* of second-order logic.

30 The Incompleteness of Arithmetic

Arithmetical truth is unaxiomatizable. This profound limitative result is due to Gödel (1931). It is perhaps the most important foundational result ever established, a beautiful triumph of the flowering of rigorous thinking in its first three decades of the twentieth century. Much has been made of Gödel's result, as we have already seen in §24.3.6. The purpose of this chapter is to provide for the philosophical beginner the most succinct and accessible proof possible of the unaxiomatizability of arithmetical truth. It is *not* Gödel's original proof that we are presenting here, for that would be fiendishly difficult for the beginner. Rather, we are presenting a much more succinct *and accessible* proof by

  (i)   appealing to the Turing–Church Thesis (see §10.3.4),
 (ii)   making prominent use, yet again, of the beautiful technique of diagonal argument, and
(iii)   setting things out in inferentialist fashion to the greatest extent possible.

Because of the compression and distillation of essentials, we believe that the reasoning set out below is within the grasp of the keen and inquiring beginner. We encourage a slow and careful reading. The resulting experience should be not just intellectual, but also aesthetic.

We use Δ for sets of sentences; φ and θ for sentences; and ψ for formulae with one free variable. The free variable is conventionally taken to be x. Recall that $\perp$ is the symbol for absurdity, and that $\Delta \vdash \varphi$ means that there is a proof whose conclusion is φ and whose premises are drawn from Δ. When $\Delta, \theta \vdash \varphi$, we shall say 'the inference from θ to φ holds *modulo* Δ'. (It is understood, of course, that θ is not in Δ.)

Because we are working with a first-order language, the relation $\vdash$ of deducibility coincides with the relation $\models$ of logical consequence. So the phrase 'follows (logically) from' can be used freely without having to specify which of these two senses it has. It should be pointed out, again with the proper measure of admiration, that *this* particular result – the completeness of *first-order logic* – is *also* due to Gödel. (He proved it in his *Doktorarbeit* at the University of Vienna [Gödel (1930)]. It was in his later dissertation at Vienna, the *Habilitationsschrift*, that he proved the *incompleteness* of *arithmetic*.)

Definition 13. *Suppose* Δ *is a set of sentences. Then* Δ *is consistent if and only if* $\Delta \nvdash \bot$.

Observation 1. *For any consistent set* Δ*, we can employ the inference rule*

$$\frac{\Delta \vdash \bot}{\bot}.$$

Note that the upper occurrence of $\bot$ is the absurdity sign in the *object language*, that is, the first-order language of arithmetic; while the lower occurrence of $\bot$ is the absurdity sign of the *metalanguage*, in which we are reasoning *about* the object language. So the inference rule in question is a metalinguistic one.

Definition 14. *Suppose* Δ *is a set of sentences in some language* $\mathcal{L}$*. Then* Δ *is complete if and only if for every sentence* φ *in* $\mathcal{L}$*, either* $\Delta \vdash \varphi$ *or* $\Delta, \varphi \vdash \bot$*.*

Definition 15. *Let* M *be any model for a language* $\mathcal{L}$*. Th(M) is the set of all sentences in* $\mathcal{L}$ *that* M *makes true. In symbols:*

$$Th(M) = \{\varphi \in \mathcal{L} | M \Vdash \varphi\}.$$

Observation 2. *For any model* M *of a language* $\mathcal{L}$*, Th(M) is consistent and complete.*

Definition 16. *The first-order language L of arithmetic is the first-order language with the identity predicate* =*, whose extralogical vocabulary consists of the name* 0*, the successor-function symbol* s*, and the binary function symbols* + *and* ×*.*

Throughout this chapter, all terms, formulae and sentences are understood to be in the first-order language of arithmetic. For present purposes, one particular model will hold our attention: the so-called *standard model for arithmetic.*

Definition 17. *The standard model for arithmetic, denoted* $\mathbb{N}$*, has for its domain exactly the natural numbers, and interprets the name (constant)* 0*, the successor symbol* s*, the addition function symbol* +*, and the multiplication function symbol* × *in the obviously correct way.*

Definition 18. *As a special case of Definition 15:* $Th(\mathbb{N}) = \{\varphi \in L | \mathbb{N} \Vdash \varphi\}$*.*

Recall Gödel's definition of *general recursive function*, which we discussed in §10.3.1. Like Turing's definition of functions computable by Turing machines, it provided a precise formal explication of the informal notion of computable function. We remarked in §10.3.1 on how Gödel's definition affords a method of proof by mathematical induction of general results about recursive functions. Theorem 7 below is one of the most important such results. The philosophical reader is asked to take it on trust, as a straightforward theorem of *mathematics*. Its proof is absolutely straighforward – it is a proof by mathematical induction. Being 'merely technical', and rather too long to include here, it can safely be omitted for the philosophical reader. (The interested reader will find a fully detailed proof of Theorem 7 in Tennant (1978).) We wish instead, in this chapter, to keep our attention focused on philosophically important *consequences* of this theorem, and, in particular, to see how, yet again, the method of 'diagonal argument' produces a remarkable result for the foundationalist.

Definition 19. *The following set of axioms defines the theory of arithmetic known as Q:*

1   $\forall x \neg sx = 0$
2   $\forall x \forall y\, (sx = sy \rightarrow x = y)$
3   $\forall x\, (x = 0 \vee \exists y\, x = sy)$
4   $\forall x \forall y\, x + sy = s(x + y)$
5   $\forall x\, x + 0 = x$
6   $\forall x\, x \times 0 = 0$
7   $\forall x \forall y\, x \times sy = (x \times y) + x$

Q is due to Raphael Robinson (1911–95). (See Tarski *et al.* (1953).)

Observation 3. $Q \subseteq Th(\mathbb{N})$.

Definition 20. *For any natural number n, the numeral for n is the term*

$$s \ldots s0,$$

with n occurrences of the successor-function symbol s. We abbreviate the numeral for n as

$$\underline{n}.$$

Theorem 7. [Representability of recursive functions in Q]
For every recursive function $f(x_1, \ldots, x_n)$ there is a formula $\varphi(x_1, \ldots, x_n, y)$ in L such that for all $k_1, \ldots, k_n$ the following two inferences hold modulo Q:

$$\frac{\varphi(\underline{k_1}, \ldots, \underline{k_n}, a)}{a = f(\underline{k_1}, \ldots, \underline{k_n})} \text{, and its converse } \frac{a = f(\underline{k_1}, \ldots, \underline{k_n})}{\varphi(\underline{k_1}, \ldots, \underline{k_n}, a)} \text{ ,}$$

where the parameter a is chosen so as to occur only in the two positions displayed.

Definition 21. *Suppose P is a (monadic) property of natural numbers. Then the characteristic function of P, called c_P, is defined by the following inference rules:*

$$\frac{P(n)}{c_P(n) = 1} \qquad \frac{\neg P(n)}{c_P(n) = 0} \ .$$

Definition 22. *Suppose that μ is an effective function defined on all (metalinguistic) sentences of the form P(n) (where n is a natural number), and that the range of μ is {0,1}. Then μ is an effective method for deciding, of any given natural number n, whether P(n), if and only if for every n the following inferences hold:*

$$\frac{P(n)}{\mu(P(n)) = 1} \qquad \frac{\neg P(n)}{\mu(P(n)) = 0} \ .$$

Definition 23. *A property P of natural numbers is decidable if and only if there is an effective method for deciding, of any given natural number n, whether P(n).*

Definition 24. *Suppose f is a function with domain D and range {0,1}. Then $\tilde{f}$ is the function with domain D and range {0,1} defined by the following inference rules (for each $d \in D$):*

$$\frac{f(d) = 1}{\tilde{f}(d) = 0} \qquad \frac{f(d) = 0}{\tilde{f}(d) = 1} \ .$$

Lemma 1. *If P is a decidable property of natural numbers, then so is $\neg P$.*

Proof. Let μ be an effective method for deciding, of any given natural number n, whether $P(n)$. Then $\tilde{\mu}$ is an effective method for deciding, of any given natural number n, whether $\neg P(n)$.   □

Definition 25. *Δ is representing if and only if for every decidable property P of natural numbers there is some unary formula $\psi(x)$ such that for every natural number n, the following inferences hold:*

$$\frac{P(n)}{\Delta \vdash \psi(\underline{n})} \ , \ and \ its \ converse \ \frac{\Delta \vdash \psi(\underline{n})}{P(n)} \ .$$

Lemma 2. *Suppose Δ is representing. Then Δ is (classically) consistent.*

Proof. Suppose for *reductio* that $\Delta \vdash \perp$, where $\vdash$ represents deducibility in classical logic. By the rule *Ex Falso Quodlibet* we have $\Delta \vdash \varphi$, for every sentence φ. So for any ψ and any n we have $\Delta \vdash \psi(\underline{n})$. It follows from the main supposition that for any decidable property P of natural numbers, and for any n, we have $P(n)$.

But this is absurd. The property of primality, for example, is decidable, but the number 4 is not prime.   □

Definition 26. Δ *is* strongly strongly representing *if and only if for every decidable property P of natural numbers there is some unary formula $\psi(x)$ such that for all natural numbers n, the following inferences hold:*

$$\frac{P(n)}{\Delta \vdash \psi(\underline{n})} \qquad \frac{\neg P(n)}{\Delta, \psi(\underline{n}) \vdash \bot} \, .$$

Observation 4. *Suppose Δ is strongly representing and $\Delta \subseteq \Delta'$. Then Δ' is strongly representing.*

Lemma 3. *Suppose Δ is consistent. Suppose Δ is strongly representing. Then Δ is representing.*

Proof. Since Δ is strongly representing, we already have the inference

$$\frac{P(n)}{\Delta \vdash \psi(\underline{n})}$$

The following proof establishes the converse inference, using only logical rules of inference and rules of inference justified by the main suppositions:

$$\frac{\Delta \vdash \psi(\underline{n}) \quad \dfrac{\overline{\quad\quad}(1)}{\neg P(n) \quad \Delta, \psi(\underline{n}) \vdash \bot}}{\dfrac{\Delta \vdash \bot}{\dfrac{\bot}{P(n)}(1)}} \text{CUT}$$

Note that the final step, which is formally one of classical *reductio ad absurdum*, is constructively acceptable, since the sentence $P(n)$ is, by hypothesis, decidable.   □

Definition 27. Δ *is* axiomatizable *if and only if there is an effective enumeration of all and only the sentences that follow from Δ.*

Definition 28. Δ *is* decidable *if and only if there is an effective method for deciding, of any sentence φ in the language of arithmetic, whether $\Delta \vdash \varphi$.*

Theorem 8. *Every decidable theory is axiomatizable.*

Proof. Suppose Θ is a decidable theory. One can effectively enumerate its theorems by listing them as follows. First, effectively enumerate all sentences

$\varphi_0, \varphi_1, \ldots$ of the language. Then generate the sought (sub-)list consisting of exactly the theorems of Θ as follows. Take each sentence φ_i in turn. Effectively decide whether φ_i is in Θ. If so, append φ_i to the list of theorems, and advance to φ_{i+1}; if not, simply advance to φ_{i+1}.   □

Theorem 9. [Janiczak] *Suppose Δ is consistent. Suppose Δ is complete. Suppose Δ is axiomatizable. Then Δ is decidable.*

(This result was first proved in Janiczak (1950).)

Proof. We seek to reveal an effective method for answering the question 'Does φ follow from Δ?', concerning any given sentence φ of the language of arithmetic.

The axiomatizability of Δ guarantees that the sentences that follow from Δ can be effectively enumerated as $\varphi_0, \varphi_1, \ldots$. Given any sentence φ in the language of arithmetic, the completeness of Δ guarantees that either φ occurs as some φ_n, or that $\neg\varphi$ does. If φ so occurs, then we are done: we answer Yes to the question 'Does φ follow from Δ?'. But if $\neg\varphi$ so occurs, then the consistency of Δ guarantees that φ does *not* so occur. So once again we are done: we answer No. Thus we can effectively determine, of any given φ, whether φ follows from Δ.   □

Theorem 10. *No set Δ is both representing and decidable.*

Proof. Suppose Δ is representing and decidable. Let $\psi_0, \psi_1, \ldots$ be an effective enumeration of all unary formulae. (There is such an enumeration.) Consider the following property of natural numbers n:

$$\Delta \not\vdash \psi_n(\underline{n}).$$

This property is decidable. For, given any natural number n, we can decide whether $\Delta \not\vdash \psi_n(\underline{n})$ as follows.

> Effectively find the unary formula ψ_n. Effectively substitute the numeral $\underline{n}$ for every free occurrence of the free variable in ψ_n. The result is $\psi_n(\underline{n})$. Since Δ is decidable, there is an effective method (say μ) for deciding, of any given natural number m, whether $\Delta \vdash \psi_m(\underline{m})$. It follows that $\tilde{\mu}$ is an effective method for deciding, of any given natural number m, whether $\Delta \not\vdash \psi_m(\underline{m})$. Now apply $\tilde{\mu}$ to decide whether $\Delta \not\vdash \psi_n(\underline{n})$.

Since Δ is representing, there is, for this effectively decidable property $\Delta \not\vdash \psi_n(\underline{n})$ of natural numbers, some unary formula ψ such that for every natural number n we can employ the rules of inference

$$\frac{\Delta \not\vdash \psi_n(\underline{n})}{\Delta \vdash \psi(\underline{n})} \quad \text{and its converse} \quad \frac{\Delta \vdash \psi(\underline{n})}{\Delta \not\vdash \psi_n(\underline{n})} \; .$$

But the unary formulae ψ occurs in the effective enumeration of all unary formulae as ψ_k, for some k. Thus the rules of inference that we may employ, for any natural number n, become (for this fixed choice of k, and for any n)

$$\frac{\Delta \nvdash \psi_n(\underline{n})}{\Delta \vdash \psi_k(\underline{n})} \quad \text{and} \quad \frac{\Delta \vdash \psi_k(\underline{n})}{\Delta \nvdash \psi_n(\underline{n})} \ .$$

Now take as an instance of n the number k. Then we may employ the rules

$$\frac{\Delta \nvdash \psi_k(\underline{k})}{\Delta \vdash \psi_k(\underline{k})} \quad \text{and} \quad \frac{\Delta \vdash \psi_k(\underline{k})}{\Delta \nvdash \psi_k(\underline{k})} \ .$$

But these rules establish the equivalence of the statement $\Delta \vdash \psi_k(\underline{k})$ with its own negation. Contradiction. $\qquad\qquad\square$

Note that this is yet another beautiful application, to devastating effect, of the diagonal method of argument. The denouement, however, is but a couple of steps away.

Theorem 11. *No set Δ is consistent, complete, strongly representing and axiomatizable.*

Proof.

$$\overbrace{\Delta \text{ consistent}, \Delta \text{ strongly representing}} \qquad \overbrace{\Delta \text{ consistent}, \Delta \text{ complete}, \Delta \text{ axiomatizable}}$$

$\vdots$ (Lemma 3)		$\vdots$ (Theorem 9)
$\underbrace{\Delta \text{ representing}}$	,	$\underbrace{\Delta \text{ decidable}}$

$$\vdots \ (\text{Theorem 10})$$
$$\bot$$

Theorem 12. *Q is strongly representing.*

Proof. Suppose P is a decidable property of natural numbers. Then its characteristic function c_P is computable. By the Turing–Church Thesis, c_P is recursive. By Theorem 7 there is a formula $\varphi(x,y)$ such that for all n the following two inferences hold *modulo Q*, with a parametric:

$$\text{(I)} \quad \frac{\varphi(\underline{n},a)}{a = \underline{c_P(n)}} \qquad \text{(II)} \quad \frac{a = \underline{c_P(n)}}{\varphi(\underline{n},a)} \ .$$

We now show that the formula $\varphi(x,\underline{1})$ strongly represents P, by establishing the two inferences

$$\text{(i)} \qquad \frac{P(n)}{Q \vdash \varphi(\underline{n},\underline{1})}$$

and

(ii) $$\frac{\neg P(n)}{Q, \varphi(\underline{n}, \underline{1}) \vdash \perp} \ .$$

Ad (i): Suppose $P(n)$. Then $c_P(n) = 1$. Substituting 1 for $c_P(n)$ in (II) above, we have that the following inference holds *modulo* Q, with a parametric :

$$\frac{a = \underline{1}}{\varphi(\underline{n}, a)} \ .$$

Putting now $\underline{1}$ in place of the parameter a, we obtain, *modulo* Q, the inference

$$\frac{\underline{1} = \underline{1}}{\varphi(\underline{n}, \underline{1})} \ .$$

But the premise is a logical theorem. Thus $Q \vdash \varphi(\underline{n}, \underline{1})$.

Ad (ii): Suppose $\neg P(n)$. Then $c_P(n) = 0$. Substituting 0 for $c_P(n)$ in (I) above, we have that the following inference holds *modulo* Q, with a parametric:

$$\frac{\varphi(\underline{n}, a)}{a = \underline{0}}$$

Putting now $\underline{1}$ in place of the parameter a, we obtain, *modulo* Q,

$$\frac{\varphi(\underline{n}, \underline{1})}{\underline{1} = \underline{0}}$$

But $Q, \underline{1} = \underline{0} \vdash \perp$. Hence $Q, \varphi(\underline{n}, \underline{1}) \vdash \perp$.   □

Corollary 1. *Th($\mathbb{N}$) is strongly representing.*

Proof. By Theorem 12, Q is strongly representing. Recall Observation 3: $Q \subseteq Th(\mathbb{N})$. By Observation 4, $Th(\mathbb{N})$ is strongly representing.   □

Theorem 13. *Th($\mathbb{N}$) is not axiomatizable.*

Proof. By definition, $Th(\mathbb{N})$ is consistent and complete. By Corollary 1, $Th(\mathbb{N})$ is strongly representing. Hence, by Theorem 11, $Th(\mathbb{N})$ is not axiomatizable.   □

APPENDIX A
The History of Western Philosophy

Ancient Philosophy

Presocratics	6th, 5th century BC	fragments
Thales	c.625–545 BC	*All things are full of gods. Water is the first principle of everything.*
Anaximander	c.610–546 BC	*On Nature*
Anaximenes	585–528 BC	fragments
Pythagoras	c.570–c.495 BC	fragments
Xenophanes	c.570–c.470 BC	fragments
Heraclitus	c.535–c.475 BC	substantial fragments
Parmenides	c.515/540 BC, fl. early 5th century BC	120 lines of a philosophical poem
Zeno	c.490–c.430 BC	fragments
Empedocles	c.490–430 BC	*On Nature* (a poem, of which about 400 lines exist)
Anaxagoras	c.500–428 BC	fragments
Leucippus	5th century BC	attributions by Democritus
Protagoras	c.490–420 BC	attributions by Plato
Democritus	c.460–c.370 BC	large collection of fragments
Gorgias	485–c.380 BC	*On What Is Not*
Thrasymachus	c.459–400 BC	attributions by Plato (in *The Republic*)
Socrates	c.469–399 BC	attributions by Plato, in his dialogues
Plato	424/3–348/7 BC	Socratic dialogues, most notably *The Republic*
Aristotle	384–322 BC	*Metaphysics; Prior Analytics; De Anima; Nichomachean Ethics*

Epicurus	341–270 BC	*Letter to Herodotus; Letter to Menoeceus; Letter to Pythocles*
Chrysippus	279 BC–206 BC	fragments
Lucretius	99–55 BC	*On the Nature of Things*
Sextus	160–210	*Outlines of Pyrrhonism; Against the Mathematicians*
Plotinus	204/5–270	*Enneads*
Porphyry	234–c. 305	*Isagoge* (introduction to logic and philosophy)
Augustine	354–430	*Contra Academicos; De Libero Arbitrio*

Medieval Philosophy

Boethius	480–524/5	*Consolation of Philosophy*
Anselm	1033–1109	*De Veritate; Proslogion*
Abelard	1079–1142	*Logica 'ingredientibus'; Theologia Christiana; Ethica*
Aquinas	1225–74	*Summa Theologica; Summa Contra Gentiles*
Duns Scotus	1265/6–1308	*Ordinatio; De Primo Principio*
Ockham	1287–1347	*Summa Logicae*

Early Modern Philosophy

Bacon	1561–1626	*The Advancement of Learning; Novum Organum Scientiarum*
Hobbes	1588–1679	*Elements of Philosophy; Leviathan*
Descartes	1596–1650	*Discourse on the Method; Meditations on First Philosophy; Principles of Philosophy*
Arnauld	1612–94	*L'Art de penser*, with Pierre Nicole; a.k.a. the 'Port-Royal Logic'

Modern Philosophy in the Age of Enlightenment, approx. 1650–1800

Spinoza	1632–77	*Ethics; Tractatus Theologico-Politicus*
Locke	1632–1704	*An Essay Concerning Human Understanding; The Two Treatises of Government*
Malebranche	1638–1715	*Search after Truth; Dialogues on Metaphysics and Religion*
Leibniz	1646–1716	*New Essays on Human Understanding; Theodicy; Monadology*
Berkeley	1685–1753	*Treatise concerning the Principles of Human Knowledge; Three Dialogues between Hylas and Philonous*
Reid	1710–96	*An Inquiry Into the Human Mind on the Principles of Common Sense*
Hume	1711–76	*A Treatise of Human Nature; Enquiries concerning Human Understanding and concerning the Principles of Morals; Dialogues concerning Natural Religion*
Rousseau	1712–78	*Emile, or On Education; The Social Contract*

Post-Enlightenment Philosophy, approx. 1790–1900

Kant	1724–1804	*Critique of Pure Reason; Prolegomena to Any Future Metaphysics; Groundwork of the Metaphysics of Morals; Metaphysical Foundations of Natural Science; Critique of Practical Reason; Critique of the Power of Judgment*
Bentham	1748–1832	*The Principles of Morals and Legislation*
Hegel	1770–1831	*Phenomenology of Spirit; Science of Logic; Philosophy of Right*
Bolzano	1781–1848	*Theory of Science*
Schopenhauer	1788–1860	*The World as Will and Representation; The Two Fundamental Problems of Ethics*

Mill	1806–73	*System of Logic; On Liberty; Utilitarianism; Considerations on Representative Government; The Subjection of Women*
Kierkegaard	1813–55	*Either-Or*
Marx	1818–83	*Das Kapital*
Brentano	1838–1917	*Psychology from an Empirical Standpoint; The Origin of the Knowledge of Right and Wrong*
Nietzsche	1844–1900	*The Birth of Tragedy; Human, All-Too-Human; The Gay Science; Thus Spoke Zarathustra; Beyond Good and Evil; On the Genealogy of Morals*

Twentieth-Century Philosophy

Peirce	1839–1914	*Pragmatism as a Principle and Method of Right Thinking*
Frege	1848–1925	*Begriffsschrift; The Foundations of Arithmetic; Grundgesetze der Arithmetik*
Husserl	1859–1938	*Logical Investigations; Ideas Pertaining to a Pure Phenomenology and to a Phenomenological Philosophy; Cartesian Meditations*
Russell	1872–1970	*The Principles of Mathematics; Principia Mathematica* (with A. N. Whitehead); *The Problems of Philosophy; Our Knowledge of the External World; Introduction to Mathematical Philosophy; The Analysis of Mind; An Inquiry into Meaning and Truth; Human Knowledge: Its Scope and Limits*
Moore	1873–1958	*Principia Ethica*
Wittgenstein	1889–1951	*Tractatus Logico-Philosophicus; Philosophical Investigations; Remarks on the Foundations of Mathematics*
Heidegger	1889–1976	*Being and Time*
Carnap	1891–1970	*The Logical Structure of the World; Logical Syntax of Language*

Popper	1902–94	*The Logic of Scientific Discovery; The Open Society and its Enemies*
Sartre	1905–80	*Being and Nothingness; Existentialism is a Humanism*
Goodman	1906–98	*Fact, Fiction, and Forecast; Languages of Art; Ways of Worldmaking*
Quine	1908–2000	*Word and Object; Roots of Reference; Pursuit of Truth; From Stimulus to Science*
Sellars	1912–89	*Empiricism and the Philosophy of Mind; Science, Perception and Reality*
Davidson	1917–2003	*Essays on Actions and Events; Inquiries into Truth and Interpretation; Subjective, Intersubjective, Objective; Truth and Predication*
Anscombe	1919–2001	*Intention*
Strawson	1919–2006	*Individuals; The Bounds of Sense; Skepticism and Naturalism: Some Varieties*
Rawls	1921–2002	*A Theory of Justice*
Dummett	1925–2001	*Frege: Philosophy of Language; Truth and Other Enigmas; The Logical Basis of Metaphysics*
Foucault	1926–84	*The Archaeology of Knowledge; The Order of Things*
Williams	1929–2003	*Problems of the Self; Moral Luck; Making Sense of Humanity*
Nozick	1938–2002	*Anarchy, State and Utopia; Philosophical Explanations*
Kripke	1940–	*Naming and Necessity; Wittgenstein on Rules and Private Language*
Lewis	1941–2001	*Convention; Counterfactuals; On the Plurality of Worlds*

APPENDIX B
Formal Results in the Theory of Probability

Axioms (1)–(3) hold for all propositions A. Axiom (4) holds for all propositions A and all propositions B.

1 $0 \le p(A) \le 1$.
2 If $\vdash A$ (i.e., A is logically true), then $p(A) = 1$.
3 If $A \vdash \bot$ (i.e., A is logically false), then $p(A) = 0$.
4 If $A \vdash B$ (i.e., A logically implies B), then $p(A) \le p(B)$.

We now proceed to prove some interesting results from these four axioms, culminating in the proof of Theorem 1 of §8.6.3.

The results are arranged, in the usual style of a mathematics textbook, as Lemmas, Theorems and Corollaries. These are convenient psychological classifications employed by mathematicians so as to indicate the relative depth or importance or usefulness of the various results. Lemmas find frequent application in the proofs of different theorems. Theorems are the 'main' statements one is interested in proving. They tend to be general, deep and elegant, and to have applications. Corollaries are usually special, interesting cases of previously proved theorems. Strictly speaking, there is no *logical* difference among lemmas, theorems and corollaries. From a logical point of view, they are all simply consequences that have been deduced from the axioms.

It is wise to try not to seek 'physical interpretations' of each and every stage of each formal proof to follow. Mathematical reasoning is perforce abstract, and it is better to seek to understand how each step works simply as a matter of formal inference. It is only when we reach a suitable theorem that we shall look for any kind of non-mathematical interpretation of the result. The interest of these investigations lies in how much one can squeeze out of the very little with which we have provided ourselves in Axioms (1)–(4).

Lemma 4. *If* $A \vdash B$ *and* $B \vdash A$ *then* $p(A) = p(B)$.

Proof. By Axiom (4) the hypotheses of the Lemma imply $p(A) \le p(B)$ and $p(B) \le p(A)$. Hence by anti-symmetry of $\le$, we have $p(A) = p(B)$. □

Thus far we have introduced only the notion of *absolute* probability. There is a companion notion of *conditional* probability, $p(A|B)$, to be read as 'the probability of A, given B'. The latter notion is defined as follows. Note that it is admissible only when $0 < p(B)$.

Definition 29. *If* $0 < p(B)$ *then*

$$p(A|B) =_{df} \frac{p(A \wedge B)}{p(B)}.$$

Theorem 14. [Bayes]
If $0 < p(A)$ *and* $0 < p(B)$, *then*

$$p(A|B) = \frac{p(B|A).p(A)}{p(B)}.$$

Proof. Under the hypotheses of the theorem we have, by definition,

$$p(A \wedge B) = p(A|B).p(B)$$

and

$$p(B \wedge A) = p(B|A).p(A).$$

By Lemma 4,

$$p(A \wedge B) = p(B \wedge A).$$

Hence

$$p(A|B).p(B) = p(B|A).p(A).$$

Dividing both sides by $p(B)$, the result follows.   □

Lemma 5. *If* $0 < p(B)$ *and* $B \vdash A$ *then* $0 < p(A)$.

Proof. Suppose $B \vdash A$. By Axiom (4), $p(B) \leq p(A)$. Now suppose $0 < p(B)$. It follows that $0 < p(A)$.   □

Theorem 15. *Suppose* $0 < p(C \wedge B)$ *and* $0 < p(A \wedge B)$. *Then*

$$p(A|C \wedge B).p(C|B) = p(C|A \wedge B).p(A|B).$$

Proof. Suppose $0 < p(C \wedge B)$. Note that $C \wedge B \vdash B$. It follows from Lemma 5 that $0 < p(B)$. By Lemma 4,

$$p(A \wedge (C \wedge B)) = p(C \wedge (A \wedge B)).$$

Hence

$$\frac{p(A \wedge (C \wedge B))}{p(B)} = \frac{p(C \wedge (A \wedge B))}{p(B)}.$$

It now follows that

$$\frac{p(A \wedge (C \wedge B))}{p(C \wedge B)} \cdot \frac{p(C \wedge B)}{p(B)} = \frac{p(C \wedge (A \wedge B))}{p(A \wedge B)} \cdot \frac{p(A \wedge B)}{p(B)}.$$

Applying the definitions of conditional probability to each of these four factors, the desired result follows. $\square$

Lemma 6. *If $B \vdash A$ and $0 < p(B)$ then $p(A|B) = 1$.*

Proof. From the deducibility hypothesis it follows that B is interdeducible with $A \wedge B$. So by Lemma 4 we have $p(B) = p(A \wedge B)$. The inequality hypothesis ensures that

$$p(A|B) = \frac{p(A \wedge B)}{p(B)}.$$

Using the previous identity to substitute for the numerator of the right-hand side, we obtain

$$p(A|B) = \frac{p(B)}{p(B)} = 1$$

as required. $\square$

Lemma 7. *If $A, B \vdash C$ and $0 < p(A \wedge B)$ then $p(C|A \wedge B) = 1$.*

Proof. Suppose $A, B \vdash C$. Then by $\wedge I$, we have $A \wedge B \vdash C \wedge (A \wedge B)$. Conversely, by $\wedge E$, we have $C \wedge (A \wedge B) \vdash A \wedge B$. Hence by Lemma 4 it follows that

$$p(C \wedge (A \wedge B)) = p(A \wedge B).$$

Now consider the following instance of the definitions of conditional probability:

$$p(C|A \wedge B) = \frac{p(C \wedge (A \wedge B))}{p(A \wedge B)}.$$

Using the previous identity to substitute for the numerator of the right-hand side, we obtain

$$p(C|A\wedge B) = \frac{p(A\wedge B)}{p(A\wedge B)} = 1$$

as required.   □

Corollary 2. *Suppose* $A, B \vdash C$, $0 < p(C\wedge B)$ *and* $0 < p(A\wedge B)$. *Then*

$$p(A|C\wedge B).p(C|B) = p(A|B).$$

Proof. The two inequalities in the hypotheses mean that Theorem 15 applies, so we have

$$p(A|C\wedge B).p(C|B) = p(C|A\wedge B).p(A|B).$$

But now the deducibility hypothesis means that the factor $p(C|A\wedge B)$ can, by Lemma 7, be set to unity.   □

Theorem 16. *Suppose that* $0 < p(H\wedge K)$; *that* $H, K \vdash E$; *and that* $p(E|K) < 1$. *Then* $p(H|E\wedge K) > p(H|K)$.

Proof. From the assumption that $0 < p(H\wedge K)$ it follows that $p(E|H\wedge K)$ exists. Given the further assumption that $H, K \vdash E$, Lemma 7 tells us that $p(E|H\wedge K)$ is indeed equal to 1.

From the assumption $H, K \vdash E$, it also follows that $H\wedge K \vdash E\wedge K$. By Axiom (4), $p(H\wedge K) \le p(E\wedge K)$. But we are assuming that $0 < p(H\wedge K)$; hence $0 < p(E\wedge K)$. These last two inequalities ensure that Theorem 15 applies, so that we have

$$p(H|E\wedge K).p(E|K) = p(E|H\wedge K).p(H|K);$$

whence, upon substitution of 1 for $p(E|H\wedge K)$ in this equation, we obtain

$$p(H|E\wedge K).p(E|K) = p(H|K).$$

But now by the assumption that $p(E|K) < 1$, we have $p(H|E\wedge K) > p(H|K)$, as required.   □

It is worth pausing to reflect on the logical relations involved among H, K and E under the hypotheses of Theorem 16. The condition $0 < p(H\wedge K)$ ensures (by Axiom (3)) that H is consistent with K. The condition $p(E|K) < 1$ ensures (by Lemma 3) that K does not logically imply E. Yet together H and K logically imply E.

This sort of situation arises when K is some body of background knowledge, and E is some empirical conjecture not implied by K, but implied (by way of a prediction) by the combination of K with some hypothesis H consistently extending K. What Theorem 16 tells us is that *if E turns out to be the case* (as predicted by H), then the probability of H given this new evidence E (conjoined with K) is higher than the probability of H when only the 'old evidence' K was given. That is, successful predictions raise the probability of a bold hypothesis that is consistent with, but logically extends beyond, what is already known.

We have just seen a Bayesian vindication of our tendency to increase our confidence in an hypothesis when it is involved in successful applications of the hypothetico-deductive method. This vindication draws on only minimal materials concerning absolute and conditional probabilities. *We have used only Axiom (4).*

Consider the following substitutions:

$$A \mapsto H$$
$$B \mapsto S \wedge K$$
$$C \mapsto E$$

in Corollary 2, yielding the following instance: Suppose $H, S \wedge K \vdash E$, $0 < p(E \wedge (S \wedge K))$ and $0 < p(H \wedge (S \wedge K))$. Then

$$p(H | E \wedge (S \wedge K)) = \frac{p(H | S \wedge K)}{p(E | S \wedge K)}.$$

We are now in a position to prove Theorem 1 of §8.6.3. We re-state it here for convenience. *Suppose*

1 $H, S, K \vdash E$;
2 $0 < p(H \wedge (S \wedge K))$;
3 $p(H | S \wedge K) = p(H | K)$; *and*
4 $p(E | S \wedge K) < 1.$

Then

$$p(H | E \wedge (S \wedge K)) > p(H | K).$$

Proof. By assumption (1), $H \wedge (S \wedge K)$ is interdeducible with $E \wedge (H \wedge (S \wedge K)))$. Hence by Axiom (4) we have

$$p(H \wedge (S \wedge K)) = p(E \wedge (H \wedge (S \wedge K))).$$

Since also

$$E \wedge (H \wedge (S \wedge K)) \vdash E \wedge (S \wedge K),$$

we have by Axiom (4) once more that

$$p(E \wedge (H \wedge (S \wedge K))) \leq p(E \wedge (S \wedge K)).$$

Now we may conclude overall that

$$0 < p(H \wedge (S \wedge K)) = p(E \wedge (H \wedge (S \wedge K))) \leq p(E \wedge (S \wedge K)),$$

whence of course

$$0 < p(E \wedge (S \wedge K)).$$

This result, along with assumptions (1) and (2), ensure that the last-mentioned instance of Corollary 2 applies. Hence we have

$$p(H|E \wedge (S \wedge K)).p(E|S \wedge K) = p(H|S \wedge K).$$

Using assumption (3) to substitute for the right-hand side, we obtain

$$p(H|E \wedge (S \wedge K)).p(E|S \wedge K) = p(H|K).$$

Given assumption (4), we conclude

$$p(H|E \wedge (S \wedge K)) > p(H|K).$$

$\square$

Bibliography

Robert Merrihew Adams and Marilyn McCord Adams, editors. *The Problem of Evil.* Oxford University Press, Oxford, 1990.

Alan Ross Anderson, editor. *Minds and Machines,* Prentice-Hall Contemporary Perspectives in Philosophy Series. Prentice-Hall, Englewood Cliffs, NJ, 1964.

Alan Ross Anderson and Nuel D. Belnap. *Entailment: The Logic of Relevance and Necessity,* Vol. I. Princeton University Press, 1975.

Saint Anselm of Canterbury. *Anselmus Cantuariensis Proslogion.* The Latin Library, www.thelatinlibrary.com/anselmproslogron.html, 1078.

Robert Axelrod. *The Evolution of Cooperation.* Basic Books, New York, 1984.

Robert Axelrod and William D. Hamilton. The evolution of cooperation. *Science,* 211:1390–1396, 1981.

A. J. Ayer. Can there be a private language? *Proceedings of the Aristotelian Society, Supplementary Volume,* 28:63–76, 1954.

Alfred J. Ayer. *Language, Truth and Logic,* 2nd edn. Gollancz, London, 1946.

Alfred J. Ayer. *Philosophical Essays.* St. Martin's Press, New York, 1963.

Jon Barwise and John Perry. *Situations and Attitudes.* MIT Press, Cambridge, MA, 1984.

George Bealer. An inconsistency in functionalism. *Synthese,* 38(3):333–372, 1978.

Eugenio Beltrami. Saggio di interpretazione della geometria non-euclidea. *Giornale di Matematiche,* 6:284–312, 1868.

Evert Beth. On Padoa's method in the theory of definition. *Koninklijke Nederlandse Akademie van Wetenschappen Proceedings Series A,* 56:330–339, 1953.

Simon Blackburn. *Essays in Quasi-realism.* Oxford University Press, Oxford, 1993.

Ned Block. Troubles with functionalism. *Minnesota Studies in the Philosophy of Science,* 9:261–325, 1978.

Ned Block. Are absent qualia impossible? *Philosophical Review,* 89:257–274, 1980.

Robert Boyd and Peter J. Richerson. *Culture and the Evolutionary Process.* University of Chicago Press, Chicago, 1985.

Robert B. Brandom. Varieties of understanding. In Nicholas Rescher, editor, *Reason and Rationality in Natural Science,* pages 27–51. University Press of America, Lanham, MD, 1985.

Robert B. Brandom. *Making It Explicit: Reasoning, Representing, and Discursive Commitment.* Harvard University Press, Cambridge, MA, 1994.

Robert B. Brandom. *Articulating Reasons: An Introduction to Inferentialism.* Harvard University Press, Cambridge, MA, 2000.

Michael Bratman, John Perry, and John Martin Fischer. *Introduction to Philosophy: Classical and Contemporary Readings*, 5th edn. Oxford University Press, Oxford, 2009.

C. A. Campbell. Has the self 'free will'? In *On Selfhood and Godhood: The Gifford Lectures Delivered at the University of St. Andrews 1953–54 and 1954–55, Revised and Expanded*, pages 158–179. George Allen & Unwin, London, 1957.

Donald T. Campbell. Downward causation in hierarchically organised biological systems. In Francisco José Ayala and Theodosius Dobzhansky, editors, *Studies in the Philosophy of Biology: Reduction and Related Problems*, pages 179–186. Macmillan, London/Basingstoke, 1974.

Donald T. Campbell. On the conflicts between biological and social evolution and between psychology and moral tradition. *American Psychologist*, 30:1103–1126, 1975.

Keith Campbell. *Body and Mind*. Macmillan, London, 1970.

Rudolf Carnap. Der Raum: ein Beitrag zur Wissenschaftslehre. *Kant-Studien Ergänzungsheft*, 56:1–87, 1922.

Rudolf Carnap. Probability as a guide in life. *Journal of Philosophy*, 44(6):141–148, 1947.

Rudolf Carnap. *Logical Foundations of Probability*. University of Chicago Press, Chicago, 1950.

Rudolf Carnap. The methodological character of theoretical concepts. In H. Feigl and M. Scriven, editors, *The Foundations of Science and the Concepts of Psychology and Psychoanalysis*, Minnesota Studies in the Philosophy of Science, 1, pages 38–76. University of Minnesota Press, 1956.

Luigi Luca Cavalli-Sforza and Marcus W. Feldman. *Cultural Transmission and Evolution: A Quantitative Approach*. Princeton University Press, Princeton, NJ, 1981.

David J. Chalmers. *The Conscious Mind: In Search of a Fundamental Theory*. Oxford University Press, New York, Oxford, 1996.

Noam Chomsky. *Aspects of the Theory of Syntax*. MIT Press, Cambridge, MA, 1965.

Alonzo Church. A note on the *Entscheidungsproblem*. *Journal of Symbolic Logic*, 1:40–41, 1936a.

Alonzo Church. Correction. *Journal of Symbolic Logic*, 1:101–102, 1936b.

Alonzo Church. Review of *Language, Truth and Logic*, by Alfred Jules Ayer. *Journal of Symbolic Logic*, 14(1):52–53, 1949.

Paul M. Churchland. Eliminative materialism and the propositional attitudes. *Journal of Philosophy*, 78:67–90, 1981.

Desmond M. Clarke. *Descartes' Philosophy of Science*. Manchester University Press, Manchester, 1982.

Paul J. Cohen. The independence of the continuum hypothesis. I. *Proceedings of the National Academy of Sciences, USA*, 50:1143–1148, 1963.

Paul J. Cohen. The independence of the continuum hypothesis. II. *Proceedings of the National Academy of Sciences, USA*, 51:105–110, 1964.

Irving Copi, Carl Cohen, and Kenneth McMahon. *Introduction to Logic*, 14th edn. Macmillan, New York, 2010.

Charles Darwin. *The Origin of Species*. John Murray, London, 1859.

Charles Darwin. *The Descent of Man, and Selection in Relation to Sex*. John Murray, London, 1871.

Donald Davidson. Mental events. In Lawrence Foster and J. W. Swanson, editors, *Experience and Theory*, pages 79–100. University of Massachusetts Press, Amherst, MA, 1970.

Donald Davidson. Radical interpretation. *Dialectica*, 27:314–324, 1973.

Donald Davidson. Knowing one's own mind. *Proceedings and Addresses of the American Philosophical Association*, 60:441–458, 1987.

Richard Davies. *Descartes: Belief, Scepticism and Virtue*. Routledge, London and New York, 2001.

Richard Dawkins. *The Selfish Gene*. Oxford University Press, Oxford, 1976.

Daniel C. Dennett. *The Intentional Stance*. MIT Press, New York, 1989.

Daniel C. Dennett. *Consciousness Explained*. Little, Brown and Co., Boston, New York, and London, 1981.

René Descartes. *Meditationes de Prima Philosophia*. Michael Soly, Paris, 1641a.

René Descartes. *Meditations on First Philosophy*, trans. *John Cottingham*. Cambridge University Press, Cambridge, 1641b.

Willis Doney, editor. *Eternal Truths and the Cartesian Circle*. Garland Publishing, New York, 1987.

Emil du Bois-Reymond. *Über die Grenzen des Naturerkennens. Die sieben Welträthsel. Zwei Vorträge von Emil du Bois-Reymond. Des ersten Vortrages achte, der zwei Vorträge vierte Auflage*. Verlag von Veit & Comp., Leipzig, 1898.

Michael Dummett. *Frege: Philosophy of Language*. Duckworth, London, 1973.

Manfred Eigen and Peter Schuster. *The Hypercycle: A Principle of Natural Self-Organization*. Springer, Berlin and New York, 1979.

Albert Einstein. Die Feldgleichungen der Gravitation. *Königlich Preußische Akademie der Wissenschaften (Berlin). Sitzungsberichte*, pages 844–847, 1915.

Albert Einstein. Die Grundlage der allgemeinen Relativitätstheorie. *Annalen der Physik*, 354(7):769–822, 1916.

Albert Einstein. Kosmologische Betrachtungen zur allgemeinen Relativitätstheorie. *Königlich Preußische Akademie der Wissenschaften (Berlin). Sitzungsberichte*, pages 142–152, 1917.

Niles Eldredge and Stephen Jay Gould. Punctuated equilibria: an alternative to phyletic gradualism. In T. J. M. Schopf, editor, *Models in Paleobiology*, pages 82–115. Freeman Cooper, San Francisco, 1972.

Herbert Feigl. *The "Mental" and the "Physical"*. University of Minnesota Press, Minneapolis, 1958.

Hartry Field. *Science without Numbers: A Defence of Nominalism*. Basil Blackwell, Oxford, 1980.

Jerry A. Fodor. *The Language of Thought*. Harvard University Press, Cambridge, MA, 1975.

Philippa Foot. The problem of abortion and the doctrine of double effect. *Oxford Review*, 5(Trinity Term):5–15, 1967.

Gottlob Frege. *Die Grundlagen der Arithmetik: eine logisch mathematische Untersuchung uber den Begriff der Zahl*. Georg Olms Verlagsbuchhandlung, Hildesheim, 1884; reprinted 1961.

Gottlob Frege. *Grundgesetze der Arithmetik. I. Band*. Georg Olms Verlagsbuchhandlung, Hildesheim, 1893; reprinted 1962.

Gottlob Frege. *Grundgesetze der Arithmetik. II. Band*. Georg Olms Verlagsbuchhandlung, Hildesheim, 1903; reprinted 1962.

Harvey M. Friedman. Higher set theory and mathematical practice. *Annals of Mathematical Logic*, 2(3):325–357, 1971.

Stephen Gaukroger. *Descartes: An Intellectual Biography*. Oxford University Press, New York, 1995.

Tamar Szabo Gendler. *Thought Experiment: On the Powers and Limits of Imaginary Cases*. Routledge, New York, 2000.

Edmund Gettier. Is justified true belief knowledge? *Analysis*, 23:121–123, 1963.

J. J. Gibson. The theory of affordances. In R. Shaw and J. Bransford, editors, *Perceiving, Acting, and Knowing: Toward an Ecological Psychology*, pages 67–82. Erlbaum, Hillsdale, NJ, 1977.

Joshua Gilder and Anne-Lee Gilder, editors. *Heavenly Intrigue: Johannes Kepler, Tycho Brahe, and the Murder behind One of History's Greatest Scientific Discoveries*. Doubleday, New York, 2004.

Kurt Gödel. Die Vollständigkeit der Axiome des logischen Funktionenkalküls. *Monatshefte für Mathematik under Physik*, 37:349–360, 1930.

Kurt Gödel. Über formal unentscheidbare Sätze der *Principia Mathematica* und verwandter Systeme I. *Monatshefte für Mathematik und Physik*, 37:173–198, 1931.

Kurt Gödel. *The Consistency of the Axiom of Choice and of the Generalized Continuum Hypothesis with the Axioms of Set Theory, Annals of Mathematics Studies, 3*. Princeton University Press, Princeton, NJ, 1940.

Kurt Gödel. On undecidable propositions of formal mathematical systems (The Princeton lectures of 1934). In Solomon Feferman, John W. Dawson, Jr., Stephen C. Kleene, Gregory H. Moore, Robert M. Solovay, and Jean van Heijenoort, editors, *Kurt Gödel: Collected Works*, vol. I, *Publications 1929–1936*, pages 346–371. Clarendon Press, Oxford, 1986.

Kurt Gödel. Ontological proof. In Solomon Feferman, John W. Dawson, Jr., Warren Goldfarb, Charles Parsons, and Robert M. Solovay, editors, *Kurt Gödel: Collected Works*, vol. III, *Unpublished Essays and Lectures*, pages 346–371. Clarendon Press, Oxford, 1995.

Nelson Goodman. *Fact, Fiction, and Forecast*. Harvard University Press, Cambridge, MA, 1955.

H. P. Grice. Meaning. *Philosophical Review*, 66(3):377–388, 1957.

H. P. Grice. Utterer's meaning and intention. *Philosophical Review*, 78(2):147–177, 1969.

Adolf Grünbaum. *The Foundations of Psychoanalysis: A Philosophical Critique*. University of California Press, Berkeley and Los Angeles, 1984.

Adolf Grünbaum. Origin versus creation in physical cosmology. In L. Krüger and B. Falkenburg, editors, *Physik, Philosophie, und die Einheit der Wissenschaften*, pages 221–254. Spektrum Akademischer Verlag, 1995.

Ian Hacking. The identity of indiscernibles. *Journal of Philosophy*, 72(9):249–256, 1975.

Ian Hacking. *An Introduction to Probability and Inductive Logic*. Cambridge University Press, Cambridge, 2001.

Edith Hamilton and Huntington Cairns, editors. *The Collected Dialogues of Plato, including the Letters*. Bollingen Series LXXI. Princeton University Press, Princeton, NJ, 1989.

Richard M. Hare. *The Language of Morals*. Clarendon Press, Oxford, 1952.

Stephen Hawking. *The Universe in a Nutshell*. Bantam Books, New York, 2001.

Geoffrey Hellman and F. Thompson. Ontology, determination, and reduction. *Journal of Philosophy*, 72:551–564, 1975.

Carl G. Hempel. Studies in the logic of confirmation I, II. *Mind*, 54:1–26, 97–121, 1945.

Carl G. Hempel. Problems and changes in the empiricist criterion of meaning. *Revue Internationale de Philosophie*, 4:41–63, 1950.

Reuben Hersh and Philip J. Davis. *The Mathematical Experience*. Burkhäuser, Boston, 1981.

Douglas R. Hofstadter and Daniel Dennett. *The Mind's I: Fantasies and Reflections On Self and Soul*. Basic Books, New York, 1981.

Jasper Hopkins and Herbert Richardson. *Complete Philosophical and Theological Treatises of Anselm of Canterbury*. The Arthur J. Banning Press, Minneapolis, 2000.

David Hume. *A Treatise of Human Nature: Being An Attempt to introduce the experimental Method of Reasoning into Moral Subjects.* John Noon, London, 1738.

Frank Jackson. Epiphenomenal qualia. *Philosophical Quarterly*, 32:127–136, 1982.

Antoni Janiczak. A remark concerning decidability of complete theories. *Journal of Symbolic Logic*, 15(4):277–279, 1950.

Julian Jaynes. *The Origin of Consciousness in the Breakdown of the Bicameral Mind.* Houghton Mifflin, New York, 1976.

Philip E. Johnson. *Reason in the Balance: The Case against Naturalism in Science, Law and Education.* InterVarsity Press, Downers Grove, IL, 1995.

V. Kagan. *N. Lobachevsky and his Contribution to Science.* Foreign Languages Publishing House, Moscow, 1957.

Robert Kanigel. *The Man Who Knew Infinity: A Life of the Genius Ramanujan.* Charles Scribner's Sons, New York, 1991.

Immanuel Kant. *Kritik der Reinen Vernunft.* Johann Friedrich Hartnoch, Riga, 1781.

Stuart A. Kauffman. *The Origins of Order: Self-Organization and Selection in Evolution.* Oxford University Press, Oxford, 1993.

Rosanna Keefe. *Theories of Vagueness.* Cambridge University Press, Cambridge, 2000.

Rosanna Keefe and Peter Smith, editors. *Vagueness: A Reader.* MIT Press, Cambridge, MA, 1996.

Anthony Kenny. *Ancient Philosophy: A New History.* Oxford University Press, Oxford, 2004.

Robert Kirk. Rationality without language. *Mind*, 76:369–386, 1967.

Robert Kirk. Zombies v. materialists. *Proceedings of the Aristotelian Society, Supplementary Volume*, 48:135–152, 1974.

Robert Kirk. *Zombies and Consciousness.* Clarendon Press, Oxford, 2005.

Robert Kirk. The inconceivability of zombies. *Philosophical Studies*, 139:73–89, 2008.

Carolyn Korsmeyer, editor. *Aesthetics: The Big Questions.* Blackwell, Oxford, 1998.

Saul A. Kripke. *Naming and Necessity.* Harvard University Press, Cambridge, MA, 1980.

Saul A. Kripke. *Wittgenstein on Rules and Private Language.* Blackwell, Oxford, 1982.

Saul A. Kripke. Semantical considerations on modal logic. *Acta Philosophica Fennica*, 16: 83–94, 1963.

Thomas S. Kuhn. *The Structure of Scientific Revolutions.* University of Chicago Press, Chicago, 1970.

Pierre Simon Laplace. *Essai Philosophique sur les Probabilités. The English translation of the sixth French edition is by Frederick Wilson Truscott and Frederick Lincoln Emory, titled A Philosophical Essay on Probabilities, published by John Wiley & Sons, New York, in 1902. It was re-issued by Dover in 1951. The original was published by V. Courcier, in Paris,* 1820.

Gottfried Wilhelm Leibniz. Meditations on knowledge, truth and ideas (1684). In Leroy E. Loemker, editor, *Gottfried Wilhelm Leibniz: Philosophical Papers and Letters*, 2nd edn, pages 291–295. D. Reidel, Dordrecht, 1969a.

Gottfried Wilhelm Leibniz. Discourse on metaphysics (1686). In Leroy E. Loemker, editor, *Gottfried Wilhelm Leibniz: Philosophical Papers and Letters*, 2nd edn, pages 303–330. D. Reidel, Dordrecht, 1969b.

Janet Levin. Functionalism. http://plato.stanford.edu/archives/fall2013/entries/functionalism/. In Edward N. Zalta, editor, *The Stanford Encyclopedia of Philosophy*. Fall edition, 2013.

David Lewis. *Convention: A Philosophical Study.* Harvard University Press, Cambridge, MA, 1969.

David Lewis. Psychophysical and theoretical identifications. *Australasian Journal of Philosophy*, 50(3):249–258, 1972.

Benjamin Libet. Unconscious cerebral initiative and the role of conscious will in voluntary action. *Behavioral and Brain Sciences*, 8:529–566, 1985.

Leonard Linsky, editor. *Reference and Modality*. Oxford University Press, Oxford, 1971.

John Locke. *An Essay Concerning Human[e] Understanding*. Tho. Baffet, London, 1689.

Konrad Lorenz. KantÃȚs Lehre vom Apriorischen im Lichte gegenwärtiger Biologie. *Blätter für Deutsche Philosophie*, 15:94–125, 1941.

Storrs McCall. Can a Turing machine know that the Gödel sentence is true? *Journal of Philosophy*, 96:525–532, 1999.

J. L. Mackie. Evil and omnipotence. *Mind*, 64:200–212, 1955.

J. L. Mackie. *The Cement of the Universe: A Study of Causation*. Clarendon Library of Logic and Philosophy, Oxford University Press, Oxford, 1974.

Gerald Massey. Indeterminacy, Inscrutability, and Ontological Relativity. *Studies in Ontology*, American Philosophical Quarterly Monograph series, 12:43–55, 1978.

D. H. Mellor. God and probability. *Religious Studies*, 5(2):223–234, 1969.

Gregor Mendel. *Versuche über Pflanzenhybriden. Zwei Abhandlungen*. Wilhelm Engelmann, Leipzig, 1866 and 1870.

Richard Montague. Deterministic theories (1962). In Richmond H. Thomason, editor, *Formal Philosophy: Selected Papers of Richard Montague*, pages 303–359. Yale University Press, New Haven and London, 1974.

G. E. Moore. The conception of intrinsic value. In G. E. Moore, *Philosophical Studies*, pages 253–275. Harcourt, Brace, and Co., New York, 1922.

George Edward Moore. *Principia Ethica*. Cambridge University Press, Cambridge, 1903.

George Edward Moore. Propositions. In George Edward Moore, *Some Main Problems of Philosophy*. Allen and Unwin Ltd, London, 1953.

Ernest Nagel. *The Structure of Science: Problems in the Logic of Scientific Explanation*. Harcourt, Brace, and World, New York, 1961.

Isaac Newton. General Scholium, from the 3rd edn of the *Principia*. William & John Innys, London, 1726.

Robert Nozick. *Philosophical Explanations*. Harvard University Press, Cambridge, MA, 1981.

Graham Oppy. Ontological arguments. *The Stanford Encyclopedia of Philosophy*, http://plato.stanford.edu/entries/ontological-arguments/. In Edward N. Zalta, editor, *The Stanford Encyclopedia of Philosophy*. Fall edition, 2011.

William Paley. *Natural Theology: Or Evidences of the Existence and Attributes of the Deity Collected from the Appearances of Nature*. Gould and Lincoln, Boston, 1867.

Blaise Pascal. *Pensées (1670)* trans. W. F. Trotter. Dent, London, 1910.

Christopher Peacocke. Deviant causal chains. *Midwest Studies in Philosophy*, 4(1):123–155, 1979.

Roger Penrose. *The Emperor's New Mind: Concerning Computers, Minds, and the Laws of Physics*. Oxford University Press, Oxford, 1989.

Roger Penrose. *The Road to Reality: A Complete Guide to the Laws of the Universe*. Jonathan Cape, Random House Group Ltd, London, 2004.

Jean Piaget. *Biology and Knowledge*. University of Chicago Press, Chicago, 1971.

U. T. Place. Is consciousness a brain process? *British Journal of Psychology*, 47:44–50, 1956.

Alvin Plantinga. *God, Freedom, and Evil*. Eerdmans, Grand Rapids, MI, 1977.

Henry Plotkin. *Darwin Machines and the Nature of Knowledge: Concerning Adaptations, Instinct and the Evolution of Intelligence*. Penguin Books, London, 1994.

Plutarch. *Life of Theseus* (AD75). In *Plutarch, Lives*, trans. Bernadotte Rerrin, pages 1–88. Loeb Classical Library, Harvard University Press, Cambridge, MA, 1914.

Henri Poincaré. *Science and Method*, trans. George Bruce Halsted, as part of *The Foundations of Science*. The Science Press, Garrison, NY, 1913.

Richard H. Popkin, editor. *The Philosophy of the Sixteenth and Seventeenth Centuries*. Routledge, New York, 1966.

Karl R. Popper and John C. Eccles. *The Self and Its Brain: An Argument for Interactionism*. Springer, Heidelberg, London, New York, 1977.

Karl R. Popper. *Objective Knowledge: An Evolutionary Approach*. Clarendon Press, Oxford, 1972.

David Premack. *Intelligence in Ape and Man*. Erlbaum Associates, Hillsdale, NJ, 1976.

Graham Priest. Two dogmas of Quineanism. *Philosophical Quarterly*, 29:289–301, 1979.

Ilya Prigogine and Isabelle Stengers. *Order Out of Chaos: Man's New Dialogue with Nature*. Bantam Books, New York, 1984.

Hilary Putnam. Minds and machines. In Sidney Hook, editor, *Dimensions of Mind*, pages 57–80. New York University Press, New York, 1960.

Hilary Putnam. Psychological predicates. In W. H. Capitan and D. D. Merrill, editors, *Art, Mind and Religion*, pages 37–48. University of Pittsburgh Press, Pittsburgh, 1967.

Hilary Putnam. Meaning and reference. *Journal of Philosophy*, 70(19):699–711, 1973.

Hilary Putnam. *Reason, Truth and History*. Cambridge University Press, Cambridge, 1981.

Hilary Putnam. 'Two dogmas' revisited. In *Realism and Reason, Philosophical Papers Vol. 3*, pages 87–97. Cambridge University Press, Cambridge, 1983.

Hilary Putnam. *Representation and Reality*. MIT Press, Cambridge, MA, 1988.

Willard Van Orman Quine and J. S. Ullian. *The Web of Belief*, 2nd edn. Random House, New York, 1970.

Willard Van Orman Quine. Two dogmas of empiricism. *Philosophical Review*, 60:20–43, 1951.

Willard Van Orman Quine. *The Ways of Paradox*. Random House, New York, 1966.

Willard Van Orman Quine. Two dogmas in retrospect. *Canadian Journal of Philosophy*, 21(3):265–274, 1991.

Willard Van Orman Quine. On simple theories of a complex world. *Synthese*, 15(1):103–106, 1963.

Martin Rees. *Just Six Numbers: The Deep Forces That Shape the Universe*. Weidenfeld and Nicolson, London, 1999.

Rupert Riedl. *Biology of Knowledge: The Evolutionary Basis of Reason*. MIT Press, Cambridge, MA, 1980.

Abraham Robinson. A result on consistency and its application to the theory of definition. *Koninklijke Nederlandse Akademie van Wetenschappen, Proceedings, Series A, Mathematics*, 59:47–58, 1956.

Hartley Rogers. *Theory of Recursive Functions and Effective Computability*. McGraw-Hill, New York, 1967.

Richard Routley. Alleged problems in attributing beliefs, and intentionality, to animals. *Inquiry*, 24(4):385–417, 1981.

David E. Rumelhart, James L. McClelland, and PDP Research Group. *Parallel Distributed Processing, vol. 1, Explorations in the Microstructure of Cognition: Foundations*. MIT Press, Cambridge, MA, 1986.

Bertrand Russell. On denoting. *Analysis*, 14(56):479–493, 1905.

Bertrand Russell. Knowledge by acquaintance and knowledge by description. *Proceedings of the Aristotelian Society*, 11:108–128, 1910.

Bertrand Russell. *The Autobiography of Bertrand Russell, 1872–1914*. George Allen and Unwin Ltd, 1967.

Gilbert Ryle. *The Concept of Mind*. Hutchinson, London, 1949.

R. M. Sainsbury. *Paradoxes*. Cambridge University Press, Cambridge, 1987.

Kevin Scharp. *Replacing Truth*. Oxford University Press, New York, 2013.

Moritz Schlick. *Allgemeine Erkenntnislehre*. Springer, Berlin, 1918.

Erwin Schrödinger. *What is Life? The Physical Aspect of the Living Cell*. Cambridge University Press, Cambridge, 1946.

John R. Searle. Minds, brains and programs. *Behavioral and Brain Sciences*, 3(3):417–457, 1980.

John R. Searle. *The Rediscovery of the Mind*. MIT Press, Cambridge, MA, 1992.

Stewart Shapiro. An 'i' for an i: singular terms, uniqueness, and reference. *Review of Symbolic Logic*, 5:380–415, 2012.

Charles Siewert. *The Significance of Consciousness*. Princeton University Press, Princeton, NJ, 1998.

Th. Skolem. Logisch-kombinatorische Untersuchungen über die Erfüllbarkeit und Beweisbarkeit mathematischen Sätze nebst einem Theoreme über dichte Mengen. *Videnskabsakademiet i Kristiania, Skrifter*, 1(4):1–36, 1919.

J. J. C. Smart. Sensations and brain processes. *Philosophical Review*, 68:141–156, 1959.

Jordan Howard Sobel. *Logic and Theism*. Cambridge University Press, New York, 2004.

Elliott Sober. *Simplicity*. Clarendon Press, Oxford, 1975.

Elliott Sober. The evolution of rationality. *Synthese*, 46:95–120, 1981.

Roy A. Sorensen. *Thought Experiments*. Oxford University Press, New York, 1992.

Florian Steinberger. What harmony could and could not be. *Australasian Journal of Philosophy*, 89(4):617–639, 2011.

Galen Strawson. *Freedom and Belief*. Oxford University Press, 1986.

Galen Strawson. *Mental Reality*. MIT Press, Cambridge, MA, 1994.

Alfred Tarski, Andrzej Mostowski, and Raphael M. Robinson. *Undecidable Theories*. North Holland, Amsterdam, 1953.

Neil Tennant. *Natural Logic*. Edinburgh University Press, 1978; (2nd rev. edn 1991).

Neil Tennant. Intentionality, syntactic structure and the evolution of language. In Christopher Hookway, editor, *Minds, Machines and Evolution*, pages 73–103. Cambridge University Press, Cambridge, 1984.

Neil Tennant. Beth's theorem and reductionism. *Pacific Philosophical Quarterly*, 66:342–354, 1985.

Neil Tennant. *Anti-realism and Logic: Truth as Eternal*. Clarendon Library of Logic and Philosophy, Oxford University Press Oxford, 1987.

Neil Tennant. Theories, concepts and rationality in an evolutionary account of science. *Biology and Philosophy*, 3:224–231, 1988.

Neil Tennant. The decoding problem: do we need to search for extra terrestrial intelligence to search for extraterrestrial intelligence? In Stuart Kingsley, editor, *SPIE Proceedings Volume 1867*. Reprinted in Brie Gertler and Lawrence Shapiro, editors, *Arguing about the mind*, pages 583–597, Routledge, Abingdon, 2007, 1993.

Neil Tennant. *The Taming of the True*. Oxford University Press, 1997.

Neil Tennant. Deductive versus expressive power: a pre-Gödelian predicament. *Journal of Philosophy*, 97(5):257–277, 2000.

Neil Tennant. On Turing machines knowing their own Gödel-sentences. *Philosophia Mathematica*, 9:72–79, 2001.

Neil Tennant. Relevance in reasoning. In Stewart Shapiro, editor, *The Oxford Handbook of Philosophy of Mathematics and Logic*, pages 696–726. Oxford University Press, New York, 2005.

Neil Tennant. Mind, mathematics and the *Ignorabimusstreit*. *British Journal for the History of Philosophy*, 15(4):745–773, 2007.

Neil Tennant. Cognitive phenomenology, semantic qualia and luminous knowledge. In Patrick Greenough and Duncan Pritchard, editors, *Williamson on Knowledge*, pages 238–256. Oxford University Press, 2009.

Neil Tennant. The logical structure of scientific explanation and prediction: planetary orbits in a sun's gravitational field. *Studia Logica*, 95:207–232, 2010.

Neil Tennant. Cut for core logic. *Review of Symbolic Logic*, 5(3):450–479, 2012a.

Neil Tennant. *Changes in Mind: An Essay on Rational Belief Revision*. Oxford University Press, Oxford, 2012b.

Neil Tennant. Aristotle's syllogistic and core logic. *History and Philosophy of Logic*, http://dx.doi.org/10.1080/01445340.2013.867144, 2014a.

Neil Tennant. The logical structure of evolutionary explanation and prediction: Darwinism's fundamental schema. *Biology and Philosophy*, http://dx.doi.org/10.1007/s10539-014-9444-0, 2014b.

Neil Tennant. Cut for classical core logic. *Review of Symbolic Logic*, forthcoming, 2014c.

Neil Tennant. Inferentialism, logicism, harmony, and a counterpoint (downloadable from http://people.cohums.ohio-state.edu/tennant9/). In Alex Miller, editor, *Essays for Crispin Wright: Logic, Language and Mathematics*. Volume 2 of a two-volume Festschrift for Crispin Wright, co-edited with Annalisa Coliva. Oxford University Press, Oxford, 2014d.

Neil Tennant. A logical theory of truthmakers and falsitymakers (downloadable from http://people.cohums.ohio-state.edu/tennant9/). In Michael Glanzberg, editor, *The Oxford Handbook of Truth*. Oxford University Press, New York, 2014e.

Stephen Toulmin. *Human Understanding: The Collective Use and Evolution of Concepts*. Princeton University Press, Princeton, NJ, 1972.

Alan Turing. On computable numbers, with an application to the *Entscheidungsproblem*. *Proceedings of the London Mathematical Society s2*, 42(1):230–265, 1937.

Alan Turing. On computable numbers, with an application to the *Entscheidungsproblem*. a correction. *Proceedings of the London Mathematical Society s2*, 43(1):544–546, 1938.

Florian von Schilcher and Neil Tennant. *Philosophy, Evolutions and Human Nature*. Routledge & Kegan Paul, London, 1984.

J. D. Watson and F. H. Crick. Molecular structure of nucleic acids: a structure for deoxyribose nucleic acid. *Nature*, 171(4356):737–738, 1953.

Otto Weininger. *Geschlecht und Charakter: Eine prinzipielle Untersuchung*. Friedrich Jasper, Vienna, 1903.

J. A. Wheeler. Law without law. In J. A. Wheeler and W. H. Zurek, editors, *Quantum Theory and Measurement*, pages 182–213. Princeton University Press, Princeton, NJ, 1983.

Alfred North Whitehead. *Process and Reality: An Essay in Cosmology*. Cambridge University Press, Cambridge, 1929.

Eugene P. Wigner. The unreasonable effectiveness of mathematics in the natural sciences. *Communications in Pure and Applied Mathematics*, 13(1):1–14, 1960.

Bernard Williams. The self and the future. *Philosophical Review*, 79(2):161–180, 1970.

Bernard Williams. Deciding to believe (1970). In Bernard Williams, *Problems of the Self: Philosophical Papers 1956–1972*, pages 136–151. Clarendon Press, Oxford, 1973a.

Bernard Williams. The Makropulos case: reflections on the tedium of immortality. In *Problems of the Self*, pages 82–100. Cambridge University Press, Cambridge, 1973b.

George C. Williams. *Adaptation and Natural Selection*. Princeton University Press, Princeton, NJ, 1966.

Crispin Wright. Scientific realism, observation and the verification principle. In G. Macdonald and C. Wright, editors, *Fact, Science and Morality*, pages 247–274. Blackwell, Oxford, 1986.

Index